STAGE FRIGHT

STAGE FRIGHT

Politics and the Performing Arts in Late Imperial Russia

Paul du Quenoy

The Pennsylvania State University Press
University Park, Pennsylvania

Library of Congress Cataloging-in-Publication Data

Du Quenoy, Paul, 1977–
Stage fright : politics and the performing arts in late Imperial Russia / Paul du Quenoy.
p.   cm.
Includes bibliographical references and index.
Summary: "Explores the relationship between culture and power in Imperial Russia. Argues that Russia's performing arts were part of a vibrant public culture that was usually ambivalent or hostile to the tumultuous political events of the revolutionary era"—Provided by publisher.
ISBN 978-0-271-05878-8 (pbk : alk. paper)
1. Performing arts—Political aspects—Russia.
2. Theater—Political aspects—Russia.
3. Performing arts—Russia—History—20th century.
4. Theater—Russia—History—20th century.
5. Popular culture—Russia—History—20th century.
6. Russia—Intellectual life—1801–1917.
I. Title.

PN2724.D8 2009
790.20947'09041—dc22
2008041655

Copyright © 2009 The Pennsylvania State University
All rights reserved
Printed in the United States of America
Published by The Pennsylvania State University Press,
University Park, PA 16802-1003

The Pennsylvania State University Press is a member of the Association of American University Presses.

It is the policy of The Pennsylvania State University Press to use acid-free paper. This book is printed on stock that meets the minimum requirements of American National Standard for Information Sciences—Permanence of Paper for Printed Library Material, ANSI Z39.48–1992.

In memory of Joe King,
A DEAR FRIEND WHO KNEW HOW TO LIVE LIFE

Contents

LIST OF ILLUSTRATIONS ix
ACKNOWLEDGMENTS xi

Introduction 1

1
"An Aspiration to Novelty":
Contours of the Performing Arts in Late Imperial Russia 15

2
"Such a Risky Time":
Arts Institutions and the Challenge of Politics 56

3
"Politics Are Death": Imperial Theater Performers 100

4
"Our Theater Will Not Strike!":
Private and Popular Theater Performers 137

5
"You Dare Not Make Sport of Our Nerves!": The Audiences 170

6
"A New Bayreuth Will Save No One":
Russian Modernism and Its Discontents 215

"Art Must Be Apolitical": A Conclusion 243

BIBLIOGRAPHY 267
INDEX 281

Illustrations

1. The Bol'shoi Theater, about 1900   17
2. Vladimir Teliakovskii, Director of the Imperial Theaters from 1901 to 1917   21
3. The interior of the Omon (Aumont) Theater, home of the Moscow Art Theater from 1902   29
4. Omon (Aumont) Theater interior, 1902   29
5. Marius Petipa, First Ballet Master of the Imperial Theaters   38
6. A scene from Maksim Gor'kii's *The Lower Depths* at the Moscow Art Theater in 1902   71
7. A caricature of Konstantin Stanislavskii as Stockmann in Ibsen's *An Enemy of the People*   101
8. Fedor Shaliapin in one of his signature roles, Modest Musorgskii's Boris Godunov   104
9. Anna Pavlova and Mikhail Fokin on the stage of the Mariinskii Theater in the early 1900s   115
10. A group of performers in the Aleksandrinskii Theater's drama troupe   123
11. Fedor Shaliapin performing at a charitable concert early in his career   134
12. Vera Komissarzhevskaia in 1903   143
13. A Congress of Dramatic Writers meeting in February 1906   162
14. Ticket prices to the Aleksandrinskii Theater, the imperial drama venue in St. Petersburg   178
15. Prices at the Mariinskii Theater, the imperial capital's main opera and ballet venue   180
16. An illustration of the typical audience in the gallery of the Aleksandrinskii Theater   182
17. Typical advertising in a publication of the Imperial Theaters Directorate   185
18. Act II of Gor'kii's *Children of the Sun* in a late 1905 production   199
19. A scene from the Moscow Art Theater production of Anton Chekhov's *The Seagull*   224

Acknowledgments

This book would not have appeared without the great deal of support and encouragement I have been fortunate to receive over the past few years. Much of the research presented in the pages that follow was conducted under the auspices of the U.S. Department of Education's Fulbright-Hays program, which funded twelve months of work in Russia and Finland in 2003–4. Georgetown University's Department of History, Graduate School of Arts and Sciences, and Center for Eurasian, Russian, and East European Studies supported me generously over the entire duration of my doctoral program, including every summer. The staff of the Russian State Theatrical Library in St. Petersburg was extremely helpful and deserves special recognition. Elena Alimova and Anna Khitrik stood out for facilitating my project, especially during a prolonged period of renovation when the library was closed to the general public but remained open to me. In Finland the staff of Helsinki University's Slavonic Library was of great help. The National Endowment for the Arts, under the leadership of its dynamic chairman, Dana Gioia, hosted me as a fellow during my last year in graduate school and offered many practical insights to inform my work. The American University in Cairo encouraged my work by inviting me to join its faculty as I approached the end of my studies. My new colleagues at the American University of Beirut showed much enthusiasm for my arrival there. Individuals play no small role in making history, and many must be acknowledged here. I could not have had a better mentor than Richard Stites, who deserves all due credit for suggesting the general topic of this study to me one evening at Martin's Tavern. His encouragement, humor, and friendship made the whole project easier and more fun than it probably should have been. Muriel Atkin's courses on Russia inspired me to pursue a Ph.D. John Dick's riotous first-year Russian-language course fortified that urge. The teaching of Charles Herber, Brother Raymond Hetu, Emmet Kennedy, and Richard Thornton convinced me to pursue history as a discipline and, more important, as a humanity. A number of friends and colleagues took the time to read and comment on various chapter and manuscript drafts, attention that improved it in many ways and helped me work out some of the inevitable rough spots. For their invaluable assistance, wonderful humor, and always great company I must thank my dissertation committee readers, David Goldfrank and Louise McReynolds. Thomas Arthur, Harley Balzer, Julijana Budjevac, Sean Foley, Murray Frame, Emmet Kennedy, Lawrence Helm, Mikail Mamedov, and the late Prince Alexis Obolensky all read and commented on the manuscript in whole or in part and deserve warm recognition. Seymour Becker and another reader who remains anonymous delivered expert critiques via Penn State University Press's peer-review process. The press's editorial director, Sanford Thatcher, showed refreshing enthusiasm for the manuscript from the beginning and guided it through its various stages of development. Masha Kirasirova was a very caring presence and reliable research assistant as the book was prepared for publication.

My parents and grandparents have always been there for me in their own ways. Many other people richly deserve thanks for sustaining my morale. The late Eve Thalis's wisdom and experience made years of Washington living as gracious as could be. Yoko and Tom Arthur, Julijana Budjevac and Lawrence Helm, and Debbie and Braxton Moncure, among many others, have made certain that I know I will always be welcomed home there. Debbie and Braxton's invitations to their beautiful Jamaican property eased several years of graduate school and junior faculty life with an elegance truly uncommon for our times. The late Joe King's expansive friendship included extending the use of his unoccupied Florida home on several occasions during the development of this book. Sally and Joe Dwinell always kept me laughing there. Marina Uchvatova and Elvira Gus'kova took excellent care of me during several long trips to Russia and, together with Mila Vergunova and Nathan Longan, made me feel as welcome and comfortable in St. Petersburg as in any other place I have lived. Nathan and Mila's suggestion that I assume the summer directorship of the Council on International Educational Exchange's St. Petersburg study program kept me coming back for a while and enabled me to put the final touches on the manuscript. Suzy and Robert Redfern-West braved the Russian winter to visit and keep up spirits and were gracious hosts throughout California, where the last pages of the first draft were written. Lynn Heffron gave a wonderful sendoff just before I took up my Fulbright. Lena and Caffey Norman are indisputably great people of our time, as are James Abely, Abraham Anderson, John Baboukis, Jelena Budjevac, Heather Burns, Katherine Cartwright, Cynthia and Ken Chase, John Dick, David Halperin, Mlada Khudolei and Peter Fleming, Lisa Khachaturian, Christine and George Loomis, York Norman, Eric Pashman, David Robinson, David Schimmelpenninck van der Oye, Irina Shuliakovskaia, Sema Soffer, George Tarnow, Countess Rhoda Trembinski, and many others who helped, encouraged, and entertained me in various ways through my long absences from the United States. Prince Obolensky, who died as I was making the last revisions to the manuscript, nourished my interest in the topic with personal anecdotes from his childhood about many of the people I have studied here. He always offered unflagging encouragement of what he called my "russizm" as well as an unforgettable song on my twenty-seventh birthday. His unique gifts included the ability to make me see Russian history beyond documents, books, and classrooms. He and Princess Selene's tireless charitable work and gracious hosting have certainly done more to help and affirm his country and its people than any academic study could.

Elissa Stankiewicz kept good homes for us and our adopted Russian cats, Sammy, Freddy, and Boots, in Russia, the United States, and Egypt. She was there for me in ways in which I hope she may one day recognize my appreciation and thanks.

My students at George Washington University, Georgetown, St. Petersburg State University, and the American Universities in Cairo and of Beirut deserve heartfelt thanks for their overwhelmingly positive and encouraging response to my teaching about Russia and other subjects. Many have become good friends, perhaps academia's greatest reward.

Note: Unless otherwise noted, dates in this book follow the Julian calendar, in use in Russia until February 1918. Transliterations from the Russian follow the Library of Congress style with slight modifications. For purposes of authenticity, in most cases I have preferred literal phonic transliterations to those common in English, French, or German use. Thus "Chaikovskii" is used rather than "Tchaikovsky," "Shaliapin" rather than "Chaliapin," and so on.

INTRODUCTION

In June 1920, assessing the international significance of the revolutionary era that had brought him to power in Russia, Vladimir Lenin adopted a theatrical idiom for one of its most important events, the Revolution of 1905. "Without the 'dress rehearsal' of 1905," he wrote, "the victory of the October Revolution in 1917 would have been impossible."[1] Political anatomy, according to Lenin's statement, borrowed in a teleological sense from the performing arts.

This book explores an inversion of Lenin's statement. Rather than question how politics took after the performing arts, its main purpose is to assess how and to what extent culture responded to power in Late Imperial Russia. Although many of the most important developments in these categories happened after 1900, I am broadly interested in the period between the reign of Alexander II (1855–81)—the era of the "Great Reforms"—and the revolutionary year of 1917. In this study I will seek to explore the impact of that period's rapid transformation and endemic turmoil on the performing arts, a category I have rather traditionally defined as organized expressions of creativity presented before audiences. Less traditionally, I have tried as much as possible to widen the category's usual focus—on opera, ballet, concerts, and "serious" drama—to include newer artistic forms thriving in Russia and elsewhere, the "new institutions of amusement and leisure" that Lewis Erenberg found to be "growing into general respectability" in modern America, for example.[2] These included "popular" theater

---

1. V. I. Lenin, "Leftwing Communism—An Infantile Disorder," in *The Lenin Anthology*, ed. Robert C. Tucker (New York: Norton, 1975), 555–56.

2. Lewis A. Erenberg, *Steppin' Out: New York Nightlife and the Transformation of American Culture, 1890–1930* (Westport, Conn.: Greenwood, 1981), 61.

(*narodnyi teatr* in Russian, so called because it was targeted at lower-class audiences), operetta, cabaret, satirical revues, pleasure garden entertainments, and, to a smaller extent because it was still in its infancy in the prerevolutionary era, film. I am interested in how Russia's performing arts culture and the individuals and institutions that brought it into being regarded their country's political life.

In the framework of a tsarist autocracy, where "power" was at least in theory monopolized by the ruler, the very concept of "politics" in society at large often suggested contentious approaches to reform, challenges to the prevailing order, a heightened spirit of political opposition, agitation for change, and eruptions of violence. Indeed, one of the most influential recent studies of Imperial Russia has argued that the projection and exercise of power depended on myriad representational idioms—including theatrical ones—designed to "elevate" Russia's autocrats into what Richard Wortman has called "the monarch's space."[3] To appreciate the nature and uses of performance from the other side of the throne, one major theme of this book will necessarily explore how theaters, performers, impresarios, audiences, and others active in the Russian Empire's cultural life articulated social and political views. Another will examine how state and civic institutions with responsibilities for and authority over culture responded to these attitudes and to events as they developed. As a work of theater history, the study seeks to determine whether changes in the performing arts themselves—by which I mean repertoire selections, theories of performance, uses of the stage, and other value-laden features—shared origins in the Russian Empire's political experience or evolved independently of it. Although much has been written about the arts in Imperial Russia, to date no scholarly work has attempted to map their political informants and meanings. That is the main task of this book.

In the early twenty-first century it is frequently argued, especially in academic circles, that culture, particularly the performing arts, is or should be imbued with some kind of social or political content. In many such milieus theater is experienced as an elite art form—a relatively expensive mode of entertainment concentrated almost exclusively in the centers of large cities. Confined to this environment, it is largely both produced and consumed by intellectuals in search of what they hope will offer higher meanings, instructive truths about life and society, and, as many of them often opine, the opportunity for people unlike themselves (usually the young or disadvantaged) to share them in some

---

3. Richard S. Wortman, *Scenarios of Power: Myth and Ceremony in Russian Monarchy from Peter the Great to the Abdication of Nicholas II* (Princeton: Princeton University Press, 2006).

meaningful way.⁴ A more radical approach, espoused by Erwin Piscator, Bertolt Brecht, and many of their contemporaries and emulators, advocates using expressive art to stimulate social change through moral messages validated by provocations to critical thought. In both cases the common understanding of theater's purpose is less to entertain than to educate, politicize, or shock. As Baz Kershaw has suggested in reference to postwar Britain's radical stage, "alternative theatre . . . may have managed to mount an effective opposition to the dominant culture, and may have modified its values."⁵ This seems to be the aspiration underlying many postmodern stage productions. Increasingly audacious directors have reinterpreted classics to impute contemporary relevance in the form of a message, theme, or social comment often absent from or tangential to the original. Some newer works for the stage try to challenge audiences through irreverence, absurdity, and other departures from accepted norms. Writing about nineteenth-century Russia, the Soviet semiotician Iurii Lotman argued that the dynamism of theater and theatrical representations "offered people new possibilities for behavior" and created "the awareness that any political turn of events was possible."⁶ He might just as easily have reaffirmed Oscar Wilde's paradoxical yet quintessentially modern aphorism that "Life imitates Art far more than Art imitates Life."

Influenced at least in part by these ideas, scholars have recently begun to study culture as a meaningful refraction of the political realities at work in modern societies. However unintentional the revelations discovered by this approach may be, their very lack of intentionality suggests an accuracy unobtainable via more traditional modes of inquiry.

This approach almost requires the arts to be territorialized by the political realm. The French sociologist Pierre Bourdieu, one of the most influential theorists on the subject, argued that modern disparities of social and political power create, define, and depend upon strategies of cultural distinction. Hierarchies of taste, in his view, function as tools that divide societies into ranked and self-perpetuating strata.⁷ Edward Said famously maintained that imperialism, one of the most nakedly political subjects in humanity's recent experience, was not

---

4. Daniel J. Wakin, "Skepticism and Praise for Change at the Met," *New York Times*, February 14, 2006, describes the "average demographic" of New York's Metropolitan Opera as "63, college educated, financially comfortable."

5. Baz Kershaw, *The Politics of Performance: Radical Theater as Cultural Intervention* (New York: Routledge, 1992), 6.

6. Jurij M. Lotman, "The Theater and Theatricality as Components of Early Nineteenth-Century Culture," in Ju. M. Lotman and B. A. Uspenskij, *The Semiotics of Russian Culture*, ed. A. Shukman (Ann Arbor: Michigan Slavic Contributors, 1984), 160.

7. Pierre Bourdieu, *Distinction: A Social Critique of the Judgement of Taste*, trans. Richard Nice (Cambridge: Harvard University Press, 1984).

only facilitated but also perpetuated in postcolonial times by the durability of Western cultural influences. According to this argument, culture can equal and, because of its less tangible qualities, perhaps even surpass the potency of military and economic methods of control.[8] In a related way Homi Bhabha's literary theories locate emerging collective identities, particularly those in the colonial and postcolonial worlds, within malleable frameworks shaped by imposed political realities and their cultural artifacts.[9]

One implication of these theoretical works is that art can offer publics a surreptitious means of resistance to external cultural-*cum*-political control. Mastery of quintessentially Western media permits cultural engagement or negotiation (Bhabha's word is "hybridization") capable of redefining real power relationships. Recent work on the performing arts in postcolonial societies has gone a step further to argue that some expressive forms, especially dramatic theater, have become open and successful forums for political opposition as well as regenerated, alternate, and often politicized identities. The historical absence of the Western-style stage from such societies carried the ironic advantage of rendering it—specifically because of its unfamiliarity and despite its cultural link to the colonizers—a rare untainted space where ideas, education, and acculturation could be explored outside the institutional legacies of imperial power persisting in civil and political establishments. Writing about modern South Africa, Loren Kruger discussed theater's viability not simply as a new mode of entertainment and education but as "a virtual public sphere" accommodating expressions of the political. In this sense it has offered an alternative to "the irredeemable agents of a repressive state," which, regardless of the political changes that followed from the abolition of apartheid in 1994, still remained "untrustworthy" institutions.[10] Other studies have observed that emerging or reemerging nations create native performing arts cultures—again largely "Western" in form—with the consciously political purposes of restoring a national identity,

---

8. Edward W. Said, *Culture and Imperialism* (New York: Knopf, 1993).

9. Homi K. Bhabha, *The Location of Culture* (New York: Routledge, 1994).

10. Loren Kruger, *The Drama of South Africa: Plays, Pageants, and Publics Since 1910* (New York: Routledge, 1999), 13, 216. For a more general study of this phenomenon in the postcolonial world, see Kruger, *Post-Imperial Brecht: Politics and Performance, East and South* (Berkeley and Los Angeles: University of California Press, 2004). To cite a specific example of this phenomenon, Shirley Apthorp, "Freedom to Raise the Roof: 'Fidelio' on Robben Island Was the Ideal Way to Celebrate a Decade of Democracy," *Financial Times*, April 1, 2004, reviews a Cape Town Opera production of Beethoven's *Fidelio* staged ten years after the abolition of apartheid and the desegregation of the company. Performed in the prison where Nelson Mandela was jailed, the staging exploded with political symbols, including recorded excerpts from Mandela's speeches played at the end of the overture, a leading tenor who physically resembled the activist politician, and, during the finale, the inclusion of a national dance and celebratory unfurling of the postapartheid South African flag.

fashioning an official new one, or advertising a state's legitimacy and the "normality" of the society over which it presides.[11]

Recent memories of the fall of communism have also left a strong impression of the potential for an oppressed society's arts community to become politicized. The relatively high esteem in which cold war–era East European performers were held by their publics and governments conferred the unique ability (for intensely controlled societies with few unpoliced expressive outlets) to make influential political statements through or alongside their art. This power enabled them to play serious roles in the peaceful revolutions of 1989. Indeed, it was the Prague actors who lent their sympathy, energy, and resources to the organization of Czechoslovakia's Civic Forum, the nucleus of that country's first postcommunist government. Actor-playwright leader Václav Havel's notoriety thrust him not only into presidential office but also into a prominent international role as a figure of conscience in human rights.[12] The Polish theatrical community's highly visible and nearly unanimous 1982 boycott of the official stage drew massive national and international sympathy to the Solidarity movement. Poland's performing artists actively allied themselves with dissent for the rest of the decade, despite martial law, and, like their Czechoslovak counterparts, made an appreciable contribution to the country's transition from communism.[13] In October 1989 the East German conductor Kurt Masur's personal renown gave him the influence to prevent the bloody suppression of dissident demonstrations in Leipzig, mass events that contributed to the collapse of the regime.[14] Recently, Belarus, the authoritarian former Soviet republic often described as "Europe's last dictatorship," has faced discreet challenges from a theatrical underground that comments on political events and has received

---

11. Brian Crow, with Chris Banfield, *An Introduction to Post-Colonial Theatre* (Cambridge: Cambridge University Press, 1996), addresses several cultural contexts. Christopher B. Balme, *Decolonizing the Stage: Theatrical Syncretism and Post-Colonial Drama* (Oxford: Clarendon, 1999), discusses practical applications. Laura L. Adams, "Modernity, Postcolonialism, and Theatrical Form in Uzbekistan," *Slavic Review* 64, no. 2 (2005), finds all three elements at work in the contemporary cultural life of the former Soviet republic. For historical examples, see Serhy Yekelchyk, "The Nation's Clothes: Constructing a Ukrainian High Culture in the Russian Empire, 1860–1900," *Jahrbücher für Geschichte Osteuropas* 49, no. 2 (2001), and Erika V. Ossipova, "Culture and Theater as Foundation for National Identity Formation in the Russian Far East," *Nationalities Papers* 33, no. 1 (2005).

12. Jarka M. Burian, *Modern Czech Theatre: Reflector and Conscience of a Nation* (Iowa City: University of Iowa Press, 2000), 181–88.

13. Kazimierz Braun, *A History of Polish Theater, 1939–1989: Spheres of Captivity and Freedom* (Westport, Conn.: Greenwood, 1996), 102–17. According to Braun, 90 percent of Polish actors participated in the boycott.

14. Gale Stokes, *The Walls Came Tumbling Down: The Collapse of Communism in Eastern Europe* (New York: Oxford University Press, 1993), 140–41, credits Masur's significant personal contribution to the collapse of the German Democratic Republic.

encouragement from Havel and the British postmodernist playwright Tom Stoppard, among others.[15]

Even the absence of politics from cultural contexts has led historians to look hard for political meanings—perhaps a natural effort if they assume such meanings *must* be there. Attempting to explain the presence of so many apolitical works in his subject of study, one historian of the mid-twentieth-century British stage has made the circular and ultimately unprovable argument that "to avoid political issues is to act politically."[16] A recent study of Russian theatrical unrest begins with the categorical observation that "all theatrical protests are political," even when they are caused by such apolitical issues as ticket prices, aesthetic qualities, or artistic innovation. Anything that "engages with an established order," however banal and in whatever way, thus "marks the evolution of social consciousness."[17] The most comprehensive history of the Ballets Russes—one of Late Imperial Russia's most sensational artistic phenomena—introduces its subject with the uncritical assumption that the Empire's performing arts culture formed "a microcosm of society at large, where politics, social relations, and artistic goals were inextricably linked."[18] A scholarly review of leisure and entertainment activities in prerevolutionary Russia insists that "by their sheer existence in an autocratic state, they were inevitably political even if they did not reveal themselves in political manifestations."[19] The pages that follow fundamentally question whether we should perceive cultures, Russian and others, in these ways; whether the performing arts are existentially and in all contexts political; and whether such terms as "all," "inextricably," and "inevitably"—absolute qualifiers now rather outmoded in historical scholarship—are appropriate to describe the relationship between culture and power.

In addition to the specific avenues of inquiry outlined above, this book will attempt to test whether conditions that appear to foster strong connections between politics and the performing arts existed in Late Imperial Russia. I began

---

15. Steven Lee Myers, "A Troupe Is a Potent Force in Belarus's Underground," *New York Times*, February 9, 2006.

16. Steve Nicholson, *British Theatre and the Red Peril: The Portrayal of Communism, 1917–1945* (Exeter: University of Exeter Press, 1999), 5.

17. Laurence Senelick, "Anti-Semitism and the Tsarist Theatre: The *Smugglers* Riots," *Theatre Survey* 44, no. 1 (2003): 68. In the same introductory paragraph, however, the author undermines his own argument by suggesting that "the root cause [of theatrical protests] *can always be construed* as political" (emphasis added), without discussing how, why, or by whom.

18. Lynn Garafola, *Diaghilev's Ballets Russes* (New York: Oxford University Press, 1989), 6.

19. Hubertus Jahn, "Fun, Leisure, and Entertainment in Russian History," *Kritika: Explorations in Russian and Eurasian History* 6, no. 4 (2005): 872. The review considers research on other topics in addition to the performing arts, but the latter nevertheless form an important part of that research.

this project with the assumption that a dramatic topography of that relationship would emerge during a period marked by rapid, turbulent change and pronounced social and political disorder. Revolutionary eras highlight and emphasize existing tensions, problems, and disappointments, the solutions to which are often dominated by passion and violence. By overturning or threatening to overturn established orders, they give birth to new ideas and aspirations in almost any field of endeavor. If Russia's performing arts community was as dominated by the country's political consciousness as scholars have traditionally maintained and as many recent theorists of the performing arts might assume, surely the connection would be easy to spot and would have reached its most fevered pitch during an impassioned and violent period. Why else do we have so many revealing cultural studies of other turbulent political contexts, including the era immediately following the Revolution of 1917?[20]

The last decades of the tsarist era, however, have recently emerged from a conventional historiography that largely accepted them as a mere prologue to 1917 and assumed that all roads led to that eventful year.[21] This mindset, along with the field's more conventional emphasis on political history, ideology, labor, and other subjects apparently more pertinent to the rise of communism, may well explain why the relationship between culture and power in prerevolutionary Russia has received comparatively less attention. If that period had been only a prelude to an "inevitable" main event, one might wonder whether its cultural milieu would be distinctive or interesting enough to warrant a full study.

Rather than explain the late imperial era as a prologue to 1917, much new literature has explored alternate paths and currents open to the Russian Empire. These works have shifted attention back to the prerevolutionary period and

---

20. To name only a few, see Mona Ozouf, *La fête révolutionnaire, 1789–1799* (Paris: Gallimard, 1976); Lynn Hunt, *Politics, Culture, and Class in the French Revolution* (Berkeley and Los Angeles: University of California Press, 1984); Emmet Kennedy, *A Cultural History of the French Revolution* (New Haven: Yale University Press, 1989); Richard Stites, *Revolutionary Dreams: Utopian Vision and Experimental Life in the Russian Revolution* (Oxford: Oxford University Press, 1989); Gordon S. Wood, *The Radicalism of the American Revolution* (New York: Knopf, 1991); James von Geldern, *Bolshevik Festivals, 1917–1920* (Berkeley and Los Angeles: University of California Press, 1993); Katerina Clark, *Petersburg, Crucible of Cultural Revolution* (Cambridge: Harvard University Press, 1995); Orlando Figes and Boris Kolonitskii, *Interpreting the Russian Revolution: The Language and Symbols of 1917* (New Haven: Yale University Press, 1999); and Nicholas McDowell, *The English Radical Imagination: Culture, Religion, and Revolution, 1630–1660* (Oxford: Oxford University Press, 2004).

21. Proponents of the older view include Leopold Haimson, "The Problem of Social Stability in Urban Russia, 1905–1914," *Slavic Review* 23, no. 4 (1964), and 24, no. 1 (1965); Haimson, ed., *The Politics of Rural Russia, 1905–1914* (Bloomington: Indiana University Press, 1979); Theodore von Laue, *Why Lenin? Why Stalin? A Reappraisal of the Russian Revolution, 1900–1930* (Philadelphia: Lippincott, 1971); and Roberta Manning, *The Crisis of the Old Order in Russia: Gentry and Government* (Princeton: Princeton University Press, 1982).

recharacterized it as a starting point for potential departures that might have led to different destinations. Abraham Ascher, one of its leading political historians, has referred to Lenin's "dress rehearsal"—the Revolution of 1905—as "a critical juncture that opened up several paths."[22] Among other categories of material supporting this conclusion, scholars have found evidence of apolitical or nonradical professional development among the intelligentsia, significant popular support for the antirevolutionary Right, and the emergence of viable parliamentarianism in the new legislative bodies that shared in the Empire's government from 1906.[23] Research on education, journalism, sexuality, law, professional life, business, charity, local government, and other rapidly changing elements of modern society has supported this new view of Late Imperial Russia and gone a long way toward proving that it had at least the potential to follow a more "normal" course of development.[24] A post-Soviet study of the last dozen years before the Bolshevik Revolution has persuasively described them as "the period when the development of nonpolitical organizations [*obshchestva*] achieved its apogee."[25] Recent work on less obvious topics, such as corporal

---

22. Abraham Ascher, *The Revolution of 1905: Russia in Disarray* (Stanford: Stanford University Press, 1988), 2.

23. See, for example, Scott Seregny, *Russian Teachers and Peasant Revolution: The Politics of Education in 1905* (Bloomington: Indiana University Press, 1989); Don C. Rawson, *Russian Rightists and the Revolution of 1905* (Cambridge: Cambridge University Press, 1995); and Alexandra Korros, *A Reluctant Parliament: Stolypin, Nationalism, and the Politics of the Russian Imperial State Council, 1906–1911* (Lanham, Md.: Rowman and Littlefield, 2002).

24. See several of the essays in Edith W. Clowes, Samuel D. Kassow, and James L. West, eds., *Between Tsar and People: Educated Society and the Quest for Public Identity in Late Imperial Russia* (Princeton: Princeton University Press, 1991); Kassow, *Students, Professors, and the State in Tsarist Russia* (Berkeley and Los Angeles: University of California Press, 1989); Louise McReynolds, *The News Under Russia's Old Regime: The Development of a Mass-Circulation Press* (Princeton: Princeton University Press, 1991), and *Russia at Play: Leisure Activities at the End of the Tsarist Era* (Ithaca: Cornell University Press, 2003); Laura Engelstein, *The Keys to Happiness: Sex and the Search for Modernity in Fin-de-Siècle Russia* (Ithaca: Cornell University Press, 1992); William G. Wagner, *Marriage, Property, and Law in Late Imperial Russia* (New York: Oxford University Press, 1994); Harley D. Balzer, ed., *Russia's Missing Middle Class: The Professions in Russian History* (Armonk, N.Y.: M. E. Sharpe, 1996); Susan P. McCaffray, *The Politics of Industrialization in Tsarist Russia: The Association of Southern Coal and Steel Producers, 1874–1914* (DeKalb: Northern Illinois University Press, 1996); Adele Lindenmeyr, *Poverty Is Not a Vice: Charity, Society, and the State in Imperial Russia* (Princeton: Princeton University Press, 1996); Mary Schaeffer Conroy, ed., *Emerging Democracy in Late Imperial Russia: Case Studies on Local Self-Government (the Zemstvos), State Duma Elections, the Tsarist Government, and the State Council Before and During World War I* (Niwot: University of Colorado Press, 1998); and Joseph Bradley, "Subjects into Citizens: Societies, Civil Society, and Autocracy in Tsarist Russia," *American Historical Review* 107, no. 4 (2002): 1094–123. An older study, Seymour Becker, *Nobility and Privilege in Late Imperial Russia* (DeKalb: Northern Illinois University Press, 1985), one of the first to use the periodizing term "Late Imperial Russia" in its title, argued that even Russia's nobility was playing an adaptive and innovative role in the Empire's modernization.

25. A. S. Tumanova, *Samoderzhavie i obshchestvennye organizatsii v Rossii, 1905–1917 gody* (Tambov: Izdatel'stvo TGU imeni G. R. Derzhavina, 2002), 9.

punishment, religious sectarianism, alcohol and temperance, and arson and firefighting, among others, has set Late Imperial Russia into even greater relief as a modernizing polity entirely capable of fitting Jürgen Habermas's definition of a transformed public sphere.[26] An important theme of the present study, which seeks a place within this new literature, is that the performing arts both reflected and played an appreciable role in a relatively nonpolitical evolutionary process that might have spared the Russian Empire its fate rather than doomed it to destruction.

From the mid-eighteenth century, Russia developed a rich and diverse cultural life centered not only in its historical capitals but also in its provincial cities and countryside. The general literature on Russian cultural history is enormous. Since 1998 two vast tomes on the subject have appeared in English, each exceeding five hundred pages.[27] A late Soviet study of prerevolutionary dramatic theater alone filled seven volumes.[28] But despite the size of the field, little direct attention has come to the performing arts' nexus with politics.[29] The mantra that Russian art and politics were/are inextricably bound together left me surprised to learn that no book-length study has yet attempted a critical examination of that relationship, especially in the politically charged and artistically explosive late imperial era. The absence of a comprehensive treatment presents the greatest lacuna that I hope this book will fill. I am particularly interested in linking cultural life to Russia's evolving public sphere, a worthwhile endeavor since the large body of recent work on tsarist-era civil society

---

26. See, for example, Abby M. Schrader, *Languages of the Lash: Corporal Punishment and Identity in Imperial Russia* (DeKalb: Northern Illinois University Press, 2003); Laura Engelstein, *Castration and the Heavenly Kingdom: A Russian Folktale* (Ithaca: Cornell University Press, 2003); Patricia Herlihy, *The Alcoholic Empire: Vodka and Politics in Late Imperial Russia* (New York: Oxford University Press, 2002); and Cathy A. Frierson, *All Russia Is Burning! A Cultural History of Fire and Arson in Late Imperial Russia* (Seattle: University of Washington Press, 2002). For Habermas's definition of a transformed public sphere, see Jürgen Habermas, *The Structural Transformation of the Public Sphere: An Inquiry into a Category of Bourgeois Society,* trans. Thomas Burger (Cambridge: MIT Press, 1989).

27. W. Bruce Lincoln, *Between Heaven and Hell: The Story of a Thousand Years of Artistic Life in Russia* (New York: Viking, 1998); Orlando Figes, *Natasha's Dance: A Cultural History of Russia* (New York: Metropolitan, 2002). A third recent work, more specific to the performing arts, Robert Leach and Victor Borovsky, eds., *A History of Russian Theatre* (Cambridge: Cambridge University Press, 1999), exceeds four hundred pages. James H. Billington, *The Icon and the Axe: An Interpretive History of Russian Culture* (New York: Knopf, 1966), remains popular.

28. E. G. Kholodov et al., eds., *Istoriia russkogo dramaticheskogo teatra,* 7 vols. (Moscow: Iskusstvo, 1977–87).

29. Lynn Sargeant, "*Kashchei the Immortal*: Liberal Politics, Cultural Memory, and the Rimsky-Korsakov Scandal of 1905," *Russian Review* 64, no. 1 (2005): 22–43, is one of the few recent contributions to this literature, which was long confined to one Soviet volume from half a century ago, A. Ia. Al'tshuller, ed., *Pervaia russkaia revoliutsiia i teatr: Stat'i i materialy* (Moscow: Iskusstvo, 1956).

has tended to neglect the arts.[30] This omission suggests the value of an attempt to bridge the two fields.

The greater part of my research lies in the primary sources chronicling the arts in late tsarist times. These texts articulate the thoughts, attitudes, and experiences of cultured Russians in the maelstrom swirling around them in the decades before 1917. Late Imperial Russia had a highly developed daily press that commented widely on culture and the arts, not only in the form of reviews, but also in editorial comment and reportage on the increasingly important business aspects of theater, which grew more commercial and professionalized over time. From 1862 articles and journals addressing theatrical life were exempt from the prepublication censorship that remained in place for most media until 1905. The major periodical covering the performing arts, *Theater and Art* (*Teatr i iskusstvo*, published from 1897 to 1918), dealt candidly and capaciously with the world of the stage, as did such short-lived competitors as *Theatrical Russia* (*Teatral'naia Rossiia*, published only in 1904–5). Monthly "thick journals"—more commonly associated with literature, painting, and other art forms—also offered important performing arts coverage. From 1890 to 1915 the Imperial Theaters Directorate (*Direktsiia Imperatorskikh teatrov*), the administration of Russia's state theaters, published an annual *Yearbook* (*Ezhegodnik*) that featured informational articles, artist rosters, performance calendars, box office receipts, and other important sources.

Happily for students of cultural life in Late Imperial Russia, many of the era's leading figures left detailed records of their lives and work. These individuals included not only performers active in every art form and setting but also their relatives, educators, employers, critics, audience members, foreign observers, administrators, and others with firsthand knowledge and experience of the performing arts. Some left diaries and correspondence. Many published their memoirs, either in the Soviet Union or, as was often the case, in emigration. Although many memoirists were famous and enjoyed privileges not shared by their less distinguished colleagues, I have made every effort to include accounts from more obscure figures. Some memoirists who enjoyed celebrity in later

---

30. Balzer, *Russia's Missing Middle Class*; Bradley, "Subjects into Citizens"; Elise Kimerling Wirtschafter, *Social Identity in Imperial Russia* (DeKalb: Northern Illinois University Press, 1997), and Madhavan K. Palat, ed., *Social Identities in Revolutionary Russia* (New York: Palgrave, 2001), leave it out, as do most of the more specific works mentioned above. Clowes, Kassow, and West, *Between Tsar and People*, include a couple of articles pertaining to arts patronage and the relationship between theater and society. V. R. Leikina-Svirskaia's older study, *Russkaia intelligentsiia v 1900–1917 godakh* (Moscow: Mysl', 1981), includes a chapter on actors. A notable and very recent exception is Murray Frame, *School for Citizens: Theatre and Civil Society in Imperial Russia* (New Haven: Yale University Press, 2006).

times, it should also be noted, occupied modest stations in the early phases of their careers and thus were not always living exceptional lives in late imperial times.

Any memoir presents information refracted through the prism of the author's own biases, inaccuracies, and other sources of retrospective subjectivity. Those published in the Soviet Union were subject to state censorship and editorial control. These factors fluctuated in focus and severity over time, but nevertheless remained present and discernible. Memoirs published in emigration often betray some degree of nostalgia or even bitterness. Yet whatever their faults, recollections in both categories contain otherwise unobtainable statements about values, ideals, creative processes, social views, political attitudes, daily lives, and their evolution in times of social and political turmoil. It would be difficult to imagine an effective study of the present subject that did not use them. As Hiroaki Kuromiya has written about recollections of the much more politicized Stalin era, "the value of these memoirs appears evident to anyone who works in the field."[31]

Russian archives also contain useful information. File (*fond*) 776 of the Russian State Historical Archive in St. Petersburg (RGIA) holds the files of the Ministry of the Interior's Main Office for Press Affairs, the principal censorship organ of the Russian Empire. Its records figure importantly in the discussions of theatrical censorship in Chapters 1, 2, and 5. File 497 holds the documentary records of the Imperial Theaters Directorate. The Russian State Archive of Literature and Art in Moscow (RGALI) holds files on individual personalities who appear throughout this study, as well as on the Russian Theatrical Society (RTO), the main professional organization for performing artists, which will be discussed in detail in Chapter 4. In addition to its impressive collection of printed materials, the State Theatrical Library of St. Petersburg holds relevant documents, as does the A. A. Bakhrushin Central State Theatrical Museum in Moscow. One major disappointment in Russian archival holdings is their paucity of documents recording the activities of private and popular theaters. Many enterprises in that category were transient and disappeared before 1917. Neither I nor, to the best of my knowledge, anyone else has been able to track down their documentary records. Since many nonstate theaters lacked permanence, and those that survived the Bolshevik Revolution were nationalized by the Soviet regime

---

31. Hiroaki Kuromiya, "Guide to Émigré and Dissident Memoir Literature," in *A Researcher's Guide to Sources on Soviet Social History in the 1930s*, ed. Sheila Fitzpatrick and Lynne Viola (Armonk, N.Y.: M. E. Sharpe, 1990), 255. Kuromiya, "Soviet Memoirs as a Historical Source" (published in the same volume), 247, argues that "one can use Soviet memoirs in a meaningful way." I believe this is at least as true for those of Late Imperial Russia.

and then either eliminated or placed under state control, such records may no longer exist.

Russia's increasing pace of modernization and rapid urbanization made its cultural life complex and multilayered in the late imperial era. Before launching into specific elements of that culture, I will first present a chapter introducing the contours of the Empire's performing arts community. My hope is that it will familiarize the reader with the development of the institutions and values that governed Russia's theaters, cultural organizations, educational establishments, financial structures, professional codes, and government authorities and how they were functioning and evolving in the last decades of the tsarist era. In the process of laying out these institutional dimensions, I will introduce the reader to many of the people who controlled, shaped, interacted with, and depended on them.

Chapter 2 will seek to explain how these institutions fared amid political turbulence, especially that of the troubled period between the Revolutions of 1905 and 1917. This chapter will attempt to present the problems and challenges they faced and describe their reactions to both individual instances of major national unrest and developments during the revolutionary period as a whole. I am interested in whether unprecedented political events forced them to alter their functions and structures. As I hope to demonstrate, turbulence created major concerns among impresarios and other arts administrators, who saw their audiences dwindle and suffered financially as a result. Government authorities exercising power over culture also betrayed a heightened sensitivity to political events. But unexpectedly, political challenges appear to have lessened rather than strengthened the degree of control that they could or were willing to exercise.

Chapters 3 and 4 will depart from institutional matters to present the people who do the most to bring the performing arts to life in any society: the performers. Although there was an appreciable movement of personnel between the imperial stages and the Empire's private and popular theaters, I felt it best to look at each group separately. As state employees, the imperial stage performers discussed in Chapter 3 not only lived noticeably different and usually more prosperous lives than their privately employed colleagues but also had to address issues of state and institutional loyalty from which private and popular stage performers were free in all but the most notional sense. One actor publicly likened the difference between imperial and nonimperial artists to the distinction between two "castes."[32] With few exceptions, virtually all imperial

---

32. Quoted in Frame, *School for Citizens*, 152.

stage performers remained satisfied with the status quo and resisted the politicization of their work, even after 1917.

Chapter 4 focuses on the problems and concerns of private and popular stage performers. Among these issues were the challenges of professional development, a process that most artists hoped would result in greater economic security and improved material conditions. Did they use their art and professional consciousness to promote social change, radical and reformist ideas, or a politicized civic mind? Or did they stay on the sidelines to tend to their own affairs and interests? My work will suggest that just as was the case with their colleagues on the imperial stage, politicizing their profession usually repelled rather than attracted them. Their public activities and concerns generally remained confined to securing stable working conditions and improvements in their professional circumstances.

Chapter 5 crosses the proscenium to the audiences. After a discussion of who went to the theater and why—itself a nuanced and illuminating subject for students of Late Imperial Russia—this chapter will examine how they responded to politics and its intrusion into a sphere that they identified primarily with entertainment. I am interested in learning the extent to which theater attendance translated into social and political awareness. Did repertoire selections and artistic content shape, highlight, or intensify the theatergoing public's engagement in political life? What role did pure diversion play in audience choices and tastes? How did audiences react when confronted with politicized messages on and off the stage? I hope to demonstrate that audiences also proved reluctant to identify entertainment with revolution and, despite a few tense moments, resisted or ignored attempts to politicize the Empire's stages.

Chapter 6 will move beyond the more tangible features of the performing arts to examine the relationship between politics and emerging theoretical concepts. This chapter will attempt to determine whether politics played a significant role in the development of Russia's avant-garde or whether the avant-garde possessed its own momentum independent of political life. The balance of my research suggests that new aesthetic concepts developed out of sync with patterns and modalities of political unrest. Typically and, I believe, revealingly, these developments failed to resonate with great critical or popular success in Russia's ever more commercialized and consumerized entertainment milieu. Radical cultural innovation does not appear to have been an especially prominent catalyst or result of radical politics.

A final chapter will summarize the results of these inquiries and seek to interpret their meanings for the relationship between culture and power in the Russian experience. To add perspective, I intend to explore how developments in Imperial Russia's performing arts culture were carried forward (or, perhaps more appropriately, left behind) after 1917 and how they are being remembered (or, perhaps more appropriately, relived) in Russia today. The evolution of the performing arts in an earlier time may well contribute to our understanding of Russia's ongoing quest for a viable civil society and to contemporary debates about the relationship between culture and power in Russia and elsewhere.

1

"AN ASPIRATION TO NOVELTY":
CONTOURS OF THE PERFORMING ARTS IN
LATE IMPERIAL RUSSIA

Prince Sergei Volkonskii did not enjoy his job as Director of the Imperial Theaters. Appointed to succeed his uncle Ivan Vsevolozhskii in 1899, this grandson and namesake of a leading Decembrist showed little enthusiasm from the beginning. "How I did not want to! How all this was not in my nature!" he opined. Later in life the prince regretted his "two unpleasant, difficult years" in the post, which were "always agonizing for me."[1]

Volkonskii's memoirs are drenched with indignities. In addition to his exhausting courtly duty of having to attend every performance at which the Imperial Family chose to appear, he suffered frequent embarrassments from his subordinates. Against them "one could not count on help from above."[2] Sergei Diaghilev, his special assistant who edited the Imperial Theaters' *Yearbook* and later became the famous impresario of the Ballets Russes, flouted Volkonskii's authority and threatened to use his court connections to take over the Directorate himself.[3] Diaghilev's temper eventually got him fired, but the atmosphere it created was not pleasant.[4] More than once Volkonskii had to change the ballets

---

1. Prince Sergei Volkonskii, *Rodina: Vospominaniia* (Moscow: Zakharov, 2002), 142. Vsevolozhskii was made Director of the Hermitage, a demotion he resented.
2. Ibid., 150, 154.
3. According to V. A. Teliakovskii, *Vospominaniia* (Leningrad: Iskusstvo, 1965), 38, Diaghilev "openly declared to his boss that he was without character and weak and that before long he would give up the directorship and hand over full powers to him, Diaghilev." Ultimately, Volkonskii claimed, it was he who had to force Diaghilev out. Volkonskii, *Rodina*, 148.
4. Prince Peter Lieven, *The Birth of the Ballets-Russes,* trans. L. Zarine (New York: Dover, 1973), 40–41. Lieven (Liven), a Directorate official, said that courtiers advised Diaghilev to refuse to resign when asked, but he was promptly fired when he followed this advice.

in the Mariinskii Theater's repertoire because the Prima Donna Matil'da Kshesinskaia, Tsar Nicholas II's former mistress, wanted it so. When she changed her mind, the tsar personally ordered Volkonskii to restore the original ballets. Volkonskii even suffered her interference in casting decisions. Upon objecting, his superior, the Minister of the Imperial Court Baron Vladimir Frederiks, told him that "by insulting Matil'da Feliksovna, you have also offended me." As a loyal subject of the tsar, Volkonskii thought it would have been "silly" to hold out. In 1901, however, he found his job much less bearable when Kshesinskaia, who had refused to appear on stage in farthingales, persuaded Nicholas II to cancel a fine that Volkonskii had imposed on her for disobeying. Already "waiting for an excuse to resign," the undermined Director quit his post.[5]

Volkonskii's short tenure proved that arts administration in Late Imperial Russia was no easy task. But before we examine rising challenges to the Empire's performing arts community, a discussion of its institutional contours at the turn of the twentieth century is in order.

The Imperial Theaters over which Volkonskii briefly presided stood at the pinnacle of Russia's arts establishment. Enjoying direct Court patronage since Empress Elizabeth began financing performing troupes in 1756, they were in every important sense "state" theaters.[6] At its height the Imperial Theater system included six main venues. As the imperial capital, St. Petersburg was adorned by the most prestigious: the Bol'shoi Kamennyi ("Great Stone," 1783) Theater and Mariinskii Theater (1860, named for Alexander II's wife, Empress Mariia Aleksandrovna) for opera and ballet, the Aleksandrinskii (1832) for Russian (and occasionally foreign) drama, and the Mikhailovskii (1833) for French (and occasionally Russian and German) drama. The Aleksandrinskii and Mikhailovskii were named for the wife and brother, respectively, of Nicholas I. Moscow offered the Bol'shoi ("Great," 1824) Theater (opera and ballet) and Malyi ("Small," also 1824, for drama). The renovation of the Bol'shoi Kamennyi Theater for use as Petersburg's Conservatory from 1886 left three major venues in the capital, with the Mariinskii considered the most prestigious.

The formal opening of the Imperial Theaters every August 30—the traditional date associated with Elizabeth's decision to finance them—launched an artistic season that usually lasted (with official Lenten breaks between 1881 and

---

5. Volkonskii, *Rodina*, 164–71.
6. Victor Borovsky, "The Organisation of the Russian Theatre, 1645–1763," in *A History of Russian Theatre*, ed. Robert Leach and Victor Borovsky (Cambridge: Cambridge University Press, 1999), 41–55. The first state-sponsored theatrical was mounted at the behest of Tsar Aleksei in 1672. The performing troupes were formally taken into the imperial household in 1759.

Fig. 1 Moscow's chief opera and ballet venue, the Bol'shoi Theater, pictured here around 1900. From V. A. Teliakovskii, *Vospominaniia* (Leningrad: Iskusstvo, 1965).

1906) until late April. On important occasions the theaters could host symbolic state functions, but these were relatively rare and mostly confined to such events as the coronation of a new tsar or the milestone anniversary of a major event in Russian history. Nicholas I, whose arrival on the throne had been challenged by the Decembrist uprising, in which Prince Volkonskii's grandfather took part, received public acclaim in the newly constructed Bol'shoi during his coronation festivities, when unmemorable opera and ballet performances were staged.[7] During his reign the Empire's new national anthem, "God Save the Tsar," was given its first public performances in the Imperial Theaters.[8] But theatrical self-aggrandizement was not always on the agenda. In 1856 Nicholas's successor, Alexander II, utilized Moscow's principal imperial stage during his coronation to present Donizetti's light comic opera *The Elixir of Love,* in which an illiterate peasant buys a bottle of wine from a quack doctor in the belief that it is a love potion that will help him win the woman he loves. Alexander III, whose reign began with his father's assassination in 1881, reverted to the patriotic idiom

---

7. Richard S. Wortman, *Scenarios of Power: Myth and Ceremony in Russian Monarchy from Peter the Great to the Abdication of Nicholas II* (Princeton: Princeton University Press, 2006), 140.

8. Ibid., 159–60. The first performance was in the Bol'shoi on Nicholas's name day, December 6, 1833. The first Mariinskii performance was on January 10, 1834. The anthem was traditionally played three times in repetition.

upon his accession with scenes from Mikhail Glinka's patriotic opera *A Life for the Tsar*, a heroic recounting of the peasant Ivan Susanin's self-sacrifice to protect the Romanov dynasty's founder, Tsar Michael, from the invading Poles in the early seventeenth century.[9] Nicholas II also included scenes from Glinka's opera when he came to the throne, but the theatrical highlight of Russia's last coronation turned out to be the semi-erotically staged ballet *The Splendid Pearl*.[10] A gala performance of *A Life for the Tsar* mounted to celebrate the tercentenary of the Romanov dynasty in 1913 drew scant attention from the house's contemporary rulers, who left after the first act, suggesting that theatrical reinforcements of official power were fading in importance.[11]

In 1804 the Imperial Theaters Directorate received a monopoly on printing advertisements and playbills in St. Petersburg and Moscow, and in 1827 its administrators were granted the power to regulate all theatrical affairs in the historic capitals. From 1843 to 1882 the theaters enjoyed an official "monopoly" on public performance in both cities.[12] These privileges were instituted both to satisfy official suspicions (substantiated or not) of unregulated theater as an agent of political dissent and ensure a large enough audience to keep the imperial stages profitable.[13] Indeed, not long before, Russia's rulers had to command often reluctant urban subjects to attend performances to guarantee revenue.[14] After the Imperial Theaters' exclusive right to entertain was abolished in 1882, their preeminence continued to be recognized with an annual subsidy set at two million rubles. This amount was nearly doubled by additional annual payments from the imperial household, nominally delivered for the use and maintenance of the tsar's box in each theater.[15]

---

9. Ibid., 277–78.
10. Ibid., 342–43.
11. Ibid., 388.
12. For a description of these powers, their evolution, and eventual abolition, see Murray Frame, "'Freedom of the Theatres': The Abolition of the Russian Imperial Theatre Monopoly," *Slavonic and East European Review* 83, no. 2 (2005), and *School for Citizens: Theatre and Civil Society in Imperial Russia* (New Haven: Yale University Press, 2006), 27. The 1827 statute allowed the authorities to determine appropriate days and times for nongovernment theatrical performances.
13. S. S. Danilov, *Ocherki po istorii russkogo dramaticheskogo teatra* (Moscow: Gosudarstvennyi Nauchno-Issledovatel'skii Institut Teatra i Muzyki, 1948), 223, records an official statement from 1858 about the harm "that might now arise in the political sense from granting full freedom to private enterprises to establish in the capitals national theaters of all types and for all estates." The importance of keeping a large enough audience was common internationally. According to F. W. J. Hemmings, *Theatre and State in France, 1760–1905* (Cambridge: Cambridge University Press, 1994), 7, ensuring the financial viability of a state-subsidized theater had been Louis XIV's rationale for granting a monopoly on drama performances in Paris to the Comédie française in 1680.
14. Borovsky, "Organisation," 49.
15. Laurence Senelick, ed., *National Theatre in Northern and Eastern Europe, 1746–1900* (Cambridge: Cambridge University Press, 1991), 381.

From 1766 Russia's Imperial Theaters were managed by a specially created Directorate. In 1826 Tsar Nicholas I placed it under the authority of the newly established Ministry of the Imperial Court. As a second-class officeholder appointed by the tsar, the Director was usually an aristocrat with prior administrative experience and some personal connection to the arts.[16] There was no systematic means of selecting a Director and thus neither a common description of the post's occupants nor a general pattern of their conduct or results. Some of Volkonskii's predecessors had been incompetent, corrupt, and abusive, while others were hospitable and engaging. Prince Mikhail Tiufiakin, Director from 1819 to 1822, was rumored to beat his male subordinates and seduce his female ones. His predecessor, Aleksandr Naryshkin, who held the post from 1799 to 1819, was known for his great kindness and generosity.[17] Some of the later Directors, whatever their mien, contributed to the theaters artistically. Stepan Gedeonov, who ran them from 1867 to 1875, coauthored several plays with the prolific dramatist Aleksandr Ostrovskii and also wrote the scenario for Nikolai Rimskii-Korsakov's opera *Mlada*. Vsevolozhskii, in the post from 1881 to 1899, produced more than a thousand set and costume designs during his eighteen years at the Directorate, many of which received critical acclaim.[18] His nephew Volkonskii continued the tradition with some unique staging of his own, including the czardas in the ballet *The Humpbacked Horse*, which won praise from no less distinguished a spectator than the visiting Shah of Persia.[19] The dancer Tamara Karsavina knew Volkonskii as "a man of refined intellect, great gifts and extensive knowledge of art, loyal and amiable."[20] The painter and designer Aleksandr Benua recalled the lavishness of his hospitality:

> A magnificent doorman in a red court frock emblazoned with a coat of arms, and a few lackeys, helped remove my coat at the entrance to the main

---

16. A. A. Mossolov, *At the Court of the Last Tsar: Being the Memoirs of A. A. Mossolov, Head of the Court Chancellery, 1900–1916*, trans. E. W. Dickes (London: Methuen, 1935), 182. There were only fifteen first-class officeholders at the time of Mossolov's tenure. The office of Director of the Imperial Theaters placed its holder in the relatively high fourth *chin* (rank) in the Court component of the Table of Ranks established by Peter I in 1722. It was equivalent to the rank of major general in the military component of the Table of Ranks.

17. Richard Stites, *Serfdom, Society, and the Arts in Imperial Russia: The Pleasure and the Power* (New Haven: Yale University Press, 2005), 156–57.

18. E. Ponomarev, "I. A. Vsevolozhskii (Ocherk ego khudozhestvennoi deiatel'nosti)," *Ezhegodnik Imperatoskikh teatrov, 1899–1900*, 31–32. P. P. Gnedich, *Kniga zhizni: Vospominaniia, 1855–1918* (Moscow: Agraf, 2000), 126, discusses his artistic contributions as well. His costume designs were used for several of Chaikovskii's ballets and operas, productions that figured among the Imperial Theaters' most prominent during his tenure.

19. Volkonskii, *Rodina*, 159.

20. Tamara Karsavina, *Theatre Street: The Reminiscences of Tamara Karsavina* (New York: Dutton, 1931), 129.

staircase. At the door of the Director's apartment a footman, also in a courtly red livery, announced the names, and the prince, standing in the first room, greeted each person who entered with the enchanting kindness of an authentic (and ever more Italian) *gran' signor,* giving various compliments to the ladies and notables. Pyramids of every kind of delicacy rose under candelabras in the dining room, and champagne flowed in torrents.[21]

When Volkonskii resigned in 1901, he was succeeded by Vladimir Teliakovskii, his deputy in charge of the Moscow Imperial Theaters. The son of a prominent military fortifications specialist and scion of a gentry family from Iaroslavl' province, Teliakovskii attended the elite Corps des pages, accepted a commission in the prestigious Horse Guards regiment, and rose to the rank of colonel before taking up his appointment to lead the Directorate's Moscow office in October 1898. His parents were drawn to the arts and frequently hosted many of Petersburg's most distinguished cultural figures, including the great composer Petr Chaikovskii. As a young child Vladimir knew the composer Anton Rubinshtein, a leader of the Russian Musical Society, director of its programs of musical instruction, and founder of St. Petersburg Conservatory. He often played piano duets with Rubinshtein's brother Nikolai, the composer, pianist, and Moscow Conservatory founder, and studied music with the composer Anatolii Liadov and several members of the Imperial Theaters' house orchestras.[22]

Teliakovskii remained in his post for the rest of the tsarist era and for the first two and a half months of the Provisional Government formed in March 1917. He was by virtually unanimous account a popular figure with progressive ideas about the arts. The writer and critic Aleksandr Pleshcheev remembered that some artists were suspicious of the new Director's military background and mocked his appointment with cruel couplets: "It is time to elevate comedy and ballet / And calm the nerves of Terpsichore! / We do not need a titled devotee, / We need the spurs of a *cavaliere.*" Yet Teliakovskii's tenure led Pleshcheev to believe that "this new, keen, and brave Director knew how to strengthen society's interest in theater, to breathe new life into it, to attract new strengths.... Wonderful artists and great actors made themselves Teliakovskii's collaborators.... There is your sergeant major and spurs. Let us recognize when we look back that Teliakovskii, at whom we laughed, now stands out as a leading and important figure."[23] The actor Iurii Iur'ev fondly remembered Teliakovskii as a

21. Aleksandr Benua, *Moi vospominaniia,* 2 vols. (Moscow: Zakharov, 2003), 2:1285.
22. Teliakovskii, *Vospominaniia,* 20–21.
23. A. A. Pleshcheev, *Pod seniiu kulis.* ... (Paris: VAL, 1936), 148–49. Terpsichore is the Greek muse of dance.

Fig. 2 Vladimir Teliakovskii, Director of the Imperial Theaters from 1901 to 1917. From V. A. Teliakovskii, *Vospominaniia* (Leningrad: Iskusstvo, 1965).

leader who "invited new directors [and] very actively promoted youth."[24] The Mariinskii's long-serving chief conductor Eduard Napravnik found him "a well-meaning, just, accessible, and approachable person."[25] Vasilii Shkafer, a tenor and stage director, recalled that "despite his dazzling official suite ... he carried himself very simply, without any shade of Madame de Pompadour [*pompadurstva*]."[26] Fedor Komissarzhevskii, who worked as a director in the Imperial Theaters, found Teliakovskii "shrewd and gifted" and placed him on par with the famed impresarios Max Reinhardt and Charles B. Cochran as "that rare combination, a sound business man who possessed artistic ideas."[27] The Director struck the famous bass Fedor Shaliapin as "a thoroughly good sort" who

24. Iu. M. Iur'ev, *Zapiski*, 2 vols. (Leningrad: Iskusstvo, 1963), 2:163.
25. E. F. Napravnik, "Vospominaniia E. F. Napravnika," in *Avtobiograficheskie, tvorcheskie materialy, dokumenty, pis'ma* (Leningrad: Gosudarstvennoe muzykal'noe izdatel'stvo, 1959), 43.
26. V. P. Shkafer, *Sorok let na stsene russkoi opery: Vospominaniia, 1890–1930 gg.* (Leningrad: Izdatel'stvo Teatra Opery i Baleta imeni S. M. Kirova, 1936), 190.
27. Theodore Komisarjevsky, *Myself and the Theatre* (London: Heinemann, 1929), 30, 21.

genuinely attracted his "sympathy and liking."[28] Benua thought he was "full of good intentions."[29] When Teliakovskii left the Directorate in May 1917, he did so "in a general atmosphere of sympathy and good wishes."[30] Upon his death seven years later, a Soviet obituary mourned him as "one of the most prominent and worthy figures of our prerevolutionary theater," "an organizer and administrator of first-class talent" who "combined with great taste an understanding of theatrical art and an aspiration to novelty, to a renewal of theatrical forms."[31]

When Teliakovskii arrived in Petersburg to take over the Directorate in 1901, he found an unenviable number of duties awaiting him. In addition to managing the artists, their temperaments, and tolerable relationships with the Imperial Family and superiors at Court, his day-to-day administrative demands were enormous. In the year before he took over, the Directorate employed a staff of 1,667, of whom 685 were artists and the rest administrative and technical personnel.[32] Together with its main offices, located in a large official building behind the Aleksandrinskii Theater and across the aptly named Theater Street from the Ministry of the Interior, the Directorate maintained separate administrative offices for both Petersburg and Moscow, the latter previously led by Teliakovskii. All set and costume design and production was done in-house. The Directorate ran the state's theatrical schools in Petersburg and Moscow, which trained students for ballet and drama (but not opera), as well as a library, printing press, photography studio, horse and carriage department, first aid centers and infirmaries, equipment shops, warehouses, and power stations. Along with the five main theaters functioning when Teliakovskii assumed his post, the Director administered the Hermitage Theater in the Winter Palace and several smaller theaters found in Petersburg's suburban palace ensembles. The Directorate had primary responsibility for determining each theater's repertoire, securing performance rights for new works, distributing roles to artists, negotiating salaries with performers and employees, and recruiting new talents.[33] Teliakovskii tried to delegate some of these responsibilities to his administrative subordinates

---

28. Feodor Chaliapin, *Man and Mask: Forty Years in the Life of a Singer,* trans. Phyllis Mégroz (New York: Knopf, 1932), 231.

29. Benua, *Moi vospominaniia,* 2:1377.

30. Vasilii Bezpalov, *Teatry v dni revoliutsii, 1917* (Leningrad: Academia, 1927), 30.

31. Quoted in D. Zolotnitskii, "Ob avtore etoi knigi," in Teliakovskii, *Vospominaniia,* 5. Teliakovskii has not been forgotten in post-Soviet times. In October 2004 a delegation from the Mariinskii Theater laid flowers on his grave to commemorate the eightieth anniversary of his death. See "Vozlozhenie tsvetov na mogilu V. A. Teliakovskogo na Serafimovskom kladbishche (28.10.04)," http://www.mariinsky.ru:8001/ru/massmedia/press/october_29_1.

32. Murray Frame, *The St. Petersburg Imperial Theatres: Stage and State in Revolutionary Russia, 1900–1920* (Greensboro, N.C.: McFarland, 2000), 22.

33. Teliakovskii, *Vospominaniia,* 22. Frame, *Imperial Theatres,* 89, correctly observes that the Directorate had "a free hand" in repertoire selections and "produced what it wanted to produce."

and, at least for the repertoires of the dramatic theaters, to artist councils and literary committees, but ultimate responsibility rested with him alone.[34] His diaries, composed between his arrival in the Moscow office in October 1898 and July 1917, came to more than fourteen thousand pages.[35]

To make Teliakovskii's job even more complicated, his tenure coincided with the emergence of privately operated performing companies. Legal in the capitals from 1882, they not only challenged the Imperial Theaters' cultural hegemony but also vied with them for audiences, artists, and box office receipts.

Movement toward an independent community of theaters was already underway long before the formal abrogation of the state monopoly on theatrical performance. Private theaters had appeared in both Moscow and Petersburg in the early eighteenth century, before the Imperial Theaters gained their monopoly.[36] Russia's provinces knew no restrictions on private entertainments. In the mid-nineteenth century 43 theaters were counted outside St. Petersburg and Moscow. By the early 1870s that figure had grown to 102.[37] Apart from their creative efforts, great landowners mounted elaborate performances on their estates, usually employing talented serfs. In 1792 Count Nikolai Sheremetev's estate theater troupe had a roster and staff of more than two hundred.[38] Its artistic milieu and those like it demanded great personal attention and professional seriousness. Some of these grandees entertained Russia's rulers and visiting foreign notables. Prince Nikolai Iusupov had his performers taught French and Italian.[39] A blacksmith's daughter whom Sheremetev trained for opera became his wife.[40]

---

34. Like Volkonskii, Teliakovskii also had to stomach some Court interference in the repertoire. Nevertheless, he generally felt that he enjoyed "full independence in artistic matters." See Teliakovskii, *Vospominaniia*, 27. Petr Gnedich, the Aleksandrinskii's chief director from 1900 to 1908, recalled the broad latitude that he and others in comparable positions had in determining repertoires. See Gnedich, *Kniga zhizni*, 255. Shkafer, *Sorok let*, 191, recalled that his colleagues "bowed before Napravnik; his authority in the theater was considered unshakable." According to Frame, *Imperial Theatres*, 52, no systematic means of repertoire selection ever emerged.

35. The diaries are filed in Gosudarstvennyi Tsentral'nyi Teatral'nyi Muzei imeni A. A. Bakhrushina (hereafter GTSTMB), f. 280, though entries from the time of his Moscow appointment in 1898 to the end of 1903 are now in print. See V. A. Teliakovskii, *Dnevniki direktora Imperatorskikh teatrov: 1898–1901, Moskva* (Moscow: Artist. Rezhisser. Teatr., 1998), and *Dnevniki direktora Imperatorskikh teatrov: 1901–1903, Sankt-Peterburg* (Moscow: Artist. Rezhisser. Teatr., 2002).

36. Borovsky, "Organisation," 42–45.

37. Frame, *School for Citizens*, 85. Of the 102 theaters functioning in the early 1870s, 61 were considered permanent.

38. N. A. Elizarova, *Teatry Sheremetevykh* (Moscow: Iskusstvo, 1944), 258–59.

39. Frame, *School for Citizens*, 39. These environments were not always so pleasant. Count Sergei Kamenskii personally whipped serf performers who made mistakes.

40. For the story of their romance, see Orlando Figes, *Natasha's Dance: A Cultural History of Russia* (New York: Metropolitan, 2002), 28–37. The marriage was kept secret until after the woman died in 1803.

In the Empire's cities private individuals could build stages and proscenia in their homes and invite spectators, often paying ones, to attend. Prince Iusupov added a lavish neorococo theater to the east wing of his palace on the Moika, complete with its own "prince's box" and a quality of performance and elegance of surroundings that would not have disgraced a minor Italian court. Admirers called it "the small Mariinskii." Napravnik, a Czech immigrant who became the real Mariinskii Theater's chief conductor in 1869, received his entrée into Russian musical life when Iusupov recruited him to play in his theater's orchestra eight years earlier.[41]

Private clubs could offer entertainments as part of their activities and, although such activities depended on official permission, they competed within the space nominally monopolized by the Imperial Theaters. The Russian Musical Society presented concerts in the Petersburg Noblemen's Club—now the Great Hall of the St. Petersburg Philharmonic—every year from its founding in 1859.[42] The Philharmonic, founded in 1802, had already been performing there for twenty-three years.[43]

Some entrepreneurs staged private performances that flouted the Imperial Theaters' monopoly, either on technicalities or outright. One magician successfully petitioned for the right to perform because his act was silent.[44] In 1865 Ostrovskii, Nikolai Rubinshtein, and other leading figures founded an artistic circle, which began entertaining Moscow with public performances three years later.[45] The Malyi Theater actress Anna Brenko received formal permission to stage excerpts from dramas in 1879 and exceeded the boundaries of that privilege to present full-length staged plays to private audiences the following year. Neither her operation nor the artistic circle's met with official sanction or any other type of government interference.[46] Indeed, an 1854 addendum to the law establishing the Imperial Theaters' monopoly permitted the Directorate to authorize private performances in exchange for a share of the profits—further evidence that the monopoly had been instituted to ensure the financial viability of the state stage.[47]

---

41. Napravnik, "Vospominaniia," 36.
42. See the appendix of performances in N. F. Findeizen, *Ocherk deiatel'nosti S.-Peterburgskogo otdeleniia Imperatorskogo russkogo muzykal'nogo obshchestva (1859–1909)* (St. Petersburg: Tipografiia Glavnogo Upravleniia Udelov, 1909).
43. Stites, *Serfdom, Society, and the Arts*, 99.
44. Louise McReynolds, *Russia at Play: Leisure Activities at the End of the Tsarist Era* (Ithaca: Cornell University Press, 2003), 225.
45. Arkady Ostrovsky, "Imperial and Private Theatres, 1882–1905," in Leach and Borovsky, *Russian Theatre*, 218–19; M. I. Andreeva et al., eds., *Russkii dramaticheskii teatr: Entsiklopediia* (Moscow: Bol'shaia Rossiiskaia Entsiklopediia, 2001), 32.
46. Frame, "'Freedom of the Theatres,'" 270–71.
47. Ibid., 254. The portion of the profits to be turned over could be as high as 25 percent.

No fewer than fourteen theaters were functioning commercially (e.g., negotiating contracts with playwrights) in St. Petersburg in 1874—eight years before the monopoly ended—while twelve operated in Moscow that year.[48]

The monopoly's fluidity led many Russians to demand its abolition. Its increasing irrelevance complemented arguments that the state's exclusive right to cultivate Russian theater in the capitals hindered artistic development by excluding external resources and talent. Enjoying the support of conservative publicists, including the influential nationalist Mikhail Katkov, in 1880 Ostrovskii suggested that the appearance of a privately run theater performing Russian dramas (such as his own) would foster greater patriotism and public support for "official nationality." This goal rose in prominence as a state priority after revolutionary terrorists assassinated Alexander II the following year. Vsevolozhskii, who became Director of the Imperial Theaters in September 1881, agreed with the critics, and the balance of opinion within the government came to favor the formal legalization of private theater. Although we have no precise record of the reasoning behind the monopoly's abolition in March 1882, it probably resulted from Alexander III's desire to renew patriotic nationalism and the growing conviction in both state and society that legally functioning private theaters would help that cause.[49]

The monopoly's elimination allowed for more regular theatrical life in the capitals, but private theaters faced numerous practical limitations. Without the business experience, notoriety, or fan base to become profitable, many early enterprises foundered. Few theatrical entrepreneurs possessed the financial resources to build new theaters. Most had to rely on existing space, which was normally rented to them by urban landlords who hoped to profit from the entertainment industry. St. Petersburg's most prominent private theater, which became the permanent home of the Literary-Artistic Circle's (after 1899 the Literary-Artistic Society) drama company, had begun life in 1879 as a venue for second-run performances of Aleksandrinskii productions. Located in a stately building on the Fontanka, its lesser status within the Imperial Theater system led the public to call it the "Malyi," or "Small," Theater, a name that continued to circulate until the premises came to house the Bol'shoi ("Great") Dramatic Theater in Soviet times. After the abolition of the imperial performance monopoly, the theater was rented successively by the entrepreneurs A. F. Kartavov (1882–85) and G. A. Arbenin (1885–95), who hosted a series of visiting companies presenting operetta, French comedy, and works of other light genres,

---

48. McReynolds, *Russia at Play*, 19.
49. Frame, "'Freedom of the Theatres,'" 274–89, concludes that "the abolition of the monopoly ... should be understood as a reaction to the perceived inability of the Directorate to promote Russian theatre."

occasionally along with more serious offerings. The actor and impresario Petr Veinberg staged "educational" performances of Sophocles' *Oedipus Rex* and *Antigone* there in February 1883. In the early 1890s it hosted visiting performances by the renowned foreign actors Ernesto Rossi, Eleonora Duse, and Sarah Bernhardt.[50] But most of its tenants were ephemeral amateur troupes.[51] The Literary-Artistic Circle's company arrived in the fall of 1895 and occupied the building until 1917, though it sublet space during its spring hiatuses. The Moscow Art Theater performed there during its St. Petersburg visits in 1903–5, and in 1906 it hosted a visiting Italian opera troupe. Likewise, from 1907 Moscow's state-owned Novyi ("New") Theater, also employed for second-run drama performances, was rented out to the impresario Sergei Zimin, who staged private opera performances there and in other locales until the end of the tsarist era.

Several less obvious venues housed emerging private theaters. Konstantin Stanislavskii, scion of the rich and artistically inclined Alekseev merchant family, kept the dramatic activities of his first theatrical venture alive after its building—a private Moscow home belonging to the Ginzburg banking dynasty—was sold to the Hunting Club. The new owners were happy to host the troupe as long as it produced a new play once a week.[52] Lidiia Iavorskaia, an actress who won fame as a leading lady of the Literary-Artistic Society's theater after initial forays in Reval and Moscow, opened her own enterprise, called the New Theater, in Petersburg in 1901, in partnership with her second husband, the journalist, translator, and cultural historian Prince Vladimir Bariatinskii. The premises were a hall—"a long, uncomfortable room," as one actress described it—on the fourth floor of a building near the Moika canal.[53] In October 1904 the entrepreneur V. A. Kazanskii opened the 480-seat Nevskii Farce in the basement of the capital's chic Eliseev department store.[54] That same year Vera

---

50. I. F. Petrovskaia and V. Somina, *Teatral'nyi Peterburg: Nachalo XVIII veka-oktiabr' 1917 goda: Obozrenie-putevoditel'* (St. Petersburg: RIII, 1994), 199–200.

51. Ibid., 215.

52. Jean Benedetti, *Stanislavski: A Life* (London: Methuen, 1988), 42. The building burned down shortly thereafter, but the arrangement continued at the Hunting Club's new premises. Alekseev used his more famous name as a professional pseudonym, which he adopted from an older amateur actor friend who also used it. The two men admired the same Bol'shoi *danseuse*, Mariia Stanislavskaia, and took her name in homage.

53. Rebecca B. Gauss, "Lydia Borisovna Yavorskaya: Her Life, Her Work, Her Times" (M.A. thesis, University of Colorado, 1992), 13–45. Born von Gubennet, the daughter of Kiev's police chief, the actress first married her secondary school history teacher, a man named Iavorskii, and continued to use his name professionally after her marriage to Bariatinskii. For the comment about her theater, see Mariia Velizarii, *Put' provintsial'noi aktrisy* (Leningrad: Iskusstvo, 1938), 222.

54. D. I. Zolotnitskii, "'Dni svobody' russkogo farsa," in *Russkii teatr i dramaturgiia epokhi revoliutsii, 1905–1907 godov: Sbornik nauchnykh trudov*, ed. A. Ia. Al'tshuller et al. (Leningrad: Leningradskii Gosudarstvennyi Institut Teatra, Muzyki, and Kul'tury, hereafter LGITMiK, 1987),

Komissarzhevskaia founded her Dramatic Theater in a back room of Eliseev's nearby rival, the Passazh (Passage) shopping arcade. Her brother Fedor, who worked as a director in her enterprise, founded his own studio theater in the basement of a friend's Moscow home in 1910. Four years later he opened a new one in another friend's drawing room, large enough to seat 160.[55] A converted ice skating rink served as the venue of Petersburg's Liteinyi Theatrical Club, which opened in 1908.[56] The capital's Conservatory hosted a private opera company founded by Prince Aleksei Tsereteli. Beginning in 1898, Count Aleksandr Sheremetev organized a private concert series that performed in the Petersburg city duma's Alexander Hall. After 1903 the pianist and impresario Aleksandr Ziloti followed the leads of the Musical Society and Philharmonic by organizing concerts of European and Russian orchestral music in the hall of the Noblemen's Club.[57] Adaptations of urban space could also go the other way: a one-thousand-seat theater taken over by the impresario V. A. Nemetti in 1902 became a bathhouse when his performing company folded seven years later.[58]

Apart from these improvisations, a few new buildings designed specifically for theatrical use appeared in urban landscapes after the Imperial Theaters' monopoly was lifted. The entrepreneur V. N. Egarev opened a new seven-hundred-seat theater around the corner from the Mariinskii, on Ofitserskaia (now Decembrists) Street in 1882. Initially called the Renaissance but later known simply by its address, 39 Ofitserskaia, it was used over the years by several enterprises, including the Dramatic Theater of Vera Komissarzhevskaia in 1906–8. In 1885 the wealthy Bakhrushin family, Moscow merchants, endowed and then rented at a below-market rate a new building on Petrovskii Alley to house a theater operated by the lawyer-turned-impresario Fedor Korsh.[59] Another new Petersburg edifice, the Panaev Theater, rose on Admiralty Embankment in 1887 and hosted a series of visiting troupes, including the Moscow Art Theater's first two visits to the capital in 1901 and 1902. Its most regular tenant, Pavel Tumpakov's Winter Bouffe, performed there from 1904 to 1912.[60]

Finance for private theaters was problematic. None enjoyed the "absolute financial security" that Prince Petr Liven, an official of the Imperial Theaters

---

131; Petrovskaia and Somina, *Teatral'nyi Peterburg*, 307. The theater was formally named Nevskii Farce the following spring.

55. Komisarjevsky, *Myself and the Theatre*, 98.
56. McReynolds, *Russia at Play*, 220.
57. Charles F. Barber, *Lost in the Stars: The Forgotten Musical Life of Alexander Siloti* (Lanham, Md.: Scarecrow, 2002), 110–12.
58. Petrovskaia and Somina, *Teatral'nyi Peterburg*, 303.
59. Frame, *School for Citizens*, 109.
60. Petrovskaia and Somina, *Teatral'nyi Peterburg*, 244.

Directorate, attributed to the imperial stage and its guaranteed annual subsidies.[61] Even the wealthiest impresarios lacked the means to offer profitable entertainment on a permanent basis. Despite its popularity Korsh's theater drained his personal resources for twenty-two years before it began to generate revenue on its own.[62] Brenko's performances depended on her wealthy husband, without whom, she wrote, "my pockets were empty."[63] In 1888 Stanislavskii used a business windfall to establish his first serious theatrical endeavor, the Society of Arts and Literature. The funds quickly went, however, and he was forced to rely on his family fortune.[64] When he and the dramatist and critic Vladimir Nemirovich-Danchenko merged their creative efforts to found the Moscow Art Theater a decade later, Stanislavskii's business and family responsibilities allowed him to devote only a small portion of his resources to the project. Investments solicited from other wealthy individuals accounted for two-thirds of the new enterprise's startup budget, and, regardless of its fiscal turns, Stanislavskii insisted on never increasing his personal support, at least partly in order to maintain the theater's independence from his own ego and financial interests.[65] Eventually the theater came to be dominated financially by the tycoon and arts patron Savva Morozov, who saved it financially after its first few seasons, and later by a board of shareholders who effectively excluded Stanislavskii from management.[66] Morozov personally bore the huge three-hundred-thousand-ruble cost of renovating the Omon (Aumont) Theater on Kamergerskii Alley when the Art Theater moved there permanently in 1902.[67] As late as December 1916—after more than eighteen years of continuous operation—Stanislavskii was still pleading family and business fiscal responsibilities to refrain from a more active financial role.[68]

A less fortunate enterprise, the Russian Private Opera—founded in 1885 by Stanislavskii's cousin-in-law, the Moscow railroad heir and arts patron Savva Mamontov—lasted two seasons and then closed for nearly a decade after its initial appearance. It collapsed after Mamontov's scandalous finances took a dramatic nosedive at the turn of the century and vanished forever in 1904.[69]

61. Lieven, *Birth of the Ballets-Russes*, 65. According to K. S. Stanislavskii, *Moia zhizn' v iskusstve* (Moscow: Iskusstvo, 1983), 339, "that which the Imperial Theaters could allow themselves, living on state means, was not available to us, a comparatively poor private theater." Tellingly, Stanislavskii's Moscow Art Theater was among Russia's most famous and generously endowed private theaters.
62. Frame, *School for Citizens*, 109–10.
63. Ibid., 88.
64. Benedetti, *Stanislavski*, 27, 62–63.
65. Ibid., 63–64; Stanislavskii, *Moia zhizn'*, 251.
66. Benedetti, *Stanislavski*, 173–76.
67. Ibid., 118–19.
68. Jean Benedetti, ed., *The Moscow Art Theatre Letters* (London: Methuen, 1991), 302–5.
69. Frame, *School for Citizens*, 113–14.

Figs. 3 and 4 The interior of the Omon (Aumont) Theater, home of the Moscow Art Theater from 1902. From Konstantin Stanislavskii, *Moia zhizn' v iskusstve* (Moscow: Iskusstvo, 1983).

The generous terms Korsh received from the Bakhrushin family spared him the fate of his earlier theatrical enterprises, which floundered in short order after they opened.[70] Ziloti's concerts depended on the fortune of his wealthy wife, his own uncompensated labor, and charitable donations from businessmen who, in addition to deriving satisfaction and social esteem from arts patronage, compelled the impresario to give their children weekly piano lessons.[71] The journalist-turned-publisher and philanthropist Aleksei Suvorin remained virtually the sole supporter of the Literary-Artistic Society's theater. Beyond its older designation as Petersburg's "Malyi" and cumbersome official name, it came to be called the Suvorin Theater and fell under his firm administrative and artistic leadership as a consequence of his financial backing. After Suvorin's death in 1912, his daughter formalized that relationship by making her direction of the theater fully independent of the Literary-Artistic Society.[72]

Enterprises without major philanthropic support depended heavily on loans and credit. Komissarzhevskaia wallowed in forty-one thousand rubles of debt after her first season alone.[73] This figure approached the forty-five thousand rubles owed by the Moscow Art Theater at the end of its first season, before it started receiving Morozov's support.[74] The character actor-turned-impresario Mikhail Lentovskii worked up sixty thousand rubles in losses by the early 1890s and, despite having started no fewer than eleven enterprises of various types in both Moscow and Petersburg, died broke in 1906.[75] Numerous failed theatrical companies had to auction off sets and costumes to pay their performers and meet other basic expenses.[76]

The precarious financial situation and short supply of reliable investors at home led some Russians to operate abroad in the hope of finding greater stability. This more than anything else was the driving force behind Diaghilev's Ballets Russes, which made Russian creativity into a kaleidoscopic international arts phenomenon. Failing to recover his position in the Imperial Theaters when Teliakovskii became Director, Diaghilev spent the next several years trying to turn profits by organizing painting exhibits.[77] His modest success in these endeavors and civic disturbances at home convinced him to move his activities to

---

70. McReynolds, *Russia at Play*, 56–57.
71. Barber, *Lost in the Stars*, 113.
72. "Khronika," *Teatr i iskusstvo* 30 (July 27, 1914): 628.
73. Iu. Rybakova, *Komissarzhevskaia* (Leningrad: Iskusstvo, 1971), 126.
74. Vladimir Nemirovitch-Danchenko, *My Life in the Russian Theatre,* trans. John Cournos (London: Bles, 1937), 198.
75. McReynolds, *Russia at Play,* 217.
76. For one such case, see "Malen'kaia khronika," *Teatr i iskusstvo* 12 (March 25, 1907): 200.
77. Teliakovskii, *Dnevniki . . . 1901–1903,* 10–12.

Paris. In 1906 he brought an exhibition of Russian pictures to the French capital, followed by concerts of Russian orchestral music the next year. Although attracted by ballet—the art form that would make him an international celebrity—in 1908 he staged Musorgskii's *Boris Godunov* (starring Shaliapin) for his growing French audience because he thought opera would produce greater profits. The first full "Russian season," including both opera and ballet, came to Paris the next season and quickly brought the new company (formally named the Ballets Russes in 1911) invitations to tour Europe and the world.[78]

Diaghilev encountered savvy competition from French impresarios, but his shrewd management and successful marketing of a colorful Russian "exotic" vied with popular Wagnerism and other more traditional offerings. The Ballets Russes quickly drew wealthy sell-out audiences and generous support from leading social figures of the Belle Époque.[79] No less important was Diaghilev's ability to exploit arts snobbery for profit, a talent he found more fruitful in the salons of Paris than those of St. Petersburg. To be "très Ballets Russes" meant to be super chic—not to know the new phenomenon was to remain provincial and limited.[80] In addition to some of Russia's leading arts patrons, within only a few years Diaghilev counted among his supporters the impresario Gabriel Astruc (who also worked as his business manager), the generous Countess de Greffuhle, Paris's noted playboy Count Boniface de Castellane and his rich but dowdy American wife, the literary matron Countess Anne de Noailles, Britain's social doyenne the Marchioness of Ripon, the hefty Aga Khan, Kaiser William II, King George V, and King Alfonso XIII of Spain.[81] Even Paris's contingent of exiled Polish grandees was willing to look past the Russian origins of the enterprise to embrace a burst of Slavic creativity.[82]

This esteem did not save the high-living Diaghilev from the occasional threat of bankruptcy; he even had to sell off the sets of his 1909 season. But it enabled him to bring some of Russia's greatest performers to the West, often for higher

---

78. For good histories, see Lieven, *Birth of the Ballets-Russes*; S. L. Grigoriev, *The Diaghilev Ballet, 1909–1929*, trans. Vera Bowen (Harmondsworth: Penguin, 1960); and Lynn Garafola, *Diaghilev's Ballets Russes* (New York: Oxford University Press, 1989).

79. Diaghilev planned his annual tours to coincide with the end of the Russian Imperial Theaters' regular seasons so the necessary performers would be available. He directly contrasted his presentations with what he thought to be Wagner's "Viking world of bearded warriors drinking blood out of skulls." Quoted in Steven G. Marks, *How Russia Shaped the Modern World: From Art to Anti-Semitism, Ballet to Bolshevism* (Princeton: Princeton University Press, 2002), 182.

80. Lieven, *Birth of the Ballets-Russes*, 94.

81. Grigoriev, *Diaghilev Ballet*, 148, called Alfonso XIII "our godfather." The first Ballets Russes appearance in London was part of George V's coronation gala.

82. Garafola, *Ballets Russes*, 285, 297. Count Potocki sat on the Ballets Russes's fund-raising committee and donated one hundred thousand francs to it in 1913.

wages than they could expect at home. Many, including the ballerina Anna Pavlova, were so enamored of their reception and received with such enchantment that they broke into free agency to accept contracts from European and American managers. Diaghilev also succeeded in hiring some of Russian's leading musicians and visual artists (Igor' Stravinskii, Sergei Rakhmaninov, Aleksandr Skriabin, Lev Bakst, Aleksandr Benua, Aleksandr Golovin, Konstantin Korovin, Natal'ia Goncharova), as well as outstanding representatives of the European avant-garde (Claude Debussy, Maurice Ravel, Erik Satie, Georges Braque, Pablo Picasso, Henri Matisse, Jean Cocteau, Coco Chanel) to charge his productions with a liveliness that bestowed well-deserved immortality. So thoroughly did he succeed that the tsarist government, despite the problems during his short tenure at the Imperial Theaters Directorate, occasionally funded the enterprise.[83]

Although some thirty-one privately operated venues in Petersburg and sixteen in Moscow were performing drama alone by 1901, most nonstate theatrical companies came and went with remarkable speed.[84] Survival depended to a great degree on market forces, audience interest, and the fluid fads of the Russian Empire's artistic life. Iavorskaia's New Theater, one of the longer lived among its private theaters, operated for five abbreviated seasons between its founding in the autumn of 1901 and bankruptcy in February 1906. In the meantime it depended heavily on her husband's princely largesse. When Komissarzhevskaia's Dramatic Theater began to function in its Ofitserskaia Street venue the season after Iavorskaia's bankruptcy, it was the fifth company to perform there in as many years.[85] Like her first theatrical enterprise, it lasted only two seasons before entering oblivion.

Many lesser enterprises lasted one season or less. An attempt to revive Iavorskaia's New Theater managed by the director Aleksandr Sanin, who had worked at both the Moscow Art Theater and the imperial Aleksandrinskii, endured for just six weeks in early 1907.[86] Three years later Sanin lasted less than a season as

83. Lieven, *Birth of the Ballets-Russes*, 220–21, reports fluctuations in official funding but notes that much of Diaghilev's early Parisian activities received Court subsidies due to the intervention of Grand Duke Vladimir Aleksandrovich, who chaired Diaghilev's committee of patrons. The Grand Duke's death in 1909 left this relationship more precarious.

84. Murray Frame, "Commercial Theatre and Professionalization in Late Imperial Russia," *Historical Journal* 48, no. 4 (2005): 1032. According to Emmet Kennedy, *A Cultural History of the French Revolution* (New Haven: Yale University Press, 1989), 174–76, thirty-five new theaters sprouted up in Paris after the January 1791 abrogation of the performance monopoly enjoyed by state-supported theaters—an action which, like the abolition of the Russian Imperial Theaters' monopoly in 1882, also greatly intensified competition for audiences and revenues.

85. Petrovskaia and Somina, *Teatral'nyi Peterburg*, 225. The first of the previous four tenants, E. A. Shabel'skaia, lasted three seasons before suffering a major financial crisis.

86. Ibid., 222–23.

the chief director of the playwright Leonid Andreev's attempt to revive the Dramatic Theater. The noted director Vsevolod Meierkhol'd's experimental cabaret, the Strand (Lukomor'e), survived for a paltry six days in December 1908 and gave only two performances before it disappeared.[87] He managed to repeat that failure with a similar theater, the House of Interludes (Dom intermedii), which gave just two performances in late 1910.[88] Nikolai Evreinov accepted his appointment as chief director of the Crooked Mirror (Krivoe zerkalo), the Strand's rival cabaret, on the condition that it remain a commercial enterprise.[89]

Professional management in this environment remained underdeveloped, and the skills and practices of private theater administrators often did little to recommend themselves. Suvorin reputedly ran his theater in an inefficient and authoritarian fashion. Tat'iana Shchepkina-Kupernik, a dramatist, translator, and great-granddaughter of the famous "serf actor" Mikhail Shchepkin, recalled that "this theater was a monarchy, and Suvorin was the monarch." "Favoritism flowered," she continued, observing that its other directors included Suvorin's son-in-law, a general whom he knew socially, and two other men identified as a "reactionary critic" and "dandyish lawyer."[90] The "monarch" used his daily media outlet, the *New Times* (*Novoe vremia*), to boost sales and attention. He even chastised its theater critics for writing too favorably about drama performances at the rival Aleksandrinskii; sometimes Suvorin wrote his own reviews when unsatisfied with the work of his journalists.[91]

Iavorskaia, despite cultivating a radical image to appeal to discontented audiences drawn from the capital's students, intelligentsia, and jaded high society, behaved about as democratically as Suvorin in administering her theater. Mariia Velizarii, an actress who lasted one season there, found her employer intolerably precious: "Iavorskaia performed the best role in every play. And the repertoire included only those plays in which there was a beautiful role for her.... Rehearsals there began not at eleven o'clock, as was done in all theaters, but at two or three in the afternoon, when the 'Princess' was 'inclined' to arrive.... [She] came around three and went to her dressing room. A footman brought breakfast to her on a silver tray. The actors sat and waited."[92] Velizarii's dissatisfaction

---

87. Edward Braun, *The Theatre of Meyerhold: Revolution on the Modern Stage* (New York: Drama Book Specialists, 1979), 90. *Lukomor'e* can be more literally translated as "cove," but most Western accounts use "Strand" for the name of the theater.
88. Ibid., 101–7.
89. Sharon M. Carnicke, "The Theatrical Instinct: A Study of the Work of Nikolaj Evreinov in Early Twentieth-Century Russia" (Ph.D. diss., Columbia University, 1979), 86.
90. T. L. Shchepkina-Kupernik, *Teatr v moei zhizni* (Moscow: Iskusstvo, 1948), 110.
91. Teliakovskii, *Vospominaniia*, 180–83; Volkonskii, *Rodina*, 144.
92. Velizarii, *Put' provintsial'noi aktrisy*, 217–19.

with these conditions led to her departure.[93] Another actor dismissed the New Theater as a "lady's enterprise" (*damskaia zateia*).[94] On the eve of starting her own theater, Komissarzhevskaia declared in a letter to a friend that she "[would] not be a leader like Iavorskaia, whose mood improves in direct proportion to the amount of champagne she has consumed."[95] A review of the New Theater's opening night described it as "half amateur."[96]

Suvorin and Iavorskaia were not exceptional cases. A press comment on the large debts accumulated by one theater placed the blame squarely on its "amateur" leadership, which lay in "inexperienced hands."[97] Evtikhii Karpov, a respected director and theorist, believed that too many theaters were led by "people who are not sufficiently educated."[98] Fedor Komissarzhevskii, who was involved in many private theatrical enterprises (including his sister Vera's) in addition to his duties in the Imperial Theaters, believed that bankruptcies were "generally the direct result of mismanagement" rather than misfortune or low appeal.[99]

Caprice loomed in music and dance as well. Zimin, reputedly "as obstinate and wilful as a child," liked to force his favorite male artists to accompany him to late night steam baths. He also insisted, in the absence of formal training or much talent, on designing the lighting for every production of his private opera company, which he micromanaged through "constant terror" during performances.[100] When the orchestra musicians of Prince Tsereteli's private opera protested a budget error that caused some of them to be slightly underpaid, he fired them all and replaced them with foreign musicians.[101] Such incidents eventually led to pressure among performers for standardized contracts offering advance payments and security deposits to guarantee that unscrupulous entrepreneurs would not cheat their employees or abscond with profits.[102] Personal conflicts could make for ugly situations. Consumed by jealous rage, Diaghilev infamously fired his *premier danseur* and sometime lover, Vatslav Nizhinskii, and

---

93. Ibid., 222–23.
94. Mikhail S. Narokov, *Biografiia moego pokoleniia* (Moscow: VTO, 1956), 119.
95. "Pis'ma V. F. Komissarzhevskoi," *Teatr* 2 (1960), 138.
96. "Homo novus," [Aleksandr Kugel'], "Novyi teatr," *Teatr i iskusstvo* 39 (September 23, 1901): 691.
97. "Khronika," *Teatral'naia Rossiia/Muzykal'nyi mir* 14 (April 2, 1905): 204.
98. "K voprosu o dramaticheskoi tsenzure," *Teatral'naia Rossiia/Teatral'naia gazeta* 37 (September 10, 1905): 1121.
99. Komisarjevsky, *Myself and the Theatre*, 36.
100. Ibid., 97–98.
101. "V. K." [V. Karatygin], "Muzykal'naia khronika Peterburga," *Zolotoe runo* 4 (April 1906): 86–87.
102. Frame, "Commercial Theatre," 1045.

Nizhinskii's new wife, Romola Pulszky, from the Ballets Russes after he learned of their marriage in 1913.[103]

Private theaters faced another structural problem in competition from Russia's growing popular theater movement, which sought to endow the performing arts with the progressive social purpose of "bettering" the urban lower classes, especially workers, through affordable and morally sound entertainment. Although no definitive legal distinction separated popular from private theaters (the matter was left for local authorities to determine), it was generally understood that the popular variety had poorer audiences, more modest facilities, and lower ticket prices.[104]

Alexander II permitted a temporary theater to perform for Moscow's lower classes as early as 1870, but the first meaningful popular theater initiative came on the heels of the abolition of the Imperial Theaters' performance monopoly ten years later.[105] Shortly after its abolition, Lentovskii, the impresario who would remain plagued by debt and bankruptcy until his dying day nearly a quarter of a century later, opened a popular theater on a refurbished estate called the Hermitage Gardens outside Moscow and another, the Arcadia, outside Petersburg. Both offered light entertainment and the allure of what their manager hoped would be the "fantastic."[106]

Subsequent popular theater endeavors came from factory owners. In 1885 a group of St. Petersburg industrialists with factories on the city's southern outskirts began offering entertainments for their employees. Its first year of activity included performances by military orchestras, acrobats, choruses, and other attractions of the "pleasure garden" variety. Formal presentations of plays were introduced in its second season. Incorporating their group in 1891 as the Nevskii Society for the Support of Popular Entertainment, they opened a small theater of about three hundred seats on the second floor of an extant wooden building, a free-standing summer theater for five hundred in 1896, and a sturdier brick theater for sixteen hundred just four years later. Throughout its existence the Nevskii Society offered a traditional repertoire of Russian classics.[107] In 1887 industrialists of the capital's Vasil'evskii Island section followed with the construction of a seven-hundred-seat theater for their workers' amusement

---

103. Diaghilev later got over it and rehired Nizhinskii for his 1916 tour of the United States, but the young dancer fell into a debilitating depression three years later.
104. E. Anthony Swift, "Fighting the Germs of Disorder: The Censorship of Russian Popular Theater, 1888–1917," *Russian History/Histoire russe* 18, no. 1 (1991): 15, 43–44.
105. Frame, *School for Citizens*, 136.
106. McReynolds, *Russia at Play*, 215; Petrovskaia and Somina, *Teatral'nyi Peterburg*, 351.
107. Petrovskaia and Somina, *Teatral'nyi Peterburg*, 260–62.

and edification.[108] Moscow businessmen emulated their Petersburg competitors. In addition to similar venues, Stanislavskii founded a theater for the workers of his family's textile plant in 1904. His personal involvement led it to be called the "Little Art Theater."[109]

High society also supported the popular theater movement. Countess Sofiia Panina, who had already funded a low-cost cafeteria and reading room for Petersburg workers, commissioned the architect Iurii Benua to design a one-thousand-seat *style moderne* theater in the capital's seedy Ligovskii district. Completed in 1903, the Ligovskii People's House became home to the General Accessible Theater of Pavel Gaideburov and his wife and business partner, Nadezhda Skar'skaia, the younger sister of Vera Komissarzhevskaia.[110] Princess Mariia Tenisheva, patroness of the World of Art group and its journal of the same name, contributed by opening a small popular theater in a school for working-class pupils. Emulating Panina, she hosted Gaideburov's touring company, "an inseparable creative organism" of the General Accessible known separately as the Wandering Theater.[111] Another society lady, V. N. fon Derviz (von der Witz), funded a six-hundred-seat theater, as well as a library, painting school, and practice rooms for poor music students. Its early seasons were dominated by amateur performers, but it hosted a small opera company in 1900–1901 and professional drama companies thereafter.[112]

On a more limited scale Russian workers themselves pioneered new theatrical enterprises, associating drama with cultural enlightenment, self-improvement, or, like their employers, morally sound diversion. Although most of these endeavors presented folk entertainments, which workers still remembered from their not-too-distant pasts as peasants, after 1900 a number of factories witnessed performances of plays commonly found on more formal stages.[113] At the Obukhov steel plant workers led by a lathe operator who had acted for a time in Nizhnii Novgorod performed and charged admission to productions of Ostrovskii, Chekhov, and Gor'kii, among other dramatists. According to one of its actors, the future Soviet film star Konstantin Skorobogatov, the theater was serious enough to inspire its participants to meet budget shortfalls out of

---

108. I. F. Petrovskaia, *Teatr i zritel' rossiiskikh stolits: 1895–1917* (Leningrad: Iskusstvo, 1990), 73.
109. Benedetti, *Stanislavski*, 85.
110. Petrovskaia and Somina, *Teatral'nyi Peterburg*, 273.
111. P. P. Gaideburov, *Literaturnoe nasledie. Vospominaniia. Stat'i. Rezhisserskie eksplikatsii. Vystupleniia* (Moscow: VTO, 1977), 221.
112. Petrovskaia and Somina, *Teatral'nyi Peterburg*, 294.
113. E. Anthony Swift, "Workers' Theater and 'Proletarian Culture' in Prerevolutionary Russia, 1905–1917," in *Workers and Intelligentsia in Late Imperial Russia: Realities, Representations, Reflections*, ed. Reginald Zelnik, International and Area Studies Research Series No. 101 (Berkeley and Los Angeles: University of California, 1999), 262–63.

their own pay and take its productions on tours to other cities. Skorobogatov was so active in it that the Obukhov management temporarily dismissed him for neglecting his factory work.[114] Petersburg printers formed a citywide theatrical troupe, though organizational problems and financial limitations soon caused it to adopt the functions of a social club.[115]

The most substantial popular theaters emerged from the efforts of Russia's Temperance Trusteeship. One of Imperial Russia's many public interest organizations, it was founded in December 1894 to provide the urban lower classes with alternatives to drinking and other sources of moral turpitude. Enjoying Ministry of Finance support in the form of subsidies from the state liquor monopoly declared earlier that year, the Trusteeship quickly expanded its operations. It officially adopted theater as a means of promoting its anti-alcohol mission in 1897 and within five years operated 102 venues Empire wide, a figure that rocketed to 361 by 1905 and 420 by 1909.[116] From the beginning, their audiences were impressive in size, nearly doubling from more than 1.6 million in 1901 to three million just two years later.[117]

The Trusteeship's principal arts venue was the Tsar Nicholas II People's House, a fifteen-hundred-seat theater that opened in Petersburg in 1900. Officially named the Tsar Nicholas II Institution for Popular Diversion, it was situated in Aleksandrovskii Park, near the Peter and Paul Fortress and just across the Neva from the city center in one direction and the working-class neighborhoods on Vasil'evskii Island and the Vyborg Side in the others. Lavished with no less than 25 percent of the Trusteeship's total annual expenditure, the People's House attracted an incredible 90 percent of all Russian popular theater viewers in 1901 and a staggering twenty million spectators between 1900 and 1910 alone.[118] Its repertoire ranged widely, including Ostrovskii and other Russian and foreign classics, as well as such provocative plays as Lev Tolstoi's *The Power of Darkness* about a womanizing peasant who has a child with his stepdaughter and then murders it at the urging of his wife. As an educational institution the People's House took advantage of its huge stage and large artist roster to present epic-scale historical tableaux. In addition to its official opening performance of Glinka's *A Life for the Tsar,* it offered flattering dramas about Peter the Great,

114. K. V. Skorobogatov, *Zhizn' i stsena* (Leningrad: Lenizdat, 1970), 50–58.
115. Swift, "Workers' Theater," 267.
116. G. A. Khaichenko, *Russkii narodnyi teatr kontsa XIX–nachala XX veka* (Moscow: Nauka, 1975), 96.
117. Ibid., 104; Gary Thurston, *The Popular Theatre Movement in Russia, 1862–1919* (Evanston: Northwestern University Press, 1998), 125.
118. Swift, "Fighting the Germs of Disorder," 3. Khaichenko, *Russkii narodnyi teatr,* 104, reports that 1,477,552 of the total 1,670,000 popular theater viewers attended the People's House in 1901.

Fig. 5 Marius Petipa, First Ballet Master of the Imperial Theaters. A Frenchman by birth, he remained employed in the Mariinskii Theater's ballet troupe from his arrival in Russia in 1847 until his death in 1910. From Marius Petipa, *Materialy. Vospominaniia. Stat'i* (Leningrad: Iskusstvo, 1971).

the eighteenth-century military hero Marshal Suvorov, the campaign against Napoleon in 1812, and the siege of Sevastopol' during the Crimean War.[119]

Education through theater was not directed solely toward audiences, for formal arts instruction also blossomed in Imperial Russia. In 1738, nearly two decades before the Russian Court began to offer regular support for theatrical performances, Empress Anna hired the French ballet master Jean-Baptiste Landé to train dance pupils in the Winter Palace. These lessons formed the nucleus of the Imperial Ballet School, which in 1836 moved into the same neoclassical building occupied by the Imperial Theaters Directorate. From Landé's time on,

---

119. Petrovskaia and Somina, *Teatral'nyi Peterburg*, 268.

instruction was supervised by imported Europeans, including a series of German dance masters, the legendary Charles Didelot (active in Russia from 1801 to 1810 and again from 1816 to 1830), and the French-born Marius Petipa, who retired from active duties in 1903 but remained on the roster of the Imperial Theaters as First Ballet Master until his death in 1910. Now called the Vaganova Ballet Academy, the school occupies the same site and continues to draw pupils from the same age group.

Ballet, which requires detailed and strenuous physical training over a dancer's entire early life, demanded the commitment of pupils from a young age, usually eight to ten. Administered in "a monastic fashion," the Imperial Ballet School imposed rigid discipline and strict regimentation on the lives of its pupils, over whom it wielded "absolute power."[120] Its personnel were infamously cruel. Varvara Likhosherstova, headmistress from 1884 to 1924, usually appears in memoirs as a mean-spirited tyrant. One witness described her to Teliakovskii, her boss, as "severe, heartless, and vindictive."[121] According to the dancer and choreographer Mikhail Fokin, she routinely read the pupils' diaries and then used the contents to humiliate them in public.[122] Instructors gave bad marks to one another's students out of professional jealousy.[123] The American dancing sensation Isadora Duncan, who observed Ballet School lessons during one of her trips to Russia and had her own ideas about the medium, found them "an enemy to nature and to Art."[124] Surviving this environment, however, brought automatic employment in the imperial dancing troupe.

Formal training for Russian actors began with the creation of the Imperial Drama School in 1776. With branches in both Petersburg and Moscow, its faculty consisted largely of active performers of the imperial dramatic stage. Until 1866 graduates enjoyed the automatic right to employment in the Imperial Theaters. Thereafter they received preferential treatment.[125]

Theaters with didactic missions included educational "studio" programs in their activities. Moscow's Philharmonic Society operated such a school under

---

120. Lieven, *Birth of the Ballets-Russes*, 64–65. For descriptions of Ballet School life in the early twentieth century, see Mikhail Fokin, *Protiv techeniia: Vospominaniia baletmeistera. Stat'i, pis'ma* (Leningrad: Iskusstvo, 1962), 36–44; and Nicolas Legat, *Ballet Russe: Memoirs of Nicolas Legat*, trans. Sir Paul Dukes (London: Methuen, 1939), 33.
121. Teliakovskii, *Dnevniki . . . 1901–1903*, 273.
122. Fokin, *Protiv techeniia*, 83.
123. Ibid., 78.
124. Isadora Duncan, *My Life* (New York: Boni and Liveright, 1927), 166.
125. Vladimir Davydov to Gnedich, n.d. [August 1904], Sankt Peterburgskii Gosudarstvennyi Teatral'nyi Muzei (SPb GTM), No. 6698/1. Davydov, a famous Aleksandrinskii comedian who taught drama courses, successfully wrote Gnedich to favor one of his students for employment in the Imperial Drama Troupe.

Nemirovich-Danchenko, who later became Stanislavskii's business partner at the Moscow Art Theater. Among his pupils were the young Meierkhol'd and the noted actress Ol'ga Knipper, who married Chekhov. Private performing arts study was widely available from Russians as well as foreigners. Stanislavskii trained in voice with the patriarch of the Komissarzhevskii artistic family, a noted tenor of the imperial stage, and in movement with a prominent dancer from the Bol'shoi ballet troupe, an uncle of the great Malyi Theater actress and Moscow Drama School graduate Mariia Ermolova.[126] Elite secondary schools, including military academies, offered arts education as part of their broadening programs of study.

Both the state stage and the emerging private and popular theatrical worlds remained open to as much talent as could be recruited for their needs and profits, regardless of where they could find it. Mikhail Shchepkin, perhaps Russia's greatest actor of the nineteenth century, was born into serfdom and came to performance through his owner's training. In 1821, at age thirty-three, admirers sponsored his freedom for the sum of four thousand rubles and enabled him to pursue a career that dominated Moscow's imperial dramatic stage for four decades.[127] Mariia Savina, the Aleksandrinskii's reigning prima donna from the 1880s until her death in 1915, learned her trade out of necessity in the extreme poverty of her childhood. An arduous provincial career led her to the capital and fame.[128] Aleksandr Lenskii, the illegitimate son of a Prince Gagarin, followed the same path from long years on provincial stages to glory at the Malyi. In the process he became "one of the most influential actors at the end of the [nineteenth] century."[129] Komissarzhevskaia studied stage techniques and music with her father and also honed her skills in the provinces before entering the imperial drama troupe and then embarking on her career in private theater.[130]

Formal musical education never became an official state responsibility, although the Imperial Theaters Directorate briefly flirted with what Teliakovskii described as an "unsuccessful" opera faculty.[131] The creation of the Russian Musical Society (RMO) in 1859, with the generous support of Grand Duchess Elena Pavlovna and other members of courtly high society, led to the country's

---

126. Benedetti, *Stanislavski*, 19.

127. For his life story, see Laurence Senelick, *Serf Actor: The Life and Art of Mikhail Shchepkin* (Westport, Conn.: Greenwood, 1984).

128. McReynolds, *Russia at Play*, 118–19.

129. Ostrovsky, "Imperial and Private Theatres," 230–31. Stanislavskii took notes on his performances.

130. Victor Borovsky, *A Triptych from the Russian Theatre: An Artistic Biography of the Komissarzhevskys* (Iowa City: University of Iowa Press, 2001), 83.

131. Teliakovskii, *Vospominaniia*, 159.

first institutionalized music lessons. In 1862 the composer Anton Rubinshtein secured their recognition in Petersburg as a conservatory designed after the European model. The Moscow Conservatory, led by his brother, Teliakovskii's childhood piano partner Nikolai Rubinshtein, opened under the Musical Society's auspices in 1866. In addition to the conservatories, which eventually increased in number to five, the Musical Society operated provincial music schools and less formal courses of instruction from 1872. By 1906 there were fifteen such schools and eleven courses.[132]

Supported by tuition fees, continuing philanthropy from its patrons, revenues from the Musical Society's annual concert series, and, beginning in 1869, state subsidies (the Society was allowed to style itself "Imperial" four years later), Petersburg Conservatory was granted the premises of the Bol'shoi Kamennyi Theater for use as an educational institution in 1889 (the theater had closed in 1886). A majority of students in Musical Society institutions were gentry or middle-class sons and daughters pursuing music lessons as part of their general education, but, despite continuing foreign recruitment, growing numbers of young Russians enrolled with the hope of pursuing professional careers.[133] Upon completing their studies, Conservatory graduates received the title "free artist" (*svobodnyi khudozhnik*), which placed them on equal footing with graduates of the Imperial Academy of Fine Arts. Beginning in 1894 they qualified for the privileged social rank of personal honored citizen (also on par with Art Academy graduates), and from 1902 male graduates were automatically taken into state service at the lowest level (*chin*) of the Table of Ranks established by Peter I.[134]

Just as in drama, talented people who had not studied within the musical education establishment could demand top billings. Shaliapin began professional life after six years of singing in his village church choir and a year of irregular private lessons in Tiflis.[135] Other leading lights worked their way up from modest positions. Grigorii Monakhov rose to prominence as one of the Mariinskii's chief stage directors after beginning his career in the prompter's box.[136] Daniil Pokhitonov likewise made the rather impressive transition from rehearsal

---

132. Lynn Sargeant, "A New Class of People: The Conservatoire and Musical Professionalization in Russia, 1861–1917," *Music and Letters* 85, no. 1 (2004): 45n.

133. Ibid., 52. Napravnik, "Vospominaniia," 39, remembered that the Mariinskii orchestra "consisted almost entirely of foreigners" when he began conducting it in the 1860s. In the early twentieth century its roster still held a large number of German, Czech, and French names.

134. Sargeant, "New Class," 42–48. Graduates employed in Musical Society institutions were entitled to a higher *chin*, two ranks above the lowest.

135. Victor Borovsky, *Chaliapin: A Critical Biography* (New York: Knopf, 1988), 42.

136. Teliakovskii, *Vospominaniia*, 164.

piano accompanist to conductor during his tenure in the Imperial Theaters. Each spring aspiring singers could appear at open auditions, where some major talents were discovered.[137]

Securing theatrical employment through patronage declined in the last decades before 1917, even if the phenomenon never quite disappeared. Despite managerial caprice, a major consequence of increasing competition and rising professional standards was that contracts went more than ever to the legitimately talented and hardworking. As Prince Liven recalled, "the theatrical life of pre-War Russia was distinguished by strict morality. It was very rarely that an actress or ballerina was a kept mistress. No Rolls-Royces or even Fords waited for the ballerinas at the stage door." In an incident described as "characteristic," the normally genial Stanislavskii fired an actress because he saw her vainly powdering her nose in public one day. "It appears you do not understand the spirit of our theatre," he told her. "It is only cocottes who powder their noses. You do not suit our tone. You had better leave."[138] Coming from a man who insisted on seventy-four rehearsals for his theater's first production, it probably was not a case of simple caprice.[139]

Direct attempts by influential people to place their favorites on stage failed with growing frequency. This was true even in the Imperial Theaters, whose prestige, lucrative compensation, and ties to the state made them the most likely targets for the ambitions of the well connected. Aleksandr Mosolov, chief of the Court Ministry's Chancellery under Nicholas II, claimed to have routinely brushed off such attempts. He told one would-be debutante, despite her note from the influential Siberian mystic Grigorii Rasputin and low-cut dress, that placing her on the stage "did not depend in any way whatever on me."[140] Pokhitonov, who witnessed much behind the scenes of the imperial opera troupe, acknowledged "rumors that one could get into the Mariinskii by having protection . . . but to my recollection these cases were very rare." Most of the beneficiaries in those rare cases did not last long without demonstrating real talent. "On this matter," he recalled, "one must credit Teliakovskii with being just."[141]

Even the clichéd selection of theatrical mistresses by members of the Imperial

---

137. D. I. Pokhitonov, *Iz proshlogo russkoi opery* (Leningrad: VTO, 1949), 128. According to Pokhitonov, about one hundred people signed up each year to try out, but only forty to fifty showed up.

138. Lieven, *Birth of the Ballets-Russes*, 63–64.

139. Frame, *School for Citizens*, 180.

140. Mossolov, *At the Court of the Last Tsar*, 153.

141. Pokhitonov, *Iz proshlogo*, 129–30.

Family was in decline. Despite her frequent appeals to high-born protectors, Kshesinskaia was already a well-regarded dancer when the future Nicholas II took up with her before he succeeded to the throne. Her talents continued to receive critical and popular acclaim as she moved on to other Romanovs. But she and those like her were exceptions proving the rule that talent mattered more than patronage. In 1905 the Mikhailovskii Theater actress Elise Baletta, a Frenchwomen who enjoyed the favor of Grand Duke Aleksei Aleksandrovich, failed to recover her position in the troupe after she had abandoned it and spent several months in Paris.[142]

Employment in the Imperial Theaters' bureaucracy also had less to do with patronage and connections. Teliakovskii's diary recorded many unsuccessful attempts by personal acquaintances and others with access to secure management positions in state arts institutions. In most cases their lack of qualifications kept them out—a factor that affected even such a prominent figure as Boris Shtiurmer, the governor of Teliakovskii's home province who in January 1916 became Premier of the Russian Empire. Fifteen years earlier he had failed to secure appointment as head of the Moscow theaters after Teliakovskii left them for the main Directorate.[143] According to Petr Gnedich, the Aleksandrinskii's chief director from 1900 to 1908, the most desirable candidates for posts in the state theaters were "men with the ability to be honest, refuse bribes, and not chase the French Theater girls and ballerinas."[144]

Growing professional seriousness had a greater impact on people already working in the performing arts. The Aleksandrinskii actor Mamont Dal'skii was temporarily dismissed from service in 1900 because he arrived too close to curtain for a performance in which he was slated to appear, forcing the Directorate to replace him. That he had nevertheless come in time did not save the actor since the administration felt that his conduct "could not be suffered in any serious theater."[145] Major stars could still get away with much—Shaliapin frequently escaped punishment for being late to rehearsals, for example—but greater expectations were increasingly present and could be applied to anyone.[146] Gnedich, who recounted the higher standards of professional conduct sought among Directorate employees, was himself ironically forced to resign when it was revealed that he had accepted a three-thousand-ruble payment just to read

---

142. V. A. Teliakovskii, "Imperatorskie teatry i 1905 god," in Teliakovskii, *Vospominaniia*, 310–14; Mossolov, *Court of the Last Tsar*, 80.
143. Teliakovskii, *Dnevniki . . . 1901–1903*, 22–33.
144. Gnedich, *Kniga zhizni*, 254.
145. Iur'ev, *Zapiski*, 1:536–37.
146. V. A. Teliakovskii, "Moi sosluzhivets Shaliapin," in Teliakovskii, *Vospominaniia*, 371.

a certain count's play.[147] In 1909 the Mariinskii's chief director, Ioakim Tartakov, a baritone who continued to appear on stage despite his more exalted duties, was fined for calling in sick for several scheduled performances.[148]

All works produced in all Russian theaters were subject to preliminary censorship. This practice had been in place from at least the seventeenth century, but formal theatrical censorship had only come about in 1804 when Alexander I assigned responsibilities for it to the recently created Ministry of Education. Seven years later, those responsibilities were transferred to the Empire's police authorities, where they remained until 1917.

Although various modes of state control over cultural expression existed throughout Russian history, censorship was governed in the last decades of the Empire by a decree (*ukaz*) promulgated at Alexander II's behest in April 1865. This legislation assigned all censorship responsibilities, except for those in ecclesiastical matters, to the Ministry of the Interior's newly created Main Office for Press Affairs (*Glavnoe upravlenie po delam pechati*). Part of the tsar's larger program of political reform, the new law softened the existing censorship regime but nevertheless left the state with substantial authority.[149] According to the decree's provisions all works bound for the theater, including plays, opera libretti, short skits, musical numbers, and other forms of staged public expression, had to be submitted to the Press Affairs Office and approved by its officials before performance. Upon review the censors could permit or deny the application or grant approval with revisions. Their decisions were subject to endorsement by the head of the Press Affairs Office, but in practice the post's occupants rarely overruled them. Once finalized, a list of approved works was published for public consumption.[150] In February 1888 another decree that was intended to be temporary in order to address just one controversial play but lasted until the end of the Empire created a second and intentionally more restrictive tier of censorship for works presented in popular theaters. The government never established

---

147. Gnedich, *Kniga zhizni*, 302–3, claimed the incident was simply a misunderstanding. According to his account, he regarded the payment as a loan and believed that Teliakovskii found fault with him not for having accepted it but for declining to produce the play. Whatever the truth, the mere appearance of impropriety made Gnedich's position untenable.

148. "V. B.," "Peterburg," *Rampa i zhizn'* 33 (November 15, 1909): 766.

149. For a good general description of the decree, see Charles A. Ruud, *Fighting Words: Imperial Censorship and the Russian Press, 1804–1906* (Toronto: University of Toronto Press, 1982), 147–48. Theaters in the constitutionally separate Grand Duchy of Finland were not subject to Interior Ministry censorship.

150. From 1865 an annual volume of decisions was published by Press Affairs. Its work was also reported in the theatrical press. "Alfavitnyi spisok dramaticheskim sochineniiam na russkom iazyke, razsmatrennym dramaticheskuiu tsenzuru i dozvolennym k predstavleniiu v dekabre 1896 goda," *Teatr i iskusstvo* 4 (January 28, 1897): 77, for example, lists works approved in 1896.

firm rules for evaluating works bound for popular stages nor determined what characteristics (other than the rather imprecise category of ticket prices) made a theater fit the "popular" category, but this mechanism was thought necessary to address the "bad tastes and sensual instincts" of Russia's lower classes.[151]

As comprehensive and, indeed, oppressive as this system may seem to have been—the government wielded the statutory power to prohibit any theatrical enterprise, including the Imperial Theaters, from performing any work for any reason—it faced many practical limitations.[152] Apart from very general language in the 1865 statute and occasional circulars addressing specific subjects, neither the Press Affairs Office nor senior Interior Ministry officials ever established an ironclad distinction between the permissible and the impermissible. Even one of the most clearly defined prohibitions, works depicting monarchs, wove between the two categories. A patriotic play called *To the Far East* was banned for popular audiences in 1904 because its staging contained a portrait of Nicholas II, beneath which reverent citizens laid wreaths.[153] Three years earlier, however, Nicholas II had personally congratulated the author of a historical tableau about Peter the Great that had been permitted for popular theaters and reportedly enjoyed by the reigning tsar.[154] In 1895 the censorship permitted a production of Aleksei Tolstoi's *Tsar Fedor Ivanovich*, a dramatization of the reign of the last, mentally handicapped ruler of the Riurikid dynasty, ostensibly because the character of the depicted monarch was thought to resemble a holy fool.[155]

---

151. The decree creating the second tier of censorship is in Rossiiskii Gosudarstvennyi Istoricheskii Arkhiv (RGIA), f. 776, op. 26, d. 42, l. 15. The memorandum suggesting it is in RGIA, f. 776, op. 1, d. 24, ll. 1a–1e. Its author, Interior Minister Dmitrii Tolstoi, acknowledged the absence of a formal definition of "popular" theater and recommended that the determination be left up to local authorities. Indeed, Petr Durnovo, a Press Affairs Office chief who later became Minister of the Interior, explicitly advised one impresario to escape popular theater censorship simply by raising his ticket prices. The "bad tastes" quote is from Konstantin Pobedonostsev, who served as Procurator of the Holy Synod, the chief state official responsible for religious matters, from 1880 to 1905. See RGIA, f. 776, op. 25, d. 340, l. 8. For the emergence of the decree, see Frame, *School for Citizens*, 140–41.

152. Ruud, *Fighting Words*, 148, does not discuss the decree's implications for theater but claims it to have been "the most methodically prepared, broadly discussed, comprehensive, and centralizing press law in the history of the state."

153. RGIA, f. 776, op. 26, d. 23, l. 57. The prohibition was not always driven by content. According to Swift, "Fighting the Germs of Disorder," 17–18, the censors were often concerned that productions involving monarchs would not be technically or artistically sufficient in depicting their august persons.

154. RGIA, op. 25, d. 603, l. 2. A. S. Suvorin, *Dnevnik* (Moscow: Novosti, 1992), 306. Peter was frequently depicted on Russian stages, especially during the bicentenary celebrations of St. Petersburg in 1903.

155. A. A. Sidorov, "Iz vospominaniia tsenzora. Nachal'niki glavnogo upravleniia po delam pechati s 1893 po 1905 g. i V. S. Adikaevskii," in N. G. Patrusheva, *Tsenzura v Rossii v kontse XIX–nachale XX veka: Sbornik vospominanii* (St. Petersburg: Bulanin, 2003), 242.

Yet Tolstoi's prequel to that play, *The Death of Ivan the Terrible,* still remained banned for popular (if not private) theaters ten years later in 1905.[156] In another paradox one censor felt that he had to "tone down" Brutus's incendiary monologue in Shakespeare's *Julius Caesar* (even though Caesar never quite wore a crown), while one of his colleagues left in all the invective directed against the reigning title character in Pushkin's *Boris Godunov.*[157]

Blasphemy—defined by any depiction of heaven or religious characters—also tended to be proscribed but often only superficially and sometimes not at all. A production of Goethe's *Faust* was allowed to go forward on the condition that its program list the role of God as "first celestial voice" and that its angels not wear costumes with wings and halos.[158] The librettist of Rimskii-Korsakov's opera *The Legend of the Invisible City of Kitezh and Maiden Fevroniia* thought it prudent to change the title character's name because she had been canonized but restored it when he learned that the censors did not care.[159] Prohibiting Russian operas during Lent also became a censorship responsibility, but this stricture faltered as well. In 1897 provincial opera companies in Tula and Riazan' were permitted to perform Russian works on the wrong side of Easter.[160] Chaikovskii's *Eugene Onegin* appeared at the Mariinskii during Lent the following year.[161]

As these cases suggest, most decisions to grant or deny permission for performance could hardly have been anything other than subjective. To make the process even more arbitrary, they were based on the review of just one of the handful of censors working in the Press Affairs Office. Since entrepreneurs had the right to resubmit a rejected work an unlimited number of times and each censor had his own biases, interpretations, moods, and whims, any new attempt opened the possibility of a favorable decision. Sergei Vereshchagin, a long-serving chief dramatic censor, admitted the system's imperfections with the candid observation that "each censor acts on his own and could easily make a mistake."[162]

The censors, moreover, were far from immune to outside influences and lobbying. Suvorin frequently used his "energy and connections" to persuade them

---

156. "K voprosu o dramaticheskoi tsenzure," 1122.
157. Thurston, *Popular Theatre,* 176; N. N. Khodotov, *Blizkoe—dalekoe* (Leningrad: Iskusstvo, 1962), 218. Khodotov, a rare radical among the capital's actors, performed the role of the False Dmitrii in a production of *Boris Godunov* and so relished delivering the character's antitsarist lines that he caused a minor scandal.
158. Gnedich, *Kniga zhizni,* 259–60.
159. Simon Morrison, *Russian Opera and the Symbolist Movement* (Berkeley and Los Angeles: University of California Press, 2002), 129.
160. "Ot redaktsii," *Teatr i iskusstvo* 7 (February 16, 1897): 121.
161. Frame, *Imperial Theatres,* 31.
162. "K voprosu o dramaticheskoi tsenzure," 1122.

to change their minds about controversial plays he wanted to produce.[163] So, too, did Iavorskaia, whose radical chic did not conflict with her use of connections (her husband, Prince Bariatinskii, had been a childhood friend of Nicholas II when his father was tutor to the children of Alexander III) to secure approval for works she wanted to stage at the New Theater.[164] Sometimes simply changing the titles of well-known works could secure their approval, if for no other reason than that the censors could not identify them under more obscure billings and lacked the time, energy, or attention to discover the truth. Rossini's opera *Wilhelm Tell* was thus permitted for popular performance under the title *Charles the Bold,* as was Meyerbeer's *Le Prophète* when it was submitted as *John of Leyden.*[165] Stanislavskii secured approval for a banned dramatization of Dostoevskii's *The Village of Stepanchikovo* under a different title and with changed character names.[166]

Direct Court influence, though relatively rare, also played a role. Alexander III personally excised lines that he found objectionable from a few plays.[167] In January 1903 his son and successor, Nicholas II, reversed censorship authorization for an Aleksandrinskii production of Gor'kii's *The Lower Depths,* finding it "unnecessary" (*lishnim*) that the work of a playwright under police observation should appear on the imperial dramatic stage.[168] The same play nevertheless retained its approval for private theaters and was approved for popular theaters in 1905. Interference from the highest levels, moreover, could work in the opposite direction. In 1895 chief dramatic censor Evgenii Feoktistov resigned from his post after Nicholas II personally overruled his decision to ban a Suvorin Theater production of Tolstoi's *The Power of Darkness.*[169] Russia's last tsar was also known to restore lines that the censors wanted to omit.[170] Ultimately, he even approved a concert version of *The Lower Depths* for the imperial stage.[171]

In addition to the arbitrary nature of the censorship regime's decisions,

163. Petrovskaia and Somina, *Teatral'nyi Peterburg,* 205; E. G. Kholodov et al., eds., *Istoriia russkogo dramaticheskogo teatra,* 7 vols. (Moscow: Iskusstvo, 1977–87), 7:302.
164. M. G. Litavrina, "Chastnye teatry Moskvy i Peterburga i provintsial'naia antrepriza na rubezhe XIX–XX vekov," in *Russkii dramaticheskii teatr kontsa XIX–nachala XX vv.,* ed. A. Nazarova and N. Orekhova (Moscow: GITIS, 2000), 177.
165. "Tsenzura pered sudom predstavitelei iskusstva," *Teatral'naia Rossiia* 41 (October 8, 1905): 1222.
166. Benedetti, *Stanislavski,* 30, 39–40.
167. Volkonskii, *Rodina,* 147–48.
168. Teliakovskii, *Dnevniki . . . 1901–1903,* 415–17. Ironically, Gor'kii's play only remained banned from imperial stages, which generally experienced the lowest degree of censorship.
169. Gnedich, *Kniga zhizni,* 205–6.
170. Frame, *Imperial Theatres,* 89.
171. S. Kara, *Varlamov* (Leningrad: Iskusstvo, 1969), 151.

over time it developed serious logistical problems. The growth of Russia's theatrical world—to say nothing of its rapidly expanding journalism and publishing industries—forced the Press Affairs Office to review a skyrocketing number of texts. It did not help that the main censorship organ remained seriously undermanned through the end of the tsarist era. At the time of the imperial performance monopoly's abolition in 1882, Press Affairs' St. Petersburg staff consisted of just nine censors, of whom only two had formal responsibilities for theater. In the thirty-five years before 1917, its staff grew to fourteen, but only one of the new hires was assigned to theatrical censorship. In the same period its budget rose a parsimonious 2 percent, from 63,996 rubles to 65,360.[172]

By the turn of the twentieth century, the sheer volume of the censors' work was overwhelming. In 1904 alone Press Affairs considered 2,360 submissions for theater, a figure marginally more daunting than the previous year's 2,334 and a 60 percent increase over the 1,418 submitted a mere thirteen years earlier in 1891.[173] To make the system work properly, each theatrical censor would have to have read and decided the fate of more than a thousand works per annum, or still nearly eight hundred after the hiring of the third dramatic censor. Unsurprisingly, many of the archived reports—required for plays that were rejected, approved subject to textual deletions, permitted after having previously been banned, or otherwise controversial—are only a few sentences long and relatively superficial in content. Reams of manuscript pages and sometimes whole submissions attracted no comment or indication that they were ever even looked at, let alone considered critically. The actual division of labor in the Press Affairs Office itself revealed its personnel's tribulations. Oskar Lamkert, a prolific reviewer of theatrical submissions, was neglecting his job as the chief posts and telegraphs censor to assist his overworked dramatic censorship colleagues, as were several other officials whose names appear in the file yet formally held responsibilities for other media.

In a vast number of cases, these few beleaguered officials decided to approve the submissions that came across their desks. Of the 2,334 theatrical works submitted to the censorship in 1903, for example, 2,085 (89.3 percent) were granted

---

172. Benjamin Rigberg, "The Efficacy of Tsarist Censorship Operations, 1894–1917," *Jahrbücher für Geschichte Osteuropas* 14, no. 3 (1966): 340–41.

173. "K voprosu o dramaticheskoi tsenzure," 1122. The 1891 figure is reported in RGIA, f. 776, op. 23, d. 1, l. 34. Hemmings, *Theatre and State*, 224, reports the same problem at the French theatrical censorship organ, located in the Third Republic's Ministry of Public Instruction and Fine Arts. In 1900 it received an impossible nine thousand submissions. Rigberg, "Tsarist Censorship Operations," 331, tracks an increase in books approved by (but not the total submitted to) Press Affairs from 1,773 in 1861 to 23,852 in 1908. According to Daniel Balmuth, *Censorship in Russia, 1865–1905* (Washington, D.C.: University Press of America, 1979), 78, print censors were responsible for forty thousand pages a year by 1875.

permission for performance. The figure dropped slightly to 88.7 percent the following year (2,094 out of 2,360), while, according to E. Anthony Swift's estimate, 86 percent of works reviewed for popular theaters between 1888 and 1915 were approved.[174] Such negligible differences hardly indicated that the censors were becoming harsher. To the contrary, Prince Nikolai Shakhovskoi, head of the Press Affairs Office from 1899 to 1905, was variously described as "a nice person," "a liberal," and even "a Red," who held his post despite reportedly having provoked the tsar's "personal antipathy."[175] Suvorin, whose repertoire was subject to Shakhovskoi's authority, described him in his diary as "a kind and reasonable man."[176] During a series of meetings about the future of censorship held in 1905, the prince advocated the abolition of the separate censorship for popular theater among other "desirable changes."[177]

Apart from the general categories noted above, banned works, particularly those prohibited for performance in popular theaters, usually dealt with explicit sexuality, related social taboos, and topics that incited or were thought to incite mass violence. Sophocles' *Oedipus Rex* was prohibited for popular audiences on account of its incest theme.[178] One censor barred Daniel Auber's opera *La Muette de Portici* from popular performance because the spurning of its heroine by her noble suitor leads to a nationalist rebellion in seventeenth-century Italy. As the censor's report noted, a performance of the opera in Brussels had been credited with stimulating the Belgian revolt of 1830.[179] The eponymous violence, cruel landlords, and "tendentiousness" of Prosper Mérimée's *La Jacquerie* prompted a general ban on the play.[180] So, too, did Gerhart Hauptmann's dramatization of the Silesian textile workers' revolt of 1844 in *The Weavers*, a work adopted as a propaganda tool by the radical Left in spite of its prohibition.[181]

---

174. "K voprosu o dramaticheskoi tsenzure," 1122; Swift, *Popular Theater*, 120. Balmuth, *Censorship*, 126, claims that Press Affairs rejected less than 1 percent of all submissions in 1865–1905. According to Hemmings, *Theatre and State*, 220, after France's Second Republic restored preliminary theatrical censorship in 1850, a nearly comparable 90.6 percent of reviewed plays were approved.

175. Gnedich, *Kniga zhizni*, 259; Sidorov, "Vospominaniia," 242. Shakhovskoi was among those killed in the August 1906 terrorist bombing of Premier Petr Stolypin's villa.

176. Suvorin, *Dnevnik*, 266. He also thought that Shakhovskoi's ill-fated superior, Interior Minister Dmitrii Sipiagin (assassinated in 1902), had "mild manners, beautiful eyes, and a pleasant voice."

177. "Ot redaktsii," *Teatr i iskusstvo* 20 (May 15, 1905): 311.

178. RGIA, f. 776, op. 26, d. 25, l. 252. According to Steve Nicholson, *The Censorship of British Drama, 1900–1968*, 2 vols. (Exeter: University of Exeter Press, 2003), 1:80, it was also banned from British stages until 1910.

179. RGIA, f. 776, op. 26, d. 21, l. 45.

180. RGIA, f. 776, op. 26, d. 24, l. 213.

181. Reginald Zelnik, "*Weber* into *Tkachi*: On a Russian Reading of Gerhart Hauptmann's Play *The Weavers*," in *Self and Story in Russian History*, ed. Laura Engelstein and Stephanie Sadler (Ithaca: Cornell University Press, 2000), 217–26. No other Hauptmann play remained prohibited.

Beyond the enormous amount of office work and the censors' relative permissiveness, mechanisms for enforcing censorship directives were weak, no matter how many works the censors wished to ban. With rising urban crime, increasingly militant labor unrest, a daring revolutionary movement, and other more pressing security matters, ensuring compliance with censorship decisions was neither a high priority nor a feasible task.[182] This was particularly true since Russia was, as Hans Rogger put it, "poorly policed" and employed far fewer law enforcement officials per capita than other major powers.[183]

The Interior Ministry's organization itself hindered efforts to make theatrical censorship work. Although the ministry's housing of the Press Affairs Office linked the main censorship organ to the Empire's police authorities, they remained functionally separate and uncoordinated. No ministerial department had specifically enumerated responsibilities for enforcing or even being aware of the censors' decisions, a task that the 1865 statute vaguely assigned to local authorities. According to Iain Lauchlan, the "police had no control over censorship"; in practice, he argues, the division of powers represented a kind of "checks and balances."[184]

The national gendarmerie did visit theaters to monitor suspects among audiences, protect high-profile spectators, and, in the Imperial Theaters, provide general security, but it simply lacked the manpower to attend and scrutinize each of the thousands of performances that went on across the Russian Empire every year.[185] Even when the police maintained a presence in theaters, their effectiveness proved slight. Seats reserved for police agents in the Imperial Theaters went largely unoccupied. The policeman most regularly on duty at the Aleksandrinskii was an elderly officer who used his official access to indulge a personal love of drama.[186] Leaving aside the issue of censorship enforcement, the

---

182. For a discussion of these issues specific to the imperial capital, see Joan Neuberger, *Hooliganism: Crime, Culture, and Power in St. Petersburg, 1900–1914* (Berkeley and Los Angeles: University of California Press, 1993).

183. Hans Rogger, *Russia in the Age of Modernisation and Revolution, 1881–1917* (New York: Longman, 1983), 56. In proportional terms Britain had seven times as many policemen as Russia, and France had five times as many around 1900.

184. Iain Lauchlan, *Russian Hide-and-Seek: The Tsarist Secret Police in St. Petersburg, 1906–1914* (Helsinki: Suomalaisen Kirjallisuuden Seura, 2002), 87–89.

185. A. T. Vassilyev, *The Ochrana: The Russian Secret Police* (London: Harrap, 1930), 37, lists theaters among several public places where suspects were followed. Reginald E. Zelnik, ed. and trans., *A Radical Worker in Tsarist Russia: The Autobiography of Semën Ivanovich Kanatchikov* (Stanford: Stanford University Press, 1986), 104, tells of a student who warned the Bolshevik worker memoirist Semen Kanatchikov and his comrades not to talk too loudly about radical literature at concerts or plays lest they "run up against a spy or a provocateur." Frame, *Imperial Theatres*, 30, establishes the general security function.

186. Teliakovskii, *Vospominaniia*, 239. Frame, *Imperial Theatres*, 123–24, reports that of the

"police presence" neither stopped a full-scale riot at the Mariinskii in October 1905 (more in Chapter 5) nor saved Premier Petr Stolypin from assassination at the Kiev Municipal Theater in September 1911. When Teliakovskii requested more policemen to help guard against disturbances in the Imperial Theaters during the national general strike that immediately preceded the Mariinskii riot, he was told that no officers were available for that purpose.[187]

"Strict control" and other purported features of a "repressive autocracy, where the arts [we]re heavily censored and policed"—characteristics upon which some scholars have relied to discuss culture and power in Imperial Russia—thus fall short of accurate.[188] Indeed, even some government institutions actively resisted the censorship's decisions, adding to the argument that the "autocracy" of which they were part was neither monolithic nor effective in its aspirations to control cultural expression. The Finance Ministry, which sponsored the hundreds of theaters operated by the Temperance Trusteeship, "continually besieged" Press Affairs with requests to broaden their repertoires.[189] So, too, did the Imperial Theaters Directorate—formally part of the tsar's own court—which struggled to secure permission for Gor'kii's *The Lower Depths*.[190]

Urban officials who believed that greater cultural life would enrich their localities added their voices. In 1905 the mayor of Moscow petitioned Press Affairs to approve a list of seventy-six works that he wanted to add to the repertoire of his city's People's House. In another illustration of the censorship's relative permissiveness, however, he may have been surprised to learn that fifty-one of them had already been approved for popular theaters, while fourteen more had never been submitted to the censorship in the first place. Only eleven (14.5 percent) had encountered prohibitions.[191]

Simply ignoring negative censorship decisions was easy and usually free of consequences. In one egregious case a 1901 Press Affairs Office memorandum revealed that the Nicholas II People's House, the flagship of Russian popular theater, had presented some seventy-five works—or nearly 40 percent of its inaugural season's repertoire—without censorship approval. The theater's

---

eleven Mariinskii, thirteen Aleksandrinskii, and seven Mikhailovskii seats reserved for the police in 1905, only three in each theater were used on a regular basis.
187. Teliakovskii, "Imperatorskie teatry," 252–58.
188. These quotations are from N. A. Gorchakov, *The Theater in Soviet Russia*, trans. Edgar Lehrman (New York: Columbia University Press, 1957), 100 (the passage discusses prerevolutionary theater); and Laurence Senelick, "Anti-Semitism and the Tsarist Theatre: The *Smugglers* Riots," *Theatre Survey* 44, no. 1 (2003): 68.
189. Swift, "Fighting the Germs of Disorder," 42.
190. Teliakovskii, *Dnevniki . . . 1901–1903*, 412–18.
191. RGIA, f. 776, op. 25, d. 783, ll. 33–34.

administration had neglected to submit most of the plays on the list, but at least a dozen had been expressly forbidden for popular audiences.[192] Because the Temperance Trusteeship operated the People's House, its sponsors in the Finance Ministry may have devised or at least sanctioned a more defiant strategy for broadening popular repertoires. Despite Press Affairs' disappointment there is no record of anything practical being done about the violations.

Government-sponsored enterprises were far from alone in flouting the censorship. Gaideburov's theater frequently performed works banned for popular performance, including Ibsen's *An Enemy of the People*, Molière's *Tartuffe*, and Schiller's *Intrigue and Love*, without consequences.[193] Iavorskaia staged Schnitzler's *The Green Parrot*, which depicts a rebellious French crowd and the murder of an aristocrat on the day of the fall of the Bastille, in her first season at the New Theater despite a censorship ban on the play.[194] A workers' drama circle at the Thornton textile plant performed Hauptmann's categorically forbidden *The Weavers*, as—to Press Affairs' frank embarrassment—had many other drama troupes.[195] Again, there is no record of any serious consequences resulting from these illegal productions.

Keeping censored lines out of staged works proved virtually impossible. In the absence of omnipresent, regular, or, as was often the case, any police monitoring, censorship deletions from theatrical texts turned into tanks of wasted ink. Aleksandr Briantsev, who worked with several theaters in the late imperial era, recalled that he and his fellow performers frequently ignored censorship deletions without sanctions.[196] According to Swift, censorship violations were "routine," and those nominally responsible for enforcing them were "unable to cope with important elements of theater such as gesture, ad-lib, intonation, makeup, and audience response."[197] The dramatic censor Mikhail Tolstoi, who noticed the abuse of these phenomena as part of his personal theatergoing, believed that censorship definitions of "decency" were "constantly violated" on Russia's stages.[198]

When punishments for disobeying censorship directives did occur, they were rare and usually limited to a fine. Iavorskaia, for example, was punished with

192. RGIA, f. 776, op. 25, d. 633, ll. 12–13.
193. Khaichenko, *Russkii narodnyi teatr*, 173.
194. Petrovskaia and Somina, *Teatral'nyi Peterburg*, 218.
195. Zelnik, "*Weber* into *Tkachi*," 218. "Ot redaktsii," *Teatr i iskusstvo* 7 (February 12, 1906): 97, cites a Press Affairs circular about censorship violations that specifically mentions *The Weavers* and its frequent performances.
196. A. A. Briantsev, *Vospominaniia, stat'i, vystupleniia, dnevniki, pis'ma* (Moscow: VTO, 1979), 51–52.
197. Swift, "Fighting the Germs of Disorder," 45.
198. RGIA, f. 776, op. 25, d. 911, l. 1.

one for performing a censored speech in the radical playwright Evgenii Chirikov's *The Jew*, a drama about the relationship between socialism and Zionism that features a pogrom during which the protagonist dies.[199] But at no time does there appear to have been a single case in which an actor or impresario was arrested or imprisoned for violating censorship directives or in which the authorities closed a theater for presenting banned or merely unapproved works. The British journalist and travel writer Maurice Baring, who often attended performances during his visits to Russia, found its theatrical censorship "childishly futile."[200]

Preliminary theatrical censorship and its practical dilemmas were also not uncommon in the era's international cultural climate. Most European nations, including republican France, employed such a system.[201] American municipalities had preliminary control over theater repertoires, and there was palpable advocacy of censorship's formal adoption for theater. In an essay published in 1900, the critic Harry Thurston Peck criticized "the moral and social decadence" of Offenbach's operettas and "wondered whether some kind of a censorship could not be established in this country; for there is no country in the world which needs a censorship so much."[202] The British Lord Chamberlain's Office actively exercised preliminary theatrical censorship powers until 1968.[203] Only shortly before the abolition of its censorial functions, the American playwright Edward Albee was required to alter or delete obscenities from the London premiere of *Who's Afraid of Virginia Woolf?*

In some cases Western censorship regimes exceeded Late Imperial Russia's in strictness. Strindberg's *Miss Julie*, a play about an unbalanced debutante who commits suicide after fornicating with her family's class-conscious valet, was permitted for Iavorskaia's New Theater in January 1906 but remained banned

199. "Khronika," *Teatr i iskusstvo* 11 (March 12, 1906): 162.
200. Maurice Baring, *A Year in Russia* (New York: Dutton, 1907), 95.
201. Although France did away with centralized national theatrical censorship in 1905, departmental prefects retained the right to prohibit controversial productions. In any case, according to John McCormick, *Popular Theatres of Nineteenth-Century France* (New York: Routledge, 1993), 110, the abolition of France's national censorship regime occurred "for purely budgetary reasons." Ruud, *Fighting Words*, 148, revealingly describes the Russian censorship law of 1865 as "'Western' both in content and in the mode of its drafting."
202. Lawrence W. Levine, *Highbrow/Lowbrow: The Emergence of Cultural Hierarchy in America* (Cambridge: Harvard University Press, 1988), 217. In a Russia-related example, according to Marks, *How Russia Shaped the Modern World*, 193, New York police officials forced the Ballets Russes to scale back the sexual content of their program during a 1916 visit. On the same tour a Kansas City official threatened to ban their performances if they proved "too rank."
203. See Dominic Shellard, *British Theatre Since the War* (New Haven: Yale University Press, 1999), 8–14, for a description of its powers, and 136–46 for the circumstances of its abolition.

from British stages for another thirty-three years.[204] A season earlier Iavorskaia had legally staged Maurice Maeterlinck's *Monna Vanna*, in which a patrician Pisan woman offers herself, clad in nothing but a mantle, to an enemy commander in order to save her besieged city. Although the sympathetic adversary ultimately refuses to despoil her virtue, the suggestion of even her seminudity was enough to keep the play off limits to British audiences until 1914.[205] British theatergoers also had to wait until that unfortunate year for lawful performances of Ibsen's *Ghosts*, a moral drama about the consequences of syphilis for healthy family living. The play had already been appearing legally in Russia for a decade.[206] A dramatization of Alphonse Daudet's novel *Sapho*, the sad tale of a young sculptor who spurns his amour when he discovers her salacious past, was permitted in Russia just after 1900 but simultaneously banned in several American municipalities. The impresario who staged it in New York was arrested.[207] Franz Adam Beyerlein's antimilitary drama *Lights Out* had dozens of performances in Petersburg in early 1906, at a time when German censors banned it "for shaking the foundations of 'military honor.'"[208] While it might go too far to call the Russian censors "open minded," they were certainly no more close minded than those in countries normally thought to be freer.

The Russian Empire entered the twentieth century with a vibrant and thriving performing arts culture—a milieu that ever-increasing numbers of its inhabitants supported and appreciated. Its effervescence was only one facet of Russia's rapid modernization, but, as in other modernizing nations, it was playing a serious role in transforming the urban landscape, amplifying the importance and desirability of entertainment, introducing unfamiliar values and ideas, and creating new opportunities for employment, investment, leisure, education, expression, identity formation, advancement, socialization, gossip, and many other

---

204. Steve Nicholson, "Unnecessary Plays: European Drama and the British Censor in the 1920s," *Theatre Research International* 20, no. 1 (1995): 33; Petrovskaia and Somina, *Teatral'nyi Peterburg*, 221. The Russian version was presented under the alternate title *Countess Julie*. Swedish and Danish censors also banned its initial productions.

205. Nicholson, *Censorship*, 1:27.

206. Dominic Shellard and Steve Nicholson, *The Lord Chamberlain Regrets: A History of British Theatre Censorship* (London: British Library, 2004), 77. Petrovskaia and Somina, *Teatral'nyi Peterburg*, 304, reports Russian censorship approval for the play in 1904. The Moscow Art Theater performed it for the first time the following year.

207. "K voprosu o dramaticheskoi tsenzure," 1120, mentions the incident in a comparative context. For a detailed history of the scandal, see John H. Houchin, *Censorship of the American Theatre in the Twentieth Century* (Ithaca: Cornell University Press, 2003), 40–52. The dramatization was reportedly "suppressed" in Boston, Baltimore, Chicago, Cincinnati, Providence, and St. Louis.

208. Petrovskaia and Somina, *Teatral'nyi Peterburg*, 197.

activities typical of modern societies. The rising commercialization of this culture contributed to paradoxes of fierce competition flourishing alongside blossoming creativity, extreme pomposity emerging together with sober professionalism, and a state struggling—not always without success—to manage its people's transition to modernity. Now that the institutional structures and mentalities of that culture have been delineated and its inhabitants introduced, we may proceed to a discussion of the tests faced by its component parts during the late tsarist era.

2

"SUCH A RISKY TIME":
ARTS INSTITUTIONS AND THE CHALLENGE OF POLITICS

On the evening of January 9, 1905, the Aleksandrinskii Theater, the principal imperial dramatic stage in St. Petersburg, presented Aleksandr Ostrovskii's light comedy *A Passionate Heart*. When the great comedic actor Konstantin Varlamov uttered his first droll lines, an indignant member of the audience jumped up on his seat and shouted, "You, Konstantin Aleksandrovich, are a good and kind man. How is it that you are not ashamed to amuse the public on such a terrible day?" Varlamov, who had been indoors since early morning, later claimed not to have known that government troops had fired on peaceful demonstrators trying to present a petition of grievances to Tsar Nicholas II that day.[1] Official figures held that 130 people had been killed and 299 wounded, though the actual number of victims on what became known as "Bloody Sunday" was probably higher.[2]

The play continued after a momentary pause, but in the second act other voices in the audience cried out, "It will be broken up, all right!" "Not on such a day!" "Lower the curtain!" "Lights!" "Enough!" These outbursts may have been connected with an unheeded threat delivered during intermission that the performance would be forcibly stopped if the theater failed to close. Regardless of the disturbance's origin, it was clear that the performance could not continue. The stagehands were too nervous to lower the curtain, however, and had

---

1. S. Kara, *Varlamov* (Leningrad: Iskusstvo, 1969), 154.
2. The most thorough account of the march is Walter Sablinsky, *Father Gapon and the St. Petersburg Massacre of 1905* (Princeton: Princeton University Press, 1976), 229–71. Abraham Ascher, *The Revolution of 1905: Russia in Disarray* (Stanford: Stanford University Press, 1988), 83–92, also covers it.

to dim the lights to ask what remained of the audience to leave. After this incident all three of the city's Imperial Theaters closed until January 13, ostensibly for a period of mourning, though the sporadic supply of electricity and gas lighting left their administration with no other practical choice.[3]

Like every other aspect of Russia's modernizing society, its varied and evolving performing arts universe could not escape the political events that rocked the Empire in the late imperial era. This chapter will seek to assess how the institutions described in the preceding pages responded to moments of confusion and unrest. Although there were many such episodes in the era under review, the most serious were those of the political crises, wars, and revolutions that characterized the period from 1905 to 1917. Its effect on expressive artistic life will form the primary, if not exclusive, focus of this chapter. When else would artistic responses to politics emerge into greater relief than during revolutionary times?

The Russian Empire rested ill at ease as it rang in the year 1905. For eleven months it had been fighting an unsuccessful war with Japan, an adversary Russian leaders had dismissed as inferior and promised to vanquish in short order. Less than two weeks before New Year's, the long besieged garrison of Port Arthur, Russia's chief base in Manchuria, surrendered to the enemy. The government's domestic opponents, who had been growing in number and daring for decades, were becoming more volatile. Since 1901 revolutionary terrorists had assassinated a sitting Minister of Education, a Governor of Finland, and two successive Ministers of the Interior, in addition to hundreds of lesser officials.[4] Waves of unrest swept over Russia's universities, while mounting military setbacks caused many political moderates to abandon their initial patriotism and become increasingly vocal in their criticism of the status quo.[5] Numerous professional and civic associations held meetings of protest, often illegal or semilegal, calling for major reforms. Their demands included comprehensive civil liberties, land redistribution, proworker economic legislation, and, most important of all, representative government.[6] Labor unrest, which had mounted over the previous few years, swelled in December 1904 after the controversial firing of four

    3. P. P. Gnedich, *Kniga zhizni: Vospominaniia, 1855–1918* (Moscow: Agraf, 2000), 282–84, and Marius Petipa, "Dnevniki 1903–1905 godov," in Petipa, *Materialy. Vospominaniia. Stat'i* (Leningrad: Iskusstvo, 1971), 105, both note that the Aleksandrinskii was closed because its electricity and gas were out.
    4. For the best study of revolutionary terrorism in Late Imperial Russia, see Anna Geifman, *Thou Shalt Kill: Revolutionary Terrorism in Russia, 1894–1917* (Princeton: Princeton University Press, 1993).
    5. Student unrest in 1905 is addressed thoroughly in Samuel D. Kassow, *Students, Professors, and the State in Tsarist Russia* (Berkeley and Los Angeles: University of California Press, 1989), 237–85.
    6. In imitation of the French Revolution of 1848, these meetings frequently took the form of "banquets" to skirt laws and police directives against mass political gatherings. For a study of the

workers from Petersburg's huge Putilov plant. By the first week of January 1905, some one hundred thousand St. Petersburg workers were on strike—more than at any previous time.[7]

In this difficult atmosphere Father Georgii Gapon, an Orthodox priest and leader of the Assembly of Russian Factory and Plant Workers, thought to mobilize the capital's workers to present an address to the tsar. On the "cold, crisp" morning of Sunday, January 9—the day of Varlamov's ill-fated appearance in *A Passionate Heart*—tens of thousands of workers set out for the Winter Palace to deliver a petition asking for redress of their grievances. Before they reached the palace, they were stopped and fired upon.

National and, indeed, international outrage knew few limits. In the days and weeks that followed the massacre, more than four hundred thousaned Russian workers, without much organization or coordination, went on strike, while many of the Empire's intellectual, professional, and student communities gathered in mass meetings to denounce the government.[8] The unrest touched off demonstrations of sympathy in many important urban centers, where they were usually suppressed by the army and police. Violent confrontations between peasants and landowners flared up in rural areas, which had also witnessed rising unrest in the years after 1900. Services of all types halted, shops closed, newspapers ceased to appear, and detachments of soldiers patrolled the streets.[9]

Russia's performing arts community suffered, especially in the troubled capital. Vera Komissarzhevskaia canceled her Dramatic Theater's scheduled performance on the evening of January 9 to mourn.[10] Lidiia Iavorskaia's New Theater announced that "performances have temporarily stopped in view of the disruption of the ordinary flow of life." The Winter Farce, the cavernous Panaev Theater, and Pavel Gaideburov's General Accessible Theater also closed, as did several smaller venues. The Empire's largest popular theater, the Tsar

---

phenomenon, see Terrence Emmons, "Russia's Banquet Campaign," *California Slavic Studies* 10 (1977): 45–86. Shmuel Galai, *The Liberation Movement in Russia, 1900–1905* (Cambridge: Cambridge University Press, 1972), comprehensively treats the general phenomenon of liberal opposition leading up to 1905.

7. The number of strikers at that time based on police reports is recorded in Gerald D. Surh, *1905 in St. Petersburg: Labor, Society, and Revolution* (Stanford: Stanford University Press, 1989), 156. For a detailed general description of Russia's situation in 1905, see Ascher, *Russia in Disarray*, 29–83. See also Victoria Bonnell, *Roots of Rebellion: Workers' Politics and Organizations in St. Petersburg and Moscow, 1900–1914* (Berkeley and Los Angeles: University of California Press, 1983).

8. Surh, *1905 in St. Petersburg*, 156, estimates that 125,000 workers were on strike in Petersburg alone on January 10. Sablinsky, *Father Gapon*, 261, surveys international reactions.

9. Ascher, *Russia in Disarray*, 92–114, discusses the wider national implications.

10. E. G. Kholodov et al., eds., *Istoriia russkogo dramaticheskogo teatra*, 7 vols. (Moscow: Iskusstvo, 1977–1987), 7:298; I. F. Petrovskaia, *Teatr i zritel' rossiiskikh stolits: 1895–1917* (Leningrad: Iskusstvo, 1990), 82.

Nicholas II People's House, held its January 9 performance but remained dark for the next four nights.[11] The New Admiralty Theater shut its doors for a full two weeks after Bloody Sunday.[12] No performances were held anywhere in Petersburg on January 14.[13]

A longer lasting difficulty grew from the challenge of staying in business in the rising tide of civil unrest. The haphazard finances, administrative irregularities, and short lifespan of most enterprises presented enough difficulty in normal times, but major upheaval made nervous urbanites reluctant to go out on the streets, let alone confine themselves to theaters and other enclosed places in hazardous city centers. Shortly after the disruption of his own performance, Varlamov wrote a friend that "the indescribable is happening here. Theaters and amusements have been closed for four days, newspapers and broadsheets are not coming out, the electricity is off, armed patrols are marching and riding around town ... the workers are striking and rebelling."[14]

In the weeks after Bloody Sunday receipts throughout the Empire "sharply declined." Several venues, including the Imperial Theaters, "gathered very small audiences" after they reopened. At the Nicholas II People's House the usually overflowing Sunday audiences were failing to appear, "something that had never happened before."[15] The popular Nevskii Farce reported "significantly smaller" publics than it usually welcomed.[16] Prince Tsereteli's opera company was still taking in "ominously parsimonious sums" in late March.[17] The Imperial Theaters Directorate acknowledged below-average receipts all through the spring.[18] The official history of the Imperial Russian Musical Society (RMO), which offered an annual concert series, recorded that it "ceased substantive performing activity."[19] Between 1905 and 1908 it gave just two concerts.[20] The composer Nikolai Rimskii-Korsakov complained that the Empire's musical events merely "dragged on their sad existence."[21] In early September the theatrical press reported that

11. "Ot redaktsii," *Teatr i iskusstvo* 3 (January 16, 1905): 41–42.
12. "Khronika," *Teatr i iskusstvo* 4 (January 23, 1905): 50.
13. "Ot redaktsii," *Teatr i iskusstvo* 3 (January 16, 1905): 42.
14. Quoted in Kara, *Varlamov*, 155.
15. "Khronika," *Teatral'naia Rossiia/Teatral'naia gazeta* 5 (January 29, 1905): 73.
16. "Khronika," *Teatr i iskusstvo* 4 (January 23, 1905): 52.
17. "Khronika," *Teatr i iskusstvo* 13 (March 27, 1905): 201.
18. "Koi pro chto," *Teatr i iskusstvo* 22 (May 29, 1905): 348.
19. N. F. Findeizen, *Ocherk deiatel'nosti S.-Peterburgskogo otdeleniia Imperatorskogo russkogo muzykal'nogo obshchestva (1859–1909)* (St. Petersburg: Tipografiia Glavnogo Upravleniia Udelov, 1909), 100.
20. I. F. Petrovskaia, *Muzykal'noe obrazovanie i muzykal'nye obshchestvennye organizatsii v Peterburge, 1801–1917: Entsiklopediia* (St. Petersburg: RIII, 1999), 258.
21. Nikolay Rimsky-Korsakov, *My Musical Life*, trans. Judah A. Joffe (New York: Knopf, 1923), 353.

the Vasileostrovskii Theater, which had been continuously rented by visiting companies since it opened its doors in 1887, would remain vacant in the 1905–6 season due to a "lack of means."[22] The radical critic Georgii Chulkov had the impression that "theaters were rarely visited" by the general public.[23]

Enterprises dependent on the support of industrialists and other businessmen were especially hard hit, as labor unrest undercut production and thus the revenues that had gone to support arts activities. Work stoppages in the Alekseev (Stanislavskii) family textile factory cost the Moscow Art Theater's budget twenty thousand rubles.[24] The ideological disillusionment of its principal patron, Savva Morozov, led him to commit suicide. As early as April 1905, the industrialist-backed Nevskii Society for the Support of Popular Entertainment could no longer pay the service on its large debt and was threatened with the auctioning of its theater.[25]

The continuing deterioration of urban calm in the fall of 1905 added to the theatrical world's woes. Rising cases of random violence, petty crime, and other forms of "hooliganism" thrived on the year's disturbances and frayed urban nerves.[26] Starting with the walkout of Moscow printers on September 20, a growing movement for a national general strike gathered steam and quickly spread to the capital and other urban centers. As the actress Valentina Verigina remembered, in an echo of Varlamov's words not long after Bloody Sunday: "Strikes flared up. Now there was no water, now no gas lights, and rehearsals went on with candles or were cancelled. The newspapers talked in different ways about demands for freedom. The Black Hundred press cursed furiously, the students worried, Cossacks roamed the city armed with whips."[27] Such conditions were hardly conducive to great performances. In addition to panicking performers, theaters often closed down for lack of light and power. Suvorin ceased operations to avoid the consequences of growing unrest.[28] The actress N. N. Otradinaia's Contemporary Theater announced its closure through the end of the season "because of strikes in the city."[29] Stanislavskii reluctantly canceled

---

22. "Khronika," *Teatr i iskusstvo* 37 (September 11, 1905): 584.
23. Georgii Chulkov, *Gody stranstvii* (Moscow: Ellis Lak, 1999), 228.
24. Jean Benedetti, *Stanislavski: A Life* (London: Methuen, 1988), 155.
25. "Khronika," *Teatral'naia Rossiia/Teatral'naia gazeta* 14 (April 2, 1905): 204.
26. Orlando Figes, *A People's Tragedy: The Russian Revolution, 1891–1924* (New York: Penguin, 1997), 188–89. Joan Neuberger, *Hooliganism: Crime, Culture, and Power in St. Petersburg, 1900–1914* (Berkeley and Los Angeles: University of California Press, 1993), 106–10, describes such violence as "an integral part of the upheaval" and "an integral feature of the revolutionary experience."
27. V. P. Verigina, *Vospominaniia* (Leningrad: Iskusstvo, 1974), 75.
28. "Uchastie Peterburgskikh teatrov v obshchei politicheskoi zabastovke," *Teatral'naia Rossiia* 44–45 (October 29, 1905): 1269–70.
29. "Benefis N. N. Otradinoi," *Teatr i iskusstvo* 6 (February 5, 1906): 82.

several performances and rehearsals, effectively ending the Art Theater's season after only a few weeks. In 1906–7 its management even entertained the idea of merging with the imperial Malyi Theater because of the previous year's financial woes.[30] Several weeks after the promulgation of the October Manifesto—Nicholas II's promise of civil liberties and an elected legislative body—the visiting British writer and travel journalist Maurice Baring was still attending performances illuminated by candlelight.[31]

Performing companies that continued to operate suffered serious disruptions. A major consequence of the printers' walkout—the first labor stoppage during the paralyzing general strike—was that such essential materials as theatrical posters, programs, sheet music, and manuscript copies ceased to appear.[32] The spreading of the strike to Russia's railroads impacted the arts as well, for neither imported texts nor expected guest performers could easily travel to and around the country. Aleksandr Ziloti canceled his concert programs because sheet music failed to arrive.[33] According to Rimskii-Korsakov, "foreign conductors refused to come" because of the turbulent situation.[34] The strike also affected the availability of Russian artists who had been touring abroad. The Mariinskii soprano Feliia Litvin appealed in January 1906 to "the impossibility of coming to us during such a difficult period" to cancel her engagements.[35] The renowned Matil'da Kshesinskaia declined to return from France for the first several months of the 1905–6 ballet season, which she considered "such a risky time."[36]

In practical terms there was little an impresario could do to improve the climate. The frequent closing of theaters was far from "a sign of solidarity with revolutionary events," as the Soviet theater historian Anatolii Al'tshuller later tried to claim.[37] Impresarios, to say nothing of their performers and audiences, were suffering and scared. Those who were also industrialists found themselves doubly cursed: the same unrest that made theatrical life impossible also targeted the normal operations of their principal sources of revenue. Many tried

---

30. Benedetti, *Stanislavski*, 170, 175.
31. Maurice Baring, *A Year in Russia* (New York: Dutton, 1907), 44.
32. Rimsky-Korsakov, *Musical Life*, 349; "V. K." [V. Karatygin], "Muzykal'naia khronika. S. Peterburg, ianvar'–fevral' 1906 g.," *Zolotoe runo* 3 (March 1906): 109.
33. Charles F. Barber, *Lost in the Stars: The Forgotten Musical Life of Alexander Siloti* (Lanham, Md.: Scarecrow, 2002), 267–68, lists the programs from 1905–6 and their notes about changes, cancellations, substitutions, and the reasons for them.
34. Rimsky-Korsakov, *Musical Life*, 353.
35. "Khronika," *Teatr i iskusstvo* 3 (January 15, 1906): 34.
36. V. A. Teliakovskii, "Imperatorskie teatry i 1905 god," in V. A. Teliakovskii, *Vospominaniia* (Leningrad: Iskusstvo, 1965), 285.
37. A. Ia. Al'tshuller, ed., *Vera Fedorovna Komissarzhevskaia: Pis'ma aktrisy, vospominaniia o nei, materialy* (Leningrad: Iskusstvo, 1964), 336.

to weather the crisis as best they could by moving their enterprises on tour abroad or to less troubled parts of Russia. Stanislavskii found the difficult autumn of 1905 a propitious time to organize the Art Theater's first foreign tour. He later claimed to have been "motivated by material need."[38] Iavorskaia investigated several possible destinations for a foreign tour, finally settling on Prague.[39] Komissarzhevskaia toured extensively in the provinces. But no matter what they did, show business faltered because of revolutionary unrest. As the impresa-rio A. A. Lintvarev expressed his disappointment, "the difficult and unforeseen events through which our motherland has survived have in a ruinous and benighted way harmed the material well being of theatrical enterprises. Many entrepreneurs have had to liquidate their businesses."[40]

The expense of coping with revolution at home and the continuing war with Japan pushed even the government to the brink of bankruptcy. The prospect of an elected Duma with budgetary powers portended additional financial pressure. Although Court expenses ultimately fell outside the Duma's reach, the heavily subsidized Imperial Theaters faced the possibility of fiscal constraints before the matter was settled. In the wake of the first revolution, their Director, Vladimir Teliakovskii, devoted much of his energy to cutting costs and increasing revenues. In early 1906 he thought of privatizing the operations of the Mikhailovskii Theater, which primarily—and unprofitably—presented French drama. He demurred when a hopeful investor told him that a project under his leadership would still cost the government at least one hundred thousand rubles per annum in subsidies.[41] Nevertheless, Teliakovskii and his superior, the Minister of the Imperial Court Baron Vladimir Frederiks, agreed that if the Directorate's financial situation worsened to the point where one of its troupes had to be eliminated, it would be that of the French Theater rather than the other candidate, the unprofitable but culturally more significant Moscow ballet troupe.[42] The Directorate's accounts never fell into such disrepair, but beginning in the spring of 1907 it began renting the Mikhailovskii to the Moscow Art Theater for its Petersburg guest performances. Beginning in the 1907–8 season the Mariinskii housed Ziloti's orchestral concerts.[43]

---

38. K. S. Stanislavskii, *Moia zhizn' v iskusstve* (Moscow: Iskusstvo, 1983), 244.
39. "Khronika," *Teatr i iskusstvo* 22 (May 29, 1905): 344.
40. "Ot redaktsii," *Teatr i iskusstvo* 5 (January 29, 1906): 65.
41. Teliakovskii, "Imperatorskie teatry," 315.
42. Ibid., 336. Ballet attendance at the Moscow Bol'shoi was poor. According to Teliakovskii, *Vospominaniia*, 74, most of its public was "incidental," and only a quarter of the seats were usually full.
43. Barber, *Lost in the Stars*, 112.

Financial woes affected the Imperial Theaters on more practical levels. The Aleksandrinskii's artistic director, Petr Gnedich, recalled that merchants often charged twice their regular prices because the Directorate was notorious for not paying its bills.[44] In the wake of 1905, Teliakovskii responded by trying to reduce and rationalize the Directorate's expenditures in this and other day-to-day areas. Its carriage department—intended to provide transportation for performers to and from the theaters but often at their disposal for personal needs—was phased out by 1907 at an impressive savings of one hundred thousand rubles. Other initiatives, such as eliminating orchestras that performed during intermissions and during dramatic performances, economized the budget as well.[45]

Finally, Teliakovskii appealed to the Directorate's fiscal troubles to convince the Court to reverse Alexander III's 1881 ban on most types of imperial stage performances during Lent. Additional performances over that forty-day religious period meant more revenue, and since performers were paid by the season rather than for in dividual appearances, the Directorate's labor costs did not rise accordingly, at least not until artist contracts came up for r enegotiation.[46] The tsar rescinded the ban in time for th e 1906–7 season despite complaints from the Holy Synod on religious grounds and from performers who had to work more for the same salaries and found themselves with less time for profitable guest appearances elsewhere.[47] So impressive were the savings from this measure that Teliakovskii eventually had to deny rumors that he planned to keep the Imperial Theaters open in the summers, too.[48]

Financial expedients did not, however, indicate the advent of a more conservative approach to the state stage. Indeed, the last decade of the imperial era saw a surprisingly large amount of work unflattering to the status quo appearing in the tsar's own theaters. After the politically and artistically radical Vsevolod Meierkhol'd was fired from Komissarzhevskaia's Dramatic Theater in late 1907, Teliakovskii rushed to hire him for the Imperial Theaters. His first commission for the state stage, Knut Hamsun's *At the Gates of the Kingdom*, was a politically radical work that dramatized the youth of an impetuous Norwegian

---

44. Gnedich, *Kniga zhizni*, 246.
45. Teliakovskii, "Imperatorskie teatry," 340–41; "Khronika," *Teatr i iskusstvo* 32 (August 6, 1906): 477–48; and Gnedich, *Kniga zhizni*, 253. In addition to their cost and reputedly bad playing, Gnedich wanted to do away with intermission orchestras because they had ceased to be fashionable in Europe.
46. "Okolo teatra," *Peterburgskaia gazeta*, March 12, 1906. Charitable and guest performances had been permitted during Lent, as, after 1898, had occasional performances of non-Russian operas.
47. "Ochevidnaia pol'za," *Peterburgskaia gazeta*, March 27, 1906. "Ot redaktsii," *Teatr i iskusstvo* 19 (May 7, 1906), supported the measure and facetiously wondered whether imperial stage performers had been "saving their strength" by not working six months of the year.
48. "Khronika," *Teatr i iskusstvo* 15 (April 14, 1913): 335. Given the success of St. Petersburg's post-1991 White Nights Festivals, one might wonder whether this was really a bad idea.

revolutionary. Neither the radical overtones of Leonid Andreev's œuvre nor his arrest for subversive political activities prevented the Aleksandrinskii from staging his plays, five of which appeared there before 1917.[49] As we shall see, performers with radical sympathies had little trouble getting contracts to work on the imperial stage.

Even at such a politically sensitive time as the tercentenary celebrations of Romanov rule in February 1913, the Mariinskii presented its premiere production (under Meierkhol'd) of Richard Strauss's opera *Elektra*, a modernist adaptation of the Sophocles play in which an evil reigning queen and her lover are brutally murdered by the queen's exiled son. Russia's theatrical press found the event "extraordinary" and "unequalled."[50] Despite the appearance of prodynasty works around it, the opera's scheduling provoked some right-wing critics to conclude that Teliakovskii, under the influence of his supposed Polish origins, was abusing his position to sabotage Russian patriotism.[51] Others simply objected to the timing of the premiere of an opera in which reigning monarchs are killed.[52] Yet it went forward without recorded incident.

Far more significant to the administration of the Imperial Theaters was the impact of international events, which led at the outbreak of World War I to the proscription of German and Austrian works, many of which were initially replaced with selections from the traditional Russian repertoire. A planned premiere of Strauss's gorgeous comedy of errors *Der Rosenkavalier* disappeared from the Mariinskii's repertoire for 1914–15.[53] Wagner's operatic tetralogy *The Ring of the Nibelung* (*Der Ring des Nibelungen*), a perennial favorite of Russian audiences since the first complete cycle was performed for them in 1907, was replaced by unconvincingly arranged "cycle" performances of Rimskii-Korsakov's operas.[54] Imperial stages actively hosted patriotic tableaux to drum up support for the war. Their audiences were treated to reverent orchestral performances

---

49. Leonid N. Andreev to M. K. Kuprina-Iordanskaia [n.d.], GTB SPb, RI/31, l. 21, records that Teliakovskii was interested in staging Andreev's *The Days of Our Lives* as early as 1908 but approached the playwright a day after he had sold the rights to another theater.

50. "Chernogorskii," "Mariinskii teatr," *Teatr i iskusstvo* 8 (February 24, 1913): 176.

51. Teliakovskii, *Vospominaniia*, 180–81. Teliakovskii came from Iaroslavl' province and hastened to note in his memoirs that he was not at all Polish.

52. Edward Braun, *The Theatre of Meyerhold: Revolution on the Modern Stage* (New York: Drama Book Specialists, 1979), 120.

53. Teliakovskii, *Vospominaniia*, 201.

54. V. P. Shkafer, *Sorok let na stsene russkoi opery: Vospominaniia, 1890–1930 gg.* (Leningrad: Izdatel'stvo Teatra Opery i Baleta imeni S. M. Kirova, 1936), 194; Hubertus Jahn, *Patriotic Culture in Russia During World War I* (Cambridge: Cambridge University Press, 1995), 141–46. Rimskii-Korsakov's operas are mostly adaptations of unrelated Russian folk tales and thus do not correspond to Wagner's *Ring*, a four-evening adaptation of German epics that the composer harmonized to tell one long story. No full *Ring* cycle was again staged in Russia until 2003.

of the national anthems of all the nations at war with Germany, often as lively preludes to the increased number of Russian works in the repertoire.[55] Despite his radical proclivities, Meierkhol'd staged a prowar pantomime entitled *The Triumph of the Powers* in 1914. Nationalist speeches from past eras frequently appeared in dramatized versions.[56] Patriotism is of course a kind of political expression, but in a time of unprecedented international crisis it was significantly this form of "politics" rather than antiwar messages or other forms of antiregime dissent that populated Russia's stages.

Although it suffered from the limitations discussed in the previous chapter, one of the principal instruments that the government wielded over cultural life was the theatrical censorship administered by the Ministry of the Interior's Main Office for Press Affairs. Since the tsarist government often responded to political unrest with strength, it is perhaps natural to assume that it adopted analogous policies in the cultural sphere. Spencer Golub, for example, has recently argued that "renewed and intensified government censorship of the arts" figured as a salient feature of state policy in the period after Bloody Sunday.[57]

A close examination of the theatrical censorship's activities, however, reveals that this was not the case. Instead the last decades of the imperial era witnessed conscious attempts to revise and reduce its authority over culture. In late January 1905 Nicholas II ordered the creation of a commission to review the standing censorship laws and suggest changes that would liberalize them. Although the timing of his decision may have been connected to the unrest following Bloody Sunday and the conciliatory spirit that led the tsar to call a few weeks later for public participation in reform, the idea of such a commission originated as part of a modest program of political changes decreed in December 1904.[58] Many government opponents found the earlier program's measures insufficient, but they had included the liberalization of local government, judicial procedures, and state policies toward ethnic and religious minorities.[59] Regardless of

---

55. Maurice Paléologue, *An Ambassador's Memoirs*, 3 vols., trans. F. A. Holt (London: Hutchinson, 1923–25), 1:128–29, recalled one such event before a September 1914 performance of Glinka's *A Life for the Tsar*, an opera that the French ambassador found "stale and frigid" but that he "had to sit through."
56. Jahn, *Patriotic Culture*, 134.
57. Spencer Golub, "The Silver Age, 1905–1917," in *A History of Russian Theatre*, ed. Robert Leach and Victor Borovsky (Cambridge: Cambridge University Press, 1999), 278.
58. For a description of the tsar's request, which called for localities and individuals to submit reformist ideas to the central government, see Ascher, *Russia in Disarray*, 112–13.
59. Ibid., 70–72. The December 1904 reform program also declared the state's intention to introduce a system of state insurance for industrial workers. According to Charles A. Ruud, *Fighting Words: Imperial Censorship and the Russian Press, 1804–1906* (Toronto: University of Toronto

the rationale and surrounding circumstances, 1905 was a gala year for reconsidering the tsarist state's approach to expressive culture.

Presided over by Dmitrii Kobeko, a noted historian and director of the Imperial Public Library, the censorship review commission included twenty-five leading cultural figures representing a variety of political views, artistic backgrounds, and social perspectives.[60] For theatrical matters its most important members were the head of the Press Affairs Office, Prince Nikolai Shakhovskoi; its chief dramatic censor, Sergei Vereshchagin; the writer and co-founder of the Moscow Art Theater, Vladimir Nemirovich-Danchenko; the vice president of the Russian Theatrical Society (RTO, the major professional organization for performers), Anatolii Molchanov; the politically radical director and popular theater enthusiast Evtikhii Karpov; the veteran Aleksandrinskii actor and long-time private theater impresario Petr Medvedev; and Aleksei Suvorin, the publisher and entrepreneur who led the theater that bore his name.

The Kobeko Commission, which met from February to December 1905, is best known for its recommendation that preliminary censorship for most printed materials be abolished—a decision that the government announced in late November and formalized by decree in April 1906.[61] Although the commission did not ultimately recommend the same fate for preliminary theatrical censorship, this appears to have resulted only from its conclusion that theatrical censorship fell outside its original mandate.[62]

Nevertheless, during sessions in May 1905 the Kobeko Commission devoted some time to discussing theatrical censorship and arrived at a consensus favoring reform. Everyone agreed that the prevailing system was arbitrary and ineffective. Nemirovich-Danchenko and Karpov both advocated the abolition of the separate censorship for popular theater, which had been implemented in 1888 as a "temporary" measure, and found that Shakhovskoi, the head of Press Affairs and in effect the Empire's chief censor, agreed with them on this point. Vereshchagin, head of the dramatic censorship, argued that "it would be desirable to create a more detailed law for dramatic censorship, as the current one has too general a character." Karpov observed that censorship decisions varied widely depending on who held the responsible offices at a given time. Molchanov stressed the importance of personal relations between entrepreneurs

---

Press, 1982), 213–14, the idea for the censorship review commission came from the reformist interior minister Prince Petr Sviatopolk-Mirskii.

60. Ruud, *Fighting Words*, 213–14.

61. Ibid., 225. It is also described by N. G. Patrusheva, "Ot sostavitel'ia," in *Tsenzura v Rossii v kontse XIX–nachale XX veka: Sbornik vospominanii*, ed. N. G. Patrusheva (St. Petersburg: Bulanin, 2003), 34.

62. "Ot redaktsii," *Teatr i iskusstvo* 20 (May 15, 1905): 311.

and local authorities, who often worked out their own variable interpretations of censorship directives. Medvedev, a conservative actor who later opposed attempts to establish autonomy for the imperial drama troupe, agreed that this could lead to arbitrary interpretations. The commission also discussed the censorship's inherent inability to prevent public demonstrations resulting from controversial content or to accomplish much by censoring individual lines. Karpov cited examples of audiences being set off by such banal material as "they are building a barracks in town" and "the students bother me most of all"—lines permitted by the censors that he believed to hold no intrinsic political significance.[63]

No one on the commission supported the outright abolition of theatrical censorship, but several members, including those who operated and directed theaters, revealingly complained that the censorship's main problem lay in its failure to exercise a positive influence on popular tastes. Suvorin felt that the censorship's relative permissiveness underserved the public interest, for "spectators go to the theater with their wives and children in the full belief that they will not see or hear anything immoral." Time and again, he argued, the content of what was permitted for Russian stages disappointed them in this expectation. According to Nemirovich-Danchenko:

> The dramatic censorship has never looked at the theater seriously. It easily allows performances of anything light, vulgar, or limited . . . theater is confined to the narrow parameters of convention, banality, and worthless plots. . . . Full freedom for the theaters and their subordination only to the law and the courts [i.e., the only state oversight of their activity that would have remained if censorship were abolished] will cause the growth of morally harmful "café-chantant" literature.[64]

The radical Karpov also supported this point, observing that "as for pornography, I dare to affirm that it is now, despite the censorship, flowering anywhere and everywhere."[65] Even for those whose avocations and livelihoods were subject to censorship control—people whom one might expect to have opposed it in principle—the problem with state power over culture was that it was not strict enough.

Similar views appeared in public discourse. Despite loud calls for political

---

63. "K voprosu o dramaticheskoi tsenzure," *Teatral'naia Rossiia/Teatral'naia gazeta* 37 (September 10, 1905): 1120–22.

64. Ibid., 1119–20.

65. Ibid., 1120.

reform in the last decades of the tsarist era, many observers, including determined critics of the status quo, stopped short of advocating theatrical censorship's abolition. In 1897 the first national congress of the Russian Theatrical Society debated the role of censorship and decided to petition only for the curtailment of the separate regime for popular theaters. Its delegates favored this step largely in the hope that the Society's members would have greater professional opportunities as the result of decreased censorship. They could live with the regular theatrical censorship in place since 1865 and the retention of a stricter separate censorship for popular fairground entertainments in which few professionals performed.[66] In other words they were more cautious than Shakhovskoi—the tsar's chief censorship official—would be only eight years later. Just a month after Bloody Sunday the editors of *Theater and Art*—no friends of the autocracy—declared: "We are far from reproaching the dramatic censor. To the contrary, it must be said openly that it is desirable to have a power charged with seeking out 'unsuitable' [*neudobnye*] plays bending to the varying influences of 'internal politics' and conforming to the changing interests of 'order'—our censorship looks carefully at the needs of the theater. It could be a lot worse."[67] In 1914 the same editors defended a provincial police chief who prohibited a play because the company performing it was not using the version approved by the censorship.[68] A columnist in *Theatrical Russia* recalled a conversation about abolishing censorship altogether with an unnamed liberal dramatist, someone "with pretensions to progressive leanings," who allegedly exclaimed, "What! What! How is that really possible? Then God knows what would show up on the stage! Without it pornography would penetrate the theaters. And if censorship were abolished, shameless spectacles would appear, in the fullest sense of the word." The author witheringly described his interlocutor as a "liberal gendarme," yet the point was clear.[69]

Other media critics not only believed that the censorship was necessary but charged that it was doing a bad job. One editorialist anticipated the comments of several Kobeko Commission members with the observation that "our stage is literally crammed with the rubbish of self-satisfied mediocrity and vulgarity. The censorship has sanctioned all of this garbage."[70] A February 1906 congress

---

66. *Trudy pervogo Vserossiiskogo s"ezda stsenicheskikh deiatelei, 9.3–23.3 1897*, 2 vols. (St. Petersburg: Nadezhda, 1898), 1216–17.
67. "Ot redaktsii," *Teatr i iskusstvo* 7 (February 13, 1905): 97.
68. "Tsenzura p'es,'" *Teatr i iskusstvo* 21 (May 25, 1914): 458–59.
69. N. Prishlii, "O dramaticheskoi tsenzure," *Teatral'naia Rossiia/Teatral'naia gazeta* 15 (April 9, 1905): 253.
70. Vl. Novoselov, "Dukh vremeni," *Teatral'naia Rossiia/Teatral'naia gazeta* 16 (April 16, 1905): 272–73.

of theatrical writers advocated censorship reform not because they found the existing system repressive but because they believed that Press Affairs "does not prevent the appearance on stage of works that are offensive to the demands of artistic taste and good morals [*dobrye nravy*]."[71] This was still a problem worthy of discussion in late 1915 when a delegate to a Moscow congress of popular theater performers accused the censorship of demonstrating its "uselessness" by permitting "vulgar things."[72] As with the directors and impresarios who objected less to the existence of censorship than to the content of what it allowed for performance, the main problem for many writers and critics was the state's willingness to approve too much material that they found objectionable on moral or aesthetic grounds. In other words it was too lenient.

Rhetoric about censorship was one matter, but how did the institution itself reflect the limited debate over its functions? Rather than toughening or even maintaining its standards for approval, a careful reading of the Press Affairs Office's judgments indicates that it became substantially more permissive over time. This transition was never more dramatic than both during and as a result of the revolutionary unrest of 1905, which paradoxically presented the most formidable challenge to tsarist authority before its collapse twelve years later. Despite the portents of disaster, the first revolution led neither to draconian tendencies nor to a more systematic approach to censorship than had previously existed. Instead the growing radicalization of social and political life both recentered the censors' views of what was impermissible and lowered the threshold of what they found permissible. The weak enforcement and frequent irrelevance of censorship decisions through the last decades of the imperial era have been noted, but comparing its evaluations of certain works before and after 1905 reveals a rapidly evolving set of values in the most important state institution with power over culture.

Put plainly, numerous works prohibited by the censorship, especially for popular theater, were permitted either during or shortly after the outbreak of the first revolution. In the months following Bloody Sunday, the Empire's more strictly censored popular stages for the first time enjoyed the legal right to present such notable plays as Shakespeare's *Hamlet, Othello, King Lear,* and *A Winter's Tale;* Goethe's *Faust;* Molière's *Don Juan;* Schiller's *Mary Stuart* and *Intrigue and Love;* Beaumarchais's *The Barber of Seville;* and Griboedev's *Woe from Wit,*

---

71. O. Dymov, "Peterburgskie teatry (pis'mo vtoroe)," *Zolotoe runo* 3 (March 1906): 106–7.

72. *Trudy Vserossiiskogo s"ezda deiatalei narodnogo teatra v Moskve, 27 dekabria 1915–5 ianvaria 1916* (Petrograd: Tipografiia L. Ia. Ganzburga, 1919), 190.

among many others.[73] A censorship ruling in August permitted Ippolit Shpazhinskii's *Princess Tarakanova*, a dark drama about the eighteenth-century pretender to the Russian throne who was abducted on the orders of Catherine the Great and left to perish in a vile dungeon.[74] It passed despite its negative depiction of a Romanov monarch, one of the taboos that had earlier commanded censorship proscription. A ban on popular performances of Tolstoi's *The Power of Darkness*—set down in 1903 despite the play's numerous earlier stagings in popular theaters—ceased to strike Press Affairs as appropriate in December 1905. "It is hardly necessary at present to consider Tolstoi a supporter of extreme ideas," the report allowing it concluded.[75] Aleksei Pisemskii's *The Partition*, an irreverent depiction of a gentry family fighting over an inheritance, was approved the same month, twelve years after its initial ban. Vereshchagin found that its once provocative characters had since become "rather caricatured" and thus uncontroversial.[76] Chekhov's *Uncle Vania*, formally prohibited for popular audiences in 1903, became permissible for them in November 1906 because the responsible censor could find no "hint of antagonism between the landowner and peasants."[77] *The Cherry Orchard*, likewise banned from popular theaters in 1903 because of its unflattering depiction of a hapless landowning family forced to sell its estate to a former serf, legally entered the popular repertoire in February 1907.[78] Newly established theaters also benefited from declining censorship after 1905. The Crooked Mirror, a cabaret venue founded three years later, suffered just two interventions in its programming before 1917: the deletion of an explicit sex scene and the removal of the word "God" from a line that suggested sacrilege.[79]

A visible pattern of censorship liberalization also occurred over the course of 1905–7 as revolutionary events were unfolding. Nikolai Garin-Mikhailovskii's *A Village Drama*, a violent work that revolves around an adulterous wife's plot to murder her husband with the help of her lover, migrated from a general performance ban in February 1905 to approval in November.[80] Ostrovskii and

---

73. A. Chargonin, "Neskol'ko slov o repertuare narodnykh teatrov," *Teatr i iskusstvo* 32 (August 7, 1905): 513–15; G. A. Khaichenko, *Russkii narodnyi teatr kontsa XIX–nachala XX veka* (Moscow: Nauka, 1975), 173; E. Anthony Swift, *Popular Theater and Society in Tsarist Russia* (Berkeley and Los Angeles: University of California Press, 2002), 118.

74. "Khronika," *Teatr i iskusstvo* 33 (August 14, 1905): 533.

75. RGIA, f. 776, op. 26, d. 24, l. 236.

76. RGIA, f. 776, op. 26, d. 12, l. 45.

77. RGIA, f. 776, op. 26, d. 25, l. 238.

78. Gary Thurston, *The Popular Theatre Movement in Russia, 1862–1919* (Evanston: Northwestern University Press, 1998), 179.

79. Barbara Henry, "Theatrical Parody at the Krivoe zerkalo: Russian 'Teatr Miniatyur,' 1908–1931" (D. Phil. thesis, Oxford University, 1996), 49n.

80. RGIA, f. 776, op. 26, d. 24, ll. 17 and 217.

Gedeonov's *Vasilisa Melent'eva*, a rare historical drama in the œuvre of the more famous of the two playwrights, struck the censors as unacceptable for popular audiences in August 1905 because it depicted Ivan the Terrible as a "monster" (*izverg*). A revised version, however, ceased to do so after the October general strike.[81] A dramatization of Aleksandr Kuprin's antimilitary novel *The Duel*, whose officer protagonist embraces radical individualism only to be cut down by his amour's husband before he can explore it, was prohibited in December 1905 but allowed in February 1906.[82] Aleksei Svirskii's *Prison*, an indictment of the criminal justice system that the censor found "an uninterrupted imitation of Maksim Gor'kii," was banned in October 1905. Surprisingly, only a few days later it was resubmitted and approved.[83] Suvorin staged it in January 1906 as a gala benefit for one of his leading actors.[84] Even Gor'kii's radicalism would not keep his works off the stage. His most famous drama, *The Lower Depths*, had been allowed for private theaters since its initial submission in 1902 and was among the many works suddenly cleared for popular theaters in 1905.[85]

Some censorship strictures remained, particularly with regard to works that portrayed violence or were thought to incite rebellion. In December 1905 Komissarzhevskaia was forbidden to produce Evgenii Chirikov's play *The Peasants* because it included riots against landowners. Oskar Lamkert, the responsible censor, described them as "agrarian pogroms."[86] At about the same time Lamkert also forbade Büchner's *Danton's Death*, a sympathetic depiction of the eponymous French revolutionary figure set at the time of his arrest and condemnation to the guillotine, on account of its "exclusively revolutionary content [with which] the author glorifies the revolution and its leaders."[87] The antimonarchical themes of Schiller's *Don Carlos* (about the Flemish revolt against Philip II of Spain and his son's supposed role in supporting it), Byron's *Sardanapalus* (in which a besieged Assyrian tyrant faces rebellion when he destroys his own besieged palace and its inhabitants), and Hugo's *Hernani* (which depicts a murder

81. RGIA, f. 776, op. 26, d. 22, l. 68 and d. 57, l. 109. According to I. F. Petrovskaia and V. Somina, *Teatral'nyi Peterburg: Nachalo XVIII veka–oktiabr' 1917 goda: Obozrenie-putevoditel'* (St. Petersburg: RIII, 1994), 255–56, it had already been presented for popular audiences in the 1890s. Significantly, Gedeonov had been Director of the Imperial Theaters from 1867 to 1875, yet his work remained subject to censorship.
82. RGIA, f. 776, op. 26, d. 24, ll. 14 and 223.
83. RGIA, f. 776, op. 26, d. 24, l. 195; "Khronika," *Teatral'naia Rossiia/Muzykal'nyi mir* 44–45 (October 29, 1905): 1272.
84. "Khronika," *Teatr i iskusstvo* 3 (January 15, 1906): 36.
85. Swift, *Popular Theater*, 118; Khaichenko, *Russkii narodnyi teatr*, 173, indicates that Gor'kii's more tendentious play *Children of the Sun* (more in Chapter 5) was, despite a scene involving a violent peasant mob, also permitted for popular audiences in 1905.
86. RGIA, f. 776, op. 24, d. 26, l. 230.
87. RGIA, f. 776, op. 25, d. 26, l. 100.

Fig. 6 The work of a radical playwright legally presented on stage: a scene from Maksim Gor'kii's *The Lower Depths* at the Moscow Art Theater in 1902. In 1905 the play was approved for popular theaters. From Konstantin Stanislavskii, *Moia zhizn' v iskusstve* (Moscow: Iskusstvo, 1983).

plot against the Holy Roman Emperor Charles V and received a riotous reception at its Paris premiere in the revolutionary year of 1830) all caused them to be barred from popular, but not private, stages in 1905–7.[88]

Depictions of contemporary revolutionary events, though relatively and perhaps significantly few in number, also encountered censorship limitations. Leonid Andreev's *To the Stars*, which relates the sorrows of a sympathetic astronomer whose son dies in prison after taking part in revolutionary events, was prohibited for presenting "the idealization of the revolution and its participants."[89] In September 1906 Vereshchagin banned Svirskii's *The Pulse of Life*, a play about the daughter of a high official who leads striking workers into battle during the October 1905 general strike. In his opinion it represented "nothing other than a call to revolution."[90] Nevertheless, the Winter Farce's production of Leonid Svetov and Vladimir Valentinov's satire *The Days of Freedom*—which featured a "cakewalk of high officials" (*sanovnyi kek-ouk*) and send-ups of Holy Synod procurator Konstantin Pobedonostsev, Petersburg's governor general Dmitrii Trepov, the short-lived interior minister Aleksandr Bulygin, a fictional officer named "Port Arthur," and similar types—was approved even though the responsible censor described it as "a harsh condemnation and mockery of the current government, verging in places on incitement to revolution."[91]

Despite the small number of cases in this category and the lack of systematized control, the range of what Russian theaters could perform undeniably widened. Theatrical censorship became far more than "a bit less oppressive."[92] Indeed, having approved nearly 90 percent of submissions before 1905, including a number of works that remained forbidden in Western nations for years or even decades thereafter, it is something of a stretch to describe it as "oppressive" to begin with. One public comment characterized the censorship's huge volume of approved material with the exclamations "How much useless work!" and "How many useless stamps!" proclaiming that state oversight of the performing arts was merely a waste of time.[93]

The fact of the post-1905 change has been minimized as a temporary phenomenon that could only have occurred because state authority weakened at

88. RGIA, f. 776, d. 26, op. 26, d. 25, l. 118, d. 24, l. 101; d. 26, l. 39.
89. RGIA, f. 776, d. 25, l. 1.
90. RGIA, f. 776, d. 26, op. 25, l. 181.
91. RGIA, f. 776, d. 826, op. 25, ll. 2–10. The phrase "a cakewalk of high officials" (*sanovnyi kek-ouk*) is from M. Iankovskii, "Teatral'naia obshchestvennost' Peterburga v 1905–1907 gg.," in *Pervaia russkaia revoliutsiia i teatr: Stat'i i materialy*, ed. A. Ia. Al'tshuller (Moscow: Iskusstvo, 1956), 176.
92. Swift, *Popular Theater*, 118.
93. "Ot redaktsii," *Teatr i iskusstvo* 20 (May 15, 1905): 312.

the time of that year's general strike.[94] The chronology does not support this interpretation. Although a number of bans were rescinded after the strike, many previously forbidden works, including the long list of plays permitted for popular theater mentioned above, had become legal earlier in the year. Nor, despite its inherent logistical and personnel problems, was there any demonstrable sign of crisis within the Press Affairs Office. The censors continued to go to work and issue decisions throughout the last turbulent months of 1905. In early 1906 they issued a circular emphasizing the "absolute duty to observe unswervingly that all dramatic works on stage are performed in strict accordance with the texts of the reviewed copies of these plays."[95] These were hardly the words of a defunct institution, even if they did reveal its sense of powerlessness. If the censors needed to make such a point about their authority, they undoubtedly believed that it was being challenged or ignored in some meaningful way. This was nothing new. What did change was their perception of the political and social climate and how it had been shaped by turbulent events that they, as Petersburg residents like any others, surely experienced in some way. The ambivalence that Shakhovskoi and Vereshchagin displayed during the Kobeko Commission's meetings also undoubtedly played a role. Some favorable censorship decisions may have resulted from the capriciousness of the process—entrepreneurs could submit a work an unlimited number of times in the hope of having a ban overturned—but Press Affairs became demonstratively more lenient than ever before.

The de facto "liberalization" of Russia's theatrical censorship remained permanent. Few approvals were later withdrawn. Once a work passed the censorship's standards, it almost always remained a permanent part of the approved repertoire either in the specific category of the theater whose administration had submitted it (e.g., imperial, private, or popular) or for all theaters if the censors accorded general approval. Chirikov's *Ivan Mironych*, another work permitted for the first time in 1905, thus became generally permissible, for, in the responsible censor's words, "if it has already been allowed once, then it would hardly be desirable to effect its removal."[96]

Among the few exceptions to this rule were World War I–era prohibitions of German and Austrian works, as well as works thought favorable to—and

---

94. Khaichenko, *Russkii narodnyi teatr*, 173; Kholodov, *Istoriia*, 312. Abram Gozenpud, *Ivan Ershov: Zhizn' i stsenicheskaia deiatel'nost': Issledovanie*, 2nd ed. (St. Petersburg: Kompozitor, 1999), 190–91, uses this argument to explain (inaccurately, as we will see in the next chapter) the appearance of Beethoven's *Fidelio* in the Mariinskii repertoire that autumn.

95. Quoted in "Ot redaktsii," *Teatr i iskusstvo* 7 (February 12, 1906): 97.

96. RGIA, f. 776, op. 26, d. 24, l. 44.

sometimes even satirical of—those countries.⁹⁷ Given the enthusiasm of Russian impresarios and audiences for removing them from repertoires on their own, however, formal censorship bans were neither always necessary nor out of character with what was happening in other Allied nations. In a comparative context Imperial Russia avoided the "somewhat stricter guard" that a British parliamentary committee recommended for theatrical censorship in its country in 1909 as well as the "increasingly stringent" government oversight of theater that Peter Jelavich has, in a less obvious example, observed in Bavaria at around the same time.⁹⁸ Even liberal deputies in Russia's Duma—the representative body that shared governmental powers from 1906—limited themselves to proposals similar to the ones endorsed by the Theatrical Society's first national congress. Like those deliberations, a Duma resolution debated in January 1914 called just for a partial curtailment of popular theater censorship.⁹⁹

The development of Russia's film industry, which in its early incarnation took direct inspiration from many of the day's leading stage dramas, only magnified the decline of state power over culture. Formal censorship never extended over film production or cinema screenings in imperial times. According to Denise Youngblood, even the exercise of informal local authority over film was "rare enough not to be a matter of pressing concern to producers."¹⁰⁰ A 1910 silent movie adaptation of Shpazhinskii's *Princess Tarakanova*—based on a play banned until just five years before—was one of Russian film's first big hits.¹⁰¹ With an estimated total of 108 million moviegoers in 1911 alone, it is difficult to exaggerate the autocratic state's powerlessness in controlling artistic expression via the new medium.¹⁰² Certainly the situation was different from that of the United States, where the Supreme Court ruled in 1915 that film was not

---

97. RGIA, f. 776, op. 26, d. 33, l. 174, records that Gnedich's play *The Assembly* was banned from 1914 because it shows Peter the Great relying heavily on German influences for his reforms. But here, too, the power of censorship proved weak. In February 1917 the work reentered the Aleksandrinskii's repertoire to honor Gnedich on the occasion of his fortieth year in artistic life. See "Khronika," *Teatr i iskusstvo* 6 (February, 5, 1917): 109. "Malen'kaia khronika," *Teatr i iskusstvo* 34 (August 24, 1914): 701, indicates a ban on a satirical play about the Austrian Court.
 98. Quoted in Steve Nicholson, *The Censorship of British Drama, 1900–1968*, 2 vols. (Exeter: University of Exeter Press, 2003), 1:70. Peter Jelavich, *Munich and Theatrical Modernism: Politics, Playwriting, and Performance, 1890–1914* (Cambridge: Harvard University Press, 1985), 247–50.
 99. "K voprosu o dramaticheskoi tsenzure," *Teatr i iskusstvo* 4 (January 26, 1914): 76. The resolution was presented by the leading Constitutional Democrat Pavel Miliukov.
 100. Denise Youngblood, *The Magic Mirror: Moviemaking in Russia, 1908–1918* (Madison: University of Wisconsin Press, 1999), 64. For a discussion of the lack of film censorship, see Louise McReynolds, *Russia at Play: Leisure Activities at the End of the Tsarist Era* (Ithaca: Cornell University Press, 2003), 276–77.
 101. Youngblood, *Magic Mirror*, 116–17.
 102. McReynolds, *Russia at Play*, 268.

protected by the first amendment's guaranteed right of free speech and where fifteen years later a comprehensive code drafted by a government official restricted Hollywood's presentation of moral, sexual, religious, and political images and themes.

Although Russia's formal censorship became less strict both during and as a result of the Revolution of 1905, more arbitrary forms of government interference in the arts remained factors in the last dozen years of the tsarist era. Many such incidents, however, provoked assertive attempts to defend what entrepreneurs and artists regarded as their rights before the law, and they received some redress. In one noteworthy controversy it was revealed that low-level police officials had been demanding "protection" payments from theaters. A consequence of the unrest and declining business resulting from Bloody Sunday was that impresarios, otherwise forced to pay off the corrupt gendarmes, now refused to go along. If their audiences were melting away because of public disorders, paying the police protection racket—extralegal though it may have been—now definitely lost any palatability. Several entrepreneurs filed lawsuits and brought their cases before the Imperial Senate, which investigated the issue and found in their favor. The theatrical press reported continuing incidents of the practice, but the fact remains that the state's highest judicial body had ruled in favor of theatrical entrepreneurs and against the police during a revolution.[103]

In a number of cases local authorities exercised, or tried to exercise, the power to cancel performances, close theaters, and interfere even in relatively minute details of show business. Some of these interventions were petty, ridiculous, or irrelevant to the content of what was being performed. Many were of the type that impresarios and artists either did not resist for expediency's sake or lacked the motivation to challenge in any meaningful way. A gendarme in Mogilev, for example, ordered Gaideburov's Wandering Theater to restore omitted Cyrillic alphabet hard signs to its avant-garde poster advertisements because some political radicals also used the modish new orthography: "Do you know who prints proclamations without hard signs?" the official asked the theater's representatives in all earnestness, "The SRs! And you, such a serious theater, are acting like them!"[104] Petersburg police officials ordered a hypnotist who may have been baffled to add the subtitle "A Parody" to an advertisement of his act originally called "The Severing of a Live Person's Head."[105] At least one performer was

---

103. "Ot redaktsii," *Teatr i iskusstvo* 2 (January 9, 1905): 25 and 35 (August 28, 1905): 553.
104. A. A. Briantsev, *Vospominaniia, stat'i, vystupleniia, dnevniki, pis'ma* (Moscow: VTO, 1979), 59–60.
105. "Khronika," *Teatr i iskusstvo* 41 (October 9, 1905): 650.

arrested for appearing drunk on stage—a violation of the Empire's law against public inebriation.[106]

Symbolic fussiness could lead to especially petty interventions. In 1912, when Russia celebrated the centenary of its historic victory over the French, the governor of Kherson province removed Beethoven's Third ("Heroic") Symphony from a concert program because it had originally been written as a paean to Napoleon. That Beethoven had angrily removed the dedication when he became disenchanted with the French emperor apparently did not matter.[107] A vice governor of Minsk expressed his disapproval for a legally produced play sympathetic to the woes of his province's Jewish population by fining newspapers that reviewed it favorably.[108] If his powers did not allow him to interfere with performances directly, he evidently felt that he could make a point by relying on his authority over the press.

Other cases of police interference were more serious. Komissarzhevskaia's Dramatic Theater found its production of Gor'kii's play *Summerfolk,* which depicts intelligentsia vacationers as self-satisfied, unengaged, and incompetent, interrupted shortly after Bloody Sunday. Despite censorship approval and twenty-three previous performances, an assistant chief of the Petersburg police ordered the rest of the run's cancellation. This dealt "a heavy blow" to Komissarzhevskaia's existing financial problems since ticket sales for the canceled performances had to be refunded.[109] Arguing that she had been within her legal rights to stage the work, the indignant actress-entrepreneuse sued the assistant chief for more than nine thousand rubles in damages. The Senate upheld her right to perform the play but, considering the police officials' appeal to the state of emergency prevailing in January, declined to award financial compensation.[110] Iavorskaia, who sued for damages over the police-ordered cancellation of her production of Lev Zhdanov's *In the Struggle,* about a conflict between a liberal professor and reactionary university administrators, encountered similar results.[111] Although the lack of financial compensation was a disappointment, both cases resulted in further legal victories over the police during a revolution. Along with the lawsuits against police protection rackets, they proved that entrepreneurs were willing and able to solve their problems through the existing order rather than devote their energies to overthrowing it.

106. "Pechal'nyi sluchai," *Teatr i iskusstvo* 47 (November 18, 1912): 910.
107. "Malen'kaia khronika," *Teatr i iskusstvo* 45 (November 4, 1912): 865.
108. "Malen'kaia khronika," *Teatr i iskusstvo* 14 (April 7, 1913): 316.
109. "Peterburgskaia khronika," *Teatral'naia Rossiia/Teatral'naia gazeta* 4 (January 22, 1905): 56.
110. Al'tshuller, *Komissarzhevskaia,* 154, 383–84n; Iu. Rybakova, *Komissarzhevskaia* (Leningrad: Iskusstvo, 1971), 97.
111. Kholodov, *Istoriia,* 7:305.

Despite these outcomes critics complained that "the arbitrariness of this power is unlimited ... any local police chief could refuse [to allow a performance] ... even if [he] did not permit *A Life for the Tsar!*"[112] The financial implications of such cancellations could not be ignored. Nemirovich-Danchenko so feared the consequences of being closed down that he pleaded with the Art Theater's student audiences not to cause trouble.[113] Business was too important. As another entrepreneur pointed out, such cases created a situation in which "the repertoire is suffering—artistically and, consequently, materially."[114] For indebted impresarios like Komissarzhevskaia, they could be harmful indeed.

Regardless of how serious incidents of police intervention may have been in fiscal terms, they were few in number and do not appear to have appreciably outlived the difficult 1905-7 period. Nor, like the censorship decisions that the government so often failed to enforce, were they always effective. The Aleksandrinskii actor Nikolai Khodotov, one of the few radicals in the imperial drama troupe, regularly ignored police bans on songs and monologues he performed. In some cases, simply leaving prohibited works off printed programs was sufficient, but he included them with everything else as he came to realize that there were no real consequences for violating the interdictions.[115] A police order banning him personally from performing at concerts for students and workers had no teeth.[116] Khodotov not only continued to appear, but he even visited police officials to argue against their prohibition of material permitted by the censorship. Although one of his interlocutors once answered that "everything permitted that comes out of your mouth sounds like something not permitted"— yet another indicator of how approved material could easily be turned into something else on stage—some of the restrictions were dropped before the police rescinded the ban on Khodotov's performances altogether.[117] The actress Nadezhda Tiraspol'skaia remembered, at least in the first edition of her memoirs, that Khodotov performed some of the same songs and poems for amused members of the extended Imperial Family, with whom the actor was on friendly terms.[118]

---

112. "Tsenzura pered sudom predstavitelei iskusstva," *Teatral'naia Rossiia* 41 (October 8, 1905): 1224.
113. Vladimir Nemirovitch-Danchenko, *My Life in the Russian Theatre*, trans. John Cournos (London: Bles, 1937), 239.
114. "A. (antreprener)," "Otkrytoe pis'mo k sovetu teatr[al'nogo] obshch[estva]," *Teatr i iskusstvo* 31 (July 31, 1905): 487-88.
115. N. N. Khodotov, *Blizkoe—dalekoe* (Leningrad: Iskusstvo, 1962), 167.
116. The ban is noted in ibid. and "Khronika," *Teatr i iskusstvo* 51 (December 18, 1905): 799.
117. Khodotov, *Blizkoe—dalekoe*, 168. The ban's formal lifting was announced in "Khronika," *Teatr i iskusstvo* 5 (February 4, 1907): 78.
118. N. L. Tiraspol'skaia, *Iz proshlogo russkoi stseny* (Moscow: VTO, 1950), 133-34, claims that

The Orthodox Church could also exercise power over theatrical matters—
"unofficial spiritual censorship," as one critic called it—although it did not formally enjoy the power to do so.[119] During the Kobeko Commission's deliberations, Molchanov mentioned a case in which Metropolitan Ionafan (Jonathan) of Iaroslavl' arranged for the prohibition of an operetta called *Poor Jonathan* lest people associate him with the work's disreputable title character. Nemirovich-Danchenko complained that Metropolitan Vladimir of Moscow had intervened to cancel the Art Theater production of Gerhart Hauptmann's *Hannele*—despite its censorship approval and frequent performances elsewhere (including popular theaters)—because one of its scenes takes place in heaven.[120] Ecclesiastical authorities in Saratov prevented a group of choral artists from performing at a wedding because they believed "mouths that sing shameless songs in the theater should not praise God in church."[121]

Such incidents were sporadic at most, but although Church interventions in the performing arts occurred less frequently than arbitrary police cancellations—and perhaps because they occurred less frequently—they continued to menace cultural life. Fedor Komissarzhevskii later claimed that the Church "had no legal right of interference" but was "privileged to act illegally when [it] wished."[122] He was referring to an October 1908 incident in which the Holy Synod, acting at the insistence of the fiery right-wing Duma deputy Vladimir Purishkevich (who later became internationally famous for helping murder Rasputin) successfully requested that the police prohibit the Dramatic Theater premiere of Oscar Wilde's *Salome*, a lascivious retelling of the story of the death of John the Baptist centered on a plot of incestuous passion and necrophilia. Outraged Holy Synod officials who attended the dress rehearsal called the production "unheard of blasphemy" and objected to its taboo (or semitaboo, given the haphazard nature of censorship on religious as well as other grounds) depiction of biblical characters.[123] The order for its cancellation arrived just three hours before curtain time.

Komissarzhevskaia's staging of the play in what has been described as a "giant

---

he did this to throw off the police. The observation, however, was omitted from the 1962 edition of her memoirs.

119. "Tsenzura pered sudom predstavitelei iskusstva," 1224.

120. "K voprosu o dramaticheskoi tsenzure," 1120–21. "Khronika," *Teatr i iskusstvo* 20 (May 15, 1905): 312, reported censorship approval for its performance at the Nicholas II People's House.

121. "Khronika," *Teatr i iskusstvo* 6 (February 5, 1912): 125.

122. Theodore Komisarjevsky, *Myself and the Theatre* (London: Heinemann, 1929), 81.

123. Rybakova, *Komissarzhevskaia*, 180; Sharon M. Carnicke, "The Theatrical Instinct: A Study of the Work of Nikolaj Evreinov in Early Twentieth-Century Russia" (Ph.D. diss., Columbia University, 1979), 24. In her letter of protest in RGIA, f. 796, op. 188, d. 7687, ll. 13–14, Komissarzhevskaia offered to change the names of the biblical characters, but this had no effect on the Synod.

scenic vagina" probably did not help its cause, even though she had full preliminary approval of both the censorship and the police to produce the work.[124] In yet another study in ambiguity, however, as many as five previous productions of *Salome* had reached Petersburg stages, albeit under different titles.[125] A month after the scandal, the dancer Ida Rubinshtein freely gave a performance of the play that included *The Dance of the Seven Veils,* an erotic set piece inspired by a scene in which Salome persuades her stepfather, Herod, to give her the head of John the Baptist on a silver platter. This was easily the most suggestive expression of the work's incest and necrophilia themes.[126] Purishkevich's important personal role in banning the play—that of an elected member of the Duma rather than an appointed official, it bears pointing out—suggests that the Church's role in cultural affairs had neither a reach nor a momentum all its own. After the cancellation he assured the media that he would have led a group of activists from the right-wing Union of the Archangel Michael to "force the performance to stop" had the premiere gone forward.[127] One exasperated newspaper editor, objecting to the actress-entrepreneuse's legal right to produce *Salome,* demanded to know "whether our theatrical censors have spiritual outlooks, Christian sensibility, and wisdom. Who allowed such a disgraceful play into the repertoire?"[128] For her part Komissarzhevskaia complained most bitterly about the incident's dire financial consequences. "It places 100 employees and me in a hopeless material position . . . and makes it impossible for me to pay the artists and stagehands the only pay on which they survive," she pleaded in vain to the procurator of the Holy Synod.[129]

A final form of extralegal censorship came from the highest political authority outside the Court, the Council of Ministers. In late 1905 it attempted to cancel *The Days of Freedom,* another controversial work approved by the censorship

---

124. Spencer Golub, *The Recurrence of Fate: Theatre and Memory in Twentieth-Century Russia* (Iowa City: University of Iowa Press, 1994), 45. Komissarzhevskaia tried to convince the Synod that the production was not offensive because it was set in the eighteenth century, included "fantastic costumes," and was intended to convey that "a woman's love for a man is stronger than death and remains alive in her even after his death." This is a dubious explanation since Salome, in exchange for an erotic dance, asks her lustful stepfather to kill John the Baptist and give her his severed head. It did not save the premiere. For the full text of her letter, see RGIA, f. 796, op. 188, d. 7687, ll. 13–14.

125. According to V. A. Vdovin, "Neopublikovannoe pis'mo V. F. Komissarzhevskoi," *Sovetskie arkhivy* 3 (1970): 116, the first censorship approval for Russian versions of the work came in October 1903.

126. Charles S. Mayer, "Ida Rubinstein: A Twentieth-Century Cleopatra," *Dance Research Journal* 20, no. 2 (1989): 34.

127. "Purishkevich i Salomeia," *Novoe vremia,* October 30, 1908. The Union of the Archangel Michael was a splinter group of the Union of the Russian People, founded in 1905 to defend the autocracy.

128. Quoted in Vdovin, "Neopublikovannoe pis'mo," 118.

129. RGIA, f. 796, op. 188, d. 7687, ll. 13–14.

despite its incendiary political content. But even in this case high-level government authority did not prove immediately effective. Performances continued for over a month after the Council issued a special circular forbidding the production. The revue only petered out after the curtain went up on it more than fifty times.[130] In 1911 Andreev's *Anathema,* a parable in which a rich man gives away all his wealth to the poor only to be murdered by them when he has no more to hand over, provoked an outcry from religious authorities and their supporters (including Purishkevich again), who found the play "abusive of God and blasphemous" and thought it cast unacceptable doubt on the Christian virtue of charity. After twenty-five performances the uproar led the Council of Ministers to ban it by special circular.[131]

Like preliminary theatrical censorship, however, the incidental power of moral indignation over the performing arts was far from unknown outside Russia and should not be exaggerated in its Russian context. To make a direct comparison, the British theatrical censorship barred Wilde's *Salome* from public performance until 1931, ostensibly because it depicts biblical characters, but really because of its sexual content. Richard Strauss's close operatic adaptation of the play disappeared from the repertoire of the Metropolitan Opera in New York after its scandalous January 1907 premiere and did not return there for twenty-seven years. The Met's board found it "objectionable and detrimental," while the influential critic Henry Krehbiel felt "stung into righteous fury by the moral stench with which 'Salome' fills the nostrils of humanity."[132] Just two years earlier the New York City vice squad had pursued arrest warrants on public indecency charges for the entire cast of George Bernard Shaw's *Mrs. Warren's Profession,* a play that presents prostitution as a means of economic emancipation for women. Two decades after *Salome* was struck from the Met's repertoire, the actress Mae West was jailed for staging a theatrical of her own inspiration with the descriptive title *Sex.* As many observers complained, Russia's state authority failed to prevent a large number of works with "immoral" or "pornographic" content from being splayed across the Empire's stages. Occasional interventions on moral grounds were at least as common in Russia as they were in other nations.

Nor, in the long term, could state power match the influence of international events over the activities of theaters and impresarios. As was the case with the

---

130. Petrovskaia and Somina, *Teatral'nyi Peterburg,* 233.
131. Ibid., 236. The Left criticized the play because it appeared to be critical of the philosophical belief in redistributing wealth.
132. The phrase "objectionable and detrimental" is from "Take Off 'Salome,' Say Opera House Directors," *New York Times,* January 27, 1907. Henry Krehbiel's quote is from "'Salome's' Reception, 1907," *New York Times,* January 7, 1934.

imperial stages, the outbreak of World War I also caused German and Austrian works to disappear from Russia's private and popular theaters, often as a consequence of management decisions and audience pressure rather than censorship and state directives. At least initially, Russia's performing arts community rallied to the government, the dynasty, and fervent prowar sentiments. This might have been expected, for much had been made of artistic patriotism in earlier eras. A serialized article written for the centenary of Russia's victory over France in 1812 proudly declared that "enflamed by the enemy with a love for the Motherland, Russian theater fulfilled its mission."[133]

When a major war again came to Russia in 1914, many theatrical enterprises rushed to repeat that achievement. Perhaps predictably, new patriotic works were often, as Stanislavskii described them, "half baked."[134] His dismissive evaluation notwithstanding, the Moscow Art Theater voluntarily removed pictures of German playwrights from its foyer and altered the repertoire of its 1914–15 season to replace German works with Pushkin plays. "This was how we expressed our response to events," its founder recalled.[135] Viennese operetta, a popular genre before 1914, was replaced throughout the Empire by French or Russian operetta, though occasionally entrepreneurs who wanted to keep profiting from the more abundant Teutonic variety retitled its works or attributed them to non-Germanic composers.[136] Fedor Korsh's theater in Moscow preceded the opening night performance of its 1914–15 season with a patriotic tableau featuring a Russian warrior, the Romanov double-headed eagle bearing the flags of Russia's allies, and a pageant of actors dressed in the combat uniforms of soldiers from nations at war with Germany. A banner above the display declared: "Great is the God of the Russian Land."[137] The Nicholas II People's House dropped its Wagner and Johann Strauss productions, dramatized fervent nationalist speeches, and staged outdoor performances mimicking the patriotic public demonstrations that had greeted the war. Many houses led their audiences in preperformance singings of "God Save the Tsar." Cabaret owners showed their colors by adding "a broad spectrum of patriotic entertainment" to their programs.[138] A typical evening at Petrograd's (as St. Petersburg was renamed in 1914) Crooked Mirror satirized Russia's enemies and offered a serious drama comparing 1914 with the much more victorious year of 1814.[139] A public opinion

---

133. Petr Iuzhnyi, "Teatr v Otechestvennuiu voinu," *Teatr i iskusstvo* 32 (August 5, 1912): 616.
134. Stanislavskii, *Moia zhizn'*, 376.
135. Ibid.; Jahn, *Patriotic Culture*, 125, 139.
136. Jahn, *Patriotic Culture*, 141–42.
137. "Khronika," *Teatr i iskusstvo* 33 (August 17, 1914): 677.
138. *Teatr i iskusstvo* 33 (August 17, 1914): 677; Jahn, *Patriotic Culture*, 105, 117, 126.
139. N. Tamarin, "Krivoe zerkalo," *Teatr i iskusstvo* 40 (October 15, 1914): 788.

survey found that a majority of Russian theatergoers considered the prospective restoration of Wagner's operas to be "inappropriate."[140]

Despite these displays the crisis of war spelled many practical problems for the performing arts. Just as the Revolution of 1905 had warped their normal operations, confusion and fear resurfaced in strength in 1914. Military deployments and steadily more exacting drafts drained large numbers of men to the front (and away from theater halls), while heightened industrial demands brought more women into the workforce and introduced the overtime, extended workdays, and night shifts that both embittered workers about their general situation and reduced their leisure time. Urban curfews initially set at eleven o'clock in the evening rendered theater performance and attendance less practical than in peacetime, while the liquor ban that followed the outbreak of war made evenings out less enjoyable.[141] Audiences became "fatally small." The theatrical press thought some venues resembled "the Arabian desert" in their emptiness.[142] Facing an urgent need of revenue, the government, following on prewar initiatives, introduced a tax on theater tickets, which in some cases doubled their prices at a time when real wages were sharply declining. Even before the war the performing community had loathed the measure as "a legal project against the theater" that "punished spectators who want to have a more artistic experience." Now it was worse.[143]

Needless to say, the war's material consequences hurt business. Not even the Imperial Theaters were immune. As early into the war as October 1914, Teliakovskii, himself a military man, told the French ambassador, "I hope to goodness we shan't persevere in this mad course."[144] Stage makeup disappeared, along with most other imported materials used by Russian theaters. Obtaining paper, printing materials, cloth, canvas, wood, paint, nails, tools, and many other essential items competed with military needs and corresponding price rises. In the first year of the war alone, the cost of some of these commodities doubled. One Petrograd theater manager tried to use the same canvases over and over by painting new backdrops on them.[145]

The physical premises of arts enterprises themselves became vulnerable commodities. As spacious locales in urban centers and transportation hubs—a

140. "Malen'kaia khronika," *Teatr i iskusstvo* 49 (December 7, 1914): 942.
141. "Fakty i zakliucheniia," *Teatr i iskusstvo* 40 (October 15, 1914): 786, notes the curfew's extension to midnight for major theaters, while cabarets and other small venues still had to close by eleven.
142. "Khronika," *Teatr i iskusstvo* 30 (July 27, 1914): 628.
143. Jahn, *Patriotic Culture*, 98, 135; "Oblozhenie Peterburgskoi dumoi teatrov," *Teatr i iskusstvo* 18 (May 4, 1914): 398; "Slukhi ob oblozhenii teatrov," *Teatr i iskusstvo* 34 (August 24, 1914): 691.
144. Paléologue, *Memoirs*, 1:166.
145. Jahn, *Patriotic Culture*, 135.

number of them, including the capital's Ligovskii People's House (which ceased its theatrical activities, including those of Gaideburov's General Accessible Theater, in 1914) and Panaev Theater, along with many of the Empire's concert halls—were converted for use as military hospitals or to serve other war-related functions. The requisitioning of several additional Petrograd theaters in August 1916 threatened the jobs of as many as five hundred performers.[146]

Even the human capital of show business began to suffer. Few foreign artists could arrive in Russia to perform, and, unless stranded elsewhere by the outbreak of war, few Russian artists could tour abroad. The Moscow Art Theater, which entered into talks to schedule its first American tour in 1913, was unable to undertake it for another ten years.[147] Touring within Russia itself became a difficult proposition, as military needs took over railways and rolling stock. A 25 percent tax on civilian rail travel burdened traveling theatrical operations.[148]

With demands at the front substantially higher than they had been during the Russo-Japanese War, men working in the performing arts often found themselves in uniform rather than costume. Within six weeks of the war's declaration, the Russian Theatrical Society reported that two hundred of its members had entered the military.[149] The press published long lists of drafted performers, as well as some who volunteered, together with numerous photographs of them martially attired. These notices eventually gave way to lists of the dead and wounded among them. The Imperial Theaters, whose artists were nominally exempt from military service, suspended the rule excusing them. A number of fit soloists were called up.[150] The Bol'shoi's orchestra lost no fewer than forty players to the draft, while the Imperial Court orchestra had to supply replacements to staff the Mariinskii's depleted pit.[151] The chief director of Sergei Zimin's opera company was summoned to active service in the first wave of draftees, as was the chief director of the Suvorin Theater. A. K. Reinek, proprietor of the Russian Dramatic Theater, was himself called up, casting doubt on the future of his enterprise.[152] The conductor Sergei Kusevitskii (Koussevitzky), later a famed director of the Boston Symphony, dissolved his orchestra after

---

146. "Rekvizitsiia teatrov," "Khronika," *Teatr i iskusstvo* 33 (August 14, 1916): 658.
147. Benedetti, *Stanislavski*, 217.
148. "Zametka," *Teatr i iskusstvo* 49 (December 7, 1914): 931.
149. "Khronika," *Teatr i iskusstvo* 36 (September 7, 1914): 725.
150. "Khronika," *Teatr i iskusstvo* 30 (July 27, 1914): 627 and 31 (August 3, 1914): 645. Those called upon included such major stars as Leonid Sobinov, Evgenii Vitting, and Fedor Lopukhov.
151. "Khronika," *Teatr i iskusstvo* 31 (August 3, 1914): 645 and 34 (August 24, 1914): 692.
152. "Khronika," *Teatr i iskusstvo* 30 (July 27, 1914): 627; "Khronika," *Teatr i iskusstvo* 48 (November 30, 1914): 914, reports Reinek being wounded and decorated.

more than half its members were drafted.¹⁵³ So many male soloists were taken from the roster of the Nicholas II People's House that the future of its opera productions came into question.¹⁵⁴ By late 1916 the Empire's stages were emptied of able-bodied men to the point that the press wondered how troupes could credibly stage plays with young characters.¹⁵⁵ Performance was not the only area in danger. Seven Petersburg Conservatory professors were drafted in the first days of the war, as were so many of the Ballet School's instructors that it was rumored to be closing.¹⁵⁶

The year 1917 brought the imperial era to an end, but the process was far from easy for Russia's stages. Both the collapse of the monarchy in February and the Bolshevik coup d'état in October halted theatrical operations for an appreciable period, while strikes, demonstrations, and related troubles tortured their work in the meantime.¹⁵⁷ In addition to continuing military needs, many theaters were requisitioned for mass meetings, most of which had little to do with their primary function. Instead their stages became forums for new government figures, labor leaders, revolutionary politicians, and others hurtled to popularity by the political situation. The state Mikhailovskii Theater was briefly taken over as a meeting place for the Petrograd Soviet, though its space ultimately proved too small to accommodate the whole body.¹⁵⁸ Zimin's opera was evicted from its premises to accommodate projects of the Moscow Soviet.¹⁵⁹ The abortive socialist rising in early July shut down the capital's theatrical life for several days.¹⁶⁰ Even mere rumors of the Bolshevik coup caused receipts to decline. In the aftermath of the communist takeover, the theatrical press—whose own days as an independent institution were numbered—reported that "Petrograd theaters are hanging by a thread."¹⁶¹ The Moscow Art Theater's October 26 performance of *The Cherry Orchard* was broken up by gunfire as revolutionaries battled forces loyal to the Provisional Government for control of the

---

153. Amy Nelson, *Music for the Revolution: Musicians and Power in Early Soviet Russia* (University Park: Pennsylvania State University Press, 2004), 13.
154. "Khronika," *Teatr i iskusstvo* 30 (July 27, 1914): 628.
155. "Kriticheskoe polozhenie teatrov," *Teatr i iskusstvo* 41 (October 9, 1916): 819.
156. "Khronika," *Teatr i iskusstvo* 30 (July 27, 1914): 628 and 32 (August 10, 1914): 660.
157. Orlando Figes and Boris Kolonitskii, *Interpreting the Russian Revolution: The Language and Symbols of 1917* (New Haven: Yale University Press, 1999), 46; "Teatr i revoliutsionnye dni v Petrograde," *Teatr i iskusstvo* 10–11 (March 12, 1917): 190–92; "Sobytiia i teatr," *Teatr i iskusstvo* 44–46 (November 12, 1917): 763.
158. N. N. Sukhanov, *The Russian Revolution, 1917*, ed. and trans. Joel Carmichael (London: Oxford University Press, 1955), 216, 224.
159. "Moskovskie vesti," *Teatr i iskusstvo* 27 (July 2, 1917): 468.
160. "Khronika," *Teatr i iskusstvo* 28–29 (July 28–29, 1917): 488.
161. "Ot redaktsii," *Teatr i iskusstvo* 44–46 (November 12, 1917): 762.

city.[162] The Bol'shoi and Malyi Theaters were sacked and severely damaged in the course of the fighting.[163] Throughout the year audiences melted away, receipts plummeted, theaters closed, and performers went unemployed.

Nevertheless, some aspects of the performing arts institution remained resistant to the year's stunning political transformations. Gnedich, the Aleksandrinskii's former chief director, remarked in July 1917 that "still, after four months of a republic, no new tasks have been undertaken in theater."[164] *Theater and Art*'s editor Aleksandr Kugel' agreed that "theater has received freedom together with all Russian society, but in fact nothing has changed."[165] Repertoires and production values registered little impact. Artists of the Ballets Russes found it "decidedly out of place" when their production of Stravinskii's *The Firebird* was altered to have the victorious hero presented with a cap of liberty and red flag instead of a crown and scepter. The original accoutrements were quickly restored.[166] A special arts conference convoked by the Provisional Government called for the preservation of the imperial symbols in what were now "state" theaters.[167] Popular enthusiasm for symbolic changes in state institutions, however, thwarted the conference's plea and many of the former Imperial Theaters' coats of arms were either removed or covered with red cloth. Their appearance on theatrical programs was abandoned in favor of a lyre.[168] The opening of the new artistic season on August 30—the traditional anniversary of the founding of the Imperial Theaters—still remained in place in 1917.[169]

Personal elements of the old regime's official arts culture also somewhat persisted. Perhaps singularly, Teliakovskii retained his long-held tsarist era post as head of the state theaters for more than two months after the tsar's abdication.[170] The Constitutional Democrat Fedor Batiushkov, who in May 1917 replaced him under the verbose title "Chief Representative of the State Theaters

---

162. Benedetti, *Stanislavski*, 236.
163. "Sobytiia i teatr," *Teatr i iskusstvo* 44–46 (November 12, 1917): 763; and "Posledniaia sobshcheniia," *Teatr i iskusstvo* 47 (November 19, 1917): 763
164. P. Gnedich, "Perelom," *Teatr i iskusstvo* 27 (July 2, 1917): 470. Russia was only proclaimed a republic in September, but the point was clear.
165. "Homo novus" [Aleksandr Kugel'], "Zametki," *Teatr i iskusstvo* 13–14 (April 2, 1917): 233.
166. S. L. Grigoriev, *The Diaghilev Ballet, 1909–1929* (Harmondsworth: Penguin, 1960), 130–31.
167. For documentation of the order and a general discussion of the removal of imperial symbols, see Figes and Kolonitskii, *Interpreting the Russian Revolution*, 49.
168. Vasilii Bezpalov, *Teatry v dni revoliutsii, 1917* (Leningrad: Academia, 1927), 39; "Khronika," *Teatr i iskusstvo* 12 (March 19, 1917): 219. The lyre is sported on Mariinskii Theater programs today even though the tsarist symbols that adorned the theater's interior have been restored.
169. "Khronika," *Teatr i iskusstvo* 32 (August 6, 1917): 543.
170. "Teatr i revoliutsionnye dni," 191, and "Malen'kaia khronika," *Teatr i iskusstvo* 10–11 (March 12, 1917): 199, report that Teliakovskii was briefly arrested, but that there had been no order for it. He was quickly released. The incident was created by a bitter Aleksandrinskii actor who felt underpaid.

for the Commissar of the Provisional Government over the Former Ministry of the Imperial Court," was the government's second choice, after Teliakovskii's immediate predecessor, Prince Sergei Volkonskii, declined an offer to return to his old post.[171] Batiushkov was hardly an unfamiliar figure in the realm of government arts administration though; since 1900 he had served as head of the Aleksandrinskii's literary committee. Nor was the succession in every way unambiguous. Teliakovskii and Batiushkov shared the Director's official apartment until September 1917.[172]

Personnel matters were not the only realm that betrayed some continuity in the relationship between culture and power after the February Revolution. Although nominally committed to "democratizing" the state theaters, the Provisional Government continued to sell tickets to them by subscription, an exclusive means that required audience members to buy tickets to numerous performances in advance. The system continued to function into the ill-fated 1917–18 season.[173] Censorship remained a factor after the tsar's abdication despite enthusiasm for its total removal and the abolition of its major prerevolutionary institution, the Interior Ministry's Main Office for Press Affairs.[174] In April 1917 the new regime ordered the Suvorin Theater not to perform "revolutionary" plays or works depicting members of the Romanov dynasty in an unflattering light. It feared their potential to cause public disturbances.[175] In July the government announced that entrepreneurs who failed to submit works for its preliminary approval would face legal sanctions. Local authorities took to the directive.[176] "Unremitting supervision" (*neoslabnyi nadzor*) of film by state authorities was introduced the same month, despite the lack of any substantial tsarist precedent.[177] Even as the authority of the Provisional Government waned in the weeks before October, it still found time to strike Merezhkovskii's *Emperor Paul I* from the repertoire of Moscow's Malyi Theater.[178] After the Bolsheviks took over,

---

171. Prince Sergei Volkonskii, *Moi vospominaniia* (Moscow: Iskusstvo, 1992), 242–43. Batiushkov's verbose title is from Murray Frame, "Theatre and Revolution in 1917: The Case of the Petrograd State Theatres," *Revolutionary Russia* 12, no. 1 (1999): 88–89.

172. "Malen'kaia khronika," *Teatr i iskusstvo* 38 (September 17, 1917): 661.

173. Murray Frame, *The St. Petersburg Imperial Theatres: Stage and State in Revolutionary Russia, 1900–1920* (Greensboro, N.C.: McFarland, 2000), 67. "Khronika," *Teatr i iskusstvo* 39 (September 24, 1917): 671, lists performances by subscription schedule.

174. "Velikaia russkaia revoliutsiia i teatr," *Teatr i iskusstvo* 10–11 (March 12, 1917): 188, and "O tsenzure p'es'," *Teatr i iskusstvo* 12 (March 19, 1917): 208, presented this most directly.

175. Petrovskaia and Somina, *Teatral'nyi Peterburg*, 214.

176. "Khronika," *Teatr i iskusstvo* 31 (July 30, 1917): 526. "Ot redaktsii," *Teatr i iskusstvo* 33 (August 13, 1917): 562, reports local preliminary theatrical censorship in Kazan'.

177. "Khronika," *Teatr i iskusstvo* 27 (July 2, 1917): 468.

178. "Moskovskie vesti," *Teatr i iskusstvo* 38 (September 17, 1917): 653.

their own reliance on theatrical censorship "remind[ed] one more and more of pre-revolutionary times."[179] It got worse from there.

Just as impresarios, administrators, directors, censors, police officials, politicians, churchmen, and others with influence over the institutional life of Russia's performing arts grappled with challenges from the political arena, unrest also confronted arts education. Universities and other institutions of higher education figured at the center of the rising urban tension from the late 1890s and continued to serve as stages for it throughout the late imperial era.[180] It may, therefore, seem logical that students and teachers of music, dance, and drama would not have approached political events in a meaningfully different way from those engaged in more conventional subjects. But their reactions, while not totally passive, remained substantially more subdued.

The nature of Russian arts education itself contributed to this distinction. The Imperial Ballet and Drama Schools—the only major institutions offering structured programs of study in those art forms—fell under the authority of the Imperial Theaters Directorate and were closely tied to its performing troupes. As we saw in the last chapter, dance graduates were guaranteed employment in the imperial ballet, while successful drama students received preferential treatment on the state stage after their automatic right to employment was terminated in 1866. From 1902 male music students who graduated from the Conservatories operated by the Imperial Russian Musical Society were guaranteed appointment to state service. The prospect of securing a livelihood in the arts and the aspiration to do so in the Imperial Theaters were not uncommon among these students and rendered many of them less likely than their university counterparts—large numbers of whom did not expect or seek state associations after graduation—to jeopardize their futures by fomenting unrest.

The demographics of performing arts students also worked against their radicalization. Ballet pupils began their studies in childhood and completed them in their late teens—the same age at which university students only began to matriculate. The ages of Drama School and Conservatory students varied to a much greater degree; many of them were either older or younger than most university students. The composer Sergei Prokof'ev entered St. Petersburg Conservatory in the autumn of 1904 at the precocious age of thirteen. He was far from alone among young people in the seriousness of his studies (Dmitrii Shostakovich

---

179. "Khronika," *Teatr i iskusstvo* 50 (December 10, 1917): 811. For a detailed study of early Soviet theatrical censorship, see Steven D. Richmond, "Ideologically Firm: Soviet Theater Censorship, 1921–1928" (Ph.D. diss., University of Chicago, 1996).

180. For a good discussion, see Kassow, *Students, Professors, and the State*, 237–85.

also matriculated at age thirteen), but most of his classmates were adults enrolled for what Lynn Sargeant describes as "vocational, rather than professional, training."[181] Like Elena Andreevna, the bored young wife and Petersburg Conservatory graduate in Chekhov's *Uncle Vania*, these students were learning to play instruments or sing more because it would help them become "accomplished" than because they planned serious careers in the arts. In 1868 nearly half of Elena Andreevna's real-life classmates (110 out of 228) studied piano, the quintessential instrument of the nineteenth-century middle classes, while the next largest number (47, another one-fifth), studied voice. Unlike in Russian universities, which until almost the end of the tsarist era rarely admitted women into regular programs of study, more than half of Petersburg Conservatory students (129 of 228) that year were female. Enrollment rose fivefold over the next half century, and the prevailing demographic trends only accelerated there and in other institutions operated by the Musical Society. In the 1904–5 academic year women and girls accounted for nearly two-thirds of the Petersburg Conservatory student body (720 of 1,137). A decade later the contingent of female students attending Kiev Conservatory, formally established in 1913, reached 68.4 percent of the total (692 of 987).[182] Of the 133 students whom Petrograd (Petersburg) Conservatory graduated in May 1917, 92 (69.2 percent) studied in the piano faculty.[183]

Mostly composed of either seekers of state arts employment or pupils too young or too old to take active part in university political movements, performing arts student bodies remained cold to radicalism. The large number of children learning ballet and proper ladies studying piano and voice did little to reverse this trend or suggest that it would be reversed in the future. The government plainly recognized these facts. In 1908, an official study of the enrollment of Jews in higher education concluded that their growing presence in music was "socially and politically harmless, diverting [them] from other, potentially far more corrosive, areas of activity." As a result the state saw no need for measures to limit their numbers, even while it upheld discriminatory policies in most university settings. Four years after the study appeared, Jews made up more than 40 percent of students at Petersburg Conservatory. By 1915 they accounted for slightly more than half of Kiev Conservatory students.[184]

The political involvement of performing arts students was long either nonexistent or too insignificant to attract comment. As for Bloody Sunday and its

---

181. Lynn Sargeant, "A New Class of People: The Conservatoire and Musical Professionalization in Russia, 1861–1917," *Music and Letters* 85, no. 1 (2004): 49.
182. Ibid.
183. "Publichnyi akt Petrogradskoi Konservatorii," *Teatr i iskusstvo* 20 (May 14, 1917): 332.
184. Sargeant, "New Class," 56, 59–60.

aftermath, "little report of it managed to creep into the fastness of the Imperial Dancing School" even though Vatslav Nizhinskii, still a student that year, was hit by a Cossack while venturing out on the streets at the wrong time.[185] Unfolding revolutionary events failed to change the attitudes of his classmates. Their main desire was to secure slight improvements in their study and living conditions, requests they frequently made in the absence of major political turmoil. In the recollection of the famed Soviet choreographer Fedor Lopukhov, who graduated from the Ballet School and entered the Mariinskii's troupe in 1905, "when the revolutionary wave reached the doorstep of the [Ballet] School . . . and the students presented their demands—very humble and useful demands—the Directorate assessed this more or less as th ough it were not a revolution."[186] Lopukhov's classmates were even happy to cooperate with the administration during troubled times. When a confrontation between the Directorate and some members of the ballet troupe led to the latter's absence from an October 1905 performance of Chaikovskii's opera *Eugene Onegin*, Teliakovskii called upon Ballet School students to appear in its dance sequences. Far from objecting on moral or political grounds—as one might expect from "conscious" students—the aspiring young dancers "were in ecstasy" to be on stage for the first time and gladly performed.[187]

The Imperial Drama School also experienced little palpable reaction to revolutionary events. In the turbulent autumn of 1905, its students asked only that they be excused from classes "in view of the general nervous situation, and also because of the absence of the professors themselves from the lectures, which had recently become so bad that it looked as though they were striking." Teliakovskii permitted them to stay home.[188] In the aftermath a student meeting requested the dismissal of one teacher who had flouted his professional duties to what the students believed to be an ex cessive degree. After reviewing the matter, the Director asked for his resignation.[189] The major concern of the drama students was to continue learning their art in a s afe, stable, and professional environment.

Petersburg's Conservatory experienced greater challenges during the Revolution of 1905, but ultimately they, too, turned out to be more professional than political in content. At first, like their fellow aspiring artists in the Imperial Ballet

185. Romola Nijinsky, *Nijinsky* (New York: Simon and Schuster, 1934), 41.
186. Fedor Lopukhov, *Shest'desiat let v balete: Vospominaniia i zapiski baletmeistera* (Moscow: Iskusstvo, 1966), 94.
187. Teliakovskii, "Imperatorskie teatry," 252–53.
188. Ibid., 243–44.
189. Ibid., 264–65.

and Drama Schools, its students did not react strongly to Bloody Sunday. The young Prokof'ev "did not notice" when it happened and in a letter to his father described the capital as "quiet."[190] His older classmates failed to respond to the brewing unrest. According to Sargeant, "the revolutionary flame did not burn very brightly. . . . Student protests were not particularly noticeable or important."[191] The only real involvement of a Conservatory student in the events of Bloody Sunday was that of a young officer enrolled for military music studies who boasted of having fired on the demonstrators. Some students demanded his expulsion, but the incident seems to have marked the limit of their political consciousness.[192]

Despite the tepid responses of music students to the emerging revolution, they did contribute to one major controversy: the temporary dismissal of the famous composer Rimskii-Korsakov from the institution's faculty in March 1905. Although the "Rimskii-Korsakov Affair" has been heralded as a major event connecting Russian culture with revolutionary politics, little about it was in fact political.[193]

In early March a student meeting addressed the general situation by demanding the cessation of classes until the following academic year, which was scheduled to begin on September 1. Along with general references to political reform, its resolution asked for better courses in music history and ensemble playing, a larger state subsidy for the Musical Society (which had founded and operated the Conservatory), more opportunities to perform publicly, and improvements in student boarding and dining facilities.[194]

Support among the student body for even these modest demands turned out to be far from unanimous. Fewer than 40 percent of the students—precisely 451 out of 1,137—voted to endorse them.[195] Prokof'ev later claimed that "our whole class disagreed . . . saying that [the students who supported the demands] were rebelling for nothing." Rather than abandon their studies, the young composer and many of his classmates wanted to continue to the end of the spring semester, realizing that "if the Conservatory closed, then both the year's studies and the money that had paid for our education would

190. Sergei Prokof'ev, *Avtobiografiia* (Moscow: Sovetskii Kompozitor, 1982), 183–84.
191. Lynn Sargeant, "Middle-Class Culture: Music and Identity in Late Imperial Russia" (Ph.D. diss., Indiana University, 2001), 217.
192. Ibid., 217.
193. See especially M. O. Iankovskii, *Rimskii-Korsakov i revoliutsiia 1905 goda* (Moscow: Gosudarstvennoe muzykal'noe izdatel'stvo, 1950).
194. Sargeant, "Middle-Class Culture," 218–19. Prokof'ev, *Avtobiografiia*, 198, lists the right to stage a monthly opera performance among these demands.
195. Lynn Sargeant, "*Kashchei the Immortal:* Liberal Politics, Cultural Memory, and the Rimsky-Korsakov Scandal of 1905," *Russian Review* 64, no. 1 (2005): 26.

disappear."[196] The most recent study of the Rimskii-Korsakov "Affair" has rightly referred to "the exaggerated myth of the conservatory revolution."[197]

It is hard to imagine that those who wanted the Conservatory to close hoped to demonstrate solidarity with authentic revolutionaries. As had the capital's audiences, for whom many of the students aspired to perform, the prevailing atmosphere of unrest convinced them that it was better to wait for more normal times to resume their studies. Since formal musical training depends on regular lessons, repetitive exercises, intense practice, and examinations based on qualitative performance, daily nerve-wracking trauma threatened distraction to say the least. Rimskii-Korsakov himself, who had not yet been touched by scandal, thought it best to close the Conservatory for these reasons, especially because a significant number of students did not wish to continue their lessons. Otherwise, he feared, those advocating closure "will either whistle at us [to disrupt lessons] or, at best, they'll carry the most popular professors out of their classes ... neither of these possibilities is particularly alluring."[198]

Rimskii-Korsakov's sentiments were shared by most of the faculty council, which had voted in favor of closing until the next academic year even before the student meeting voiced its opinion.[199] The director of the Conservatory, A. R. Berngard, and other members of the Musical Society's Petersburg committee, however, were only willing to close until March 15 and said nothing about the other student demands. When the Conservatory attempted to open for business on March 16, students who wanted to continue studying found the building blocked by a crowd of the more insistent among their classmates who had decided to take matters into their own hands. The police made sure that those willing to study could enter, but the next day the protesters broke in and vandalized the classrooms.[200]

If the Conservatory were to remain open at this point, there was no way it could have offered solid instruction. This was the main point of a controversial open letter from Rimskii-Korsakov to Berngard published the next day and heralding the composer's scandal. After briefly recounting the uneasiness among his students, he reproached the director: "Is a normal course of instruction possible in such conditions? I find it impossible, as do many other instructors.

196. Prokof'ev, *Avtobiografiia*, 196.
197. Sargeant, *"Kashchei the Immortal,"* 43.
198. V. V. Yastrebtsev, *Reminiscences of Rimsky-Korsakov*, trans. Florence Jonas (New York: Columbia University Press, 1985), 354. The official history of the Musical Society, albeit not an objective source, also gives this explanation. See Findeizen, *Ocherk deiatel'nosti*, 97.
199. Marina Mikheeva, "Sankt Peterburgskaia Konservatoriia i 1905 god," http://www.conservatory.ru/rus/ history_cons1905.shtml.
200. Sargeant, "Middle-Class Culture," 220–21.

The Conservatory authorities—the Director, the Inspectors, the Directorate of the [Russian] Musical Society—look at it differently, untroubled by events that make the government itself stop to think." Deriding the responsible Musical Society officials as "amateurs and dilettantes," he found "the actions of the Conservatory administration inexpedient, anti-artistic, and callous from a moral point of view" and believed it his "duty to protest."[201] Although Rimskii-Korsakov had once allegedly described himself as a "vivid Red," he claimed in his memoirs that his greatest concern at the time was for the well-being of his students.[202] The composer's personal views have in any case been described as subordinate to his "comfortable, quiet, and apolitical life."[203] The embarrassed Berngard resigned as a result of the fiasco, but the board of the Musical Society's Petersburg committee nevertheless voted to dismiss Rimskii-Korsakov for his public insubordination and expelled the students who had taken part in the disruptions.[204]

The nature of the dispute was essentially professional—Rimskii-Korsakov had departed from the established rules governing the conduct of Conservatory professors and was punished for it. His dismissal, however, set off a firestorm of protest. Several of his colleagues, including the well known composers Aleksandr Glazunov and Anatolii Liadov and the prominent conductor Feliks Blumenfel'd—all of them former students of his—resigned their Conservatory professorships.

Much of the public outrage found corresponding expression in professional terms. Several editorials about the scandal argued that Russia's musicians had grown into a group sufficiently cohesive and responsible to govern itself without input from the Musical Society's leaders, none of whom were working performers. Comparing the board of directors' administrative judgments to "the croaking of frogs" and "the bacteria of bureaucracy, ruining the organism," one commentator declared that "it is not musicians who are in charge of affairs, but certain officials who have brought to the sacred matter of art the ignorance of dilettantism and the vulgarity of careerism."[205] Another listed the board members' names and ranks and concluded that they "say nothing either to musicians or to lovers of music." Instead they held their posts because musicians had not

---

201. Translation as quoted in Yastrebtsev, *Reminiscences*, 355. The reference to the government almost certainly pertains to its decision, made official on March 18, to close all universities until September 1.
202. Rimsky-Korsakov, *Musical Life*, 346–47. The phrase "vivid Red" is from Yastrebtsev, *Reminiscences*, 351.
203. Sargeant, "Middle-Class Culture," 224.
204. Yastrebtsev, *Reminiscences*, 356.
205. A. Koptiaev, "Muzykal'nyi biurokratizm i kompozitory," *Teatral'naia Rossiia/Muzykal'nyi mir* 13 (March 26, 1905): 179.

been confident enough to take charge: "Our artistic and educated society believes so little in its own strengths.... Free artists and scholars willingly submit to bureaucrats as though their influence were insufficient. And here are the results!"[206] A third comment found it "silly to say that the fate of Russian music is not decided by musicians, composers, or artists, but by people who pay 10 rubles for the right to be members of the Musical Society."[207]

The thrust of these opinions said far less about the relationship between art and politics than it did about the relationship between society and art. The Musical Society, like many other independent civic groups, received state subsidies but was far from being a captive organ of the tsarist government. It was a voluntary association of the type that mushroomed in the late imperial era and gave Russians a greater role in public life. Theoretically, those who objected to autocratic government and heavy-handed state institutions should have looked—and in almost every other context did look—to such associations as alternative sources of action and authority.[208] But in this case, criticisms of the Musical Society revolved around how it operated and arrived at decisions, a discourse that turned it into "an unexpected villain of Russian cultural life."[209] Indeed, there is no evidence that the government's educational, police, or other high institutions planned, ordered, encouraged, or even necessarily approved of Rimskii-Korsakov's dismissal. Neither the composer himself nor the most vociferous critics of the scandal ever leveled such an accusation. What is remarkable is the extent to which unrest contributed to the development of professional consciousness among musicians. As we shall see in Chapter 4, the disruptive effect of political events on Russian cultural life complemented a larger, apolitical process of professionalization. It is, however, sufficient to say that this development found expression in the debate about the nature of the Musical Society and its powers in the wake of Rimskii-Korsakov's dismissal.

Despite the professional emphasis of the scandal's public discussions, it presented the radical camp with an irresistible opportunity to make a political point.

---

206. "3, 14," "Tiazhkii urok," *Teatral'naia Rossiia/Muzykal'nyi mir* 14 (April 2, 1905): 193–94. Several of the Musical Society's board members had high civil service or Court ranks. Its St. Petersburg committee chairman, P. N. Cheremisinov, was an actual state councilor, as was another member, D. A. Filosofov (cousin of the symbolist intellectual). The committee's deputy chairman, A. M. Klimchenko, was a privy councilor. A. S. Taneev held the courtly rank of *gofmeister*, while Princess A. A. Obolenskaia's husband was a *shtalmeister*. The author's invective spared I. A. Persiani, who voted against dismissing Rimskii-Korsakov, and Berngard, who resigned.

207. G. Agraev, "Pozornoe sobytie," *Teatral'naia Rossiia/Muzykal'nyi mir* 14 (April 2, 1905): 196.

208. For the best recent discussion of this development, see Joseph Bradley, "Subjects into Citizens: Societies, Civil Society, and Autocracy in Tsarist Russia," *American Historical Review* 107, no. 4 (2002).

209. Sargeant, *"Kashchei the Immortal,"* 24.

The actual motivation that led Rimskii-Korsakov to confront the Musical Society's leadership—his concern for his students and realization that the Conservatory could not function effectively in a climate of serious unrest—left a circle to be squared. But a premier institution of arts education had fired Russia's leading composer for publicly taking the side of student protesters against authority figures in higher education. Critics of the government thus had the opportunity both to adopt Rimskii-Korsakov as a martyr for their cause and, by conflating the Musical Society's leadership with everything they detested about the government, rail against the status quo. They found in the composer's dismissal "a surrogate for broader debates over the relationship between educated society and the autocratic state." The Musical Society, though not an organ of government, stood out as something to which the intelligentsia could "transfer its anger."[210] One contributor to *Theatrical Russia* did this quite explicitly in a short satirical playlet entitled *At the Conservatory (A Bureaucracy in 1 Act)*. Presenting its day-to-day operations as a drama populated by administrators, it depicted the institution as a government organ, a soulless "Department of Music" in which the musician-professor is merely "a desk official." "We need attentive functionaries," its caricature of the Musical Society's Petersburg committee chairman P. N. Cheremisinov declaims, "not geniuses."[211]

To make politicizing the scandal even more convenient for radicals, a previously scheduled performance of Rimskii-Korsakov's short opera *Kashchei the Immortal* was due to take place in the hall of Komissarzhevskaia's Dramatic Theater only eight days after his dismissal. Some critics attempted to read the work as a political text. Its fairy-tale plot revolves around a sorcerer king who will enjoy immortality and eternal rule for as long as his daughter remains incapable of love. The king's machinations against the determined suitor of a foreign princess he holds captive backfire and instead cause his icy daughter to fall for the young man. Foiled in his attempt to seduce the captive princess, whom events reunite with her suitor, and seeing his daughter shed real tears over her unrequited love for the handsome hero, the king dies to a chorus of his people singing, "Go forth in freedom!"

Since the opera was composed around the turn of the century and had premiered at the Moscow industrialist and arts patron Savva Mamontov's private opera in 1902, it is imprecise to perceive it as a conscious metaphor for the Revolution of 1905. Nevertheless, a larger-than-expected crowd gathered and used the curtain calls to honor the composer as a political figure. Representatives of

---

210. Ibid., 23–25.
211. "Pek" [V. A. Ashkinazi], "V Konservatorii (Biurokratiia v 1-m deistvii)," *Teatral'naia Rossiia/Muzykal'nyi mir* 14 (April 2, 1905): 203–4.

various trade unions, professional groups, and other radicalized organizations spoke enthusiastically about Rimskii-Korsakov's artistic talent, its meanings for Russian culture, the importance it held for their ideals of liberty, and the folly of arts officialdom for having fired him. A Soviet theater historian called the demonstration "one of the brightest pages in the history of artistic intelligentsia's social movement in the years of the first Russian revolution."[212] When Rimskii-Korsakov came on st age for his bow, he was presented with seven wreaths, including two addressed "To a Fighter" and "To a Great Artist and Citizen."[213] He later remembered the evening as an "enormous political demonstration" that expressed "pent-up indignation against the general régime."[214] The police, concerned about the demonstration's character, ordered the closing of the theater before a projected second part of the program, which was to consist of concert pieces.[215] Governor General Trepov even ordered a temporary ban on Rimskii-Korsakov's music lest performances of it stimulate further political demonstrations.[216]

Regardless of the plaudits Rimskii-Korsakov received, he steadfastly refused to embrace the revolutionary cachet attributed to his actions and motivations. Those present at the *Kashchei the Immortal* performance probably considered it a gesture of modesty when he replied to the audience ovations with, "Thank you very much. Believe me, I did not deserve this," but the statement expressed what appears to have been running through his mind.[217] In his memoirs he described the performance-demonstration as an "exaggeration of my services and my quasi-extra courage." As for his general lionization by the Left, he "wanted only to see how soon it would end. My position was unbearable and absurd."[218] A week after the performance when Cheremisinov wrongly claimed in a press interview that Rimskii-Korsakov had "led the movement of students at the Conservatory who decided to strike" and observed that "such a point of view could be called political," the composer angrily refuted the suggestion that his actions had anything to do with either fomenting unrest or politics in general. Decrying Cheremisinov's statement as "an explicit public denunciation," he declared, "I find it beneath me to try to justify myself." The incident may have

212. Iankovskii, "Teatral'naia obshchestvennost'," 151.
213. Yastrebtsev, *Reminiscences*, 358.
214. Ibid., 357; Rimsky-Korsakov, *Musical Life*, 348.
215. Rimsky-Korsakov, *Musical Life*, 347.
216. Frame, *Imperial Theatres*, 125, quotes Trepov's order, which argued that "in consequence of the growing discontent in several strata of society with regard to the dismissal of N. A. Rimsky-Korsakov from the staff of professors of the St. Petersburg Conservatory, any public performance of his musical works may give cause for undesirable demonstrations."
217. Yastrebtsev, *Reminiscences*, 358.
218. Rimsky-Korsakov, *Musical Life*, 347–48.

frustrated a conciliatory offer to rehire the composer in early April, which he dismissed out of hand for the time being.[219]

Until his death in 1908, Rimskii-Korsakov stayed out of public life and even expressed regret for his passing involvement in it. He reflected on the peformance-demonstration of *Kashchei the Immortal* as a sensational event, "the like of which I never saw before or since." Nor had he particularly enjoyed the evening: "I left the theater with a headache. I confess that I would never attend such an event a second time."[220] Over a year later he regretted that "if only I could have foreseen the consequences of my letter to Bern[g]ard—how they would exaggerate its importance—I never would have written it."[221]

The brief ban on the composer's music died out in short order—yet another example of the gap between government aspirations to control cultural expression and the practical limitations they faced. Summer concerts regularly performed Rimskii-Korsakov's works, and neither the Imperial Theaters Directorate nor the responsible court officials paid much attention to the controversy.[222] A few months later Teliakovskii eagerly met him to discuss the Bol'shoi premiere of his opera *Lord Governor (Pan Voeveda)*, scheduled for that autumn.[223] Another of his operas, *The Tsar's Bride*, was revived at the Mariinskii in mid-September, less than three weeks into the new season. The curtain went up on a third work of his, *The Snow Maiden*, eleven times at the Mariinskii in 1905–6, making it the house's most frequently performed opera that year.[224] Yet another Rimskii-Korsakov opera, *Sadko*, was proposed for 1905–6 but postponed for technical reasons.[225] His thoroughly Wagnerian *The Tale of the Invisible City of Kitezh and Maiden Fevroniia*, a work in which Teliakovskii had expressed interest during *Lord Governor*'s run, premiered with much success in February 1907.[226] Rimskii-Korsakov's last opera, *The Golden Cockerel*, which depicts an ineffectual king who brings about his own destruction by provoking an Eastern land to war, eventually passed the censorship and was planned for a production on the imperial stage at the time of his death. The work's thinly veiled references to Nicholas II and his

219. Quoted in Yastrebtsev, *Reminiscences*, 361.
220. Ibid., 357.
221. Ibid., 390.
222. Rimsky-Korsakov, *Musical Life*, 348.
223. Teliakovskii, "Imperatorskie teatry," 328; *Ezhegodnik Imperatorskikh teatrov*: 16 (1905–6, chast' II): 89.
224. *Ezhegodnik Imperatorskikh teatrov*: 16 (1905–6, chast' II): 84–130. Its conductor Feliks Blumenfel'd was one of the other Conservatory composers who had resigned in solidarity with Rimskii-Korsakov.
225. N. A. Rimskii-Korsakov, *Letopis' moei muzykal'noi zhizni* (St. Petersburg: Glazunov, 1909), 359.
226. Yastrebtsev, *Reminiscences*, 403; Shkafer, *Sorok let*, 205. Shkafer, who directed the production, called it a "decisive success" and recalled that Rimskii-Korsakov was lavishly praised by Teliakovskii and other officials. See Rimsky-Korsakov, *Musical Life*, 350, on the early plans to stage it.

war with Japan thus proved too uncontroversial to be permanently proscribed. It premiered at Zimin's private opera in Moscow in September 1909.[227]

As did students in universities and most other institutions of higher education, aspiring musicians overwhelmingly favored the resumption of normal studies in the autumn of 1905.[228] Although they continued to meet to discuss the situation and demanded educational reforms along professional lines, their statements and goals remained muted in both v olume and political content, even during the October general strike.[229] The young Prokof'ev, who had shown no great interest in events earlier in the year, recalled that he "probably heard about strikes and demonstrations a few times, but was not aware of the true nature of things."[230]

Nevertheless, in November the Musical Society bowed to the prevailing mood and amended its charter to allow the institutions it managed to elect directors to three-year terms.[231] In practice it thus granted their faculties the same power that university professors had regained from the government's August 1905 decision to reinstate the election of rectors—a right established by the educational reforms of the 1860s but abrogated in the University Charter of 1884.[232] Also like university professors, who were government employees, conservatory faculty members received the right to state pensions in 1905.[233]

Rimskii-Korsakov, his colleagues who had resigned in solidarity at the time of his dismissal, and the students expelled for creating the disturbances in March all returned to Petersburg Conservatory shortly thereafter. From then on students had a greater say in administrative decisions. On December 5 Glazunov, one of those who had resigned, was elected director in a near-unanimous vote.[234] Cheremisinov, who had publicly accused Rimskii-Korsakov of having led the student unrest earlier in the year, in turn resigned from the Musical Society's leadership, as did another member who had voted to dismiss the composer.[235]

---

227. Yastrebtsev, *Reminiscences,* 420, 442–43. The composer complained about some c ensorship deletions from the work but observed that the lines he thought would be most offensive were still left in. It is perhaps telling tha t Rimskii-Korsakov chose an episode in foreign policy, rather than domestic affairs, to satirize the regime, if that was his main intention.

228. For a description of the general attitude of students at this time, see Kassow, *Students, Professors, and the State,* 248.

229. *Teatr i iskusstvo* 40 (October 2, 1905): 631, reports such a meeting.

230. Prokof'ev, *Avtobiografiia,* 183.

231. Sargeant, "Middle-Class Culture," 240–44.

232. Ascher, *Russia in Disarray,* 197–98, discusses the restoration of this right.

233. Sargeant, "New Class," 47.

234. Petrovskaia, *Muzykal'noe obrazovanie,* 121. In Yastrebtsev, *Reminiscences,* 377, Rimskii-Korsakov pithily observed that there was "only one negative vote, obviously [Glazunov's] own."

235. According to Yastrebtsev, *Reminiscences,* 377, they were subsequently elected h onorary members.

Although the Society continued to administer the conservatories and its other schools and programs, the major effect of the Revolution of 1905 was to elevate the professional role of its faculty musicians, who when all was said and done achieved the same status as their university colleagues. Indeed, rather than defend its independence, some voices in Russian cultural life argued that music education was such a "serious affair" that it was "high time the government took it into its hands."[236]

The Musical Society's administrative changes heralded unprecedented expansion. Between 1906 and 1914 it opened new conservatories in Khar'kov, Saratov, and Kiev, raising the total number from two to five. In the same short period it added seven new provincial music schools and eight less-formal music courses to those it already operated, a rate of almost one per year in each category.[237] Enrollment showed no signs of slowing. When Saratov Conservatory opened in September 1912, it immediately had one thousand students ready to begin their studies.[238]

Regardless of the Society's liberalization and expansion, Rimskii-Korsakov—the reluctant hero of the radical intelligentsia—was less than pleased with the results of the reform. After watching Petersburg Conservatory's greater autonomy come into practice in the last years of his life, he found the students "too immature for real freedom" and charged that "they've turned the Conservatory into a saloon. How disgusting!"[239]

If Russia's institutions of arts education—like its theaters—failed to embrace an active political role in late imperial times, much of the reason lay in the attitudes of the students whom they were training and the intensifying professional ethos that governed their atmospheres. They appear to have shared what Samuel Kassow has described as "an ideology of student professionalism" characterizing academia in the last dozen years of the imperial era.[240] Many of the aspiring artists studying in these institutions became the actors, dancers, and musicians who populated the Empire's cultural life, the colleagues of stage performers already active in it. Like the institutions with which they worked and interacted, and like any other set of urban residents, performers were also confronted by disruption and uncertainty. The next two chapters will explore how they responded to and were impacted by the politics of late tsarist Russia.

236. "O Russkom Muzykal'nym Obshchestve," *Teatr i iskusstvo* 23 (June 8, 1914): 498.
237. Sargeant, "New Class," 45n.
238. "Khronika," *Teatr i iskusstvo* 33 (August 12, 1912): 627.
239. Yastrebtsev, *Reminiscences*, 380.
240. Kassow, *Students, Professors, and the State*, 399.

3

"POLITICS ARE DEATH":
IMPERIAL THEATER PERFORMERS

In early 1901 Konstantin Stanislavskii took the financially strapped Moscow Art Theater on its first tour to St. Petersburg in the hope that the capital's avid theatergoers would fill its coffers.[1] The highlight of the tour, the Art Theater production of Ibsen's *An Enemy of the People*, featured Stanislavskii himself in the leading role of Stockmann, a principled doctor who reports the truth about his spa town's contaminated waters even though it means its economic ruin and his family's ostracism from the community.

The play's first performance on March 4 was inauspiciously timed. Earlier that day a troop of Cossacks had violently dispersed a student demonstration in front of Kazan' Cathedral, less than a mile away on the city's central avenue, Nevskii Prospekt. By evening word of the incident had spread, and many students who had been there were in Stanislavskii's audience. When he uttered the line "one should never wear a new coat when he goes out to fight for freedom and truth," he recalled, "the hall rose with such a crash of applause that the action had to be stopped. A few people leapt from their seats and threw themselves over the footlights to shake my hand." In the actor-director's opinion they were "searching thirstily for a hero."[2]

Stanislavskii had not anticipated that his lines would provoke this response. As he later confessed in a passage omitted from English editions of his memoirs: "We the performers of the play and its roles, standing up on the stage, were

---

1. K. S. Stanislavskii, *Moia zhizn' v iskusstve* (Moscow: Iskusstvo, 1983), 244.
2. Ibid., 257.

Fig. 7 "One should never wear a new coat when he goes out to fight for freedom and truth." A caricature of Konstantin Stanislavskii as Stockmann in Ibsen's *An Enemy of the People*. From Konstantin Stanislavskii, *Moia zhizn' v iskusstve* (Moscow: Iskusstvo, 1983).

not thinking about politics. On the contrary, the demonstrations caused by the performance appeared to us unexpectedly. For us Stockmann was neither a political man nor a protest orator, but merely an idealistic, honest, and just person, a friend of his homeland and people, such as every truthful and honest citizen of a country should be."[3]

Stanislavskii's ingenuousness about the relationship between culture and power was not unique. Most of Russia's theatrical community spent the last decades of the tsarist era in precisely the same frame of mind. As this chapter and the next will demonstrate, the overwhelming majority saw political events as obstacles

3. Ibid., 257.

to their work, hindrances to their careers, and unfortunate disturbances that they hoped would pass.

Nowhere was this truer than in the Imperial Theaters. Their performers had "made it" in every sense. Imperial stage artists were Russia's highest paid, most famous, most pampered, and most steadily employed performers. Their audiences, though far from uniformly elite in social composition (as we shall see in Chapter 5), were nevertheless the country's most exclusive and prestigious. Imperial performers were lavished and publicized with honorific recognition from the government and called upon to favor its ceremonial functions. The titles "Honored Artist of the Imperial Theaters" (for drama and ballet), "Ballerina" (for ballet), and "Soloist of His Majesty" (for opera and ballet) were crafted for the most distinguished of them, as was a series of decorations.[4] The titles or more general designation "Artist of the Imperial Theaters" appeared proudly on their calling cards. The great bass Fedor Shaliapin recalled that identifying himself in this way "was very flattering to me."[5] Exceptional service was rewarded with membership in the prestigious Orders of St. Anne and St. Stanislav, also bestowed on distinguished civil servants and business and professional leaders.[6] From 1839 accomplished performers were entitled to classification as hereditary honored citizens (*potomstvennye pochetnye grazhdan'e*), a privileged stratum of urban dwellers.[7] Male performers were nominally exempt from military service. After performing for a requisite period of time, most artists could look forward to generous state pensions.[8] The Imperial Theaters Directorate maintained an entire photography department to create, advertise, and popularize images of its stars. Until 1907 state carriages transported them between their homes and the theaters, and many abused this privilege to enjoy free

---

4. Murray Frame, *The St. Petersburg Imperial Theatres: Stage and State in Revolutionary Russia, 1900–1920* (Greensboro, N.C.: McFarland, 2000), 33. "Khronika," *Teatr i iskusstvo* 2 (January 12, 1897): 30, records the awarding of a series of medals to performers who had appeared at Nicholas II's coronation celebrations the previous year. "Khronika," *Teatr i iskusstvo* 6 (February 9, 1897) reports, for example, Mariia Savina's promotion to Soloist of His Majesty.

5. Fedor Shaliapin, "Stranitsy iz moei zhizni," in F. I. Shaliapin, *Povesti o zhizni* (Moscow: Iskusstvo, 1960), 108.

6. "Khronika," *Teatr i iskusstvo* 17 (April 24, 1905): 264, for example, notes that the veteran dancer Feliks Kshesinskii (Matil'da Ksheshinskaia's father) was awarded the Order of St. Anne, second class. According to Seymour Becker, *Nobility and Privilege in Late Imperial Russia* (DeKalb: Northern Illinois University Press, 1985), 91, the first degree of these orders, which conferred hereditary nobility, was rarely granted to artists.

7. Marc Slonim, *Russian Theater: From the Empire to the Soviets* (Cleveland: World Publishing, 1961), 48.

8. Marius Petipa, "Dnevniki 1903–1905 godov," in Petipa, *Materialy. Vospominaniia. Stat'i* (Leningrad: Iskusstvo, 1971), 68, thought his nine-thousand-ruble-a-year pension "wonderful" and "marvelous" and did not know how he was going to spend it all.

local transportation.⁹ Especially accomplished artists had the privilege of periodic benefit performances, which gave them a substantial cut—often more than half—of the evening's box office receipts. When the legendary ballet master Marius Petipa retired from active service in February 1903, he received 3,884 rubles out of the 7,045 his retirement benefit had realized.¹⁰ The popular actress Vera Komissarzhevskaia exclaimed "I can die now!" after devoted admirers carried her home from one of her benefits before she left the imperial drama troupe in 1902.¹¹

Despite the trend toward greater professionalization, well-connected artists used or abused their talents and popularity to exercise informal authority in the Imperial Theaters and win other favors. The dancer Nikolai Legat warmly wrote of Tsar Nicholas II: "I received many presents from him, and I knew I could always count on his gracious patronage if I got into difficulties." After Legat tore a tendon during a performance, Prince Sergei Volkonskii, Director of the Imperial Theaters from 1899 to 1901, sent his personal Swedish masseur to care for him.¹² As we saw in Chapter 1, the ballerina Matil'da Kshesinskaia, Nicholas II's mistress when he was heir to the throne, more than once appealed to him and other members of the imperial family to alter the ballet's repertoire to her own liking and effectively caused Volkonskii's resignation. Volkonskii's successor, Vladimir Teliakovskii, referred to the influential veteran actress Mariia Savina as "the other Director" and his "colleague in power," complaining that when she made a decision about a performance, "the director only signed off— and his signature was a pure formality, hardly even necessary."¹³ Savina's power was so great that she refused to participate in an artist repertoire council—established by the Directorate in 1903 to broaden the artists' administrative input— because it threatened to limit her private influence.¹⁴ In the words of the Aleksandrinskii Theater's artistic director Petr Gnedich, who spent several years dealing with her, Savina "always had ways to get what she wanted."¹⁵ As Julie

---

9. V. A. Teliakovskii, "Imperatorskie teatry i 1905 god," in V. A. Teliakovskii, *Vospominaniia* (Leningrad: Iskusstvo, 1965), 340; *Teatr i iskusstvo* 32 (August 6, 1906): 477. The abuse was long tolerated; the carriage department was abolished in 1907 only because of budget constraints.

10. Petipa, "Dnevniki," 71–72. Petipa remained titular First Ballet Master until his death in 1910. Collective artistic bodies, including the theaters' orchestras and choruses, usually received an annual benefit.

11. N. L. Tiraspol'skaia, *Iz proshlogo russkoi stseny* (Moscow: VTO, 1950), 124.

12. Nicolas Legat, *Ballet Russe: Memoirs of Nicolas Legat*, trans. Sir Paul Dukes (London: Methuen, 1939), 37–39.

13. Teliakovskii, *Vospominaniia*, 98–103; M. G. Svetaeva, *Mariia Gavrilovna Savina* (Moscow: Iskusstvo, 1988), 266.

14. Teliakovskii, "Imperatorskie teatry," 299.

15. P. P. Gnedich, *Kniga zhizni: Vospominaniia, 1855–1918* (Moscow: Agraf, 2000), 275–76, 299–300.

Fig. 8 Imperial Russia's highest-paid artist: Fedor Shaliapin in one of his signature roles, Modest Musorgskii's Boris Godunov. From *Bol'shoi teatr* SSSR (Moscow: Gosudarstvennyi akademicheskii Bol'shoi teatr SSSR, 1976).

Buckler has illustrated in reference to opera, the power of stage celebrity loomed every bit as strongly in Imperial Russia as it did in Europe and America.[16]

Beyond their fame many imperial stage artists did well financially, even in the early phases of their careers. Just one year after the young soprano Mariia Kuznetsova-Benua entered the Mariinskii Theater's opera troupe in 1904, she received a contract worth six thousand rubles per annum, nearly twenty times the average yearly income of a skilled industrial worker and only slightly less than that of a ministerial department director.[17] Experienced artists earned more, often over ten thousand rubles. Four days after the Bloody Sunday massacre of demonstrating workers disrupted his performance, the great (in girth as well as accomplishment) comic actor Konstantin Varlamov wrote a friend that he was "living as loud and large as usual. I earned 15 thousand last year, spent it all, and worked up another 4 thousand in debt."[18] When the twenty-nine-year-old Shaliapin renegotiated his contract in 1902, only six years after his debut on the imperial operatic stage, he topped Russia's theatrical salary scale with a sensational 36,800 rubles a year for five years. His next renegotiation raised that amount to 50,000. It reached 60,000 in 1912 and peaked at a projected 80,000 for 1917–18.[19] Savina once asked the Imperial Theaters Directorate for an extra 15,000 rubles to pay her debts, even though she had just married the wealthy theater enthusiast and vice president of the Russian Theatrical Society Anatolii Molchanov and was thought (at least in Russia) to be "'the richest actress in the world.'"[20]

Older artists often kept their positions and salaries even when their stage appearances were rare. In the 1904–5 season three actresses and two actors on

---

16. Julie A. Buckler, *The Literary Lorgnette: Attending Opera in Imperial Russia* (Stanford: Stanford University Press, 2000), 84–94.

17. "Khronika," *Teatr i iskusstvo* 33 (August 14, 1905): 522. Gerald D. Surh, *1905 in St. Petersburg: Labor, Society, and Revolution* (Stanford: Stanford University Press, 1989), 23–25, cites a calculation that the average Petersburg worker made 314 rubles a year in 1900. Industrial wages were probably not much higher five years later. Hans Rogger, *Russia in the Age of Modernisation and Revolution, 1881–1917* (New York: Longman, 1983), 45, lists the average department director's annual salary as seven thousand rubles.

18. Quoted in S. Kara, *Varlamov* (Leningrad: Iskusstvo, 1969), 155.

19. V. A. Teliakovskii, *Dnevniki direktora Imperatorskikh teatrov, 1901–1903: Sankt-Peterburg* (Moscow: Artist. Rezhisser. Teatr., 2002), 257; Teliakovskii, "Moi sosluzhivets Shaliapin," in V. A. Teliakovskii, *Vospominaniia*, 373–74; "Khronika," *Teatr i iskusstvo* 1 (January 6, 1913): 3 and 4 (January 22, 1917): 66. The 1917–18 figure was obviously not realized because revolution intervened.

20. Svetaeva, *Savina*, 247. "Khronika," *Teatr i iskusstvo* 27 (July 6, 1914): 579, reports her signing a contract for twenty-four thousand rubles in 1914–15. It is unclear whether her request about the debt was granted, but that she would even ask is nevertheless significant. Molchanov was the Theatrical Society's Vice President and in practice its Chief Executive in the place of the honorary president, Grand Duke Sergei Mikhailovich.

the Aleksandrinskii Theater's active roster did not appear on stage at all.[21] The aged mezzo-soprano Mariia Kamenskaia, a Soloist of His Majesty who debuted in 1874, made just six appearances in the 1905–6 season, five of them in the tiny role of Tat'iana's nurse in Chaikovskii's *Eugene Onegin*.[22] Although standard contracts prohibited imperial stage artists from performing elsewhere during the regular season, they were free to accept lucrative private engagements at other times. In practice, however, some took on extra work during the season with impunity, relying on their personal connections, strong personalities, fame, and lack of administrative oversight to avoid the consequences.[23]

Performers of the Imperial Theaters resisted and often resented the political maelstrom swirling around them at the end of the tsarist era. Nothing that would attack the source of their prestige, frighten their audiences into staying home, disrupt their work on stage, and fray their nerves off of it was likely to attract their sympathies. On the contrary, virtually all accounts—regardless of when or where they were published—stress their indifference or aversion to politicizing themselves and their careers. The dancer Tamara Karsavina sympathetically remembered her fellow performers as "so conservative at heart, so indifferent to politics, usually so loyal to the Court of which we were in a way a modest part."[24] Referring to the tsar, Legat proudly wrote that "we were his servants, his employees, as an aesthetic institution we were his property."[25] Recalling the opera troupe's first official gathering after the summer break in 1905, the rehearsal accompanist and conductor Daniil Pokhitonov was "astonished by the degree to which artists of the Imperial Theaters lived outside of politics: would that someone had mentioned the events of the first Russian Revolution, then happening in the country.... No, only embraces, kisses, and the hum of voices."[26] Shaliapin confessed that he did not understand how the revolutionary song "The Little Cudgel" ("Dubinushka") could be considered controversial, despite its lines: "The time has arrived, and the people have risen / They straighten their twisted backs / And hurling their eternal yoke from off their shoulders / They raise up their cudgels against their foes." "What nonsense!" he retorted to a concerned

---

21. "Spisok artistov Imperatorskikh teatrov," *Ezhegodnik Imperatorskikh teatrov* 15 (1904–5, chast' II): 1–8. Two of the actresses had been at the Aleksandrinskii since the 1840s.
22. "Spisok artistov Imperatorskikh teatrov," *Ezhegodnik Imperatorskikh teatrov* 16 (1905–6, chast' II): 9; Teliakovskii, "Imperatorskie teatry," 344.
23. Teliakovskii, *Vospominaniia*, 53–57.
24. Tamara Karsavina, *Theatre Street: The Reminiscences of Tamara Karsavina* (New York: Dutton, 1931), 190.
25. Legat, *Ballet Russe*, 33.
26. D. I. Pokhitonov, *Iz proshlogo russkoi opery* (Leningrad: VTO, 1949), 71.

friend who tried to explain that the police would come if he sang it at a concert for workers.[27] Whether Shaliapin grasped the song's potential political significance when he performed it for the patrons of Moscow's elite Metropol' restaurant and again on the stage of the Bol'shoi Theater is uncertain yet doubtful.[28]

Practical responses to the revolutionary events of 1905—Imperial Russia's most politicized moment before 1917—reflected these anecdotes. Bloody Sunday itself was largely an abstraction in the minds of most imperial stage artists. No one had expected the massacre, but the capital's performing arts community appeared especially aloof. The artist Aleksandr Benua, then a young set designer at the Mariinskii, remembered his ignorance of the demonstration: "No one in our circle knew exactly what the workers wanted," he confessed.[29] The ballet debutante Elena Smirnova recorded the day's events in her diary as "a rising of unskilled workers [*chernorabochikh*]."[30] Kshesinskaia sensed something was wrong on January 9 but still went to a dinner party lest her hostess, the dancer Vera Trefilova, be distraught should no other guests arrive.[31] Petipa, formally retired but still a presence in ballet life, recorded the day with the simple diary entry: "The workers don't want to work. A very difficult moment for Russia. Lord, save the Emperor."[32]

Surprise and confusion presented these artists with significant challenges as they tried to follow normal routines and maintain scheduled engagements. Although the Mariinskii's benefit for the dancer Ol'ga Preobrazhenskaia and the Mikhailovskii Theater's double bill of French comedies went undisturbed, the Aleksandrinskii's evening performance of Ostrovskii's *A Passionate Heart*, as we saw in the last chapter, fell victim to the passions of the day. Varlamov was struck dumb when interrupted by an agitator who appealed to his sense of moral indignation.[33] The scandal terrified all the artists on stage. The aged actress Nadezhda

27. Shaliapin, "Stranitsy," 200–203.
28. Maksim Gor'kii depicted the Metropol' performance in his novel *Zhizn' Klima Samgina* (*The Life of Klim Samgin*). For the Bol'shoi rendition and its controversy, see Teliakovskii, "Imperatorskie teatry," 292–96. Shaliapin sent Teliakovskii the lyrics a few days later but did not indicate why. Shaliapin to Teliakovskii, December 4/17, 1905, in F. I. Shaliapin, *Literaturnoe nasledstvo. Pis'ma. Stat'i. Vyskazyvaniia. Vospominaniia o F. I. Shaliapine*. 2 vols. (Moscow: Iskusstvo, 1960), 1:404. Boris Gasparov, *Five Operas and a Symphony: Word and Music in Russian Culture* (New Haven: Yale University Press, 2005), 190–91, suggests that the song's undulating rhythm and other lyrics had a psychosexual meaning that may have appealed to the early twentieth-century avant-garde.
29. Aleksandr Benua, *Moi vospominaniia*, 2 vols. (Moscow: Zakharov, 2003), 2:1433.
30. Quoted in Fedor Lopukhov, *Shest'desiat let v balete: Vospominaniia i zapiski baletmeistera* (Moscow: Iskusstvo, 1966), 121n.
31. Matil'da Kshesinskaia, *Vospominaniia* (Moscow: Olimp, 2002), 137.
32. Petipa, "Dnevniki," 105.
33. Kara, *Varlamov*, 154.

Vasil'eva, who had started her stage career in ballet thirty-five years before, "fell into a faint," while the young Liubov' Shuvalova "went into hysterics."[34]

Like all the capital's residents and their unfortunate colleagues at the Aleksandrinskii, imperial stage artists drifted through the next few weeks in a state of confusion and doubt. Benua recalled that "rumors were going around that there could be a general strike at any moment. Revolution could already be felt in the air in connection with the difficult position on the Japanese front and the staggering impression everyone had of the bloodletting."[35] "We were afraid all day," Smirnova lamented to her diary, "I don't think I'll go to the theater."[36] Varlamov confided to the same friend to whom he had written about "living large" that "we don't know how and when it will end."[37]

Were imperial stage performers in any way sympathetic to political action and rhetoric in these dangerous times? Only a few moved out of their general passivity to react in at least a personal way to tragedy. The dancers Anna Pavlova and Iosif Kshesinskii (Matil'da's elder brother) criticized the government's handling of the Bloody Sunday demonstration during a ballet rehearsal.[38] The dramatic soprano Valentina Kuza briefly left the imperial opera troupe after being sentenced to two weeks of house arrest for showing "impertinence" to soldiers, possibly after remarking that they had "fired on their brothers."[39] Nikolai Khodotov, an actor in the drama troupe noted for his radical sympathies, claimed that he opened his apartment as a first-aid center for victims of the day's violence.[40] Preobrazhenskaia requested permission to take up a charitable collection for the families of dead workers.[41] Many artists of the Imperial Theaters, including "even the most cautious of them," contributed to charitable funds to help the injured and families of the dead and imprisoned.[42]

---

34. Gnedich, *Kniga zhizni*, 283.
35. Benua, *Vospominaniia*, 2:1441.
36. Quoted in Lopukhov, *Shest'desiat let*, 121–22n.
37. Quoted in Kara, *Varlamov*, 155.
38. Lopukhov, *Shest'desiat let*, 122; and Gosudarstvennyi Tsentral'nyi Teatral'nyi Muzei imeni A. A. Bakhrushina (GTSTMB), f. 280/16, l. 5141.
39. "Khronika," *Teatr i iskusstvo* 4 (January 23, 1905): 50, and 5 (January 30, 1905): 65; Pokhitonov, *Iz proshlogo*, 41; Lopukhov, *Shest'desiat let*, 122; and M. Iankovskii, "Teatral'naia obshchestvennost' Peterburga v 1905–1907 gg.," in *Pervaia russkaia revoliutsiia i teatr: Stat'i i materialy*, ed. A. Ia. Al'tshuller (Moscow: Iskusstvo, 1956), 143–44. Kuza's first name was Evfrosiniia, but she went by Valentina, after the heroine of Meyerbeer's opera *Les Huguenots*.
40. N. N. Khodotov, *Blizkoe—dalekoe* (Leningrad: Iskusstvo, 1962), 174.
41. Lopukhov, *Shest'desiat let*, 122. The benefit never materialized.
42. A. Ia. Al'tshuller, "Aleksandrinskii teatr v 1895–1907 godakh," in *Russkaia khudozhestvennaia kul'tura kontsa XIX–nachala XX veka (1895–1907)*, 4 vols. (Moscow: Nauka, 1968–81), 1:151.

Despite these incidents and gestures, most artists wanted to stay out of the way. A number of them took that sentiment to its literal extreme by fleeing either from at least the turbulent cities or Russia altogether. This was an especially feasible option for wealthier performers, who were more likely to have both the means to travel and the influence not to lose their careers as a result. Benua, expecting an imminent general strike and "all kinds of other complications and disorders," left with his family and spent more than two years abroad, mostly in Paris, living off his inheritance. He remembered the trip as "a kind of flight."[43] Kshesinskaia, who had formally retired from the ballet in the 1903–4 season with the understanding that she could return for guest appearances in "her" roles, canceled scheduled performances after receiving threatening letters.[44] After a tour in Poland, she decamped to Cannes until March 1906, sending to Russia for her servants and poodle when she realized how long her stay abroad would be.[45] Among other adventures she claimed to have spotted the refugee Father Georgii Gapon, organizer of the January 9 workers' march, playing roulette at the same wheel as the liberal Grand Duke Nikolai Mikhailovich, who cracked wise at the disgraced priest's expense.[46] Ironically, she thus found herself closer to political personalities than she had probably expected. Shaliapin, on tour in Western Europe in the spring of 1905, sought engagement after engagement to delay going home. He found Monte Carlo an opportune place to explore his "pain for the dear motherland, which is now truly in a tragic situation," and told Teliakovskii revealingly but probably not insincerely that he "would be very happy to hear how you are doing and that you are surviving."[47] Moving on from the Riviera, he wrote the Director that despite all the bad news from home, "it is good to be abroad, wonderful to be in Paris."[48] Upon his return he bought the painter and set designer Konstantin Korovin's estate so that he could spend what he hoped would be a quiet summer there.[49]

Members of the French drama troupe had the additional temptation of returning to their native land and its thriving theater scene. Faced with the alternative of Petersburg's unpredictability and intermittent turmoil, which "strongly repelled" them, several left. Suzanne Munte, Henri Rousselle, and Elise Baletta,

43. Benua, *Vospominaniia*, 2:1441–78.
44. Petipa, "Dnevniki," 106.
45. Kshesinskaia, *Vospominaniia*, 137–39.
46. Ibid., 140–41.
47. Shaliapin to Teliakovskii, February 25/March 10, 1905, in Shaliapin, *Literaturnoe nasledstvo*, 1:401.
48. Shaliapin to Teliakovskii, [March 29/]April 11, 1905, in ibid., 1:402.
49. Teliakovskii, "Shaliapin," 381.

all leading lights of the troupe, went home before the start of the next season.[50] Lawsuits filed by the Directorate did not stop them.[51]

In another scheduling mishap the renowned Wagnerian soprano Feliia Litvin, who had family connections to France and frequently traveled abroad for guest engagements, could not return because of railroad strikes and requested release from her contract.[52] Several of her performances had to be canceled. That same month, Kshesinskaia's continuing absence forced the Directorate to give one of "her" roles, Lise in *La fille mal gardée,* to her rival, Preobrazhenskaia. This enraged the prima ballerina *assoluta* at a distance, and her fans sabotaged the performance by sneaking live chickens on the stage, causing a great scandal.[53] The incident may have been a factor in Kshesinskaia's return to the capital in March, but neither her presence in Petersburg nor the influence of her partisans at Court could reverse the redistribution of her signature roles. Her informal power was at an end.

For many other artists of the Imperial Theaters, professional life in times of political crisis reflected more normality than controversy. Relations between the artists and their administrators remained rosy, even at the most contentious political moments. A run of Gnedich's play *Winter,* which opened in February 1905, was one of the hits of the season. The evening after its premiere, a large group of Aleksandrinskii actors fêted their administrator in style at the fashionable restaurant Cuba to celebrate his twenty-five years in artistic life. They partied until four in the morning over a dinner of lamb chops and filet of sole, washed down with Pommery sec.[54] When a group of seventy artists touring the Caucasus went unpaid by local impresarios, they revealed their priorities by petitioning the region's viceroy to intercede on their behalf.[55]

Despite the flight phenomenon the Revolution of 1905 saw relatively few artists leave service before retirement—an action that might have signaled displeasure with the tsarist government or protested against prevailing political and social conditions. The painter Valentin Serov, after all, resigned from the Imperial Academy of Fine Arts just after Bloody Sunday because its president,

---

50. Teliakovskii, "Imperatorskie teatry," 310–11.
51. "Khronika," *Teatr i iskusstvo* 3 (January 15, 1906): 34. The damages sought in the lawsuits were denominated in francs.
52. "Khronika," *Teatr i iskusstvo* 3 (January 15, 1906): 34. Litvin's stepfather was French. When her mother married him, she later wrote, "I became a Frenchwoman." Feliia Litvin, *Moia zhizn' i moe iskusstvo* (Moscow: Muzyka, 1967), 29.
53. Teliakovskii, "Imperatorskie teatry," 285–89. The ballet was and remains known in Russia as *A Useless Precaution* (*Tshchetnaia predostorozhnost'*).
54. Gnedich, *Kniga zhizni,* 285.
55. "Khronika," *Teatr i iskusstvo* 29 (July 17, 1905): 456.

Grand Duke Vladimir Aleksandrovich, had been the titular commander of the troops who fired on the demonstration. But Serov had no counterparts in the Imperial Theaters or, for that matter, among his fellow Academy painters. The performing artist rosters published in the Imperial Theaters' *Yearbook* reported that in the turbulent period between September 2, 1904, and September 1, 1906, only nineteen principal artists out of the approximately four hundred employed in the Petersburg opera, ballet, and drama troupes departed.[56] At less than 5 percent over two years, this was hardly a large or abnormal attrition rate, and there is no indication that any of the artists departed for political reasons. Eight of them left after at least twenty years of service, the usual length of time before retirement with pension.[57] Nor was there any shortage of aspiring performers—in September 1905 the theatrical press reported that seventy-three youths had auditioned for the Imperial Drama School's incoming class.[58] That same month Shaliapin importuned Teliakovskii to accept an eager young female acquaintance into the Bol'shoi Theater's opera troupe.[59] A May 1906 report on the Mariinskii's annual opera auditions noted "just as many seekers of the government pie [*okhotnikov do kazennego piroga*] as ever."[60]

The participation of imperial stage artists in public life beyond the proscenium had limits. Of 104 performers active in the Aleksandrinskii's 1904–5 season, only twelve signed a February 1905 petition entitled "The Needs of the Russian Theater (A Declaration of Stage Performers)," coincidentally published on the same day of Gnedich's fête, in which members of the performing arts community called for greater protection of theater's existing legal rights, the abolition of the stricter censorship of popular theaters, and stronger measures to protect their own economic interests.[61] Few took part in chaotic summer 1905 meetings

---

56. "Spisok artistov Imperatorskikh teatrov," *Ezhegodnik Imperatorskikh teatrov* 15 (1904–5, chast' II): 1–8; and 16 (1905–6, chast' II): 1–9. Imperial Theater contracts always began or ended on September 1.

57. Ibid., 1–9. Two of these, Alfred Bekefi and Aleksandr Shiriaev, received farewell benefit performances and thus definitely retired. Romola Nijinsky, *Nijinsky* (New York: Simon and Schuster, 1934), 46, recalls the twenty-year tenure.

58. "Khronika," *Teatr i iskusstvo* 37 (September 11, 1905): 585. Training at the Drama School entitled graduates to preferential treatment in hiring for the imperial stage. Nineteen were accepted. In 1912, a roughly comparable twenty-three students were accepted. "Khronika," *Teatr i iskusstvo* 38 (September 16, 1912): 715.

59. Shaliapin to Teliakovskii, September 1/14, 1905, in F. I. Shaliapin, *Literaturnoe nasledstvo*, 1:403.

60. "V. K." [V. Karatygin], "Muzykal'naia khronika Peterburga," *Zolotoe runo* 5 (May 1906): 68. The identification of employment at the Mariinskii as a "government pie" only highlights the largesse that many imperial stage performers received.

61. "Nuzhdy russkogo teatra (Zapiska stsenicheskikh deiatelei)," *Slovo*, February 12, 1905; *Teatr i iskusstvo* 7 (February 13, 1905): 98–99. "Spisok artistov Imperatorskikh teatrov," *Ezhegodnik Imperatorskikh teatrov* 15 (1904–5, chast' II): 1–8, lists a total of 112 artists in the dramatic troupe. Of these,

at which, as we will see in greater detail in the next chapter, Petersburg theatrical intellectuals, influenced by the formation of all sorts of professional unions over the course of the revolutionary year, attempted to create the Union of Stage Performers (*Soiuz stsenicheskikh deiatelei*). The Directorate's rare public comments about its artists said almost nothing about their political lives or convictions. One typical news item reported that its officials were thinking about prohibiting performers from going to casinos, for "the artists, spending whole nights in an a tmosphere of excitement and tobacco smoke, were far from the peak of their calling."[62] Management's sensitivities were hard to describe as political.

Intense periods of unrest continued to provoke disquiet. In the days leading up to the national general strike that convulsed the Empire in October 1905, Shaliapin requested leave to go south for a few w eeks because radical groups had threatened to kill him if he performed.[63] The theatrical press noted "an epidemic of falling" around the same time, when such ordinarily poised actresses as Savina and Vera Michurina-Samoilova demonstrated what spectators took to be obvious signs of stress by becoming distracted and stumbling on stage.[64] Karsavina described the whole autumn of 1905 as "a nightmare."[65]

Unlike the period immediately after Bloody Sunday, the charged atmosphere of the general strike prompted at least the notion that artists of the Imperial Theaters would become involved in bu rning political questions. The press addressed the issue head-on in early October when *Theatrical Russia*'s editor I. O. Abel'son asked Savina whether the performing ar ts community should take part in the Liberation Movement. The actress replied: "In my opinion theater must not and cannot if it wants to remain itself. The serious dramatic stage must not be an ar ena for topical reviews, if that were even possible. . . . To demand from it intensiveness, a hastened tempo in th e teaching of freedom loving ideas, is to deprive it of its stability, its durability. . . . As is well known, art does not like trouble."[66]

---

six had left service effective September 1, 1904, and were included only as a forma lity, as was one actress who transferred to the Moscow dramatic troupe effective the same date. One actor was on leave that season. Two of those who had left service effective September 1, 1904, Aleksandr Kashirin and Pavel Samoilov, signed the petition.

62. "Khronika," *Teatr i iskusstvo* 33 (August 14, 1905): 522.
63. Teliakovskii, "Imperatorskie teatry," 235.
64. "Khronika," *Teatr i iskusstvo* 40 (October 2, 1905): 632.
65. Karsavina, *Theatre Street*, 190.
66. I. Osipov [I. O. Abel'son], "Beseda s M. G. Savinoi," *Teatral'naia Rossiia* 41 (October 8, 1905): 1218–19.

The activity of Savina's colleagues during the "October Days" reveals that she spoke for almost all of them. Although some scholars have described events in the Imperial Theaters during the general strike as overtly political, a closer inspection reveals that this was far from the case.[67] The renowned Soviet choreographer Fedor Lopukhov, who debuted as a dancer that season, later admonished his readers: "There is no need to exaggerate the ballet troupe's role in the revolutionary movement. . . . We took no direct part in it; of those people I knew, none moved in underground circles."[68]

Unrest among the artists derived from the sense that increasing civil strife jeopardized their work and physical safety. The first stirrings of this mood appeared among Lopukhov's colleagues in the ballet troupe on October 13—perhaps not coincidentally, the same day on which the city's Soviet of Workers' Deputies first met—when some of them refused to rehearse "in view of the extremely uneasy conditions in the city." Many of the dancers' families grew concerned for their well-being and wanted them to stay home. Teliakovskii thought it prudent to pay the artists small bonuses for continuing to work in the parlous conditions.[69] The next day a delegation of ballet performers asked Teliakovskii's permission to hold a general meeting for the troupe to discuss "questions about their needs." The Director declined to allow it but nevertheless permitted a meeting to elect ten delegates with whom he would meet.

When 183 members of the ballet troupe assembled on the morning of October 15, however, pandemonium reigned. For seven hours the cacophonous dancers held the meeting they were not supposed to have.[70] At times it showed slight hints of politicization, though nothing that could be described as coherent. The young dancer and budding choreographer Mikhail Fokin accused the stage director Nikolai Sergeev of spying for the Directorate, prompting the latter to leave in a huff. Iosif Kshesinskii spoke "fervently in favor of a strike." Teliakovskii cheekily referred to the young dancer Petr Mikhailov, elected to the delegation to be sent to the Directorate, as "the local ballet Robespierre." Some dancers criticized Teliakovskii and his administrative subordinates for being "wealthy" and looking upon their jobs as a means of social self-promotion.[71]

67. Orlando Figes, *A People's Tragedy: The Russian Revolution, 1891–1924* (New York: Penguin, 1997), 189; Frame, *Imperial Theatres*, 129; Richard Stites, *Serfdom, Society, and the Arts in Imperial Russia: The Pleasure and the Power* (New Haven: Yale University Press, 2005), 517, concludes that "political revolution in the theater," albeit "pallid," skipped the earlier period he writes about to arrive in 1905.
68. Lopukhov, *Shest'desiat let*, 120.
69. Teliakovskii, "Imperatorskie teatry," 237.
70. Ibid., 238–41.
71. Ibid., 241–43; Lopukhov, *Shest'desiat let*, 122–23.

In the end the meeting's resolutions turned out to be apolitical. Lopukhov recalled that the participants talked "less about political questions, and more about creative and economic ones."[72] First, the artists demanded Petipa's return to active service, as well as the return of the dancer Alfred Bekefi and the recently retired Second Ballet Master, Aleksandr Shiriaev. That Petipa had turned eighty-seven in 1905 did not appear to make an impression. Neither had the much celebrated retirements of the other two artists—Bekefi's January 1906 benefit performance celebrated both his farewell and his fortieth year of service, while Shiriaev was one of the retirees who left after twenty years on stage.[73] Second, the ballet troupe wanted an extra day off each week. Their most significant demand was to share authority over day-to-day administration—decisions about the distribution of roles, salaries and raises, and the selection of stage directors and their assistants—a process to be supervised by an elected "ballet bureau."[74] In other words they wanted the Directorate to expand and formalize the more casual power arrangements that leading ballet artists already enjoyed. Karsavina, elected to the bureau that day, later claimed that its purpose was merely "to raise the standard of art to its adequate height," a task that she as a leading young dancer felt qualified to accomplish.[75]

The meeting's elected delegation presented a more formal statement of its resolutions to the Directorate on the morning of Sunday, October 16, the day of the next scheduled ballet performance. It warned against official reprisals: "If there are any repressive actions against our resolutions by the administration, we have in mind the ability and the means to fight."[76] Teliakovskii spent the day at the tsar's residence at Peterhof and could not receive the delegation. Frustrated and hoping to make their point, several of the meeting's leaders, including Fokin, Mikhailov, Karsavina, and Pavlova, attempted to prevent the ballet from taking part in the matinee performance of Chaikovskii's opera *The Queen of Spades*. Significantly, the core agitators were all young dancers with hurtling reputations and vaulting egos to match—precisely the type who expected to benefit the most from sharing the Directorate's powers. Running

---

72. Lopukhov, *Shest'desiat let*, 123.
73. Lynn Garafola, *Diaghilev's Ballets Russes* (New York: Oxford University Press, 1989), 4, claims that they were "forced out of the company for political reasons," but there is no evidence of this, nor, in light of the advanced ages and long and honored service of all involved, should there be.
74. Teliakovskii, "Imperatorskie teatry," 242; and Lopukhov, *Shest'desiat let*, 123. Saturdays were already holidays in all the Imperial Theaters. According to Teliakovskii, *Dnevniki . . . 1901–1903*, 266, Shiriaev had only reluctantly accepted his 1902 promotion to Second Ballet Master and may well have been glad to retire in 1905, after twenty years of service.
75. Karsavina, *Theatre Street*, 190–91.
76. Teliakovskii, "Imperatorskie teatry," 248.

Fig. 9 Artistic radicals? Anna Pavlova and Mikhail Fokin on the stage of the Mariinskii Theater in the early 1900s. During the Revolution of 1905, they hoped to gain more self-direction for the ballet troupe but quickly declared their loyalty to the Imperial Theaters Directorate when put to the test. Pavlova became a Ballerina at the end of the 1905–6 season. Fokin became First Ballet Master in 1910. Neither remained in Russia after 1917. From Marius Petipa, *Materialy. Vospominaniia. Stat'i* (Leningrad: Iskusstvo, 1971).

around to the dressing rooms of the ballet artists performing that day, most of whom had no interest in striking, they did their best to upset their colleagues and, in some cases, physically prevented them from making their entrances. "Laughter, threats, tears, and curses were audible" backstage, and the chorus was forced—not without success—to improvise the opera's second act pastorale.[77]

Contrary to what the ballet "strikers" may have expected, few of their colleagues were impressed by their antics. Even as they tried to obstruct the ballet's participation in *The Queen of Spades*, some of the opera singers cursed and dumped water on them. The laconic Smirnova observed that "the stupid ballet dancers are rebelling."[78] The Directorate tackled the "strike" with an equally farcical "lockout" by canceling the evening ballet performance and substituting youths from the Ballet School for the regular artists in *Eugene Onegin*'s dances the next evening. As we have seen, while the young students gladly made their debuts—showing exactly how little they cared about the agitators' presumed goals—about 150 rank-and-file ballet artists, the "great majority" in Karsavina's account, sent Teliakovskii a signed statement denouncing the strikers and their provocative actions.[79] As it turned out, no signatures had been attached to either the October 15 meeting's original resolutions or the accompanying threat to strike; they had merely been delivered with a separate sheet of paper listing the signatures of the 183 dancers who had attended at the meeting—not an endorsement of the core agitators' resolutions or subsequent threat to "fight" reprisals.[80]

The denouement of the ballet strike thus saw the Mariinskii's dancers overwhelmingly affirm their loyalty to the Directorate. Even some of the leading strikers joined in. When Teliakovskii met with the assembled troupe on October 20, Fokin and Pavlova, who helped wreak havoc during *The Queen of Spades* four days earlier, denied that there had ever been a strike or even a plan to strike. Instead they insisted that the ballet artists had failed to appear only because certain officials and stage directors misunderstood the situation and overreacted.[81] Another alleged strike supporter, the young dancer Sergei Legat, committed suicide on the night of October 18. Although Karsavina and Iosif Kshesinskii later claimed that he did so from a profound sense of guilt about "betraying" his fellow activists, there is no evidence that this was the case.[82] An inquest found that the capital's fevered conditions, intensified by the turbulent last days

---

77. Ibid., 248–49; Karsavina, *Theatre Street*, 194.
78. Quoted in Lopukhov, *Shest'desiat let*, 122n.
79. Teliakovskii, "Imperatorskie teatry," 252–53; Karsavina, *Theatre Street*, 195.
80. Teliakovskii, "Imperatorskie teatry," 248.
81. Ibid., 261.
82. Karsavina, *Theatre Street*, 195; I. F. Kshesinskii, "1905 god i balet," *Zhizn' i iskusstvo* 51 (1925): 7.

of the general strike and the disarray surrounding the promulgation of the October Manifesto, exacerbated Legat's already delicate emotional state. Several witnesses who saw him before his death described his "extremely nervous condition" and claimed that "he walked around in the crowds all day, yelled in the streets, and generally left the impression of an abnormal and overwrought person."[83] His brother and fellow dancer, Nikolai Legat, who found his body, and friend Romola Nizhinskaia blamed the suicide on Sergei's "mad and hopeless infatuation" and "desperately unhappy love affair" with Mariia Petipa, daughter of the retired Ballet Master, who was eighteen years Legat's senior.[84] Petipa herself confirmed that Sergei was overwrought and that she locked him in his room, where he slashed his throat. Her father's diary reported the same story.[85] The most recent Russian reference work on twentieth-century ballet confirms this explanation of Legat's suicide.[86] At least one other member of the ballet troupe, Vasilii Kiselev, also lost his sanity at about the same time and required psychiatric care.[87] Pavlova canceled a subsequent appearance because she was "very distressed" and incapable of performing. Nevertheless, in early November a new ballet delegation visited Teliakovskii's apartment to thank him for settling the dispute and assure him that the rank and file "were not in solidarity with the minority's opinion."[88] Petipa described the prospective "ballet bureau" to his diary as "an idiotic enterprise."[89]

The quick resolution of this "tempest in a teapot," as Lopukhov later described the "strike" episode, returned relative calm to the ballet troupe.[90] Karsavina recalled that "life resumed its normal course, and our inglorious épopée finished with a fatherly admonition."[91] There was some residual tension, however. At another "ballet bureau" meeting in late November, Kshesinksii intervened in an argument between Pavlova and the dancer Aleksandr Monakhov. When Monakhov accused the small minority who favored the strike of doing so only to serve their own interests, Kshesinskii struck him in the face.[92] In a curious inversion of the incident's political implications—and another demonstration of

83. Teliakovskii, "Imperatorskie teatry," 257.
84. Legat, *Ballet Russe*, 45; Nijinsky, *Nijinsky*, 42.
85. Petipa, "Dnevniki," 110.
86. Arsen Degen and Igor Stupnikov, eds., *Peterburgskii balet, 1903–2003: Spravochnoe izdanie* (St. Petersburg: Baltiskii dom, 2003), 166.
87. Teliakovskii, "Imperatorskie teatry," 257; Lopukhov, *Shest'desiat let*, 124.
88. Teliakovskii, "Imperatorskie teatry," 264, 275. Pavlova's absence caused the performance's cancellation.
89. Petipa, "Dnevniki," 110–12. He was, however, flattered by the demand for his return.
90. Lopukhov, *Shest'desiat let*, 122.
91. Karsavina, *Theatre Street*, 201.
92. Teliakovskii, "Imperatorskie teatry," 278.

the lack of political awareness among Russian performers—Monakhov called his rebellious assailant a "Black Hundred," a member of the reactionary groups that professed staunch and often violent support for the autocracy.[93] The next day a group of angry dancers declared to Teliakovskii that they would no longer work with Kshesinskii. Although the Director was apprehensive of Kshesinskaia's reaction—"the Japanese did not fight with such persistence and strength," he wrote of the once formidable ballerina—her brother was fired on the spot.[94] When Kshesinskaia organized a benefit performance for the St. Petersburg Society for the Care of the Mentally Ill in April 1906 and invited her brother to make a "comeback" in it, fifty-five other dancers refused to appear. The would-be striker thus himself became the victim of a strike.[95]

The imperial opera troupes, as well as Moscow's ballet, endured comparatively less trouble. Delegations from their orchestras and choruses approached Teliakovskii in mid-October 1905, but they only requested "in a reserved and extremely correct manner" the same salary and pension increases they had always requested and would continue to request until 1917.[96] None of these approaches had subversive overtones; they merely resembled the usual economic demands often made by unappreciated supporting musicians in any society's arts institutions. If politics intruded on their activities at all, it involved gestures of loyalty. During a scene change in a January 1911 performance of Musorgskii's *Boris Godunov* with Nicholas II and other members of the Imperial Family in attendance, the Mariinskii chorus "protested" by raising the curtain, falling to its knees, and singing "God Save the Tsar" six times rather than the usual three repetitions demanded by Court ritual.[97] On the eve of the February Revolution of 1917, it protested again by refusing to sing in full voice during a performance of Rimskii-Korsakov's *May Night*.[98]

The opera soloists made no recorded effort to confront the Directorate or otherwise secure greater power. Nevertheless, the general tension affected their work. During a performance of Wagner's *Lohengrin* on October 18, 1905—the evening after the promulgation of the October Manifesto, which guaranteed civil liberties and an elected legislature—an altercation in the audience became violent. Within a matter of minutes most of the orchestra and all but one soloist fled the theater, as did most of the audience. The brave young soprano

---

93. *Peterburgskaia gazeta*, November 27, 1905. Kshesinskii returned the insult—and confused the political meanings even more—by calling Monakhov a Black Hundred.
94. Teliakovskii, "Imperatorskie teatry," 279–82.
95. Ibid., 289–92.
96. Ibid., 263, 266–72.
97. Shaliapin, "Maska i dusha," in Shaliapin, *Povesti o zhizni*, 321–24.
98. "K intsidentu s khorom v Mariinskom teatre," *Teatr i iskusstvo* 9 (February 26, 1917): 171.

Kuznetsova-Benua was pregnant and only in her second season with the opera troupe, but she courageously returned to the stage to inform the few lingering spectators that the performance could not continue because "many of the artists have become nauseous." To try to end the evening on a positive note, she and a few chorus members, accompanied by the dozen or so musicians who remained in the orchestra pit, led the remaining audience in singing "God Save the Tsar" the ritual three times.[99]

The turbulence of the Revolution of 1905 found its way into the imperial drama troupe, although only one of its members, Nikolai Khodotov, "the great ham actor" as Vladimir Nabokov called him, approached radicalism.[100] His fellow performer Iakov Maliutin remembered him only as "a secret friend of revolutionaries."[101] But Khodotov hid fugitives from the law—subversive students, worker activists, illegal Jewish residents of the capital, deputies of the St. Petersburg Soviet, and even entire revolutionary meetings—in his apartment.[102] As we learned in the last chapter, he defied police bans to sing revolutionary ditties, read subversive poetry at popular concerts, and labored to make their performance legal.[103] Savina, who worked with him frequently on the Aleksandrinskii stage, teased him about being the "Socialist of His Majesty," a play on the "Soloist" title given to accomplished opera and ballet artists.[104]

Khodotov's "extreme" (his word) views distinguished him sharply from his fellow artists.[105] A recent institutional history of St. Petersburg's Imperial Theaters rightly describes his politics as "exceptional" for that milieu.[106] As did virtually every other observer, Khodotov noted the absence of political or social conviction from the imperial drama troupe. "The Revolution of 1905," he recalled with disappointment about that turbulent period, "caught employees of the stage unprepared. Even the most cultured and free thinking among them followed the course of events with astonishment and tried their best to stand on the sidelines of the revolutionary movement." Despite his zeal, Khodotov

---

99. V. B. Bertenson, *Za 30 let (listki iz vospominanii)* (St. Petersburg: n.p., 1914), 276–79; Teliakovskii, "Imperatorskie teatry," 255–56; Gnedich, *Kniga zhizni*, 289; "Uchastie Peterburgskikh teatrov v obshchei politicheskoi zabastovke," *Teatral'naia Rossiia* 44–45 (October 29, 1905): 1270.

100. Vladimir Nabokov, *Pnin* (New York: Vintage, 1989), 27.

101. Ia. O. Maliutin, *Aktery moego pokoleniia* (Leningrad: Iskusstvo, 1959), 257.

102. Ibid., 260; Khodotov, *Blizkoe—dalekoe*, 167, 173–74, 229–30; Iu. M. Iur'ev, *Zapiski*, 2 vols. (Leningrad: Iskusstvo, 1963), 2:85; and N. L. Tiraspol'skaia, *Zhizn' aktrisy* (Leningrad: Iskusstvo, 1962), 159.

103. Khodotov, *Blizkoe—dalekoe*, 161, 167–68, 173; Iur'ev, *Zapiski*, 2:85–86; Maliutin, *Aktery*, 260; and T. L. Shchepkina-Kupernik, *Teatr v moei zhizni* (Moscow: Iskusstvo, 1948), 159–60, 392.

104. Iur'ev, *Zapiski*, 2:86.

105. Khodotov, *Blizkoe—dalekoe*, 180.

106. Frame, *Imperial Theatres*, 134.

considered himself politically naïve and deferred to the tutelage of the radical geologist L. I. Lutugin, whom he credited with having "an enormous influence on my political views and convictions," and his brother, the painter V. I. Lutugin, in whom the actor found "a second father, a brother, and [perhaps more curiously] a nanny." The Lutugins introduced their pupil to leading political dissidents and played a major role in directing and supervising his subversive activities.[107]

Motivating his colleagues at the Aleksandrinskii to become more politically engaged frustrated the eager Khodotov. "The slogan 'art for its own sake,'" he lamented, "served as the main stimulus for professional unity, and it was unbelievably difficult to divert them from this path." His only option was to "agitate ideologically."[108] Few were willing to listen. Desperately wanting to accomplish something meaningful during the October Days, however, he tried to disrupt the Aleksandrinskii's operations. Although Teliakovskii never realized who was behind the delivery of an incendiary proclamation to the theater just before a performance of Ostrovskii's *The Heart Is Not a Stone*, Khodotov took full credit. Aimed at stoking his colleagues' social consciousness, it declared:

> Artist citizens! You are teachers of the people. You preach living words, the beginnings of true happiness, of freedom. You are obliged at this decisive moment to adhere to all courageous struggles for the freedom and happiness of Russia. Violence will take from you the ability to say what now must be said from the stage. There is a single, honest way for you to fulfill your duty to yourselves and the motherland: proudly keep your silence. Let those who see in your acting only a source of fun and comfort understand that the artist is before all else a citizen. Let your silence sound a loud call to the last decisive struggle for those who learn from you. Let the curtain go down! Let it go up only when free Russian citizens enjoy the right to greet you openly as free apostles of the free word, as comrades in the struggle for the people's freedom.[109]

This bold challenge did more to increase the actors' sense of confusion and danger than elevate their civic consciousness. The wholly unsympathetic Varlamov, once again slated to appear in an Ostrovskii play on a troubled day, tore

---

107. Khodotov, *Blizkoe—dalekoe*, 168.
108. Ibid., 179–80.
109. Ibid., 180; an abbreviated version appears in T eliakovskii, "Imperatorskie teatry," 239. "Uchastie Peterburgskikh teatrov," 1270, reported that a delegation of actors' representatives from the Suvorin Theater learned that the Aleksandrinskii's scheduled performance "would not take place because of the actions of one actor," presumably Khodotov.

up his copy in disgust.[110] Khodotov, seeing that his initial provocation had little effect, resorted to more forceful means. He told the famous Vladimir Davydov that if he appeared, "progressive Russia will never forgive you ... you are continuing to comfort the public at a time when innocent blood lies on the streets and the better people of Russia are fighting for the right to live in human conditions." This persuaded Davydov to cancel his appearance and ask Gnedich for a week of leave, explaining that "the difficult events of the last few days are reflected ever more heavily in the soul of every Russian. We actors are already nervous people by profession and, seeing the dear Motherland's horrors and woes, are making ourselves sick with nervousness. Dark thoughts do not give us the ability to carry out our tasks as we must.... In such conditions it is unthinkable to perform."[111] Getting to Varlamov was another matter. "I simply intimidated Varlamov." "Uncle Kostya!" he claimed to have threatened in pure bluff, "I know that if you even just appear on stage, a bomb will be thrown by workers of the Obukhov factory. Committees of the Putilov and Obukhov workers have decided to sacrifice you for the great revolutionary cause." Varlamov called in sick.[112]

In the absence of the two major leads, the Directorate decided to replace the play with the standby production, Ostrovskii's *The Forest*. But Khodotov so "electrified" its leading performers that they "could not be of any use."[113] Teliakovskii knew only that Pavel Lenskii (stage name of Prince Pavel Telepnev-Ovchina-Obolenskii), who was to play the lead character Neschastlivtsev ("Unhappy"), was so "sick with nerves... that letting him onto the stage would have been quite risky." The Director had to go in person to Anastasiia Nemirova-Ral'f's dressing room to comfort her after she "fell into hysterics." Neither performer recovered; the Aleksandrinskii went dark.[114]

Coercion worked in this difficult moment. The next day a group of about fifteen Aleksandrinskii actors requested that the theater close for a few days because "all the artists found themselves in such a nervous state that they positively could not perform." The Director told them to have a general meeting to discuss the matter. Its written report, signed by Savina and Davydov as "authorized agents of the troupe," made the same request, again citing the artists' inability to perform "in their current states of mind." Teliakovskii, the city police chief V. A. Dediulin, and the chief of the Imperial Cabinet Prince Nikolai Obolenskii

110. Kara, *Varlamov*, 161–62.
111. Davydov to Gnedich, October 14, 1905, SPb GTM, No. 1178.
112. Khodotov, *Blizkoe—dalekoe*, 82, 181. Khodotov liked this story so much he told it twice in his memoirs. There is no evidence to suggest that it was founded in fact.
113. Ibid., 181.
114. Teliakovskii, "Imperatorskie teatry," 240.

agreed, though the city's Governor General, Dmitrii Trepov, crudely told the Director, his old comrade from the Horse Guards regiment, to force the performers to appear at gunpoint.[115]

Reality circumvented Trepov's forceful suggestion. As the request to close fell on a Saturday (the Imperial Theaters remained dark on the Sabbath eve), no performance was scheduled. The Directorate, faced with the ballet's agitation the next afternoon (October 16) and an additional plea from the nervous dramatic performers, preemptively canceled the Aleksandrinskii's Sunday evening show.[116] Another performance of *The Forest* went forward without incident the following night. The next day, having learned of the October Manifesto's promulgation, an actors' meeting on the Aleksandrinskii stage called for Teliakovskii. When he arrived, he was greeted with "feelings of faithful subordination to the sovereign." The Director graciously responded that he was glad to receive such a declaration and reminded the artists that they could help improve the theater by taking more active part in the repertoire council he had created two years earlier. They had never managed to elect one on their own, and the Directorate had no choice but to appoint its members. Expressions of gratitude for his sensitivity were followed by hurrahs, handshakes, kisses, and the proposal that he be carried home on the shoulders of some of the sturdier actors. He declined the suggestion, observing that there were already enough demonstrations in the streets.[117]

A day later the troupe assembled and asked Gnedich to compose an address to the sovereign on its behalf:

> On October 17 the flowering of national art began by the will of your Imperial Majesty. Now the possibility to serve the stage freely and to carry the torch of good, beauty, and truth—which must be the guiding star in the development of humanity—has been given to us, free artists. With ecstasy we accept this news in the house of our August Master and we are ready, Lord, to serve great and beautiful dramatic art with renewed strength, giving to it all our knowledge, thought, and gifts.[118]

Afterward they sang "God Save the Tsar."[119] Infuriated radicals denounced the address as servile and called for a boycott of the Imperial Theaters—significantly

---

115. Ibid., 243–45.
116. Ibid., 249; Gnedich, *Kniga zhizni*, 288. The French Theater's performance was also canceled on October 16, though there was no sign of trouble there.
117. Teliakovskii, "Imperatorskie teatry," 254–55; *Peterburgskaia gazeta*, October 23, 1905.
118. Gnedich, *Kniga zhizni*, 289.
119. "Uchastie Peterburgskikh teatrov," 1270.

Fig. 10 A group of performers in the Aleksandrinskii Theater's drama troupe. *From left to right:* Petr Medvedev, Vladimir Davydov, Mariia Savina, Konstantin Varlamov, and Ekaterina Zhuleva. They were not disposed toward engaging in political life. Medvedev angrily declared it "dishonest" to seek autonomy for performers of the Imperial Theaters. Davydov and Varlamov had to be threatened before they would agree not to perform on stage. Savina publicly stated that the performing arts community "must not and cannot" take part in politics. From V. A. Teliakovskii, *Vospominaniia* (Leningrad: Iskusstvo, 1965).

targeting the performers rather than the institutions of what officially remained an autocratic government.[120] Khodotov found the address an expression of the troupe's "social bankruptcy."[121] One arts journalist angrily jeered at the "liveried state actors" for their absence from political life even as it reached a fevered pitch.[122]

Although Teliakvoskii reminded the troupe that it could elect the repertoire council in place since 1903, his gesture had little resonance. Several weeks after

---

120. Teliakovskii, "Imperatorskie teatry," 262–63; Richard G. Thorpe, "The Management of Culture in Revolutionary Russia: The Imperial Theaters and the State, 1897–1928" (Ph.D. diss., Princeton University, 1990), 40.
121. Khodotov, *Blizkoe—dalekoe*, 195.
122. "A." [E. A. Solov'ev], "Spasite teatr!" *Teatral'naia Rossiia*, 44–45 (October 29, 1905): 1265–66.

the promulgation of the October Manifesto, the press reported that no elections had taken place and suggested that "reactionaries" within the troupe had derailed the council for their own purposes.[123] Periodic meetings on the subject came to nothing, at least partly because the troupe's heavyweights continued to see it as a threat to their substantial informal power. The actor Grigorii Ge complained to Teliakovskii in late December that the meetings were drawing less than half the troupe and none of its stars.[124] Some artists outright opposed the idea. Savina, realizing what an elected council with real power could mean for her informal authority, refused to work with it unless she had the final word in its decisions.[125] When Khodotov delivered an impassioned speech in favor of the fullest and most active possible form autonomy, the veteran actor Petr Medvedev—a former impresario whose provincial troupes had introduced many stars of the imperial stage to their profession—exploded, "Get out of this theater! With such views it is dishonest to serve the one who feeds you and pays you!" Many of the other performers present applauded and cheered.[126] A New Years' editorial comment pronounced the council "stillborn."[127] "Routine reigns," wrote another disappointed proponent of autonomy.[128]

The troupe finally succeeded in electing a council in January 1906, but it merely chose the same people whom Teliakovskii had appointed in earlier years. Unsurprisingly, their recommendations for the repertoire just regurgitated many of the Directorate's traditional choices.[129] Khodotov believed that the council's chairman, the debonair Vasilii Dalmatov, opposed autonomy in principle and used his position to be "the first person to wreck it." At one meeting, Dalmatov admonished its proponents that "politics is not an actor's affair. His affair is to act well. . . . I have never been my own gendarme and do not recommend that you be."[130]

These attitudes persuaded the small number of activists to give up, and the elected repertoire council never amounted to much. According to the actor Iurii Iur'ev, the Aleksandrinskii troupe's "first definitive general meeting" only

---

123. *Peterburgskaia gazeta*, December 1, 1905.
124. Teliakovskii, "Imperatorskie teatry," 299. Ge claimed that a maximum of forty out of more than one hundred members of the troupe ever showed up.
125. Ibid., 299.
126. Khodotov, *Blizkoe—dalekoe*, 195. On Medvedev's career, see Murray Frame, *School for Citizens: Theatre and Civil Society in Imperial Russia* (New Haven: Yale University Press, 2006), 85–86.
127. "Khronika," *Teatr i iskusstvo* 1 (January 1, 1906): 2.
128. Nik[olai] Arbenin, "Ob avtonomii Imperatorskikh teatrov," *Teatr i iskusstvo*, 1 (January 1, 1906): 11.
129. Teliakovskii, "Imperatorskie teatry," 300; *Peterburgskaia gazeta*, January 6, 1906, editorialized that "the selection does not recommend the council's taste."
130. Khodotov, *Blizkoe—dalekoe*, 194–95.

occurred after the collapse of the monarchy in March 1917.[131] It still took the performers more than two months to create an autonomous council, a feat accomplished after the 1916–17 season had concluded. Even then its founding statute subordinated all its activities to Teliakovskii's replacement as head of the state theaters under the Provisional Government, Fedor Batiushkov.[132]

Although state drama troupes acquired the right to elect their artistic directors after the February Revolution, they merely voted to retain their standing tsarist-appointed chiefs. Evtikhii Karpov, a dramatist, theorist, and stage director, continued on at the Aleksandrinskii. He had first served as its chief director from 1896 to 1900 and returned to the post in 1916. Karpov's Moscow counterpart, the actor and dramatist Prince Aleksandr Iuzhin-Sumbatov, was also elected to keep his position. He had been appointed chief director of Moscow's Malyi Theater in 1909. To make the gesture toward autonomy even weaker, almost as soon as the ill-fated 1917–18 season began, the Aleksandrinskii's autonomous regime was reportedly failing as a consequence of disorganization and apathy on the part of the artists. Many appeared to think its main purpose was to allow them to work in other theaters during the season, something they were formally forbidden to do under the old regime. Within just a few weeks it ceased to function, and the frustrated Batiushkov threatened to eliminate autonomy in all the state theaters.[133]

As Murray Frame has suggested, the autonomy movement failed "not because of any repression on the part of the [Imperial Theaters] Directorate, but because the desire for it among the artists was not strong enough."[134] Teliakovskii's provision for an elected repertoire council in 1903 and subsequent reminder that the artists could do something practical with it suggest that he had encouraged steps toward a more participatory administration, perhaps one that could relieve the burdens of his job. Indeed, the greatest portent of state action against autonomy in pre-Soviet times came from the Provisional Government organ that replaced the Directorate with the intention of democratizing the state stage. Only the Bolshevik coup d'état of October 1917, which resulted in something altogether different, prevented Batiushkov from following through with his threat to end the autonomy newly enjoyed by the state theaters. Even when the prospect of greater authority was handed to imperial stage performers in times of unprecedented political upheaval, they showed little enthusiasm for it.

131. Iur'ev, *Zapiski*, 2:239.
132. Murray Frame, "Theatre and Revolution in 1917: The Case of the Petrograd State Theatres," *Revolutionary Russia* 12, no. 1 (1999): 88–89.
133. Ibid., 89–90; "Khronika," *Teatr i iskusstvo* 39 (September 24, 1917): 671 and 41 (October 8, 1917): 708.
134. Frame, *Imperial Theatres*, 132.

The long-term careers of Imperial Theater artists speak further to their absence from political life. Perhaps nothing could reveal this better than the professional trajectories of the small number of artists associated with disorders in the theaters or opposition politics in general. One might expect that the Directorate or higher organs of the tsarist government would have retaliated against them for engaging in subversive activities or politically motivated insubordination. Bronislava Nizhinskaia, the dancer Vatslav Nizhinskii's sister, made such an accusation in her memoirs.[135] It has been accepted uncritically even though Nizhinskaia was a fourteen-year-old student at the time of the 1905 ballet "strike" and could have had no firsthand knowledge of state decisions on arts personnel.[136]

A close examination indicates that there were virtually no official punishments for expressions of political dissent, which suggests that the government either did not take the performers' activities too seriously or turned a blind eye to them for aesthetic reasons. Kuza, whose January 1905 departure from the opera roster may have resulted from an altercation with soldiers, returned to the Mariinskii for thirty performances the following season and remained there until her premature death in 1910.[137] Whatever "impertinence" she may have shown failed to keep her well-regarded Aida and Brünnhilde from the public for long. Iosif Kshesinskii, the only artist of the Imperial Theaters ever dismissed in connection with political events, was fired only because he had assaulted another dancer. Nevertheless, in 1914 even he was readmitted to the ballet troupe.[138]

Kshesinskii's fellow agitators kept their hands to themselves and continued to appear in major roles. Many went on to dazzling careers. Pavlova—a leader of the strike movement, one of the dancers who disrupted the ballet's performances during it, and the alleged initiator of the argument that cost Kshesinskii his position—was still named a Ballerina at the end of the 1905–6 season.[139] She remained on the Mariinskii roster until 1910, when she took a leave of absence to begin an international career as an independent performer and occasional collaborator of Sergei Diaghilev's Ballets Russes. Thereafter, she returned to the imperial stage for guest performances. She even received government subsidies

---

135. Bronislava Nijinska, *Early Memoirs*, trans. Irina Nijinska and Jean Rawlinson (New York: Holt, Rinehart, and Winston, 1981), 155.

136. Garafola, *Ballets Russes*, 5, accepts it as proof of "repressive actions." Vatslav Nizhinskii was less than a year older and still attending the ballet school, so there was probably nothing he could have told his sister.

137. "Spisok artistov Imperatorskikh teatrov," *Ezhegodnik Imperatorskikh teatrov* 16 (1905–6, chast' II): 9.

138. Kshesinskaia, *Vospominaniia*, 141, claims that her influence got her brother back on the imperial stage, though she does not specify whether that was true in 1914 or only for the 1906 benefit she organized.

139. Keith Money, *Anna Pavlova: Her Life and Art* (New York: Knopf, 1982), 63.

for her international tours.¹⁴⁰ According to the dance critic Aleksandr Pleshcheev, the Directorate and the tsar himself hoped to have her back on a more permanent basis after her planned return to Russia in 1914. Only the outbreak of World War I prevented this by stranding her abroad.¹⁴¹ Her fellow strike supporter Karsavina, who remarked on the absence of retribution after the events of 1905, was elevated to Ballerina in 1909 and continued to dance at the Mariinskii until 1918, shortly before she fled Soviet Russia.¹⁴²

Fokin, another strike leader alleged to have taken part in disrupting *The Queen of Spades*, continued his dancing career and began to stage ballets as well. His productions of *Eunice* and *Chopiniana* (*Les Sylphides*) appeared on the Mariinskii stage in February 1907. After their success the Directorate commissioned a third ballet, *Le Pavillon d'Armide*, to be staged in full accordance with Fokin's innovations in dance.¹⁴³ The young choreographer was pleasantly surprised by the Directorate's enthusiasm and "enchanting attitude." As he later reminisced, "never, nowhere did I enjoy such luxury, such possibilities, as we were given under these state 'bureaucrats' . . . I felt full freedom of creation."¹⁴⁴

Although Fokin's productions for the Ballets Russes made him an international celebrity, he complemented that success at home with *The Egyptian Nights* (*Cléopâtre*), the sublime set piece *The Dying Swan* (a solo created for Pavlova), a revised version of *Chopiniana*, and the lusty ballet sequence in Wagner's *Tannhäuser*, among other productions that later graced foreign as well as Russian stages.¹⁴⁵ Rather than remember the choreographer's controversial past, Teliakovskii assiduously defended his protégé from the intrigues of resentful fellow artists, who regarded Fokin as an "incapable fantasist" and tried to shoot down his rising star.¹⁴⁶ In October 1910, the Director formally appointed him, at the youthful age of thirty, to replace the deceased Petipa as First Ballet Master. Just a month later Fokin had enough confidence to ask Teliakovskii to discipline more conventional dancers who refused to work in his productions, twenty-three of

---

140. Ibid., 77, observes that her 1908 tour through Europe was funded "principally by the Imperial Theatres."
141. A. A. Pleshcheev, *Pod seniiu kulis* . . . (Paris: VAL, 1936), 12.
142. Karsavina, *Theatre Street*, 202.
143. Mikhail Fokin, *Protiv techeniia: Vospominaniia baletmeistera. Stat'i, pis'ma* (Leningrad: Iskusstvo, 1962), 92–100.
144. Ibid., 101, 105.
145. In addition to the productions mentioned here, Fokin choreographed thirteen others for the Mariinskii between 1905 and 1910. For the complete list, see Garafola, *Ballets Russes*, 379–87.
146. Teliakovskii, *Vospominaniia*, 171, 457. On the eve of the first Mariinskii performance of Fokin's Polovtsian Dances in Borodin's *Prince Igor*, the director Nikolai Sergeev, the "spy" from the October 1905 meeting, stormed into Teliakovskii's office declaring, "This certainly isn't dance!"

which premiered at the Mariinskii between the time of his appointment and flight from Soviet Russia seven years later.[147]

Perhaps the most noteworthy dismissal of an imperial stage performer—Nizhinskii's forced resignation from the Mariinskii ballet troupe in January 1911—resulted not from political rebelliousness but from a prolonged and well-documented pattern of professional irresponsibility over his four seasons of employment.[148] His appearance on stage in a revealing pair of tights—revealing enough to scandalize an audience eager to see his first performance of the leading role in Adolphe Adam's *Giselle*—was merely the straw that broke the camel's back. According to his future wife, such a dismissal "had never before happened in the annals of the Imperial Ballet."[149] The incident caused him to leave the country to concentrate fully on his rising career with Diaghilev's enterprise. Neither the circumstances of Nizhinskii's departure from the Imperial Theaters nor their impact on his life provoked greater political awareness. "My business is to dance and to dance well," he told reporters after the incident, noting that the tights were part of the costume for his Paris performances.[150] He later wrote that "politics are death" and asserted in the wake of 1917: "I dislike revolutions. I find the victory achieved by this means a horror—I consider it the victory of godless animals. . . . I don't want to be mixed up in politics."[151]

Talent outweighed politics on the other stages, too. Khodotov, the Imperial Theaters' most outspoken radical and the agitator who caused the cancellation of Aleksandrinskii performances in October 1905, remained on stage with no consequences. Indeed, in the 1905–6 season only one other actor appeared more frequently than he.[152] Teliakovskii and Gnedich continued to solicit his views of young artists, and in August 1906 he received a one-thousand-ruble bonus to his contract.[153] Khodotov later recalled that Aleksandr Krupenskii, the Directorate's

---

147. Fokin to Teliakovskii, November 8, 1910, in Fokin, *Protiv techeniia*, 375–76. The list of productions for this period is in Garafola, *Ballets Russes*, 387–92. One of the works, for Glinka's opera *Ruslan and Liudmila,* premiered shortly after the Bolshevik coup, but it was planned earlier and was Fokin's last production in Russia.

148. RGIA, f. 497, d. 3, ed. khr. 2223, ll. 10–60, brims with reports of missed performances and rehearsals, chronic tardiness, increasingly suspicious requests for "vacations," and frequent administrative warnings and fines.

149. Nijinsky, *Nijinsky,* 119–22, recalls that members of the Imperial Family in attendance may have been offended, but Dowager Empress Mariia Fedorovna later denied it and asked a mutual friend to pass on her regrets about the matter to Nizhinskii.

150. Quoted in Peter Ostwald, *Nijinsky: A Leap into Madness* (New York: Lyle Stuart, 1991), 46.

151. Vaslav Nijinsky, *The Diary of Vaslav Nijinsky,* trans. Romola Nijinsky (London: Quartet Encounters, 1991), 26, 65, 86.

152. "Spisok artistov Imperatorskikh teatrov," *Ezhegodnik Imperatorskikh teatrov* 16 (1905–6, chast' II): 7. Khodotov appeared 101 times, 8 fewer than V. F. Mel'nikov.

153. Khodotov, *Blizkoe-dalekoe,* 195–96, 217; "Khronika," *Teatr i iskusstvo* 32 (August 6, 1906): 478.

office administrator for St. Petersburg from 1907 to 1914, "saved me many times from the denunciations of the Okhrana and the police."[154] In 1908 the Directorate allowed Khodotov to stage his own play, *At the Crossroads*, in which he hoped to expose "the sick condition of Russian society and cultural life during the period of reaction" and "stir up the wallowing intelligentsia to cry out the pain that mildewed reality had inflicted." His work failed to accomplish those potentially political goals, but the Directorate was not put out. A second play on the same theme, *Miss Vulgarity*, appeared at the Aleksandrinskii the following year, even if it did produce "booing à la P urishkevich" and struck the critics as a "vacuous performance" that was "strange to see . . . on the serious stage."[155]

The private-stage actor Aleksandr Mgebrov, a former artillery officer who deserted his unit to become a Socialist Revolutionary Party activist and was later arrested for participating in revolutionary circles, claimed that his radical politics kept him off the imperial stage when the Directorate showed an interest in recruiting him in 1913.[156] But there is neither any proof to substantiate his allegation nor any logical reason to expect there to be. Mgebrov's account only suspects that the police played some role in sabotaging his dreams. Since he also thought his father's connections would help get him into the drama troupe, the state theaters may simply not have appreciated his talent.[157]

Whatever the explanation for Mgrebov's difficulties, the Directorate had long recruited other talents known for oppositionist sympathies. The playwright Aleksandr Ostrovskii had been fired from the civil service (he was a trained lawyer) and placed under police observation in the last years of Nicholas I's reign. Yet his eventual fame as a playwright helped him overcome any stigma that may have been incurred. In 1884—shortly after he successfully lobbied for the abolition of the Imperial Theaters' performance monopoly—he was granted a state pension to reward his contributions to Russian drama.[158] Three years later Ivan Vsevolozhskii, then Director of the Imperial Theaters, appointed him head of the repertoire committee at Moscow's Malyi Theater. "I have never been so happy in my life!" the playwright wrote after receiving the news.[159]

---

154. Khodotov, *Blizkoe-dalekoe*, 214–15.
155. Ibid., 205, 215–16; S. Matov [S. S. Mamontov], "Gospozha poshlost'," *Rampa i zhizn'* 33 (November 15, 1909): 768. Both plays quickly vanished from the repertoire. As we saw in Chapter 2, Purishkevich was a driving force behind the cancellation of the Dramatic Theater production of Wilde's *Salome*.
156. A. A. Mgebrov, *Zhizn' v teatre*, 2 vols. (Leningrad: Academia, 1929), 1:150 and 2:7–9.
157. Mgebrov, *Zhizn' v teatre*, 1:150. That his connections failed further indicates the decline in official favoritism noted in Chapter 1.
158. Kate Sealey Rahman, "Aleksandr Ostrovsky—Dramatist and Director," in *A History of Russian Theatre*, ed. Robert Leach and Victor Borovsky (Cambridge: Cambridge University Press, 1999), 168.
159. Quoted ibid., 177. Ostrovskii died just five months later.

Boris Gorin-Goriainov, a private-stage actor who participated in violent attempts to disrupt performances in private and popular theaters during the 1905 general strike, joined the Aleksandrinskii's roster with no problems six years later. He found Teliakovskii "obliging and friendly" during the contract negotiations.[160] Ekaterina Korchagina-Aleksandrovskaia, a radical actress who began in private theaters and went on to be elected to the Supreme Soviet in 1936, became a member of the Aleksandrinskii's prerevolutionary "old guard."[161] Karpov, the artistic director confirmed in his post by that theater's troupe in May 1917, had held his tsarist-era administrative appointments there despite his arrest for illegal involvement in the Populist movement of the 1870s and the several years of prison and exile that followed. His continuing agitation did not interfere with his tenure in the Aleksandrinskii's top post in the 1890s or his return to it in 1916. Nor did it stop the government from appointing him to its censorship review commission, which met over the course of 1905 and reached a consensus favoring the abolition of preliminary censorship for most publications as well as a reform of theatrical censorship.[162] The Malyi chief director Iuzhin-Sumbatov held his post from 1909 despite his outspoken membership in the liberal Constitutional Democratic Party and formal regulations prohibiting state officials from belonging to political parties in general. Batiushkov's liberal political affiliations, which helped position him to take over from Teliakovskii after the February Revolution, had not interfered with his appointment as head of Aleksandrinskii's literary committee in 1900. From these cases it is clear that personal political convictions played little role in state arts employment decisions, even in a nominally autocratic state.

Likewise, the director Vsevolod Meierkhol'd's radical views and associations did not stop Teliakovskii from rushing to hire him after Vera Komissarzhevskaia fired the director, whose innovations (see Chapter 6) had been disastrous for her private theater. His first production was Knut Hamsun's politically radical *At the Gates of the Kingdom*. It was so bad that the press called it "a real 'scarecrow.'"[163] Both Savina, who found it "noxious," and the male lead asked to be taken out of the rest of its run.[164] Even the artistically and ideologically sympathetic Khodotov found it "very bad" and recalled that "neither the acting nor the production was understood by the press or the public."[165] But despite the

160. B. A. Gorin-Goriainov, *Aktery: Iz vospominaniia* (Moscow: Iskusstvo, 1947), 121–23.
161. Slonim, *Russian Theater*, 225.
162. Laurence Senelick, ed., *National Theatre in Northern and Eastern Europe, 1746–1900* (Cambridge: Cambridge University Press, 1991), 410n; Al'tshuller, "Aleksandrinskii teatr," 134.
163. *Peterburgskaia gazeta*, October 1, 1908.
164. Teliakovskii, *Vospominaniia*, 170–71.
165. Khodotov, *Blizkoe—dalekoe*, 217.

director's personal views, the play's overtly political content, and the production's failure, Teliakovskii gave Meierkhol'd a whole year to produce *Tristan and Isolde* at the Mariinskii—one of the most important operatic premieres in Russian theatrical history and a production that has influenced the staging of Wagner in Russia ever since.[166] The director staged sixteen additional productions in the Imperial Theaters before 1917.

Fedor Shaliapin, who sang "The Little Cudgel" at popular concerts and on the Bol'shoi stage just before the December 1905 uprising in Moscow, went unpunished. Although the Minister of the Imperial Court, Baron Frederiks, wanted to fire him after the Bol'shoi incident, Teliakovskii persuaded the minister not to punish his friend, Russia's highest paid artist, arguing: "The revolutionary party would be very happy to have a leading artist and singer in its ranks . . . he is a big name not only in Russia, but all over the world. We cannot forbid him to sing . . . he will electrify the public so much that the police will have to close one theater after another."[167] Shaliapin, the Director also noted, was scheduled for four upcoming benefit performances. A repressive political act was not worth losing the revenue he was sure to produce in those appearances and future stage productions. Teliakovskii even threatened to resign if Shaliapin were dismissed. Empress Aleksandra and the chief of the Imperial Cabinet, Prince Obolenskii, supported Teliakovskii's position and the bass went unpunished.[168] In May 1910 the tsar named him a Soloist of His Majesty.[169]

With the exception of the handful of artists mentioned in the few previous pages, the extent of imperial stage performers' detachment from politics emerges from clumsy attempts to impute prorevolutionary motives and sentiments to them, particularly those who remained in Russia after 1917 and were honored by the Soviet regime. A biographer of the tenor Ivan Ershov claimed that he "recognized the monstrous injustice of the social order" and learned "that politics and art are inseparable" because he appeared in productions of Beethoven's *Fidelio* and Rimskii-Korsakov's *The Snow Maiden*. Ershov's participation must have indicated his real feelings, we are told, for the first opera celebrates a sympathetic prisoner's liberation from tyranny while the second, the work of

---

166. Rosamund Bartlett, *Wagner and Russia* (Cambridge: Cambridge University Press, 1995), 96–99. Meierkhol'd's use of dance and rhythm were among his productions' more influential characteristics. Sergei Eisenshtein's 1940 Bol'shoi production of Wagner's *Die Walküre* employed them notably, as did Vladimir Mirzoev's historic production of the same composer's *Der Ring des Nibelungen*, which premiered at the Mariinskii in 2003.

167. Teliakovskii, "Imperatorskie teatry," 293–95.

168. Ibid., 294–96.

169. Teliakovskii to Shaliapin, May 2/15, 1910, in Shaliapin, *Literaturnoe nasledstvo*, 1:650.

a composer who had become politically controversial, depicts a weak tsar.[170] Since it was the Directorate that decided to stage those works and assigned the tenor suitable parts in them, however, this explanation is unsatisfactory. Teliakovskii had wanted to stage *Fidelio* at least from the time of his appointment as Director of the Imperial Theaters in 1901. *The Snow Maiden*'s eleven performances made it the Mariinskii's most frequently performed opera in the turbulent 1905–6 season.[171]

Some artists' participation in charitable concerts that benefited striking workers, political prisoners, and their suffering families caused them to be labeled revolutionary sympathizers. Khodotov naturally drew much praise from the new regime as a conscientious "actor-citizen."[172] A late Soviet era biographer of Savina argued that the actress's appearance in such concerts along with Khodotov and other radical performers bestowed revolutionary credentials despite her public statements about art not liking trouble and jealously guarded authority in the drama troupe.[173]

Whether these few instances of "political" charity should be applied generally to the whole of Russia's performing arts culture is a doubtful proposition. Charitable activities are not necessarily barometers of political conviction. Many political radicals, including Lenin, disapproved of them. It was always possible for compassionate people who had no political convictions, kept them private if they did, or even outright opposed political agendas to use their talents to help those in need. Lopukhov recalled that social convictions among the Mariinskii ballet troupe "sprouted from our own thoughts, outside of any organized rubric."[174] Actors of the French Theater, hardly revolutionary sympathizers given the number who left the country or failed to return in 1905, voluntarily took up a collection for unemployed provincial artists.[175] The patriotic soprano Kuznetsova-Benua, who sang "God Save the Tsar" to calm the Mariinskii after its October 1905 disturbance, appeared just a few weeks later as one of the best-received performers in a concert for the families of needy workers, an evening that ended with

---

170. Abram Gozenpud, *Ivan Ershov: Zhizn' i stsenicheskaia deiatel'nost': Issledovanie*, 2nd ed. (St. Petersburg: Kompozitor, 1999), 190.

171. Teliakovskii, *Dnevniki . . . 1901–1903*, 125, records the Director's early interest in Beethoven's opera. See "Sezon 1905–1906 gg.," *Ezhegodnik Imperatorskikh teatrov* 16 (1905–6, chast' II): 84–130, for that season's list of performances. Despite the politically charged atmosphere, the leading review of *Fidelio*, published in an uncensored journal, said nothing about the opera's political implications and focused exclusively on artistic details. M. Nesterov, "Mariinskii teatr," *Teatr i iskusstvo* 40 (October 2, 1905): 633–34.

172. Al'tshuller, "Aleksandrinskii teatr," 1:152.

173. Svetaeva, *Savina*, 243–45.

174. Lopukhov, *Shest'desiat let*, 121.

175. "Khronika," *Teatr i iskusstvo* 4 (January 22, 1906): 50. They raised 478 rubles and 500 francs.

young audience members singing the "Marseillaise" and "Varsovienne."[176] Even Khodotov, despite his well-known radical affiliations, greeted the outbreak of World War I with benefit performances of militantly nationalist speeches by the conservative nineteenth-century general Mikhail Skobelev.[177] Davydov ended a reading of patriotic poems in August 1914 by exclaiming his optimistic hope that Russian forces were about to take Königsberg.[178] Mariinskii singers voted unanimously to donate 2 percent of their salaries to soldiers' families in 1914, while all the imperial performing troupes supported military hospitals.[179]

In other cases artists might have had different motives for participating in such concerts. The Italian-born soprano Medeia Figner-Mei, a Soloist of His Majesty, nervously reported to Teliakovskii that a "delegation" sporting red armbands had visited her apartment and threatened her with bodily harm if she failed to appear in a concert for amnestied political prisoners and revolutionary students. After Frederiks heard this and similar stories involving other artists, he suspended the rule barring them from appearing in independent charitable concerts during the season. Although many did subsequently perform for charity, Teliakovskii claimed that more than a few took advantage of the Court Minister's good intentions to appear for profit in private engagements bogusly billed as philanthropic endeavors.[180] When a number of scheduled performers failed to appear at a Mariinskii benefit for unemployed actors, prompting the audience to demand a refund, the press criticized "the frivolous artists of the Imperial Theaters—such sated, satisfied, and blithe people."[181] Still, a large number of imperial stage performers seemed patriotic enough to secure the right to appear in charitable performances during the Russo-Japanese War and World War I. Teliakovskii, who remained suspicious of their true intentions, recalled that "this bacchanalia continued without any restraint right up to the revolution and finally turned into downright speculation."[182]

Shaliapin performed for charitable causes with goals so various that interpreting his activities as consistent political commitment, as Soviet scholars did, defies logic. His appearance in a 1903 concert performance of Arrigo Boito's *Mefistofele*, one of his signature roles, raised six thousand rubles for the right-wing Patriotic Society.[183] Two years later he wrote to the leftist organizers of a

176. V. V. Yastrebtsev, *Reminiscences of Rimsky-Korsakov*, trans. Florence Jonas (New York: Columbia University Press, 1985), 376.
177. Frame, *Imperial Theatres*, 139–40.
178. "Khronika," *Teatr i iskusstvo* 33 (August 17, 1914): 678.
179. "Khronika," *Teatr i iskusstvo* 34 (August 24, 1914): 692 and 39 (September 28, 1914): 771.
180. Teliakovskii, "Imperatorskie teatry," 331–33.
181. "Ot redaktsii," *Teatr i iskusstvo* 2 (January 8, 1906): 17.
182. Teliakovskii, *Vospominaniia*, 54.
183. Ibid.

Fig. 11 Fedor Shaliapin performing at a charitable concert early in his career. Shaliapin's charitable activities encompassed a wide range of causes and provoked much speculation—most of it inaccurate—about his political beliefs. From V. A. Teliakovskii, *Vospominaniia* (Leningrad: Iskusstvo, 1965).

very different concert that he was "happy with all my soul to go to the aid of the poor."[184] During World War I, he personally funded two military hospitals for wounded soldiers.[185]

Wavering from Right to Left to patriotic rendered Shaliapin's political convictions subject to gossip and inference rather than fact. One of the bass's biographers has noted that "many of his most innocent actions were transformed into political issues ... all sorts of groups and factions wanted to be able to claim Chaliapin as 'their man.'"[186] When he canceled a scheduled appearance in Glinka's monarchist opera *A Life for the Tsar* on the opening night of the Mariinskii's 1906–7 season, the Left applauded what it presumed to be an expression of his antigovernment sentiment. The extreme Right vilified him for

---

184. Shaliapin to Glazunov and Rimskii-Korsakov, November 23/December 6, 1905, in Shaliapin, *Literaturnoe nasledstvo*, 1:403.
185. Hubertus Jahn, *Patriotic Culture in Russia During World War I* (Cambridge: Cambridge University Press, 1995), 120.
186. Victor Borovsky, *Chaliapin: A Critical Biography* (New York: Knopf, 1988), 349.

being unpatriotic. In truth he had a toothache.[187] Conversely, when the bass remained kneeling on stage (as the direction required him to be) during the imperial opera chorus's "protest" performance of "God Save the Tsar" between scenes of *Boris Godunov* in January 1911, the same Left castigated him as a "lackey," "blackguard," "traitor," and "serf" who had indulged in an unacceptable demonstration of "loyal subjecthood" (*vernopodannichestvo*). But in fact he had no foreknowledge of the incident and failed to react because he was stupefied by the surprise. After he explained the whole story to Gor'kii, the exiled writer decided they could still be friends.[188] While on tour with the Ballets Russes in London two years later, he punched out a striking chorus member who tried to stop him from making a stage entrance. According to one version of the story, he only returned to perform with the incensed chorus after arming himself with two pistols, which he carried in his costume's pockets.[189] "Politics," Shaliapin later wrote, "have interested me less than anything. My whole nature revolts against them."[190]

Radical critics and some Soviet theater historians recognized that most imperial stage artists remained on the sidelines and condemned them for it. One angry journalist, evoking the Imperial Theaters' perceived social exclusivity, complained that "the actor is only a minstrel [*skomorokh*] for the bored nobility, the actress a gift to the noble harem."[191] An official history of the Aleksandrinskii published for the theater's centennial in 1932 recorded that "the theater reacted weakly to events."[192] The Soviet theater historian Anatolii Al'tshuller described its prerevolutionary performers as "politically passive, socially inert people" despite his individual praise for Khodotov.[193] Varlamov's biographer concluded that the fun-loving star was "a personality, but not a citizen and, what is more, not an actor-citizen."[194] One of Savina's biographers accused her of "political conservatism" and concluded that she resisted the Aleksandrinskii's autonomy movement and radicalism in general because she "could not

187. Teliakovskii, "Shaliapin," 383–88; Shaliapin to Stasov, September 23/October 6, 1906, *Literaturnoe nasledstvo*, 1:388.

188. Shaliapin, "Maska i dusha," 322–26; Teliakovskii, "Shaliapin," 393–406; see also Shaliapin and Gor'kii's correspondence in Shaliapin, *Literaturnoe nasledstvo*, 1:336–42. The publicist A. V. Amfiteatrov accused him of "loyal subjecthood."

189. Borovsky, *Chaliapin*, 40–41.

190. Feodor Chaliapin, *Man and Mask: Forty Years in the Life of a Singer*, trans. Phyllis Mégroz (New York: Knopf, 1932), 175.

191. "I. K." [I. M. Knorozovskii], "Kul'turnoe prosvetlenie teatra," *Teatral'naia Rossiia* 42–43 (October 22, 1905): 1242.

192. Petr Kogan, "Teatr v epokhu reaktsii," in *Sto let: Aleksandrinskii teatr—teatr gosdramy, 1832–1932. Sbornik stat'ei*, ed. Ia. O. Boiarskii (Leningrad: Direktsiia Leningradskikh gosudarstvennykh teatrov, 1932), 294.

193. Al'tshuller, "Aleksandrinskii teatr," 151.

194. Kara, *Varlamov*, 155.

step over new historical thresholds."¹⁹⁵ Ershov's biographer concluded that the tenor, "thinking that art should preserve its 'purity,' avoided politics.... Theater was for him a di stinct means of escape from everyday life, a romantic transformation of reality."¹⁹⁶

Imperial stage artists reacted to political turbulence with a mixture of confusion, fear, flight, nervousness, nausea, aloofness, and, even if some did feel personal compassion for the suffering and took modest measures to help, a general desire to avoid disorder. Even at the most difficult moments, they hardly "walked off their jobs" in protest.¹⁹⁷ It was dramatically far from the case that they "joined the revolutionary movement."¹⁹⁸ Instead they wanted to continue to enjoy their prosperous lives and stable careers untouched by politics and unthreatened by civic unrest. In the most tempestuous moments many lost or were deprived of their ability to perform on stage—the defining feature of their livelihood and professional identity. One, Sergei Legat, probably committed suicide as a result of revolutionary turmoil. That almost all of his colleagues should have disliked radicalism should be no surprise.

The Soviet film star Ivan Perestiani, who began his acting career in the troupe of Iavorskaia's New Theater, recalled that "the bureaucratic performers of the Imperial Theaters remained completely indifferent."¹⁹⁹ Although this chapter has suggested some nuance, the actor's comment invites an inquiry into a broader range of performers in Russian theatrical life, those who populated the Empire's diverse scene of private and popular theaters of which Perestiani was a part. It is to this subject that we now turn.

195. I. I. Shneiderman, *Mariia Gavrilovna Savina, 1854–1915* (Leningrad: Iskusstvo, 1956), 286.
196. Gozenpud, *Ershov*, 270.
197. W. Bruce Lincoln, *Sunlight at Midnight: St. Petersburg and the Rise of Modern Russia* (New York: Basic, 2000), 192, wrongly makes this observation of "the entire corps de ballet of the Imperial Mariinskii Theater."
198. Frame, *Imperial Theatres*, 129. Figes, *People's Tragedy*, 189, included "actors of the Imperial Theatre in St Petersburg" among many groups involved in "a national strike against the autocracy."
199. I. N. Perestiani, *75 let zhizni v iskusstve* (Moscow: Iskusstvo, 1962), 194.

4

"OUR THEATER WILL NOT STRIKE!":
PRIVATE AND POPULAR THEATER PERFORMERS

While on tour in Geneva, the future Russian and Soviet film director Vladimir Gardin encountered the city's bustling community of exiled Russian radicals. One evening he happened upon Lenin delivering a speech exhorting his audience to revolution. The Bolshevik leader's rhetoric baffled the young actor. Approaching the speaker afterward, Gardin asked exactly what he had meant by "revolution." Lenin smiled condescendingly and said, "You just heard my speech. Tell me what seems unclear to you and I'll explain it."[1]

Most performers on Russia's private and popular stages shared Gardin's weak grasp of the political challenges confronting their society. Gardin's fellow Dramatic Theater actor Mikhail Narokov lamented that he, "like the majority of actors, remained in the prison of indifference toward social questions."[2] The young actress Valentina Verigina recalled that such problems "did not especially alarm me, a carefree and egotistical youth. It did not touch upon those close to me and was happening somewhere far away."[3] Ivan Perestiani, the actor at Lidiia Iavorskaia's New Theater who criticized imperial stage performers for their passivity, claimed his colleagues in private theater "settled in the wings ... motionless in the face of current events, not understanding their meaning and significance."[4] Boris Gorin-Goriainov, one of the few actors who did turn to

---

1. V. R. Gardin, *Zhizn' i trud artista* (Moscow: Iskusstvo, 1960), 80.
2. Mikhail S. Narokov, *Biografiia moego pokoleniia: Teatral'nye memuary* (Moscow: VTO, 1956), 139–40.
3. V. P. Verigina, *Vospominaniia* (Leningrad: Iskusstvo, 1974), 59–60.
4. I. N. Perestiani, *75 let zhizni v iskusstve* (Moscow: Iskusstvo, 1962), 194.

radicalism, remembered the Empire's acting community as "an inert apolitical mass devoid of any conscious social purpose."[5] The impresario Vladimir Nemirovich-Danchenko described his actors' political tendencies as "something anti-revolutionary, or even quite apolitical."[6] His business partner Konstantin Stanislavskii wrote: "I do not want to stir up either the revolutionaries or the reactionaries." His theater's mission was "not a political but an artistic question."[7]

These sentiments were not confined to the accounts of working stage professionals. As one critic alleged, "the indifference of today's artists to politics flows exclusively from their social backwardness.... The Russian performing community now roams on a path of unenlightened darkness."[8] Another accused performers of being "satisfied and idle" and bemoaned the need for "new, willing actors" to enliven the theater's slight presence in social and political life.[9] To a great degree the passivity characteristic of imperial stage performers extended beyond the purview of the state theaters.

As we saw in Chapter 1, few theaters in private hands enjoyed the means to offer permanent, secure employment. Financial concerns remained central in the life of the Russian actor. As early as 1876, six years before the abolition of the Imperial Theaters' monopoly on performances in the capitals, actors concerned about their economic conditions founded a mutual assistance society. This organization became the nucleus of the Russian Theatrical Society (RTO), created in 1894 to alleviate the needs of impoverished stage performers. Democratically structured and offering membership to any adult of either sex and any background who paid the annual five-ruble membership fee, by 1902 it had an officially recorded national membership of 4,444.[10] One of its principal activities, and the main subject of its governing council's weekly meetings, was distributing loans and grants to needy artists and troupes who were connected to the Society. In 1903 it devoted more than forty-six thousand rubles to this purpose.[11] Just over a decade later its total expenditures on grants and loans had more than doubled to ninety-three thousand rubles.[12] In addition to this form

---

5. B. A. Gorin-Goriainov, *Aktery: Iz vospominaniia* (Moscow: Iskusstvo, 1947), 100.
6. Vladimir Nemirovitch-Danchenko, *My Life in the Russian Theatre*, trans. John Cournos (London: Bles, 1937), 257.
7. Jean Benedetti, ed., *The Moscow Art Theatre Letters* (London: Methuen, 1991), 251.
8. "I. K." [I. M. Knorozovskii], "Kul'turnoe prosvetlenie teatra," *Teatral'naia Rossiia/Muzykal'nyi mir* 42–43 (October 22, 1905): 1242.
9. "Pek" [V. A. Ashkinazi], "Osvobozhdenie," *Teatral'naia Rossiia/Muzykal'nyi mir* 44–45 (October 29, 1905): 1261.
10. RGALI, f. 641, op. 1, ed. khr. 163, l. 30.
11. RGALI, f. 641, op. 1, ed. khr. 163, l. 29.
12. "Khronika," *Teatr i iskusstvo* 4 (January 26, 1914): 76. For an overview of the Theatrical Society's

of philanthropy, the Theatrical Society maintained retirement facilities for elderly theater professionals and established an information and employment agency for performers seeking work.[13]

The foci of the Theatrical Society's national congresses held in Moscow in March 1897 and March 1901 were predominantly material. Discussion revolved around increasing educational opportunities for performers, gaining government financial assistance for theatrical enterprises, standardizing contracts and other administrative aspects of show business, and securing better pay for artists.[14] Although delegates also mentioned the abstract issue of raising the aesthetic qualities and social values of dramatic art, many of their comments in these areas were directly linked to enhanced material conditions. By "improving the condition of the artist," the actress and honorary chairwoman of the 1897 congress Nadezhda Medvedeva proclaimed, "we ourselves will make him more capable of work and will in this way elevate the theater."[15]

Most of the Theatrical Society's efforts to improve professional conditions bore fruit. Beginning in 1895 the imperial government subsidized it with an annual grant of five thousand rubles, an amount doubled to ten thousand from 1899 and later augmented by benefit performances and other activities sponsored by the Directorate of the Imperial Theaters.[16] The subsidy remained subject to the State Council's (and, after 1906, the State Duma's) annually renewed approval, but was given each year until 1917.[17] In January 1903 the Society issued

---

organizational structure, see Murray Frame, *School for Citizens: Theatre and Civil Society in Imperial Russia* (New Haven: Yale University Press, 2006), 154–57. Most decisions were made by a simple majority vote of its membership, which met in an annual general assembly in St. Petersburg. Council members were elected by secret ballot for three-year terms staggered so that one-third of the seats were contested each year. Grants and loans were available to artists who had been Theatrical Society members for at least two years and working in the creative aspects of theater for at least five years as well as to entire troupes if two-thirds of their members had belonged to the Society for at least two years.

13. Frame, *School for Citizens*, 157.

14. For the full record of the conference, see *Trudy pervogo Vserossiiskogo s"ezda stsenicheskikh deiatelei, 9.3–23.3 1897*, 2 vols. (St. Petersburg: Nadezhda, 1898). See also the translated excerpts in Laurence Senelick, ed., *National Theatre in Northern and Eastern Europe, 1746–1900* (Cambridge: Cambridge University Press, 1991), 407–10. For a firsthand account, see V. A. Michurina-Samoilova, *Shest'desiat let v iskusstve* (Leningrad: Iskusstvo, 1946), 49–50. The congresses were held in Moscow rather than St. Petersburg, site of the annual general assembly meetings, in order to introduce an element of geographic diversity to the delegates.

15. "Rech' N. N. Medvedevoi," *Teatr i iskusstvo* (March 16, 1897): 206.

16. "Khronika," *Teatr i iskusstvo* 8 (February 23, 1914): 172, reports one such benefit, in which the entire proceeds of a Mariinskii performance of Wagner's *Die Meistersinger von Nürnberg* were given to the Theatrical Society.

17. RGALI, f. 641, op. 1, ed. khr. 148, l. 1, and ed. khr. 22, l. 3. "Ot redaktsii," *Teatr i iskusstvo* 5 (January 29, 1906): 66, reports the State Council's approval for that year.

a standardized contract for all private theatrical enterprises and required impresarios to leave a security deposit with the Society to safeguard against fraudulent employment practices.[18]

Government patronage grew in volume and importance. Ivan Vsevolozhskii, Director of the Imperial Theaters from 1881 to 1899, was among the Society's charter members. State cultural institutions were placed at its disposal. Every February one of Petersburg's imperial theaters hosted a benefit masked ball on its stage.[19] In 1895 the Society, in what its leadership described as a "joyous event," came under the tsar's personal patronage. Five years later Grand Duke Sergei Mikhailovich assumed the Society's presidency, and several other members of the Imperial Family and Court became honorary members.[20] In 1904 the government allowed the Society to style itself "Imperial." Eventually membership in the honorific orders granted to distinguished imperial stage performers became available to their colleagues on the private stage.[21] In 1916 the Society secured government approval to make November 22 an annually observed "Actors' Day."[22]

As the Theatrical Society's founders and members recognized, the finances of Russia's private and popular stages ranged from comparatively poor to precarious. Without the state theaters' permanent subsidies, unparalleled prestige, and enduring institutional traditions, it could hardly be otherwise. Pavel Orlenev, a typical actor at the Suvorin Theater, one of the most prestigious private venues, earned three hundred rubles a month during the season—substantially less than performers in the Imperial Theaters, who could easily command almost twice as much even at the beginning of their careers.[23] In 1904 he turned down an offer to join Komissarzhevskaia's company because touring abroad independently promised a higher income.[24] When the young director Nikolai Petrov left the Moscow Art Theater for the Aleksandrinskii in 1915, his income increased

18. Murray Frame, "Commercial Theatre and Professionalization in Late Imperial Russia," *Historical Journal* 48, no. 4 (2005): 1045–47. The degree of compliance is unknown.

19. "Khronika," *Teatr i iskusstvo* 8 (February 23, 1897): 150. "Khronika," *Teatr i iskusstvo* 1 (January 5, 1914): 4, reports a forthcoming Theatrical Society benefit at the Mariinskii Theater.

20. Frame, *School for Citizens*, 168.

21. "Khronika," *Teatr i iskusstvo* 1 (January 6, 1913): 3, reports the Order of St. Stanislav, second class, being awarded to the Korsh Theater actor A. I. Charin.

22. "Po povodu 'akterskogo dnia,'" *Teatr i iskusstvo* 46 (November 13, 1916): 923.

23. Pavel Orlenev, *Zhizn' i tvorchestvo russkogo aktera Pavla Orleneva opisannye im samim* (Moscow: Academia, 1931), 86. According to "Khronika," *Teatr i iskusstvo* 33 (August 14, 1905): 522, the young soprano Mariia Kuznetsova-Benua earned six thousand rubles in 1905–6, her second season at the Mariinskii Theater. "Khronika," *Teatr i iskusstvo* 6 (February 5, 1906): 82, reported that the actor Kondrat Iakovlev, formerly a Suvorin performer, had negotiated an initial contract at the Aleksandrinskii worth sixteen thousand rubles over three years.

24. Orlenev, *Zhizn' i tvorchestvo*, 244–69.

nearly fivefold.²⁵ Even Vsevolod Meierkhol'd, a well-known actor, director, and theorist who had managed his own itinerant theatrical company, was poorly remunerated in relative terms. The forty-five hundred rubles that Komissarzhevskaia paid him to serve as her theater's chief director for the 1906–7 season registered at the low end of entry level for young performers in the Imperial Theaters.²⁶ After the actress-entrepreneuse fired Meierkhol'd in late 1907, he too found more lucrative employment in the Imperial Theaters.

Many performers drifted from one short-term contract to another in a hand-to-mouth existence that they supported with steady employment in the "real world" or hoped to overcome by entering the rosters of the Imperial Theaters. Even legally contracted work was unreliable. Memoirs and the theatrical press were replete with complaints about unpaid or underpaid wages. One student of the matter observed that "in reality an actor's contract guarantees nothing to anyone, neither to the actor nor to the entrepreneur."²⁷ Sometimes their day jobs rather than their artistic calling brought them into direct contact with political events. The young New Theater actor Grigorii Baranskii was killed in the Bloody Sunday massacre of 1905, not because he was protesting, but because his day job as a reporter with the *Stock Exchange Gazette*, a leading Petersburg daily newspaper, put him in harm's way.²⁸ A happier case was that of the future film star Konstantin Skorobogatov, who began his acting career in the semi-professional drama circle of his workplace, the Obukhov steelworks.²⁹ Mariia Velizarii, an actress who tired of the poor management, self-indulgence, and unpredictability she encountered under Iavorskaia, eventually escaped to steadier employment in the imperial drama troupe.³⁰ Fedor Shaliapin importuned the Imperial Theaters Directorate to hire the tenor and director Vasilii Shkafer in 1904, pleading that Shkafer and other members of the Moscow industrialist Savva Mamontov's private opera (Shaliapin's own former employer) were "almost starving" on their miserable salaries.³¹ Shkafer was accepted, but he had been "eagerly" (*okhotno*) trying to get into the Imperial Theaters since at least the fall of 1901, when he had been unemployed with no other prospects.³² Vladimir

25. N. V. Petrov, *50 i 500* (Moscow: VTO, 1950), 77.
26. Vsevolod Meierkhol'd, *Perepiska, 1896–1939* (Moscow: Iskusstvo, 1976), 62.
27. N[ikolai] Arbenin, "Provintsial'nyi teatr," *Teatr i iskusstvo* 4 (January 28, 1897): 73.
28. "Khronika," *Teatr i iskusstvo* 3 (January 16, 1905): 42; "Peterburgskaia khronika," *Teatral'naia Rossiia/Teatral'naia gazeta* 4 (January 22, 1905): 55–56.
29. K. Skorobogatov, *Zhizn' i stsena* (Leningrad: Lenizdat, 1970), 50–58.
30. M. I. Velizarii, *Put' provintsial'noi aktrisy* (Leningrad: Iskusstvo, 1971), 217–23.
31. Shaliapin to Teliakovskii, n.d. [1904], in Fedor Shaliapin, *Literaturnoe nasledstvo. Pis'ma. Stat'i. Vyskazyvaniia. Vospominaniia o F. I. Shaliapine*, 2 vols. (Moscow: Iskusstvo, 1960), 1:401.
32. Vladimir Teliakovskii, *Dnevniki direktora Imperatorskikh teatrov, 1901–1903: Sankt-Peterburg* (Moscow: Artist. Rezhisser. Teatr., 2002), 113.

Teliakovskii, Director of the Imperial Theaters from 1901 to 1917, regularly attended private theaters incognito to seek out new talents to hire away from impresarios who could not compete with the Directorate's salary offers.[33]

Disappointment was a common companion of the daring and often reluctant few who moved from the Imperial Theaters to the uneven milieu of Russia's private and popular stages. Evtikhii Karpov, who in 1900 left his position as chief director of the Aleksandrinskii to resume work in private and popular theaters, held a variety of positions, but all, save a stint at the Suvorin Theater, were unsuccessful. In 1916 he returned to the Aleksandrinskii.[34] Aleksandr Sanin left no record of his feelings about becoming jobless when his attempt to revive the New Theater failed in short order in 1907. Since he had left the state stage after five successful years to do so, he probably regretted that decision. Eventually he found his way to the Ballets Russes. A tenor who left the Moscow Bol'shoi in 1902 to work on Russia's few private operatic stages begged (unsuccessfully) to be readmitted to the Imperial Theaters just a few months later.[35] Pavel Samoilov, a member of the imperial drama troupe and a son, grandson, nephew, and cousin of performers in the Imperial Theaters, left for the private stage in 1904. But apart from a season at Komissarzhevskaia's Dramatic Theater and one season each at the failed revivals of the Dramatic Theater and the New Theater, he had no steady stage employment until he returned to the Aleksandrinskii in 1920.[36] Komissarzhevskaia, who had felt compelled by the reigning prima donna Mariia Savina's intrigues to leave the Aleksandrinskii in 1902, encountered even greater disappointments in her floundering Petersburg enterprises, always heavily in debt and requiring the support of taxing provincial and foreign tours. The last of these, to Turkestan, led to her premature death from smallpox, a demise that her erstwhile collaborator Meierkhol'd described as one of "quiet despair."[37]

---

33. Vladimir Teliakovskii, *Vospominaniia* (Leningrad: Iskusstvo, 1965), 192–93.

34. I. F. Petrovskaia and V. Somina, *Teatral'nyi Peterburg: Nachalo XVIII veka-oktiabr' 1917 goda: Obozrenie–putevoditel'* (St. Petersburg: RIII, 1994), 223. Karpov also returned briefly to the Suvorin Theater in 1914–15.

35. Teliakovskii, *Dnevniki . . . 1901–1903*, 462–63.

36. Kholodov et al., eds., *Istoriia russkogo dramaticheskogo teatra*, 7 vols. (Moscow: Iskusstvo, 1977–87), 7:354, 367–68; M. I. Andreeva et al., eds., *Russkii dramaticheskii teatr: Entsiklopediia* (Moscow: Bol'shaia Rossiiskaia Entsiklopediia, 2001), 405. Samoilov's paternal grandparents and father were noted imperial stage artists, as were three of his aunts and two of his cousins.

37. Quoted in Aleksandr Gladkov, *Meierkhol'd*, 2 vols. (Moscow: Soiuz teatral'nikh deiatelei, 1990), 2:325. Several accounts concur that Komissarzhevskaia left the Aleksandrinskii because of Savina. Teliakovskii, *Dnevniki . . . 1901–1903*, 382, records that her "incomprehensible" departure was caused by her belief that "as long as Savina rules at the Aleksandrinskii Theater, there is nothing for her, Komissarzhevskaia, to do on the Imperial stage." For other firsthand accounts see N. V. Turkin, *Komissarzhevskaia v zhizni i na stsene* (Moscow: Zolotosvet, 1910), 103; Theodore Komisarjevsky, *Myself and the Theatre* (London: Heinemann, 1929), 25; T. L. Shchepkina-Kupernik, *Teatr v moei zhizni* (Moscow: Iskusstvo, 1948), 342.

Fig. 12 Vera Komissarzhevskaia, pictured here in 1903, the year after she left the imperial stage and a year before she began her first private enterprise, the Dramatic Theater. Her private theater initiatives were financial failures. From A. Ia. Al'tshuller, ed., *Vera Fedorovna Komissarzhevskaia: Pis'ma aktrisy, vospominaniia o nei, materialy* (Leningrad: Iskusstvo, 1964).

More desperate times called for desperate measures. When social turmoil disrupted theatrical operations, impresarios normally withheld pay from performers for days when the show did not go on.[38] Standard contracts allowed this, but performers quickly learned that external disturbances equaled lost wages. In 1905 theaters that continued to pay despite the cancellation of performances, including the Tsar Nicholas II People's House and Prince Aleksei Tsereteli's private opera company, suffered financially as a result.[39] The outbreak of World War I in 1914 led to declining revenues, abbreviated contracts, reduced wages, and scarcer employment opportunities. Theatrical wages not infrequently fell by 50 percent or more during the war years.[40]

Many entrepreneurs appealed to disorder to reduce the rosters of their theaters. The impresario A. A. Lintvarev, whom we have already encountered as an observer of Bloody Sunday's deleterious effects on the business aspects of theater, hastened to point out that many of his colleagues had no choice but to "leave hundreds of stage performers without work, and that means without a crust of bread."[41] Since Lintvarev claimed to be unable to pay some of his own actors, he knew well of what he wrote.[42] Nor was he alone. After only its first season in 1904–5, Komissarzhevskaia's Dramatic Theater, forty-one thousand rubles in debt, had to let go fifteen of its thirty-seven performers and two of its three directors.[43] When it went out of business in 1908, its actress-entrepreneuse could only pay her last director, Nikolai Evreinov, by giving him use of the empty hall.[44] Not even the Suvorin Theater, a veritable model of stability in Petersburg's theatrical universe, could escape such pressures. In February 1906 it declined to renew contracts with thirty-two performers—about one-third of its roster—"in view of the reduction of the budget."[45] Within a month of the declaration of war in 1914, it repeated this measure, dropping thirty-five of its eighty-nine performers as revenue collapsed.[46]

These economic challenges found public expression. Less than three weeks after Bloody Sunday, the editors of *Theatrical Russia* published a questionnaire

---

38. "Ot redaktsii," *Teatr i iskusstvo* 4 (January 23, 1905): 50; "Khronika," *Teatral'naia Rossiia/Teatral'naia gazeta* 5 (January 29, 1905): 73.
39. "Ot redaktsii," *Teatr i iskusstvo* 4 (January 23, 1905): 50.
40. "Teatral'nyi krizis v Peterburge," *Teatr i iskusstvo* 33 (August 17, 1914): 676. Supporting musicians in some cases accepted a 75 percent pay cut.
41. "Ot redaktsii," *Teatr i iskusstvo* 5 (January 29, 1906): 65.
42. Velizarii, *Put' provintsial'noi aktrisy*, 233–34.
43. Iu. Rybakova, *Komissarzhevskaia* (Leningrad: Iskusstvo, 1971), 126.
44. Sharon M. Carnicke, "The Theatrical Instinct: A Study of the Work of Nikolaj Evreinov in Early Twentieth-Century Russia" (Ph.D. diss., Columbia University, 1979), 84.
45. Kholodov, *Istoriia*, 7:304; "Khronika," *Teatr i iskusstvo* 8 (February 19, 1906): 113.
46. "Khronika," *Teatr i iskusstvo* 33 (August 17, 1914): 677.

requesting biographical information about performers. In addition to personal data and brief explanations of how the respondents had come to theater, the artists were probed in detail about their earnings from work on the stage, other sources of income, standard of living, and level of satisfaction with their profession.[47] The journal did not subsequently publicize the results of this survey or the degree of participation it received, but the questionnaire's clear purpose was to assess and quantify the material conditions in which performers lived and worked.

This inquiry anticipated the performers' most direct and frequently mentioned public statement, "The Needs of the Russian Theater (A Declaration of Stage Performers)." Published in the liberal newspaper *The Word* and the journal *Theater and Art* in February 1905, it called for the abolition of special censorship of popular theaters (but not preliminary theatrical censorship in general); an end to arbitrary police interventions to cancel performances; and such general democratic rights as freedom of conscience, expression, and association.[48] The statement was followed by 211 signatures.

Despite their timing and apparently political character, the exigencies presented in "The Needs of the Russian Theater" were strikingly phrased more in economic than political terms. The call to abolish stricter popular theater censorship aimed to improve those enterprises' financial viability by broadening their repertoires. This only echoed a call from the Theatrical Society's 1897 congress to drop the special censorship regime for all theaters except fairground entertainments (see Chapter 2), a measure intended to ensure greater employment opportunities for performers.[49] Eliminating the police's arbitrary power to cancel performances meant to guarantee that theaters would not face financial disaster after investing in officially approved productions suddenly taken off by order of local authorities. Talk of free association centered on plans to form a professional Union of Stage Performers (*Soiuz stsenicheskikh deiatelei*), a step that the manifesto's supporters thought necessary to alleviate their "pitiful existence." Since, in their opinion, the "lamentable economic condition . . . [did] not provide material security for stage performers," these were all important goals.[50] Nor, given both the Press Affairs Office chief Prince Shakhovskoi's support for abolishing special popular theater censorship and the Imperial Senate's rulings in favor of impresarios who suffered police intervention in their

47. "K artistam," *Teatral'naia Rossiia/Teatral'naia gazeta* 5 (January 29, 1905): 61–62.
48. "Nuzhdy russkogo teatra (Zapiska stsenicheskikh deiatelei)," *Slovo*, February 12, 1905; *Teatr i iskusstvo* 7 (February 13, 1905): 98–99.
49. *Trudy pervogo Vserossiiskogo s"edza*, 1:216–17.
50. "Nuzhdy russkogo teatra," 98–99.

repertoires (discussed in Chapter 2), were these demands particularly out of step with the prevailing sentiment even within government institutions.

How accurately did "The Needs of the Russian Theater" express political consciousness among stage performers? Referring to its demands' purportedly "liberal-bourgeois character," one Soviet theater historian struggled to describe them as "modest, but nevertheless political."[51] The actress Ekaterina Korchagina-Aleksandrovskaia claimed in her Soviet-era memoirs that she signed the declaration to rail "against all those deathly obstacles with which the tsarist government tried to surround the theater."[52] Several other performers known for their radical sympathies, including the Aleksandrinskii actor Nikolai Khodotov, signed it as well.

It is doubtful that the declaration's politicized language represented a majority of Russia's, or even Petersburg's, performing artists. Indeed, a number of the 211 signers were not stage performers at all but intellectuals with theatrical interests—critics (including *Theater and Art*'s editor Aleksandr Kugel'), entrepreneurs (Stanislavskii's partner, Vladimir Nemirovich-Danchenko), dramatists (the playwright Osip Dymov and Iavorskaia's husband, Prince Vladimir Bariatinskii), or theorists (Ivan Shcheglov). Those who signed were in any case a tiny minority of the 4,444 Theatrical Society members counted in 1902 and an even punier segment of the more than ten thousand stage performers Murray Frame estimates to have been working in Russia in 1899.[53]

No precise figures measure exactly how many performers were active in Petersburg (where both publications that carried the declaration were published) in the early years of the twentieth century, but if we accept Frame and Vera Leikina-Svirskaia's estimate that an "average" private or popular theater employed about thirty performers, the capital's thirty or so active enterprises would have employed roughly nine hundred stage artists.[54] This figure does not include the nearly four hundred principal performers of the capital's Imperial Theaters, of whom only twelve (all from the Aleksandrinskii's drama troupe) signed the declaration, or the unemployed. Even if all 211 signers had been

---

51. M. Iankovskii, "Teatral'naia obshchestvennost' Peterburga v 1905–1907 gg.," in *Pervaia russkaia revoliutsiia i teatr: Stat'i i materialy*, ed. A. Ia. Al'tshuller (Moscow: Iskusstvo, 1956), 147.

52. E. P. Korchagina-Aleksandrovskaia, "Stranitsy zhizni," *stat'i i rechi, vospominaniia* (Moscow: Iskusstvo, 1955), 45.

53. Frame, *School for Citizens*, 150.

54. Frame, "Commercial Theatre," 1032, establishes that fourteen theaters and seventeen pleasure garden enterprises with theatrical components functioned in St. Petersburg in 1901, as did twelve theaters and four pleasure gardens in Moscow. See also V. R. Leikina-Svirskaia, *Russkaia intelligentsiia v 1900–1917 godakh* (Moscow: Mysl', 1981), 197. Komissarzhevskaia, for example, employed thirty-seven performers in her first season in 1904–5. Some companies were larger—the Tsar Nicholas II People's House employed about one hundred performers.

St. Petersburg stage performers—and many were neither performers nor based in Petersburg—they would still have accounted for only about fifteen percent of the capital's working performing community and less than one-fourth of its nonimperial artists. To give another sense of scale, in August 1905 the actor Kazimir Bravich estimated that the year's straitened financial circumstances would bring unemployment to three hundred Petersburg stage performers in the following season, a figure almost 50 percent higher than the number of those who had signed "The Needs of the Russian Theater" the previous February.[55] As Elise Wirtschafter has observed in her study of tsarist-era social identity, the "very small proportion" of other professionals associated with politicized public statements might give "undue weight to activist, self-conscious subgroups who propagated images of political struggle and social commitment."[56] Like people working in other professions, most Russian stage performers expressed no sympathy for even modest political reform. When they did, it is not unreasonable to assume that many of them "were merely caught up in the euphoria of the moment and were simply repeating the political mantra of other organized occupational groups."[57]

The circumstances of the declaration's composition cast further doubt on its reliability as a political indicator. It credited no author or authors, but stage artists do not appear to have taken part in writing it. According to Khodotov, his political mentor, L. I. Lutugin, a radical geologist, Mining Institute professor, and leading figure of the engineer and technicians' union, played the principal role in drafting the document and presided over "all meetings of performers and dramaturges in my Kolomenskoi apartment in 1905."[58] No other evidence corroborates Khodotov's claim, but the high volume of Lutugin's activism was well known.[59] The phenomenon of political radicals "tutoring" performing artists in politics, moreover, was not an isolated one, despite Lenin's patronizing treatment of Gardin in Switzerland. Verigina recounted that the Moscow Bolshevik martyr Nikolai Bauman came regularly to her rehearsals, although his identity remained unknown (or unrecognized) until after his death.[60] The Menshevik Lev Deich gave regular lessons in radical politics to the actors of

55. K. V. Bravich, "Chto delat'?" *Teatr i iskusstvo* 32 (August 7, 1905): 504.
56. Elise Kimerling Wirtschafter, *Social Identity in Imperial Russia* (DeKalb: Northern Illinois University Press, 1997), 88–91. During the Revolution of 1905, her research demonstrates, "only a minority of professionals actually spoke out."
57. Frame, *School for Citizens*, 197.
58. N. N. Khodotov, *Blizkoe—dalekoe* (Leningrad: Iskusstvo, 1962), 168.
59. Leikina-Svirskaia, *Russkaia intelligentsiia*, 44, describes Lutugin as "one of the most energetic figures" in the engineer and technicians' union.
60. Verigina, *Vospominaniia*, 76.

Iavorskaia's New Theater, as did an incognito revolutionary known to his audience only as "Comrade Dem'ian." Gorin-Goriainov recalled that such visitors "explained day after day the difference between the SD and SR programs, the difference between the Bolsheviks and Mensheviks, and the difference between the liberals and monarchists and the revolutionary parties. For us this was an elementary school of political literacy."[61]

Despite conscious efforts to radicalize the capital's theatrical community, most stage performers failed to respond. Involvement in the revolutionary underground or the constitutionalist Liberation Movement had been virtually imperceptible among performing artists. Outspoken political or social statements from them were rare, limited for the most part to Iavorskaia's pointed refusal to appear in a November 1900 Suvorin Theater production of Viktor Krylov and Savelii Litvin's anti-Semitic play *The Smugglers*.[62] Even that gesture, however, was condemned by a large number of her fellow performers in the company, who signed a resolution charging that she had behaved "despicably" (*podlo*) and that they would no longer work with the actress. Shortly thereafter Suvorin dismissed her for breach of contract, a decision for which a majority of the company's actors expressed support.[63] Stanislavskii's profession of total surprise at the audience reaction to his March 1901 performance of Ibsen's *An Enemy of the People* was noted in the last chapter.

Sometimes the social and political sentiments of performing artists could be downright reactionary. The actor Nikolai Vekhter, a delegate to the Russian Theatrical Society's 1897 congress, called for the legal exclusion of Jews from performing because he feared they "threaten our national Russian influence."[64] At the 1901 congress the actress Pelageia Strepetova argued to an applauding audience of fellow performers that Jewish stage artists should at least be denied residency rights in Petersburg and Moscow because they would create unwelcome competition in an already crowded field.[65] One performer's anti-Semitism thus found expression in the material concerns that were increasingly important to the profession at large. Strepetova's fellow delegates registered their agreement when they voted to reject a resolution calling for equal residency rights for Jews—hardly the public stance that one might expect from the politically enlightened. "These are the consequences of playing at actors' democracy," the press opined.[66]

61. Gorin-Goriainov, *Aktery*, 101, 115.
62. Shchepkina-Kupernik, *Teatr v moei zhizni*, 133; I. F. Petrovskaia, *Teatr i zritel' rossiiskikh stolits: 1895–1917* (Leningrad: Iskusstvo, 1990), 80.
63. A. S. Suvorin, *Dnevnik* (Moscow: Novosti, 1992), 298, 309.
64. Senelick, *National Theatre*, 409. Vekhter himself was a baptized Jew.
65. Frame, "Commercial Theatre," 1045.
66. "Stesnenie promysla," *Teatr i iskusstvo* 12 (March 18, 1901): 242. The vote was 170 to 117.

Khodotov recalled that when he presented the text of "The Needs of the Russian Theater" to the theatrical community, "the modest demands of this petition were considered extremely bold and terrible by the majority of stage performers."[67] Its publication certainly stimulated no discernible rise in political consciousness. To the contrary, theatrically minded intellectuals continued to register their disappointment. Six weeks after the declaration appeared, one radical critic opined that "the light of art glimmers faintly. . . . To put it precisely, there is no socially actualized life among [performers]."[68] Sergei Svetlov, a trained physician who worked as a director in popular theater, noted that while other professional groups were taking part in politics, "the actor alone is silent." "The actor, a fighter for the truth, for the best ideals of life," he lamented, "is turning into a pitiable buffoon [*figliar*], a comedian." Deploring the theatrical profession's apparent lack of social commitment, Svetlov wondered whether there were "enough actors capable of forming a core of future fighters for social interests?"[69] As late as August 1917, a featured article in *Theater and Art* maintained that the stage "must be outside of politics" and urged performers "to throw themselves into their work, carrying our civic spirit into that and not squandering it at political meetings and on the street."[70] An inquiry into the difference between "bourgeois" and "proletarian" art in the revolutionary year concluded that "there is only one consideration in art: talented or untalented."[71]

Performers normally wanted to remain employed and weather political crises as best they could. For Gardin, who encountered a dismissive Lenin in Geneva, "theatrical life went on in its own way." His main objectives in 1905 were to overcome stage fright and perfect his technique—essential professional accomplishments if he were to enjoy success on the stage.[72] Skorobogatov, who was fired for his involvement in a strike at the Obukhov plant—an event in which he participated as an industrial worker rather than an actor—ironically looked to his developing theatrical identity to replace his lost job. "One exit remained," he thought after his dismissal, "to find an entrepreneur who would take me into his troupe." Although Skorobogatov continued to do intermittent factory work, he left behind his workplace radicalism to be in the limelight and built a major career.[73] The dramatist Evgenii Chirikov, a friend of Gor'kii and favorite

67. Khodotov, *Blizkoe—dalekoe*, 182–83.
68. "Vl. Sh.," "Iskusstvo i obshchestvo," *Teatr i iskusstvo* 13 (March 27, 1905): 205.
69. S. Svetlov, "Obshchestvennye zadachi soiuza stsenicheskikh deiatelei," *Teatr i iskusstvo* 22 (May 29, 1905): 348–49.
70. B. Glagolin, "Teatr i revoliutsiia," *Teatr i iskusstvo* 32 (August 6, 1917): 547–48.
71. N. Malkov, "Iskusstvo burzhuaznoe i proletarskoe," *Teatr i iskusstvo* 28–29 (July 16, 1917): 530.
72. Gardin, *Zhizn' i trud*, 78.
73. Skorobogatov, *Zhizn' i stsena*, 61–70.

of radicals, entered the theatrical press during the first revolution only to demand to know why the Theatrical Society was selling copies of his plays without his permission and without paying royalties.[74] At least part of the reason lay in the Society's own fiscal problems, which, since it depended on membership dues and charitable contributions, resulted from the worsened economic position of its members that year. Its leadership debated scaling back philanthropic activities, but the argument that the acting community had fallen on harder times than ever defeated the proposal.[75]

Resisting political commitment and avoiding even the appearance of radical coloration was a common reaction. Petrov, a director who profitably moved from the private stage to the Imperial Theaters, "stayed in a neutral position" with respect to politics, mainly to avoid conflict with his family, all of whom adopted various ideologies.[76] Writing in the 1950s, the actor Narokov apologetically recalled that he had "stayed far on the sidelines of events and like an ordinary narrow-minded person perceived them with repulsion, not examining them in my inner thoughts. But I consider myself a typical representative of the acting community. From my description one can to a degree imagine ... the actor's renunciation, alienation, and disorganization, dooming actors either to be quite on the sidelines or to trudge along at the tail of the social movement."[77] No matter how regretful he later claimed to be about his lack of political engagement, in August 1906 he wrote Meierkhol'd, his director at the time, "it is not good that politics exist."[78]

Even for performers who were inclined to take up politics at times of unrest, the idea that it should play a major role in their work remained at best notional. "Our political worldview was just beginning to form, we fit poorly in political programs," Gorin-Goriainov recalled in a way not so surprising for someone who equated the visits of revolutionary activists with elementary school.[79] When Perestiani's colleagues attended political meetings, "they would go and applaud even though many speeches were chaotic, not always clear, and most importantly, both pointless and senseless."[80] Pavel Gaideburov, whose popular enterprises attempted to foster social integration and acculturate the lower classes to the world of the stage, vaguely acknowledged a social role for his art form: "All the social conditions that surrounded us ... led to the conviction that art

74. "Ot redaktsii," *Teatr i iskusstvo* 17 (April 24, 1905): 263.
75. RGALI, f. 641, op. 1, ed. khr. 74, ll. 53–54.
76. Petrov, *50 i 500*, 13.
77. Narokov, *Biografiia*, 143.
78. Meierkhol'd, *Perepiska*, 69.
79. Gorin-Goriainov, *Aktery*, 100.
80. Perestiani, *75 let v iskusstve*, 193–94.

was given to humanity to hasten the movement of life toward its possible perfection." Yet at the same time he resisted the idea that outside forces or individuals should set a political agenda for his theater or the performing arts in general: "No one, of course, except we ourselves, could teach us what role this debt to art played in our actions, in our practical lives."[81] Being an artist of conscience was easily an apolitical avocation.

When Russia's stage performers detected threats to their economic conditions, few appealed to radical measures. Agitation connected with the surging labor movement may in an abstract sense have "increased the possibilities for some form of unionization that could balance the power of the entrepreneur," but such possibilities rarely extended to strikes or other confrontational tactics.[82] Mariia Velizarii, who toured with the troupe of Lintvarev, the same impresario who had detailed the theatrical community's financial woes in *Theater and Art*, recorded her frustration with trying to persuade fellow performers to strike when their wages went unpaid. "Only six people listened to me," she recalled, "the others signed a paper to the effect that they agreed to render their labor to strengthen the entrepreneur Lintvarev and would wait for their desired wages for an indefinite time." Instead the thoroughly bourgeois threat of a lawsuit helped the impresario find the cash.[83]

Breathing life into the Union of Stage Performers faced major challenges from artist apathy. Although "The Needs of the Russian Theater" called for such an organization in early 1905, the Russian Theatrical Society had already discussed it at its 1897 congress and resolved to draft a charter at its next meeting four years later.[84] This failed to happen, but the straitened economic circumstances caused by Bloody Sunday hastened the union's development in 1905. Its driving force, however, was a small group of theatrically minded intellectuals who found the Society's leadership too slow to act. Their first organizational meetings unfolded without the substantial participation of working performers. A typical meeting in July 1905 gathered only twenty or thirty people, mostly theatrical journalists, stagehands, and other technical personnel who identified with the capital's proletariat. According to observers "there was not one actor there."[85]

81. P. P. Gaideburov, *Literaturnoe nasledie. Vospominaniia. Stat'i. Rezhisserskie eksplikatsii. Vystupleniia* (Moscow: VTO, 1977), 128.
82. Louise McReynolds, *Russia at Play: Leisure Activities at the End of the Tsarist Era* (Ithaca: Cornell University Press, 2003), 68.
83. Velizarii, *Put' provintsial'noi aktrisy*, 233–34.
84. *Trudy pervogo Vserossiiskogo s"ezda*, 1:152; RGALI, f. 641, op. 1, ed. khr. 74, ll. 7–8; Leikina-Svirskaia, *Russkaia intelligentsiia*, 205.
85. "Soiuz stsenicheskikh deiatelei (Soedinennye zasedaniia komissii po vyrabotke proekta ustava i deputatov ot peterburgskikh i okrestnykh teatrov)," *Teatr i iskusstvo* 29 (July 17, 1905): 463.

Many performers toured in the provinces or abroad during the summer and would have been unable to attend these meetings, but the small number who did emphasized such economic matters as creating a pension fund and starting a union-managed theatrical enterprise to employ jobless performers. The latter goal lay behind Bravich's warning that three hundred stage performers would remain unemployed through the next winter.[86] Svetlov, who had agitated for the theatrical profession's greater commitment to social and political affairs, shifted his focus to welcoming stagehands and other working-class employees. This would broaden the project out of necessity to include "every useful member of the profession."[87] Despite these efforts, an attempt to create a working charter failed because "from the expected representatives of the troupes, almost no one appeared."[88]

Setbacks for the organization of a "politicized" stage performers' movement provoked disappointment from those who found artists insufficiently committed. One observer acknowledged the economic imperatives for the union project but urged that social and political questions appear on its agenda: "Let the economic, professional, and day-to-day functions of the union be worked out in their turn. But to rest on this is impossible and unworthy of stage performers."[89] After the unproductive summer meetings a certain Pokhilevich complained that performers had failed to be "seized by the new current, and because of that life is passing them by." Urging greater political consciousness, he implored them to recognize "above all our proper position among the citizens of Russia."[90]

The tepid intrusion of politics into the discourse of professionalization still failed to rouse the performing community. On the contrary, at least one anonymous actor took offense to it. Replying to a union meeting announcement that stressed the importance of its participants' "moral outlook," he tartly declared that "an actor's morality, like that of other citizens, is subordinate to the laws of the country's government."[91] Ultimately, the Theatrical Society had to address the concerns of the capital's suffering performers. In addition to holding a benefit

---

86. "Protokoly zasedanii kommisii po organizatsii soiuza stsenicheskikh deiatelei (Zasedanie 30-go aprelia 1905 g.)," *Teatr i iskusstvo* 20 (May 15, 1905): 319; K. V. Bravich, "Chto delat'?" *Teatr i iskusstvo* 32 (August 7, 1905): 504; "Protokol sobraniia stsenicheskikh deiatelei," *Teatral'naia Rossiia/Muzykal'nyi mir* 36 (September 3, 1905): 1099.

87. "Soiuz stsenicheskikh deiatelei," *Teatr i iskusstvo* 29 (July 17, 1905): 464.

88. "Khronika," *Teatr i iskusstvo* 31 (July 31, 1905): 490.

89. "Rigoletto," "Kakoi soiuz nam nuzhen?" *Teatral'naia Rossiia/Teatral'naia gazeta* 15 (April 9, 1905): 256.

90. A. Pokhilevich, "Chto delat'?" *Teatr i iskusstvo* 31 (July 31, 1905): 488–89.

91. "Mneniia i otzyvy," *Teatr i iskusstvo* 20 (May 15, 1905): 306.

concert to boost revenues, it organized a "Committee of Actors' Salvation" tasked with evaluating and responding to the profession's economic challenges.[92]

In order to succeed, the Union of Stage Performers had no choice but to adopt material concerns as its primary raison d'être. Despite his earlier exhortations to political radicalism, Svetlov admitted at a September 1905 meeting that "the surrounding conditions of life, fraught with all sorts of surprises, must naturally worry stage workers." Subsequent speakers identified the union project directly with economic concerns. The actor Boris Nevolin maintained that a strong union was desirable "if one suggests uniting with the exclusive goal of economic security." The meeting's secretary, A. V. Leifert, viewed "a manifestation of solidarity" as "the only way to guard against the consequences of the crisis." Since those consequences were largely economic, he was probably not using the word "solidarity" in its modern political sense. An actor called Sazonov even called for the inclusion of theatrical impresarios in the union because of their "existential importance to the organization of performances for profit."[93] So much for balancing entrepreneurial power. Indeed, when a similar proposal surfaced in 1912, the press conceded that it might be a good idea, for "sooner or later theater will doubtlessly become a capitalist enterprise. We should reconcile ourselves to it now."[94]

Shifting to an economic focus had some results. After the September 1905 meeting the press announced that the embryonic Union of Stage Performers had 471 members—still only a minority of Russia's theater artists, but more than twice the number of those who had signed "The Needs of the Russian Theater" seven months earlier, and far more, indeed, than had attended the quasi-politicized and unsuccessful organizational meetings.[95] The creation that same month of the Actors' Mutual Aid Circle as an outgrowth of the Theatrical Society's Committee of Actors' Salvation, a body charged with alleviating unemployment and related economic problems, added some high-profile names to the relief effort. Among its leaders were Vera Komissarzhevskaia, the Aleksandrinskii actor Vasilii Dalmatov, and *Theater and Art*'s editor Aleksandr Kugel'. So fundamentally did it focus on economic matters that Soviet critics later denounced its creation as a

---

92. "Khronika," *Teatr i iskusstvo* 31 (July 31, 1905): 490; "Komitet akterskogo spaseniia," *Teatr i iskusstvo* 32 (August 7, 1905): 503.
93. "Protokol sobraniia," 1099–100.
94. "Proekt E. N. Razsokhinoi," *Teatr i iskusstvo* 9 (February 26, 1912): 189.
95. "Listok ob"edineniia," *Teatr i iskusstvo* 37 (September 11, 1905): 598. Professional associations for stage performers in other nations also attracted small minorities. Membership in the British Actors' Association, founded in 1891, peaked eight years later, when only an estimated 13 percent of the nation's performers belonged. See Michael Sanderson, *From Irving to Olivier: A Social History of the Acting Profession in England, 1880–1983* (New York: St. Martin's, 1984), 96.

conscious effort on the part of the Theatrical Society's "reactionary leadership" to "distract the acting masses from participation in the political struggle."[96] What really happened was that the theatrical profession, confronted by revolutionary unrest and an attendant economic crisis, responded with an independent attempt to solve its problems outside the political realm.

Before the Actors' Mutual Aid Circle could do much work, the looming general strike of October 1905 presented radicals with another chance to solicit the loyalty of the performing arts community. Actors in some theaters discussed joining the strike to show solidarity with the workers and the political aims of the tsarist government's opponents. For the most part these efforts had few results. The closing of various theaters resulted much more frequently from the unsettled conditions and consequent nervousness among performers. As the actress Valentina Verigina remembered Moscow that month, "we were swallowed up by art, but could not fail to hear the rumble of approaching events." Her reaction to a tense confrontation on the city's central Tverskaia Street was to run away from it so fast that she fell down and hurt herself.[97] A meeting of Suvorin Theater performers voted overwhelmingly against participating in the general strike; only four actors supported the measure. Nevertheless, the prevailing unrest convinced Suvorin to keep his theater dark for the next few days.[98]

The troupe of Komissarzhevskaia's Dramatic Theater also considered striking, but some of its members complained about the prospect of losing their pay as a result. Even the troupe's radicals justified its October 12 performance because Gor'kii's play *Children of the Sun*, which portrays an out-of-touch and ineffectual intelligentsia circle that almost gets lynched by the very peasants it idealizes, was scheduled to have its Petersburg premiere that night.[99] Despite their enthusiasm the play's director Nikolai Arbatov recalled that its second performance "went unevenly as a consequence of the elevated mood of the artists." Dress rehearsals were "cancelled as a consequence of political events," and the nervous actors voted to skip two shows. Some of Komissarzhevskaia's actors made a virtue of a necessity by declaring their absence to be a sign of solidarity with the general strike and pledged to give one day's wages to the strike fund. Others wanted to reopen because they feared that their "material well-being does not allow for

---

96. Iankovskii, "Teatral'naia obshchestvennost'," 165; K. Semenova, "'Pamiatnye zapiski' rezhisserskogo upravleniia teatra V. F. Komissarzhevskoi," in Al'tshuller, *Pervaia russkaia revoliutsiia*, 325.

97. Verigina, *Vospominaniia*, 75–76.

98. "Uchastie Peterburgskikh teatrov v obshchei politicheskoi zabastovke," *Teatral'naia Rossiia* 44–45 (October 29, 1905): 1269–70.

99. N. I. El'iash, "Tvorchestvo V. F. Komissarzhevskoi i P. N. Orleneva," in *Russkii dramaticheskii teatr kontsa XIX–nachala XX vv.*, ed. A. Nazarova and N. Orekhova (Moscow: GITIS, 2000), 200.

a continuation of the strike." The loss of just two days' wages was enough of a financial shock to dissuade them from wanting to remain absent for any reason. They were overruled, however, by a majority who "favored closing the theater, motivated by the fact that any performances were unthinkable at a time when almost all of Russia had stopped and found itself in a terribly unsettled and tense condition."[100] Politics was not the major factor.

According to Gorin-Goriainov, the buzz about "theater's participation in the brewing general strike" found little resonance among his colleagues. Instead, he recalled, "it frightened many people." Even members of the capital's performing arts community who had been inclined to politicize their profession at other times opposed striking. Kugel', a signer of "The Needs of the Russian Theater" and editor of one of the periodicals that published it, asked an assembly of actors, "Do you know what a strike is? Have you thought about what will happen to your families? . . . A strike is hunger, poverty, unemployment!"[101] This attitude earned Kugel' denunciation as a "propagandist" and "typical bourgeois liberal" by one Soviet theater historian, but his speech nevertheless reflected and informed the prevailing mood.[102] Narokov, who attended several meetings about the union project held in October, later claimed that "nothing came of this undertaking. Three meetings devoted to the union's organization were torn apart by different groups of actors. The meetings ended every time because of the incredible noise, shouts, and wild behavior made by 'rebels.'"[103] He later remembered 1905 for its "terror-filled days, when dark forces carried out bloody violence in the streets."[104] Aleksandr Briantsev, touring southern Russia with Gaideburov's Wandering Theater (a component of the same impresario's General Accessible Theater), found himself stranded in Khar'kov with the rest of the troupe. Although he and his fellow performers found unfolding events there "interesting," they took no part in them. Their main concerns were to stay out of the way and return to Petersburg.[105] Naturally, such attitudes were not conducive to forming a disciplined political stance.

Faced with a rejection of the strike by most of the capital's performing community, the small minority of radicals who still favored participating in it resorted to coercion. But few even among them demonstrated a deep awareness of politics. As Gorin-Goriainov haplessly recalled, "it was believed that there

---

100. Semenova, "'Pamiatnye zapiski,'" 323–24.
101. Gorin-Goriainov, *Aktery*, 101, 103.
102. Iankovskii, "Teatral'naia obshchestvennost'," 156, 170.
103. Narokov, *Biografiia*, 143.
104. Ibid., 137.
105. A. A. Briantsev, *Vospominaniia, stat'i, vystupleniia, dnevniki, pis'ma* (Moscow: VTO, 1979), 67.

was a center trying assiduously to give the revolutionary movement some necessary organization and planning. But we actors of course knew nothing and about this center and could not have known [about it]."[106] Narokov also captured their confusion: "This period demanded a clear vision of the essence of events and their roots. To us, the majority of actors, this was not understood then because of our semi-literacy."[107]

Receiving instructions from "Comrade Dem'ian," the agitator who adopted the role of political missionary to Petersburg's theaters, a small group of left-wing actors formed a "fighting retinue" to enforce participation in the general strike. Their actions were likely driven by the St. Petersburg Soviet's declaration: "Comrades, those workers who do not wish to stop working, despite the resolutions of the Soviet of [Workers'] Deputies, should be removed from their jobs. Those who are not for us are against us, and against them the Soviet of Deputies has decided to apply more extreme methods—force."[108] At the same meeting where Kugel' spoke against a strike, some young radicals tried to intimidate representatives from the many theaters unwilling to close their doors. "We'll see!" and "You will be forced to do it!" echoed in their conversations with actors who declared, "Our theater will not strike!"[109]

"When it became clear that a strike in the theaters would not proceed smoothly by legal means," Gorin-Goriainov remembered, "the question arose of forcibly ending performances in those theaters that did not voluntarily cancel them."[110] Approaching the Suvorin Theater peaceably, the strike delegation's request that the running performance cease elicited only a curt refusal from the management. The radicals persisted, only to be confronted by a group of angry actors, one of whom brandished a revolver. As a last resort the agitators hurled flasks of hydrogen sulfide into the hall. The poison gas was too diffuse to harm anyone, but the commotion and the chemical's putrid, rotten egg smell convinced the audience to "rush out." The same tactic worked at the Panaev Theater, where a performance of an operetta called *Fireflies* ended in a mélange of hydrogen sulfide and a dance number.[111]

Not all these attempts at disruption were successful. When agitators tried to stop the show at the Nevskii Farce, its "rather reactionary" troupe, which had "militated strongly against the strike," chased them from the wings with

106. Gorin-Goriainov, *Aktery*, 100.
107. Narokov, *Biografiia*, 151.
108. Quoted in Abraham Ascher, *The Revolution of 1905: Russia in Disarray* (Stanford: Stanford University Press, 1988), 217–18.
109. Gorin-Goriainov, *Aktery*, 104.
110. Ibid., 104–5.
111. Ibid., 108–10.

hammers, metal slide rules, and other blunt objects. One of the agitators was seriously injured.[112] Ironically, several of the Nevskii Farce's performances ended with the "Marseillaise."[113] But when it came to overt participation in political life, the troupe's players had their limits. Likewise, when agitators arrived at the Conservatory, where Prince Tsereteli's private opera company was performing, the burly tenor Lev Klement'ev ran around in full costume and makeup yelling, "Beat them, the scoundrels." The police arrested some of the "striker-terrorists," but in both cases, as well as at the Suvorin Theater (where at least one of their opponents wielded a firearm), the performers were willing to get violent in order to stop the strike from penetrating their places of work.[114] In another Petersburg venue, the popular Nicholas II People's House, "not only did no one think about striking, but the artists were even extremely rude to delegates from other theaters." Indeed, performers there were so reluctant to take part in events that only twelve out of the troupe's one hundred or so members bothered to sign up for the Actors' Mutual Aid Circle, apolitical though it was.[115]

It should be no surprise that the Theatrical Society's leadership seized hopefully onto the promulgation of the October Manifesto to hail Count Sergei Vitte, the country's new premier and an honorary member of the Society, as "the builder and first leader of a renewed Russia."[116] Social and political stability, its leaders and members realized, was crucial to their professional interests. Few performers were impressed by one Moscow *intelligent*'s admonition that theater people should look for heroes among "those fighters who gave their lives in the struggle with autocracy."[117]

Negative attitudes toward striking and other forms of political radicalism were confirmed by a general meeting of performers that assembled on October 20 at the Panaev Theater, one of the venues closed down by force a few days before. A journalist reported that when the subject of joining the Liberation Movement came up, "voices broke out . . . loudly demonstrating that politics and art are 'two incompatible things,' that actors should not appear in citizens' roles."[118] Kugel', who had discouraged participation in the general strike a few days before, slightly reversed himself and argued that the Union of Stage Performers should

---

112. Ibid., 110.
113. D. I. Zolotnitskii, "'Dni svobody' russkogo farsa," in *Russkii teatr i dramaturgiia epokhi revoliutsii, 1905–1907 godov: Sbornik nauchnykh trudov*, ed. A. Ia. Al'tshuller et al. (Leningrad: LGITMIK, 1987), 132.
114. Gorin-Goriainov, *Aktery*, 111–12.
115. "Khronika," *Teatral'naia Rossiia* 44–45 (October 29, 1905): 1272–73.
116. Ibid., 1272.
117. "Bel' ami" [B. Lebedev], "Iz Moskvy," *Teatr i iskusstvo* 51–52 (December 25, 1905): 795.
118. "A." [E. A. Solov'ev], "Spasite teatr!" *Teatral'naia Rossiia* 44–45 (October 29, 1905): 1265.

adopt a political character and support the goals of the Liberation Movement. Although he presented this idea as an imperative of the stage performers' "economic and artistic interests," he found himself publicly denounced by actors who accused him of using his prominence and leadership role in the Actors' Mutual Aid Circle to impose his views by "*force majeure.*"[119] Only eighty people signed the meeting's resolution.[120] The number of performers willing to make a political statement thus declined over the course of Russia's first revolution.

Performer apathy had attracted negative comment at earlier times. Shortly before the Theatrical Society's 1897 congress, one performer felt chagrined by the public view that "an actor is a lackey." He realized that this derived from the "abnormality" (*nenormal'nost'*) of working conditions, but the prevalence of this perception during the 1905 general strike provoked more vitriol from those who thought stage performers should adopt an active role in politics.[121] As a columnist for *Theatrical Russia* bitterly mourned, the Russian performing arts community

> has remained on the sidelines of the great tasks of the century.... It has not been concerned with the Liberation movement at all... the theater alone has not taken part in the general struggle for freedom of thought.... It is a shame to admit it, but it is a fact: among servants of stage art there is not enough cultural force to inspire battle.... Russian theater has shamefully stayed out of life [and] remains an obtuse, apathetic spectator of events that it does not understand, of attitudes that it does not share, of a heroism with which it is incapable of ennobling itself.[122]

If it could not change, it would be "condemned to tedious vegetation [*tomitel'noe proziaban'e*]."[123] E. A. Solov'ev, who covered the October 20 Panaev Theater meeting, vented his ire on the actors more directly: "Russian performers have played a pitiful role. There was no political strike by actors.... Even in the theaters that called themselves committed, the theaters of the intelligentsia, events caught the troupes entirely unawares. The interpreters of Ibsen and Gor'kii could not consciously relate to a movement that seized even the darkest elements of the working masses." Offering a revealing insight into why some

---

119. "Uchastie Peterburgskikh teatrov," 1271–72. The French phrase is original.
120. Leikina-Svirskaia, *Russkaia intelligentsiia*, 206–7.
121. N[ikolai] Arbenin, "Provintsial'nyi teatr," *Teatr i iskusstvo* 6 (February 9, 1897): 113–14.
122. "I. K." [I. M. Knorozovskii], "Kul'turnoe prosvetlenie," 1242.
123. "I. K." [I. M. Knorozovskii], "Da zdravstvuet svoboda!" *Teatral'naia Rossiia* 44–45 (October 29, 1905): 1260.

theaters had closed during the general strike, Solov'ev continued his diatribe with the sarcastic observation that "the [lack of] electricity and the Cossacks, forcing the public to stay home, saved the reputation of the Russian actor." He called on performers to "save the theater" by "fighting not for the stomach, but for the death of a regime that is killing theatrical affairs" and appended a list of fifty cities and towns where pogroms had taken place to change the minds of "those who think sacred art has nothing in common with politics."[124] "A circus or a theater—a trained animal or an actor—isn't it all the same?" another sharp comment asked.[125]

Despite these complaints the relationship between "sacred art" and politics remained elusive. Alongside the denunciations of radical critics, those interested in theatrical affairs could read reports of disruptions throughout the Empire and their effect on the profession. In Tambov seventy performers lost work because civic disturbances had brought a halt to that provincial city's stage life. A successful theater in Ekaterinoslav foundered for the same reason, depriving its entire troupe of employment. In faraway Baku performances that had been bringing in full receipts suddenly drew neither audiences nor revenues.[126] An operetta artist broke a contract with a Russian theater in Harbin to escape the "unsettled state of affairs in the Far East."[127] *Theatrical Russia*'s editors could only wonder what the professional community could do to help the provinces' suffering performers.[128]

Even without this news performers in the capitals had enough turbulence to worry about. The Dramatic Theater continued to have problems "because of current political events."[129] The outbreak of the December 1905 uprising in Moscow, which shut down that city's theatrical life for several weeks, drove performers everywhere into paroxysms. Narokov recalled that he and many of his colleagues viewed it as "a useless and dangerous caprice."[130] Bravich called for his fellow performers to respond with unspecified "energetic measures," but this only "created a panic among the artists," even though they were several hundred miles away. Komissarzhevskaia suspended further performances "until life returns to a more normal condition" and promised to pay the troupe half its wages to keep rehearsing.[131] Yet, in another illustration of tolerated or at least

124. "A." [E. A. Solov'ev], "Spasite teatr!" 1265.
125. N[ikolai] Arbenin, "Kakoi teper' nuzhen teatr?" *Teatr i iskusstvo* 5 (January 29, 1906): 75.
126. "Khronika," *Teatral'naia Rossiia* 44–45 (October 29, 1905): 1272.
127. "Khronika," *Teatr i iskusstvo* 5 (January 29, 1906): 66.
128. "Khronika," *Teatral'naia Rossiia* 44–45 (October 29, 1905): 1272.
129. Semenova, "'Pamiatnye zapiski,'" 326–27.
130. Narokov, *Biografiia*, 143.
131. Semenova, "'Pamiatnye zapiski,'" 328–29.

irrelevant radicalism, Bravich had no problem joining the Imperial Malyi Theater's dramatic troupe after Komissarzhevskaia entered bankruptcy; he remained there until shortly before his death in 1912.[132]

The centrality of economic concerns among Russia's performing arts community only increased after the storm of the first revolution subsided. As members of the Union of Stage Performers continued to talk about a charter and organizational structure, several subgroups within the Empire's theatrical community emerged with their own union projects, virtually all of which focused on material concerns. In January 1906 the city's prompters formed a union, followed in the summer by the chorus of Prince Tsereteli's private opera company.[133]

Theatrical writers also talked about a union pr oject. Petr Veinberg, one of its organizers, concluded that "all those gathered are united in th eir striving to improve their material position, to have the possibility to work freely and undisturbed without forever thinking about a crust of bread . . . we cannot deny that material considerations are one of the existing indices here."[134] The union's proponents demanded that the performing arts community "take measures" against people "using the literary property of others in bad faith," that is, those who violated what we today call intellectual property rights by not paying royalties.[135] Khodotov, who had pretensions to being a playwright in addition to his acting career, attempted to inject politics by urging the creation of "an organized circle called to fight against the reaction in art." But he found few willing to listen.[136] One of the congress's rare "political" statements came from a certain Shukhmin, who suggested that entrepreneurs should not be permitted to schedule Saturday performances because requiring artists to work on the Sabbath eve violated their freedom of conscience.[137]

The project for a theatrical writers' union appears to have been conceived as nonoppositional or at least uncontroversial, moreover, for its meetings included the Ministry of the Interior's chief dramatic censor Sergei Vereshchagin, one of the main figures charged with evaluating the suitability of the writers' plays for Russian stages. The congress's official photograph featured him among the other

---

132. "K. V. Bravich," *Teatr i iskusstvo* 47 (November 18, 1912): 915.
133. "Soiuz suflerov," *Teatr i iskusstvo* 5 (January 29, 1906): 66; "Khronika," *Teatr i iskusstvo* 27 (July 2, 1906): 417.
134. "Vserossiiskii s"ezd dramaticheskikh i muzykal'nykh pisatelei," *Teatr i iskusstvo* 8 (February 19, 1906): 124.
135. O. Dymov, "Peterburgskie teatry (pis'mo vtoroe)," *Zolotoe runo* 3 (March 1906): 106–7.
136. Khodotov, *Blizkoe—dalekoe*, 206.
137. "Vserossiiskii s"ezd dramaticheskikh i muzykal'nykh pisatelei," *Teatr i iskusstvo* 9 (February 26, 1906): 134.

participants in his spotless civil service uniform.[138] By the eve of World War I, the theatrical writers' main ambitions included increasing their honoraria payments to the point where *Theater and Art*'s editorial board believed that they threatened the financial stability of many enterprises.[139] When the outbreak of conflict led to the disappearance of German and Austrian works from repertoires, the union protested not for cultural or political reasons but on the behalf of translators who lost royalty income.[140] As Frame has suggested, the theatrical profession's general attitude provides "further testimony that the relationship between state and civil society in late tsarist Russia was not necessarily antagonistic."[141] Joseph Bradley's general argument that Russian civic associations "presented an opportunity for a pragmatic, advantageous reciprocal relationship with the imperial government," one that enabled their members "to promote and pursue the same goals as their counterparts in Europe and North America," does not seem at all out place with respect to the performing arts, even during a revolutionary time.[142]

The defense of material interests in a professional context continued with the charter of the Union of Stage Performers, finally drafted in March 1906 and approved in June. There was no question about the Union's economic function. Its main responsibilities were to manage a pension fund, savings and loan bank, and health and unemployment insurance plans. The principal sources of financial support were to be membership dues and donations.[143] Despite its union structure, however, its functions and activities were not meaningfully different from those adopted or planned by the Theatrical Society in the 1890s. And, since the government formally legalized trade unions, professional associations, and similar organizations in March 1906, the Union's creation violated no law.

Precise qualifications for membership defeated attempts to include potentially more radical elements, such as stagehands, technicians, and other "proletarian" theatrical employees. Instead they established firm professional prerequisites. Union members had to have worked in a creative theatrical occupation for at least three seasons or for two seasons if they had formal theatrical training.[144] The membership rules thereby excluded nonartists, including many of the theatrical

---

138. Ibid., 135.
139. "Ob obshchestvakh dramaticheskikh pisatelei," *Teatr i iskusstvo* 16 (April 20, 1914): 358.
140. "Khronika," *Teatr i iskusstvo* 30 (July 27, 1914): 628.
141. Frame, *School for Citizens,* 170–71.
142. Joseph Bradley, "Subjects into Citizens: Societies, Civil Society, and Autocracy in Tsarist Russia," *American Historical Review* 107, no. 4 (2002): 1120–21.
143. Frame "Commercial Theatre," 1036–38; Leikina-Svirskaia, *Russkaia intelligentsiia,* 207.
144. Leikina-Svirskaia, *Russkaia intelligentsiia,* 207.

Fig. 13 A Congress of Dramatic Writers meeting in February 1906, as covered by the journal *Theater and Art*. Some of the leading figures of Russian theater appear in the photo. At the far left in the first row is Prince Aleksandr Iuzhin-Sumbatov, a Constitutional Democratic Party member who, despite his oppositionist affiliation, served as artistic director of the Malyi Theater from 1909 and was elected to remain in that post in 1917. Aleksandr Kugel', editor of *Theater and Art*, is third from left in the front row. The actor and dramatist Nikolai Arbenin, who lamented the lack of desire for autonomy in the imperial drama troupe, is fourth from the left. Fifth from left in the same row sits Petr Gnedich, dramatist and artistic director of the Aleksandrinskii Theater from 1900 to 1908. Evtikhii Karpov, a radical who served time in Siberian exile but nevertheless led the Aleksandrinskii from 1896 to 1900 and again from 1916, is seventh from left. Sergei Vereshchagin, the Interior Ministry's chief dramatic censor, is fifth from right in the second row. Note his civil service uniform. The congress notably included members of the government bureaucracy, suggesting that state and civil society were far from irreconcilable. From *Teatr i iskusstvo* 9 (February 26, 1906), 135. Author's private collection.

intellectuals who had tried to influence the Union's organization and character in the first place, and amateurs thought insufficiently acculturated into the life of the Russian stage to count as professionals. Within twelve months the Union's membership grew to more than six hundred and increased in the years before 1917. The Russian Theatrical Society's overall membership reached six thousand by the time of the Bolshevik Revolution.

In the intervening eleven years neither entity became politicized. Their charters and missions never changed in any way beyond administrative reorganizations, and they neither adhered to the Union of Unions, which attempted to coordinate the professional intelligentsia politically, nor voiced support for the liberal and radical political groupings into which the pre-1905 opposition evolved.[145] After the collapse of the monarchy in 1917, the Union of Stage Performers declared its primary interest to be "the defense of material and artistic interests and the elevation of art in Russia."[146] This was essentially the same message that the Theatrical Society had elaborated at its first national congress twenty years earlier and that its members had talked about ever since. The Society's official reaction to the Bolshevik Revolution—an event that portended its end as an independent institution of the Empire's growing civil society—was its sarcastic declaration that "we have already lost Russia in sacrifice to the socialist paradise."[147] One member pleaded with his colleagues: "Don't force the theater into the political struggle."[148] Michael Sanderson's words about early twentieth-century British performers apply perfectly well to their contemporaries on the Russian stage: "Actors, in the main, were not political animals. Still less were they associated with radical, Left, or trade-union sympathies."[149]

To dampen leftist hopes further, neither concern nor enthusiasm about including "proletarian" theater employees in the union project ever produced tangible results. A November 1917 resolution drafted by a meeting of Petrograd stagehands announced that their "political immaturity" prevented them from either supporting or opposing the Bolshevik coup d'état. They declared that they would continue at their jobs, for they were "materially dependent on every working day . . . and for that reason we cannot accept responsibility for the cessation of performances."[150] Like the performers, their primary motivations were economic, even in a time of intense political crisis.

---

145. Ibid., 203, 207, 222.
146. "Teatr v revoliutsionnye dni Petrograda," *Teatr i iskusstvo* 12 (March 19, 1917): 209.
147. "Pomnite o 22 noiabria!" *Teatr i iskusstvo* 47 (November 19, 1917): 782.
148. Mikhail Murav'ev, "Sokhranite teatr!" *Teatr i iskusstvo* 44–46 (November 12, 1917): 764.
149. Sanderson, *From Irving to Olivier*, 95.
150. RGIA, f. 497, op. 6, ed. khr. 5129, l. 8.

If stage performers were so unwilling to involve themselves in politics in the late imperial era, is there any justification for Soviet claims that they "stood side by side with the working class"?[151] The assertion that "many joined the general strike" is simply untenable after a close reading of the available accounts.[152] Performer activity in organized national politics was limited to just one individual, an amateur baritone elected to the State Duma in 1912 after having left the stage to serve as a district marshal of the nobility in his home province. He sat as a member of the Center-Right Octobrist Party.[153] The moderation of his engagement, to say nothing of its singularity, only reinforces the idea that the performing arts formed a notable exception to Harley Balzer's claim that "most professions joined the assault on autocracy." Certainly private and popular theater artists contradicted the contention that "unions of the intelligentsia directed most of their efforts not at obtaining improved economic conditions but at abolishing the autocracy."[154] Even the more balanced suggestion that divisions between factions of performers represented "a considerable obstacle to coordinated action" belies the true isolation in which radicals of the stage found themselves.[155] Gary Thurston's judgment that performers in popular theaters were "for the most part skittish toward revolution" seems broadly applicable to Russia's entire performing community.[156] So do Amy Nelson's recent observation that "musicians did not take a particularly active role in politics during these chaotic [prerevolutionary] years" and Kendall Bailes's argument that thorough inquiries "call into question the cohesiveness of the professional intelligentsia as a revolutionary force."[157]

To justify their depiction of Russian performing artists as revolutionary activists, the Soviets later seized onto those who had shown almost any degree of sympathy to their cause, however symbolic. They were aided somewhat by memoirists who remained in Russia after 1917. Velizarii, who had tried to stand up to Lintvarev over unpaid wages and threw herself into the theatrical life of

---

151. Iankovskii, "Teatral'naia obshchestvennost'," 182.
152. G. A. Khaichenko, *Russkii narodnyi teatr kontsa XIX–nachala XX veka* (Moscow: Nauka, 1975), 171.
153. "Khronika," *Teatr i iskusstvo* 49 (December 2, 1912): 962.
154. Harley D. Balzer, introduction to *Russia's Missing Middle Class: The Professions in Russian History*, ed. Harley D. Balzer (Armonk, N.Y.: M. E. Sharpe, 1996), 15; Ascher, *Revolution of 1905*, 142.
155. Richard G. Thorpe, "The Management of Culture in Revolutionary Russia: The Imperial Theaters and the State, 1897–1928" (Ph.D. diss., Princeton University, 1990), 47.
156. Gary Thurston, *The Popular Theatre Movement in Russia, 1862–1919* (Evanston: Northwestern University Press, 1998), 207.
157. Amy Nelson, *Music for the Revolution: Musicians and Power in Early Soviet Russia* (University Park: Pennsylvania State University Press, 2004), 6; Kendall E. Bailes, "Reflections on Russian Professions," in Balzer, *Russia's Missing Middle Class*, 50.

early Soviet Russia, proudly recalled that she was once "almost arrested" for reading subversive poems in the home of a liberal merchant.[158] The dramatist and theatrical personality Tat'iana Shchepkina-Kupernik, a great-granddaughter of the famous "serf actor" Mikhail Shchepkin, was ordered to appear in court over the publication of writings that "insulted the authorities," though she failed to show up and was not punished.[159] Korchagina-Aleksandrovskaia's daughter claimed that the actress became a political radical after performing in Gor'kii's *Children of the Sun* at the Dramatic Theater, the production in which she made her Petersburg debut.[160] The symbolist poet and dramatist Aleksandr Blok carried a red flag in one (and only one) demonstration and in a 1908 article called on artists to "do their duty," though he failed to explain what it was.[161] Iavorskaia allegedly yelled, "To the barricades! To the barricades! Why are you sitting there and what are you waiting for?!" after a Cossack knocked off her hat during the general strike.[162] Revenue from some of her theater's charitable performances supported strike committee funds and may have reached the coffers of the Social Democratic press.[163] At one benefit performance she denounced "the slavery of the theater, against which it will be almost impossible to fight until the whole hated and untalented old regime falls."[164]

Despite her histrionics on and off stage, Iavorskaia proved an inconvenient heroine after the revolution. Fleeing Soviet Russia in February 1919, possibly to escape an arrest warrant, she denounced the Bolshevik regime, in her words "a foreign and enemy yoke," at least as harshly as she had denounced the tsarist one.[165] A 1956 study claimed that "the radicalism of the New Theater's leader L[idiia] Iavorkskaia and her husband [Prince Vladimir] Bariatinskii was very limited, they were casual fellow travelers of the revolution."[166] Instead of lionizing Iavorskaia, one of the few performing artists who did speak out publicly against the tsarist government, retrospective Soviet honors fell largely to the other grande dame of the Silver Age private theater scene, Vera Komissarzhevskaia.

158. Velizarii, *Put' provintsial'noi aktrisy*, 234–35, 265–68.
159. Shchepkina-Kupernik, *Teatr v moei zhizni*, 345.
160. E. Aleksandrovskaia, "Vospominaniia o materi," in Korchagina-Aleksandrovskaia, "Stranitsy zhizni," 177.
161. Aleksandr Blok, "Tri voprosa," *Zolotoe runo* 2 (1908): 55. William Richardson, "*Zolotoe Runo*" *and Russian Modernism, 1905–1910* (Ann Arbor: Ardis, 1986), 111–12, believes that the tepidity of these actions rendered Blok "ineffectual" as both a revolutionary and a spiritual leader.
162. Gorin-Goriainov, *Aktery*, 117.
163. Ibid., 99; Petrovskaia and Somina, *Teatral'nyi Peterburg*, 216–17.
164. "G. Ch." [G. I. Chulkov], "Benefis L. B. Iavorskoi," *Novaia zhizn'* (February 1, 1906).
165. Rebecca B. Gauss, "Lydia Borisovna Yavorskaya: Her Life, Her Work, Her Times" (M.A. thesis, University of Colorado, 1992), 62–63; *The Times* (London), June 17, 1919, 8.
166. Iankovskii, "Teatral'naia obshchestvennost'," 166.

Having died in 1910, Komissarzhevskaia was not around to experience or comment on the Bolshevik Revolution and its meanings for Russian culture and society. Making her into a posthumous revolutionary icon was no difficult task, especially in periods when her artistic innovations, interest in "decadent" symbolist drama, and work with the officially "unpersoned" Meierkhol'd did not contradict official Soviet cultural policy. The same study that trashed Iavorskaia's shallow commitment to the revolutionary movement lauded Komissarzhevskaia's "passionate ideas of liberation."[167] Aleksandra Brushtein, an avid theatergoer who attended many Dramatic Theater performances, later wrote that the actress "was especially close to the revolution . . . her revolutionary sympathies were widely known in those years."[168] Nadezhda Tiraspol'skaia, who had performed alongside Komissarzhevskaia at the Aleksandrinskii, remembered her as the "standard bearer" of "progressive youth."[169] Commemorating the twentieth anniversary of her death, the once prominent Bolshevik leader Aleksandra Kollontai grandiloquently accorded Komissarzhevskaia "an honored place among the names of those who made possible the victory of revolutionary ideology and the contemporary construction of socialism."[170] In 1959 the theater that had housed Komissarzhevskaia's enterprise for its first two seasons was renamed in her honor. Some recent Russian scholarship continues to present Komissarzhevskaia as someone who "lived for social movements, ideas of revolution."[171]

Much evidence suggests that Komissarzhevskaia's political sympathies were considerably less definitive than these plaudits supposed. Although her efforts for political causes later attracted much attention, the scope of her philanthropy, like that of many other artists, reached virtually every suffering group in Imperial Russia. Komissarzhevskaia put on charitable concerts and performances for the unemployed, their families, poor students, sick children, pogrom victims, literacy programs, impoverished actors, teachers, exiles, and the inhabitants of a town destroyed by a devastating fire, among others.[172] None of this was out of step with the types of philanthropy generally favored by performing artists.

---

167. Ibid., 152–53.
168. Aleksandra Ia. Brushtein, *Stranitsy proshlogo* (Leningrad: Iskusstvo, 1952), 77.
169. N. L. Tiraspol'skaia, *Iz proshlogo russkoi stseny* (Moscow: VTO, 1950), 125.
170. A. Kollontai, "Molodezh' zvala ee solntsem," in *Vera Fedorovna Komissarzhevskaia: Pis'ma aktrisy, vospominaniia o nei, materialy,* ed. A. Ia. Al'tshuller (Leningrad: Iskusstvo, 1964), 251.
171. El'iash, "Tvorchestvo V. F. Komissarzhevskoi," 200. The theater is still named for her today.
172. A. Ia. Al'tshuller, "V. F. Komissarzhevskaia i ee dramaticheskii teatr v 'Passazhe,'" in *Russkaia khudozhestvennaia kul'tura kontsa XIX–nachala XX veka (1895–1907),* 4 vols. (Moscow: Nauka, 1968–81), 1:104; Komisarjevsky, *Myself and the Theatre,* 85; Mary C. Resing, "Vera Fedorovna Kommissarzhevskaia [sic]: A Life in Performance" (Ph.D. diss., University of Michigan, 1997), 36; Khodotov, *Blizkoe—dalekoe,* 153–54, has the story about the burned village.

The actors of the Suvorin Theater who refused to strike in October 1905 and resisted the radicals who forced the evacuation of their theater donated a percentage of their annual income to help starving peasants.[173] "Various revolutionary organizations" approached Gaideburov for support at different times, but as he recalled, "individual actors and even entire troupes made similar requests, having fallen for one reason or another into a disastrous position."[174]

World War I witnessed "a massive outburst of patriotism" among performing artists, many of whom became involved in war-related philanthropy. The Theatrical Society decided in the early days of the war that its philanthropic activities should support the wounded rather than its standard activities. It even opened a hospital for them in its Moscow office.[175] The actors of the Moscow Art Theater donated 2 percent of their salaries to support a military hospital, as did the Nezlobin Theater's performers.[176] Petrograd's Stray Dog cabaret supported its own military hospital with the proceeds from benefit performances. Actresses, ballerinas, and sopranos joined society ladies in becoming nurses. The popular singer Nadezhda Plevitskaia organized concerts to benefit soldiers, as did the former Mariinskii soprano Mariia Dolina, whose concerts produced more than three hundred thousand rubles in the first two years of the war alone. Dolina was so admired that she received government decorations and even had an army unit named after her.[177] Philanthropy could come from almost any quarter. In 1916 the theatrical troupe of the Finnish Life Guards regiment put on charitable dramatic performances to benefit widows and orphans.[178] Although such activities served a united, national purpose, they were, in Hubertus Jahn's description, "exercises in patriotic fervor" that at least partly "promoted reactionary ideas of hierarchy and traditional order."[179]

Komissarzhevskaia's charitable activities were thus not out of step with those of others in her milieu before and after her death. Nor were they confined to financial help. In the weeks before the general strike the actress-entrepreneuse played a leading role in the Actors' Mutual Aid Circle. Significantly, she shared her responsibilities with the conservative Aleksandrinskii actor Vasilii Dalmatov. As we saw in Chapter 3, Khodotov, probably the Imperial Theaters' only

173. "Khronika," *Teatr i iskusstvo* 40 (October 2, 1905): 632.
174. Gaideburov, *Literaturnoe nasledie*, 129.
175. "K chrezvychainynomu sobraniiu chlenov Teatral'nogo Obshchestva v Petrograde," *Teatr i iskusstvo* 34 (August 24, 1914): 692; "Khronika," *Teatr i iskusstvo* 37 (September 14, 1914): 740.
176. "Khronika," *Teatr i iskusstvo* 34 (August 24, 1914): 694.
177. Hubertus Jahn, *Patriotic Culture in Russia During World War I* (Cambridge: Cambridge University Press, 1995), 85, 100, 106, 116, 138. "Khronika," *Teatr i iskusstvo* 33 (August 17, 1914): 677, reports the noted soprano Mariia Kuznetsova-Benua's decision to become a nurse.
178. Petrovskaia and Somina, *Teatral'nyi Peterburg*, 259.
179. Jahn, *Patriotic Culture*, 117–18.

radical and Komissarzhevskaia's lover besides, later accused Dalmatov of being "the first person to wreck" the imperial drama troupe's autonomy movement and bitterly recalled his admonition that "politics is not an actor's affair."[180]

Even participation in charitable concerts with potentially radical overtones failed to define Komissarzhevskaia's politics in any convincing way. Benefits for amnestied political prisoners in which she appeared also included Mariia Savina, the Aleksandrinskii's conservative prima donna whose intrigues had driven the younger actress from the imperial stage and who argued publicly that the theatrical community should stay out of politics. Like her rival and other artists, Komissarzhevskaia performed at such events at least in part because she desired to help those in need, though she may also have done so to affect a radical chic image to appeal to her leftist audience and create publicity.[181] Her brother Fedor, who worked closely with her at the Dramatic Theater, claimed that her "extraordinarily generous" charitable donations left her broke at the time of her death.[182]

While these philanthropic activities reflected the actress's expansive humanity and genuine concern for the lot of the suffering—qualities she shared with a broad cross-section of the Empire's performing arts community and society in general—the strength of her personal political convictions may be doubted. When she received a letter from the Bolshevik Central Committee member and fundraiser Leonid Krasin, Komissarzhevskaia uncharitably asked the messenger, "Have you seen this despot recently?" Describing her first meeting with Krasin in 1903, she recalled him asking, "Are you a revolutionary?" "I was stunned," she admitted, "and could not answer anything."[183] Yet responding to the Bolshevik's eloquent pleas for financial help for a vaguely progressive cause—pleas that also helped him extract money from bankers, officials, and the wealthy industrialist and arts patron Savva Morozov—Komissarzhveskaia gave him concert proceeds that helped buy a printing press for the Bolshevik paper *The Spark* (*Iskra*). Similarly, the Bolshevik activist Agrippina Kruglova persuaded Komissarzhevskaia to donate the receipts of a performance of Chekhov's *The Seagull* to help establish a "cultural enlightenment center" run by Petersburg Social Democrats to hide clandestine political activities.[184]

---

180. Khodotov, *Blizkoe—dalekoe*, 194–95.
181. Resing, "Kommissarzhevskaia," 46, 60. Victor Borovsky, *A Triptych from the Russian Theatre: An Artistic Biography of the Komissarzhevskys* (Iowa City: University of Iowa Press, 2001), 156, makes the same argument about her repertoire selection.
182. Komisarjevsky, *Myself and the Theatre*, 85. Her theater's financial difficulties probably also had something to do with it.
183. A. Serebrov [A. N. Tikhonov], *Vremia i liudi: Vospominaniia, 1898–1905* (Moscow: Moskovskii rabochii, 1955), 93–94.
184. A. I. Kruglova, "Ona pomogla nam," in Al'tshuller, *Komissarzhevskaia*, 252.

In neither case is it clear that Komissarzhevskaia knew the ultimate purpose or political significance of her largesse. Telling Gor'kii about her first impression of the suave Krasin, she confessed that "there is no way I could ever have thought that this was a revolutionary."[185] When the fugitive Menshevik president of the St. Petersburg Soviet Georgii Khrustalev-Nosar appeared seeking shelter in her home, she had no idea who he was. But she helped him nevertheless because she saw before her not a political dissident with whom she felt solidarity, but a person in need at a time of distress.[186] Brushtein's observation that the revolutionary side of Komissarzhevskaia was "offensively little revealed" may thus have been grounded in solid fact rather than feigned indignation.[187]

Komissarzhevskaia and others like her proved that it was possible to be "a sensitive barometer to all the changes in the life of society" without being politically "conscious" or holding any well-defined convictions.[188] In Arkady Ostrovsky's recent words "the revolution for Komissarzhevskaia had ethical, rather than political meaning."[189] Indeed, her most memorable political statement came after she twisted her ankle while descending from the dais at the October 20, 1905, meeting of performers at the Panaev Theater: "I'm not lucky in politics," she quipped.[190]

Regardless of artist attitudes toward politics in the late imperial era, no study of a performing arts culture would be complete without examining another vital barometer of the prevailing mood, the audience. It is to the other side of the proscenium to which we must now devote our attention.

---

185. Maksim Gor'kii, *Polnoe sobranie sochinenii*, 25 vols. (Moscow: Gosudarstvennoe Izdatel'stvo khudozhestvennoi literatury, 1968), 17:55.

186. Komisarjevsky, *Myself and the Theatre*, 85. The laudatory Soviet literature on Komissarzhevskaia is silent about this episode.

187. Brushtein, *Stranitsy*, 77.

188. Borovsky, *Triptych from the Russian Theatre*, 132.

189. Arkady Ostrovsky, "Imperial and Private Theatres, 1882–1905," in *A History of Russian Theatre*, ed. Robert Leach and Victor Borovsky (Cambridge: Cambridge University Press, 1999), 245.

190. Rybakova, *Komissarzhevskaia*, 98.

5

"YOU DARE NOT MAKE SPORT OF OUR NERVES!":
THE AUDIENCES

On October 18, 1905, a riot broke out at the Mariinskii Theater. That evening its opera troupe was presenting Richard Wagner's early and most Italianate work, *Lohengrin*. Nothing about the plot was especially incendiary in the context of Russian social and political life. Elsa, the daughter of a tenth-century Duke of Brabant, is implicated in the murder of her younger brother, the realm's rightful heir, who has mysteriously disappeared. When her accuser asks Henry the Fowler, King of the Germans, to condemn her, an unknown champion appears from the mists in a boat drawn by a swan. Victorious in a trial of single combat and merciful to his opponent, the knight proves the girl's innocence and offers to marry her on the condition that she never ask his name or origins. She agrees, but the banished accuser returns to plant seeds of suspicion about the champion in Elsa's mind and plot his murder. After the wedding the overwrought damsel breaks down and asks her champion's identity. Although she then saves him from the murder plot, and despite his promise to lead an army against invaders upon the morrow, the knight ends the opera by identifying himself as Lohengrin, son of the Holy Grail King Parzifal (Percival in Arthurian legend and Parsifal in a later Wagner opera), and disappears into the mists from whence he came. In the denouement he magically transforms the swan that draws his boat into the missing heir, freeing the boy from a curse that had been placed on him to frame Elsa, and leaves Brabant to its rightful ruler.

The performance's only unusual feature was that late the previous evening Tsar Nicholas II had promulgated the October Manifesto, a decree promising the Russian people substantial civil liberties and an elected legislative body. Arriving in the middle of a paralyzing national general strike, news of the government's concessions called forth a huge outburst of relief and cheer. Tens of thousands of citizens came out into the Empire's streets in delirious celebration. Striking workers returned to their jobs. Many believed that Russia was entering a new era of liberty. The press hailed the success of a "peaceful national revolution" and warmly greeted the manifesto as "the first step toward a Russian constitution." Even such conservative defenders of the autocracy as Petersburg's Governor General Dmitrii Trepov could say that "now a new life will begin."[1] The painter Il'ia Repin captured the tumultuous mood in a large canvas entitled simply, if somewhat anachronistically, *October 17, 1905*.[2] It shows a vast, ecstatic crowd of all ages and urban social strata extending from Palace Square into a deep background framed by the Admiralty and St. Isaac's Cathedral, noted Petersburg landmarks. The figures in the foreground are smiling, laughing, singing, and holding aloft a defiant prisoner who raises shattered fetters into the air. A few people look as though they are in prayer or serious contemplation. Only one frowning, brow-furrowing man in a civil service uniform at the painting's extreme right seems unhappy.

Not everyone proved to be such a great fan of the promised reforms. Defenders of the autocracy despised the manifesto as a concession that had been forcibly extracted from the tsar by disloyal and rebellious subjects. Some of them reacted violently. Many liberal politicians and intellectuals continued to mistrust the government and remained skeptical of its intentions; others needed to see the reform project work in practice to be convinced. Uncompromising radicals, who watched the wind blow out of their sails with every worker who picked up his tools, had no reason at all to welcome reform. The St. Petersburg Soviet responded to the manifesto by calling for a continuation of the general strike. Few listened, however, and almost all of Russia's labor organizations independently decided to resume work before the Soviet endorsed that step effective on October 21.[3]

The radical Left's determination to disrupt the status quo and attack symbols of the regime brought havoc to the audience assembled at the Mariinskii on the first evening after the announcement of the October Manifesto. Vasilii Bertenson, a physician who bought a ticket on the spur of the moment to hear the

---

1. Quotes from Abraham Ascher, *The Revolution of 1905: Russia in Disarray* (Stanford: Stanford University Press, 1988), 229–31.

2. Repin's painting is set in daylight. The manifesto reached the public just before midnight on October 17, and the scene depicted on the canvas could therefore only have taken place the following day.

3. Ascher, *Revolution of 1905*, 232. The Soviet's vote was on October 20. It called, superfluously as it turned out, for the workers to end the strike at noon the following day.

beautiful young soprano Mariia Kuznetsova-Benua, noted that the theater was only half full. Such poor attendance was uncommon for performances of Wagner's operas at the Mariinskii in those years but attributable that evening to the recent turbulence and excitement. Just after the curtain went up on *Lohengrin*'s second act, two representatives from a meeting of "students and 'conscious' comrades" demanded that the management end the performance and close the theater.[4] They were told that Trepov and the Minister of the Imperial Court, Baron Vladimir Frederiks, had ordered the theater to operate that evening. Only Frederiks, as the minister responsible for the Imperial Theaters, could countermand those instructions. The representatives departed, muttering that they would take matters into their own hands.[5]

A few minutes later someone in the theater's upper reaches jolted the audience from its Wagnerian raptures with a shout of "Down with the autocracy!"[6] Bertenson, sitting in the parterre stalls, heard other patrons respond with cries of "Shut up, young man!" and "What impertinence!" A spectator whom he took to be a professor stood up in his box and began to make a speech about the manifesto. No sooner had he begun than annoyed and unsympathetic audience members yelled, "Out with him!" and, "Shut his mouth!" A few officers lunged into the orator's box and rounded on him with their fists. Others leapt from their seats and drew their swords. A number of people called for the orchestra to calm the crowd by playing "God Save the Tsar," while a smaller number of dissenters hissed the suggestion.

Total panic ensued. Eduard Napravnik, the house's chief conductor since 1869, fled his podium, followed by most of the orchestra and singers. Many patrons rushed to leave, some hurdling over row after row of parterre seats to get out faster.[7] Those in the upper tiers tried to rush down the theater's narrow staircases. On one side their exit was blocked by a huge, drunk, redheaded merchant who stood menacingly on the landing and with one hand swung his chair at them shouting, "All right, you revolutionaries, bring it on, I'll smash you to splinters! . . . Really, to scandalize an Imperial Theater when full freedom has now been given everywhere! Here are your rights, you ungrateful swine!" A young female student pleaded with the theater's security guards to stop the brawl, but not enough were on hand.[8] The officers beating up the professor

---

4. V. B. Bertenson, *Za 30 let (listki iz vospominanii)* (St. Petersburg: n.p., 1914), 276–77.
5. V. A. Teliakovskii, "Imperatorskie teatry i 1905 god," in V. A. Teliakovskii, *Vospominaniia* (Leningrad: Iskusstvo, 1965), 255.
6. Ibid.; Bertenson, *Za 30 let*, 277.
7. Teliakovskii, "Imperatorskie teatry," 255–56; Bertenson, *Za 30 let*, 277.
8. Bertenson, *Za 30 let*, 278–79.

were armed and dangerous after all! Nevertheless, the unfortunate academic got away and the guards managed to subdue the surly merchant, who, in an inebriated attempt to reason, insisted that he was "helping you against the hooligans!" According to the Director of the Imperial Theaters Vladimir Teliakovskii, "the final commotion came when chairs from the boxes were thrown into the parterre like grenades and bombs."⁹

As a measure of calm returned, the small audience remaining in the hall again asked for "God Save the Tsar." Kuznetsova-Benua announced that the artists were too "nauseous" to continue the performance but led those remaining in a performance of the national anthem. Bertenson recalled "deafening applause" before everyone left.¹⁰ "Thus ended the first day of freedom," Teliakovskii sarcastically remembered.¹¹ The box office offered full refunds.¹²

What did Russian audiences want in the late imperial era? One cannot approach this question effectively without looking at who they were. Russia's performing arts had traditionally been an elite form of entertainment, confined in the eighteenth century to state theaters in the capital cities and, in the countryside, to the estates of wealthy landowners who coveted the trappings of European high culture and relied on talented serfs to populate their ranks of players. Professional and semiprofessional theatrical companies sprouted throughout Russia's provinces in the mid-nineteenth century, but in the capitals theatrical entertainment remained dominated by the Imperial Theaters, which held a de jure monopoly on performances there until March 1882. Emerging private and popular theaters competed for their audiences as well as their performers. The popular fairground booth form of theater—the *balagan*—was simple in content and derided as provincial and backward by "cultured" Russians. The very word "*balagan*" was thought a "derogatory appellation" and an "antonym for real theater and art."¹³

As Russia entered the reigns of its last two tsars, theatrical exclusivity was on the wane. Although more socially diverse audiences crowded urban theaters in earlier times,¹⁴ by the early twentieth century they had ceased to be the sole province of the Empire's upper strata. The theater historian Ira Petrovskaia

---

9. Teliakovskii, "Imperatorskie teatry," 256.
10. Bertenson, *Za 30 let*, 279; Teliakovskii, "Imperatorskie teatry," 256–57.
11. Teliakovskii, "Imperatorskie teatry," 257.
12. Bertenson, *Za 30 let*, 279.
13. E. Anthony Swift, *Popular Theater and Society in Tsarist Russia* (Berkeley and Los Angeles: University of California Press, 2002), 29.
14. Richard Stites, *Serfdom, Society, and the Arts in Imperial Russia: The Pleasure and the Power* (New Haven: Yale University Press, 2005), 186.

probably exaggerated when she wrote that "everyone went to the theater just as everyone read a newspaper" in Late Imperial Russia, but she is correct to suggest that there was no "average theatergoer."[15]

The Imperial Theaters, particularly those of Petersburg, have long been depicted as insufferably exclusive institutions, "citadels of glamour" that remained the province of an extremely wealthy and well connected few.[16] E. Anthony Swift has described them as remote institutions, "high temples of the Westernized culture of Russia's privileged classes" and "symbols of the expanding cultural gap between the elite and the common people."[17] Murray Frame's institutional history of the Petersburg Imperial Theaters argues that they "were broadly exclusive institutions" and that, for example, "ninety-nine per cent of the population of the imperial capital had no access, or only a limited possibility of access, to the opera."[18]

These conclusions rely largely on the way in which access to the Imperial Theaters was sold. From 1884 tickets to most performances were available to season subscribers, who bought seats to a large number of performances far in advance. Ballet subscriptions initially allowed buyers to only purchase tickets to most of a season's performances, usually forty to fifty.[19] Opera subscriptions typically included ten performances—still a substantial expense if one wanted pricey seats, and at least theoretically a bar to urban audiences who were anything less than affluent.

The aura that surrounded subscriptions and the audiences who held them is a common trope in memories of ballet and opera performances in Imperial Russia. Ballet subscribers constituted the famous "balletomanes," aesthetes who by virtue of the sales policy attended all or most performances and were thought to have formed the most precise and scrutinizing appreciation of the art form. Many combined their artistic interest with romantic attachments (usually unrequited) to the ballerinas. Listen to Teliakovskii's description of them at the height of their prominence:

> They entered the hall with a special assurance, exchanging a few words of greeting among themselves and with representatives of the theater administration; the ushers bowed especially low to them, which the balletomanes

---

15. I. F. Petrovskaia, *Teatr i zritel' rossiiskikh stolits: 1895–1917* (Leningrad: Iskusstvo, 1990), 4, 46.
16. The phrase "citadels of glamour" is from N. A. Gorchakov, *The Theater in Soviet Russia*, trans. Edgar Lehrman (New York: Columbia University Press, 1957), 3.
17. Swift, *Popular Theater*, 17.
18. Murray Frame, *The St. Petersburg Imperial Theatres: Stage and State in Revolutionary Russia, 1900–1920* (Greensboro, N.C.: McFarland, 2000), 67, 83.
19. Teliakovskii, "Baletomany," in Teliakovskii, *Vospominaniia*, 432–33.

answered with an imperceptible nod upwards, as important people usually convey greetings. The balletomane never took his seat right away. At first he—if his subscription seats were in the first row—spoke a few friendly words to the musicians in the orchestra, and sometimes even offered a handshake. . . . On ballet days the whole Mariinskii Theater turned into a temple of carefree joy and love. . . . There were people of the sovereign's suite, courtiers, generals of full rank and physique, gilded youths, department directors, former governors and governors-general, retired generals and admirals, people from the financial world, former and current *rentiers*, editors and newspaper employees, student youths, and, finally, those whose profession and origins could not be fully determined by the others.[20]

The ballerina Tamara Karsavina remembered theirs as a "very curious world with its own culture," in which subscription seats were passed down by inheritance.[21] The young music student Sergei Prokof'ev thought Mariinskii subscriptions were "prized like treasure" and also commented on their heritability.[22] The French ambassador Maurice Paléologue rubbed elbows with "a brilliant audience" populated by "the upper and propertied classes."[23] The touring American dancer Isadora Duncan, a frequent guest in Russia in the first decades of the twentieth century, "saw the most beautiful women in the world, in marvelous décolleté gowns, covered with jewels, escorted by men in distinguished uniforms." More salaciously, she encountered officers "who would have given anything to be allowed to make love to me," but who "bored me so by the first words they said to me, that they even froze my senses to the very centre of desire."[24]

These impressions are naturally subjective, and a close examination reveals that neither they nor the simple fact of the subscription sales policy reflected the whole truth about Imperial Theater audiences. Subscribing was unnecessary to be among them, if for the simple reason that the box office usually failed to sell out, either by subscription or single-ticket sales. A detailed reading of the season schedules published in the Imperial Theaters' *Yearbook*, which listed each performance's receipts, shows that in the 1905–6 season 86 out of 131 ordinary opera performances and all regular ballet performances failed to sell out

20. Teliakovskii, "Baletomany," 416–17.
21. Tamara Karsavina, *Theatre Street: The Reminiscinces of Tamara Karsavina* (New York: Dutton, 1931), 150–53.
22. Sergei Prokof'ev, *Avtobiografiia* (Moscow: Sovetskii Kompozitor, 1982), 241.
23. Maurice Paléologue, *An Ambassador's Memoirs*, 3 vols., trans. F. A. Holt (London: Hutchinson, 1923–25), 1:166.
24. Isadora Duncan, *My Life* (New York: Boni and Liveright, 1927), 164, 171.

the Mariinskii Theater.[25] In most cases plenty of nonsubscription tickets to the Empire's premier operatic and ballet stage were available to the general public. Even then demand was insufficiently high to fill the entire house, a dilemma that Western theatrical companies selling tickets via subscription still face today.[26] Moscow's Imperial Theaters were even less crowded. Teliakovskii, who led them from 1898 to 1901, found their audiences "casual" (*sluchaino*) and estimated that no more than one-fourth of their seats were normally taken.[27]

Attendance at the ballet, whose performances almost never sold out, was particularly poor. Prince Petr Liven, a balletomane who became an official of the Imperial Theaters Directorate in 1903, recalled a "half-empty auditorium" and observed that the art form "survived only feebly."[28] Early in his tenure as Director, Teliakovskii hoped to alleviate this situation. Believing that the theaters "could not exist for one handful of privileged people" and that their "deficit could be corrected only if a large public attended," he increased the number of nonsubscription ballet performances and replaced the traditional subscription option of buying tickets to most of the season's performances with three series of ten performances each, which no single subscriber would be allowed to combine. Although some old guard fanatics got around the new rules, the subscription reform succeeded in expanding and diversifying the audience.[29] Nonsubscribers, who could always simply buy unsold tickets to any performance, had greater opportunities to attend: in the 1904–5 season the number of ballet performances sold in subscriptions fell to thirty-four of that season's total of forty-eight; in 1905–6 the figure dropped further to twenty-six of forty-two.[30] Within four years of Teliakovskii's arrival, in other words, nearly 40 percent of ballet performances came to be sold exclusively via single-ticket sales, whereas virtually none had been a few years earlier. The existence of subscriptions had not automatically excluded the general public, but in a meaningful sense "a new audience appeared, who had never attended the ballet before."[31]

---

25. "Sezon 1905–1906 gg.," *Ezhegodnik Imperatorskikh teatrov* 16 (1905–6, chast' II): 84–130. Full receipts for an evening equaled approximately thirty-six hundred rubles for both art forms. The figures presented here do not include benefit performances, which charged higher prices, and a couple of stray performances for which the receipts were unreported.

26. New York's Metropolitan Opera, which offers almost all its performances for initial sale by subscription, functioned at 85 percent capacity in the 2005–6 season, a figure low enough to persuade its management to make ambitious and popularizing reforms.

27. Teliakovskii, *Vospominaniia*, 74.

28. Prince Peter Lieven, *The Birth of the Ballets-Russes*, trans. L. Zarine (New York: Dover, 1973), 56.

29. Teliakovskii, "Baletomany," 434–49. Teliakovskii remembered performances as early as the 1902–3 season at which the "new" audience shouted down the balletomanes when they booed and hissed innovations in productions.

30. Frame, *Imperial Theatres*, 67.

31. Teliakovskii, *Vospominaniia*, 76.

Audience diversity also stood as a n otable feature of imperial opera and drama performances. No precise figures exist, but large numbers of students, workers, intellectuals, and casual spectators easily attended. Dr. Bertenson simply went to the box office and bought his ticket to the unfortunate performance of *Lohengrin* in October 1905, which, as he recalled, was half empty. The evening's circumstances probably accounted for the smaller crowd he observed, but plenty of evidence corroborates the existence of incidental audiences in the late imperial era. The Obukhov steelworker and future actor Konstantin Skorobogatov proudly bought a ticket to Wagner's *Tristan and Isolde* at the Mariinskii when he became interested in high culture. Finding himself more attracted to drama, he used his weekly bonus of fifty kopeks to attend Sunday afternoon plays at the Aleksandrinskii.[32] In his poor art student days Petr Gnedich, who eventually became that theater's artistic director, bribed its ushers fifty kopeks to sit in empty parterre seats.[33] A relative of Prokof'ev had a subscription to the Mariinskii, enabling the budding composer to go to the opera.[34] The young actress Valentina Verigina frequently attended Moscow's Imperial Theaters when she was barely surviving as a poor dr ama student.[35] The theater scholar Victor Borovsky's father, another poor student, simply snuck into the Mariinskii without paying. Caught by an usher on one occasion, he claimed to know Fedor Shaliapin, who was singing that evening. Presented to the great bass with what the usher recognized as an obvious lie, the elder Borovsky was delighted when Shaliapin, picking up on his trick, burst out, "Of course he knows me," and told the usher to let him in and give him the best seat he could find.[36] Shaliapin himself wrote after 1917 that "hotheads of the populace recently said that the theatre with its high prices is a bourgeois amusement. I frankly state that this is not true." "Being Imperial," he maintained without a self-conscious hint of paradox, "the theatres were also for the people."[37] This comment was as subjective

32. K. Skorobogatov, *Zhizn' i stsena* (Leningrad: Lenizdat, 1970), 46–48.
33. P. P. Gnedich, *Kniga zhizni: Vospominaniia, 1855–1918* (Moscow: Agraf, 2000), 43.
34. Prokof'ev, *Avtobiografiia*, 241.
35. V. P. Verigina, *Vospominaniia* (Leningrad: Iskusstvo, 1974), 44, 61.
36. Victor Borovsky, *Chaliapin: A Critical Biography* (New York: Knopf, 1988), xiv–xv.
37. Feodor Chaliapin, *Pages from My Life: An Autobiography,* trans. H. M. Buck (New York: Harper and Brothers, 1927), 211. None of these observations would have been out of place in other modernizing societies. One need only think of the (in)famous and largely working-class *loggionisti* of Milan's La Scala. According to Jim Davis and Victor Emeljanow, *Reflecting the Audience: London Theatregoing, 1840–1880* (Iowa City: University of Iowa Press, 2001), 226, "London theatre audiences in the mid-nineteenth century were so diverse that generic definitions are clearly inappropriate." Lawrence W. Levine, *Highbrow/Lowbrow: The Emergence of Cultural Hierarchy in America* (Cambridge: Harvard University Press, 1988), 86, finds nineteenth-century American opera audiences "*simultaneously* popular and elite." Original italics.

Fig. 14 Ticket prices to the Aleksandrinskii Theater, the imperial drama venue in St. Petersburg, advertised for the 1913–14 season. It offered modest seating options for as little as five kopeks. From the author's private collection.

as any other observation about Imperial Theater audiences, but it nevertheless stands as the impression of one their favorite artists.

Prices to individual performances were not uniformly prohibitive. While the best seats in the Imperial Theaters—located in sections where such elite spectators as Paléologue and Duncan perched—were costly, a significant portion of tickets were affordable to the urban middle class, students, and, in the case of Skorobogatov and others, even workers. The galleries, the cheapest sections of the theaters, were so affordable that Petrovskaia's study of Moscow and Petersburg audiences cedes them almost entirely to students.[38] Enough "progressive youths" got in to adopt the affecting young Vera Komissarzhevskaia as "their own standard bearer" before she left the Aleksandrinskii's drama troupe in 1902.[39] During the randomly chosen 1913–14 season seats in that theater's upper reaches could be had for as little as s eventeen kopeks and were discounted to a mere five kopeks for students.[40] Komissarzhevskaia's brother and director Fedor, who also mounted productions there, described the theater as "not expensive."[41] In comparison, prices for tickets to the Obukhov workers' theater company in which Skorobogatov acted ranged from ten kopeks to one ruble.[42] The writer and critic Aleksandr Pleshcheev enumerated "journalists, playwrights, merchants, and actors" among the Aleksandrinskii's habitués, while the avid theatergoer Aleksandra Brushtein described them collectively as "the third estate."[43] The actor Iurii Iur'ev recalled that his audiences were often casually dressed, for the Aleksandrinskii "was not at the center of Petersburg society's attention."[44] Marc Slonim accepted the imperial dramatic stage's description as a "theater for the people" into which "educated men and women from the lower and middle classes infused new blood."[45] Richard Stites has identified it even in the 1830s and 1840s "as the theatrical gathering place for a broad cross-section of the urban population."[46]

---

38. Petrovskaia, *Teatr i zritel' rossiiskikh stolits*, 173.

39. N. L. Tiraspol'skaia, *Iz proshlogo russkoi stseny* (Moscow: VTO, 1950), 125.

40. *Plany i tseny v Imperatorskikh teatrakh* (St. Petersburg: Tipografiia Imperatorskikh Sankt Peterburgskikh teatrov, 1913). Gerald D. Surh, *1905 in St. Petersburg: Labor, Society, and Revolution* (Stanford: Stanford University Press, 1989), 23–25, cites a calculation that the average Petersburg worker made 314 rubles a year in 1900. Seventeen kopeks was probably not prohibitive.

41. Theodore Komisarjevsky, *Myself and the Theatre* (London: Heinemann, 1929), 35.

42. Skorobogatov, *Zhizn' i stsena*, 51.

43. A. A. Pleshcheev, *Pod seniiu kulis.* . . . (Paris: VAL, 1936), 148; Aleksandra Brushtein, *Stranitsy proshlogo* (Leningrad: Iskusstvo, 1952), 245.

44. Iu. M. Iur'ev, *Zapiski*, 2 vols. (Leningrad: Iskusstvo, 1963), 1:370.

45. Marc Slonim, *Russian Theater: From the Empire to the Soviets* (Cleveland: World Publishing, 1961), 90, 65.

46. Stites, *Serfdom, Society, and the Arts*, 186.

Fig. 15 Prices at the Mariinskii Theater, the imperial capital's main opera and ballet venue. Like the Aleksandrinskii Theater, it offered affordable tickets that nonelite spectators bought and enjoyed. From the author's private collection.

Opera and ballet could also be relatively inexpensive. In 1913 the Mariinskii Theater's cheapest seats sold for forty-seven kopeks on weekdays and twenty kopeks for Sunday opera and ballet performances. Since the ballet danced only on Sundays and odd Wednesdays, two-thirds of its performances were thus subject to substantial discounts, which scaled the theater's entire range of prices.[47] At about the same time average cinemas charged their large, socially diverse audiences a comparable twenty to fifty kopeks for floor seats and two to four rubles for boxes.[48] Low prices undoubtedly helped the tenor Ivan Ershov build up a huge following among the "laboring intelligentsia" and become "the most beloved singer and artist of Petersburg students," difficult feats if those groups could rarely or never attend his performances in an era before radio or widespread commercial recordings. His biographer noted that "it was not hard for [them] to get in, for they filled the theater's gallery and comprised the basic group of Ershov's fans."[49]

Even the "glamorous" balletomane clique could not escape cultural modernity's social homogenization. The dance historian Roland Wiley has found references to its elite character "more convenient than accurate" and noted that its members were "drawn from all social and economic classes," a claim borne out by Teliakovskii's inclusion of "student youth" in his description of its typical members.[50] The famous dancer and choreographer Mikhail Fokin recalled one longtime subscriber, a modest clerk named Sil'vo, who held subscription seats in the gallery. Upon the fan's death Fokin visited his small apartment in an unfashionable neighborhood to retrieve his bequest to the Imperial Theaters, a book collection that became the nucleus of the Ballet School's library. Far from being surprised, Fokin observed that "such ballet fans, modestly sitting in the cheapest seats in the balcony, were at that time numerous."[51]

Incidental factors did threaten, at least superficially, to keep lower class audiences away from the Imperial Theaters and the centrally located private theaters. Urban geography alone presented serious obstacles. Most Russian workers dwelled in peripheral communities on the outskirts of major cities and worked ten or more hours a day. Without widespread vehicle ownership or reliable

47. *Plany i tseny v Imperatorskikh teatrakh.*
48. Denise Youngblood, *The Magic Mirror: Moviemaking in Russia, 1908–1918* (Madison: University of Wisconsin Press, 1999), 43. According to RGIA, f. 497, op. 6, ed. khr. 4604, l. 8, in 1900 seats in the stalls of the Aleksandrinskii also cost between two and four rubles.
49. Abram Gozenpud, *Ivan Ershov: Zhizn' i stsenicheskaia deiatel'nost': Issledovanie*, 2nd ed. (St. Petersburg: Kompozitor, 1999), 272–73.
50. Roland John Wiley, *Tchaikovsky's Ballets: "Swan Lake," "Sleeping Beauty," "Nutcracker"* (Oxford: Clarendon, 1985), 11.
51. Mikhail Fokin, *Protiv techeniia: Vospominaniia baletmeistera. Stat'i, pis'ma* (Leningrad: Iskusstvo, 1962), 80.

Fig. 16 An illustration of the typical audience in the gallery of the Aleksandrinskii Theater. Its patrons were well known for their social diversity, and its prices were low. From V. A. Teliakovskii, *Vospominaniia* (Leningrad: Iskusstvo, 1965).

public transportation, walking from home or factory to the center of town and back again was impractical and difficult, especially during the awful winters, when most performances were staged. The arrival of trams connecting the outer districts with urban centers undoubtedly improved mobility, but the trip remained long.[52]

Standard repertoires presented another potential barrier. Even the most "conscious" workers had limited educations that did not allow them to share the highbrow cultural contexts, requisite language skills, and sophisticated artistic tastes of urban Russia's upper and middle classes. How many workers could be expected to attend performances at the imperial Mikhailovskii Theater when most of them were in French? The worker memoirist Semen Kanatchikov later admitted that "the music played at the concerts or theaters failed to impress

---

52. Brushtein, *Stranitsy,* 246–47; Luigi Villari, *Russia of To-Day* (Boston: Millet, 1910), 45.

me; we did not understand it and dismissed it as lordly amusement for the privileged." One of Kanatchikov's machinist colleagues thought the performing arts "very fine" yet maintained that "they aren't accessible to us workers. Right now all those things are for the idlers, parasites, and loafers."[53]

Nevertheless, workers, students, and other poor urban residents were enjoying the performing arts to a much greater degree than ever before. Teliakovskii frequently received letters from people in these groups asking for more non-subscription performances and discounted tickets, requests to which he claimed to have responded in a constructive way.[54] Even Kanatchikov's comments about the *lack* of appeal that the arts held for him and his comrades ultimately resulted from their exposure to them.

If poorer social groups were appearing in the Imperial Theaters, the importance of those venues as places of socialization for "high society"—the plot-turning meetings and ritualized courtships depicted in nineteenth-century novels—was in decline. According to Teliakovskii, interest in serious theater among top officialdom, courtiers, and the highest stratum of the aristocracy fell to the point where people in these categories "often asked me the most unexpected questions, proving that history and art were perfectly foreign to them. High society had a poor understanding of even the plots." "The majority of the public attending the Imperial Theaters," the Director recalled, "consisted of gentry of average prosperity, the intelligentsia, the bureaucratic world, the merchantry, and young students."[55] This audience was certainly not proletarian, but it was nevertheless far from exclusive.

Instead of reinforcing an outmoded social hierarchy, audience composition reflected the broad economic and social changes brought on by rapid industrialization, commercialization, and other facets of urban modernity. To middle-class Russians the Imperial Theaters offered chances to mix and identify with elites by engaging in what at least symbolically remained an elite activity, to capture some of the "*bon ton*" that the actor Iur'ev ascribed to ballet, for example.[56] This heightened their sense of belonging, status, and social mobility, in addition to their evolving senses of self and individuality. For less-well-off elements, the Imperial Theaters offered opportunities for cultural self-improvement, a common desire among workers and students. Knowledge of the artistic world promised an entrée into the realm of culture and ideas that they coveted and identified

---

53. Reginald E. Zelnik, ed. and trans., *A Radical Worker in Tsarist Russia: The Autobiography of Semën Ivanovich Kanatchikov* (Stanford: Stanford University Press, 1986), 103, 106.
54. Teliakovskii, *Vospominaniia*, 77.
55. Ibid.
56. Iur'ev, *Zapiski*, 1:369.

with social respectability and self-actualization. Premieres of innovative new productions, which became more common after 1900, stimulated their interest. As the French sociologist Pierre Bourdieu theorized in reference to cultural consumption, "the manner of using symbolic goods, especially those regarded as the attributes of excellence, constitutes one of the key markers of 'class' and also the ideal weapon in strategies of distinction."[57] Late Imperial Russia offered an arsenal of such weapons, especially in cultural life.

Even the Imperial Theaters' advertising sponsors reflected the broadening audience of the state stage. Chic *couturiers* and exclusive shops attracted potential customers in official publications; but so, too, did the publisher of the telephone book, soap salesmen, life insurance companies, a hose manufacturer, and a champagne purveyor who felt compelled to explain the meanings of "sec," "very dry," and "brut," not improbably for consumers who were partaking of his product for the first time.[58]

Russia's private theaters were often no less exclusive than its imperial stages, whose audiences and performers they shared. Indeed, in some cases private theater prices far exceeded those of their imperial counterparts. When the Moscow Art Theater toured to Petersburg in the first years of the twentieth century, it charged sell-out audiences a whopping twenty-six rubles for front-row seats, compared to the four rubles that the Aleksandrinskii charged for the best places in its stalls in 1900. At two rubles, seventy kopeks, places in the Art Theater's gallery cost three times more than the most expensive upper-tier seats at the capital's principal imperial dramatic theater.[59] Like the Imperial Theaters, moreover, the Art Theater and a number of other enterprises also sold tickets by subscription, a practice that endured until 1917.[60]

But here, too, hefty prices do not tell the whole story. According to Stanislavskii's business partner Vladimir Nemirovich-Danchenko, the Art Theater "attracted all strata of the population," including "the whole advanced youth," which "in particular, considered the Art Theatre its own." In some cases young

---

57. Pierre Bourdieu, *Distinction: A Social Critique of the Judgement of Taste*, trans. Richard Nice (Cambridge: Harvard University Press, 1984), 66.
58. *Plany i tseny v Imperatorskikh teatrakh*. For a wider array of such advertisements, see the last pages of any issue of *Ezhegodnik Imperatorskikh teatrov*.
59. Petrovskaia, *Teatr i zritel' rossiiskikh stolits*, 79. According to RGIA, f. 497, op. 6, ed. khr. 4604, l. 8, in 1900 the top price for seats in the Aleksandrinskii's gallery was ninety kopeks.
60. "Khronika," *Teatr i iskusstvo* 7 (February 11, 1901): 147, reports the Art Theater's subscription seats selling out in two days. "Khronika," *Teatr i iskusstvo* 9 (March 3, 1913) announces the opening of subscriptions for Zimin's private opera company. "Khronika," *Teatr i iskusstvo* 5 (January 29, 1917): 96, reports the Art Theater's plan to end subscription sales in the hope of boosting revenues, which had suffered because of World War I.

Fig. 17 Typical advertising in a publication of the Imperial Theaters Directorate. The ad at the top of the page is for a wine and cigar shop. Beneath it is an ad for a wine and champagne company. At the lower left its Russian customers are helped by definitions of "sec," "very dry," and "brut." From the author's private collection.

people did not even have to purchase tickets. Nemirovich-Danchenko recalled accommodating as many as five hundred nonpaying students who stole into the theater's upper reaches for one performance: "We winked at it; after all, they were the student youth."[61]

Other notable private venues, such as the Suvorin and Korsh theaters, attracted an "essential public" that "consisted of the bourgeoisie and intelligentsia," with audiences becoming more diverse for less-expensive late-run performances and revival productions.[62] Korsh's enterprise offered cheap matinee tickets that allowed large numbers of lower-class spectators to attend.[63] At the same time the dramatist Tat'iana Shchepkina-Kupernik observed among Suvorin's audiences "elderly officials, ladies covered in jewels, and gilded youths from the Guards regiments."[64] The avid theatergoer Aleksandra Brushtein, on the other hand, thought Suvorin's public "a rank lower" than the Aleksandrinskii's, but the precision and significance of such impressionistic remarks could be dubious.[65]

Vera Komissarzhevskaia's two successive theatrical enterprises, which operated between 1904 and 1908, also attracted a varied public, though the blanket label of "intelligentsia" is most often applied to her spectators.[66] The better seats accommodated well-off figures from Petersburg's arts community and wealthier theatergoers. Students and less-established intelligentsia types crowded the balconies. Brushtein recorded "segments of the foremost workers of Petersburg factories" maintaining a presence there as well.[67] Nothing could have illustrated the social divide in Komissarzhevskaia's audience better than the demonstration that accompanied the premiere of Gor'kii's *Summerfolk* in September 1904. The play, which depicts ineffectual intelligentsia members on vacation, drew furious protests from the front of the theater, where many of the capital's leading cultural figures jeered and hissed. The crowd in the balcony cheered Gor'kii and his excoriation of their social betters in the stalls. As one spectator remembered, "the aesthetes booed, cursed, and stomped their feet. The amphitheater

61. Vladimir Nemirovitch-Danchenko, *My Life in the Russian Theatre*, trans. John Cournos (London: Bles, 1937), 238.
62. Petrovskaia, *Teatr i zritel' rossiiskikh stolits,* 11; I. F. Petrovskaia and V. Somina, *Teatral'nyi Peterburg: Nachalo XVIII veka–oktiabr' 1917 goda: Obozrenie-putevoditel'* (St. Petersburg: RIII, 1994), 205.
63. Murray Frame, *School for Citizens: Theatre and Civil Society in Imperial Russia* (New Haven: Yale University Press, 2006), 133.
64. T. L. Shchepkina-Kupernik, *Teatr v moei zhizni* (Moscow: Iskusstvo, 1948), 108.
65. Brushtein, *Stranitsy,* 78.
66. Victor Borovsky, *A Triptych from the Russian Theatre: An Artistic Biography of the Komissarzhevskys* (Iowa City: University of Iowa Press, 2001), 156, employs this description.
67. Brushtein, *Stranitsy,* 78.

and gallery drowned them out with applause."⁶⁸ Evidently this audience was not homogenous in its attitudes and values.

Lidiia Iavorskaia's New Theater, which also presented leading "idea" plays targeted at "socially conscious" audiences, enjoyed the patronage of the "lower ranks of high society," including many a disaffected nobleman, "bourgeois" types who wanted to be shocked, and the ubiquitous angry intellectuals.⁶⁹ Students were often admitted gratis and attended in substantial numbers. Boris Gorin-Goriainov, one of its more radical actors, believed that it "resembled a kind of political club," whose membership transcended generation and social position.⁷⁰

Even popular theaters, nominally oriented toward lower-class audiences, did not avoid social differentiation. Critics maintained that many of their spectators were not poor at all but were middle-class and even wealthy people who craved entertainment and did not hold up their noses to lower prices or less exalted surroundings, people who "came not so much to be distracted from drinking as to spare their pocketbooks the expense of drinking in *cafés-chantants*."⁷¹ Consider the visiting Italian journalist Luigi Villari's assessment of the public at the largest popular theater in Russia, the Tsar Nicholas II People's House: "The majority of the *habitués* are not workmen at all. There are shopkeepers, *employés* of the lower ranks, soldiers and non-commissioned officers, and even a few officers, mostly with families, University students, and a crowd of miscellaneous persons of various classes. The 'horny-handed sons of toil' are few and far between, and do not seem to be quite at their ease; they feel themselves to be intruders."⁷² Villari concluded that the theater was "not altogether answering to the purpose for which it was intended." By including a more diverse assortment of spectators, it instead represented "wasted good intentions."⁷³ Paléologue found the People's House chic enough to invite a party of titled aristocrats and Russia's foreign minister, Sergei Sazonov, to a performance of Massenet's *Don Quichotte* there in 1916.⁷⁴ According to one recent study, popular theater became "a vehicle

---

68. A. Serebrov [A. N. Tikhonov], *Vremia i liudi: Vospominaniia, 1898–1905* (Moscow: Moskovskii rabochii, 1955), 96.
69. Petrovskaia, *Teatr i zritel' rossiiskikh stolits*, 79.
70. B. A. Gorin-Goriainov, *Aktery: Iz vospominaniia* (Moscow: Iskusstvo, 1947), 99–100.
71. Gary Thurston, *The Popular Theatre Movement in Russia, 1862–1919* (Evanston: Northwestern University Press, 1998), 149.
72. Villari, *Russia of To-Day*, 45. According to G. A. Khaichenko, *Russkii narodnyi teatr kontsa XIX–nachala XX veka* (Moscow: Nauka, 1975), 104, the People's House attracted 90 percent of Russia's popular theater spectators in 1901, though this figure certainly declined with the proliferation of popular theaters in subsequent years.
73. Villari, *Russia of To-Day*, 45. Petrovskaia and Somina, *Teatral'nyi Peterburg*, 264, agree that the audience was predominantly middle class.
74. Paléologue, *Memoirs*, 2:208.

for amusement and education that reached the middle class more readily than the target audience: peasant workers."[75] The theorist Ivan Shcheglov enthusiastically described popular theater audiences of the 1890s stretching "from the officer to the lowliest worker, from the fashionable woman with a lorgnette in the first row to the grandmother in a shawl."[76]

Leaving such editorializing aside, there were practical reasons for more heterogeneous audiences to attend popular theater. Despite their intended purpose of providing low-cost entertainment, ticket prices could still be rather high, especially for premieres and gala events.[77] While not excluding lower-class audiences completely, simple economics and greater middle- and upper-class awareness of cultural events promoted the attendance of those with more disposable income. Popular theaters, moreover, often featured the very same artists whom elite and middling audiences would otherwise have had to pay more to admire on the imperial stages. One season-opening performance of Glinka's *A Life for the Tsar* at the Mariinskii attracted disappointingly few patrons, at least partly because Shaliapin was performing in concert at the popular New Summer Theater that same night. Hearing Russia's greatest male voice trumped a stale B-cast presentation of one of the repertoire's more familiar operas, however opulent the surroundings. "Of course one would rather have seen Shaliapin," a tactless critic admitted in his review. Feeling that the performance "went drearily" before a "half empty" theater, he mourned for "the poor opera! Poor Glinka!"[78]

Smaller popular venues also attracted variegated audiences. Pavel Gaideburov, director of the General Accessible Theater, proudly remembered that "the doors of our theater were open to all, however they were dressed: in a worker's apron, a peasant caftan, a German dress, or a brilliant uniform."[79] The critic and editor of the journal *Theater and Art* Aleksandr Kugel' found in popular theaters a "living example of the equalization of the social strata," an unlikely observation if they attracted only one of them.[80] Social distinctions in Russian theater crowds remained, but the composition of those crowds increasingly resembled what the symbolist poet and novelist Andrei Belyi plausibly saw in cinema audiences:

---

75. Patricia Herlihy, *The Alcoholic Empire: Vodka and Politics in Late Imperial Russia* (New York: Oxford University Press, 2002), 14.
76. Quoted in Petrovskaia and Somina, *Teatral'nyi Peterburg*, 252.
77. Petrovskaia, *Teatr i zritel' rossiiskikh stolits*, 77.
78. M. Nesterov, "Mariinskii teatr," *Teatr i iskusstvo* 36 (September 4, 1905): 571. *A Life for the Tsar* traditionally opened every opera season on August 30, the conventional date of the founding of the Imperial Theaters in 1756.
79. P. P. Gaideburov, *Literaturnoe nasledie. Vospominaniia. Stat'i. Rezhisserskie eksplikatsii. Vystupleniia* (Moscow: VTO, 1977), 222.
80. "Homo Novus" [Aleksandr Kugel'], "Narodnyi teatr," *Teatr i iskusstvo* 2 (January 13, 1908): 25.

"aristocrats and democrats, soldiers, students, workers, schoolgirls, poets, and prostitutes."[81]

Social diversity extended to the audiences drawn by cabaret, vaudeville, and other forms of "miniature" theater beginning to spread to Russia in the first decade of the twentieth century, a medium sometimes known as "*estrada*." With prices as low as fifty kopeks—the same amount that would buy floor seats in cinemas, decent tickets to popular theaters, and modest places at private and Imperial Theaters—it is hard to call them categorically "elite venues for an in-crowd."[82] In Liudmila Tikhvinskaia's description their audiences consisted of "painted coquettes, nannies with their charges, the soldier with the cook, active and retired generals, students with models and other students, shopkeepers and skilled workers, petit bourgeois women in kerchiefs and rich women in expensive furs," types who "ran the gamut of urban citizenry."[83]

Even if the diverse audiences inhabiting Russia's cultural universe represented what one critic called a "mass audience [with] no individual opinion, no fixed ideals," they shared one salient characteristic: they wanted to be entertained.[84] Recent attempts to characterize theater halls as "symbolic parliaments," "courts of public opinion," or similar spaces where a restless and unfree people lacking other forums articulated dissent miss this larger truth.[85] The journalist E. A. Solov'ev, whom we have already met as a critic of political indifference among performers, optimistically described the theater as "the only place where the Russian citizen feels himself to be a citizen." Yet in the cauldron of the Revolution of 1905, even he complained that "the public attends the theater as though nothing has happened. What an unfeeling, heartless, uncultured, and socially undeveloped audience!"[86]

The more relevant story is that, as did the performers who entertained them, audiences reeled back from political events and found in them a reason to abjure

---

81. Quoted in Yuri Tsivian, *Early Cinema in Russia and Its Cultural Reception,* trans. Alan Bodger (New York: Routledge, 1994), 35.

82. The price of fifty kopeks is from Petrovskaia, *Teatr i zritel' rossiiskikh stolits,* 98. The phrase "elite venues for an in-crowd" is from Swift, *Popular Theater,* 137.

83. Liudmila Tikhvinskaia, *Kabare i teatry miniatur v Rossii, 1908–1917* (Moscow: Kul'tura, 1995), 176; Louise McReynolds, *Russia at Play: Leisure Activities at the End of the Tsarist Era* (Ithaca: Cornell University Press, 2003), 221.

84. Quoted in Frame, *School for Citizens,* 133. The comment was written in 1887, years before many of the late imperial era's leading theaters appeared.

85. Swift, *Popular Theater,* 95; Elise Kimerling Wirtschafter, *The Play of Ideas in Russian Enlightenment Theater* (DeKalb: Northern Illinois University Press, 2003), 23; Julie A. Buckler, *The Literary Lorgnette: Attending Opera in Imperial Russia* (Stanford: Stanford University Press, 2000), 52.

86. "A." [E. A. Solov'ev], "Teatr i sobytiia," *Teatral'naia Rossiia/Teatral'naia gazeta* 22 (May 28, 1905): 375–76.

infusions of discord into cultural life. To the distress of the Empire's performing community, urban disturbances persuaded many theatergoers to stay home. The widespread closure of theaters during periods of unrest limited audience attendance, but Russian theaters lost much of their public as a result of continuing disorder and popular fear even after they reopened. As we have seen, this happened predictably enough to threaten the jobs of many performers and even the existence of several theaters. The official history of the Imperial Russian Musical Society explained poor attendance at its concerts in times of strife with the assertion that "the audience's attention was paralyzed and focused in a different direction."[87] The administration of the state theaters noticed declining attendance for the same reason: "Political events," Teliakovskii wrote, "naturally distracted public attention from the theater to a significant degree."[88]

Just as radical critics opined the lack of political commitment among performing artists, their ire did not spare audiences, many of whom, they believed to their disgust, shared the priorities of the entertainers. As the journalist Solov'ev continued his bitter observations in 1905: "The country is on fire, the country is going through a crisis, . . . but in the capital of this country, music is played in the pleasure gardens and applause and peals of laughter resound. . . . History is making its harsh judgment. And the public watches farces and amuses itself with comics' cartwheels and the opening of leading ladies' hearts." "This," he concluded, "is not a society."[89] Another prominent arts critic, the symbolist intellectual Dmitrii Filosofov, began to think of theater as "a place of crude diversion for the satisfied crowd."[90] The editorial staff of *Theater and Art* felt the same way, judging that "society is indifferent to the sufferings of Russia [and] passively follows the path that the bureaucracy has shown it . . . always happy to have fun, go out, and celebrate."[91] How dare it! In early 1906 the same editors castigated the "heartless audience" of the Mariinskii Theater for demanding refunds when several expected performers failed to appear at a benefit performance for unemployed actors.[92] The pleasure of the evening mattered more to that audience than the fate of the out-of-work actors, and the theatrically minded intelligentsia hated them for it.

87. N. F. Findeizen, *Ocherk deiatel'nosti S.-Peterburgskogo otdeleniia Imperatorskogo russkogo muzykal'nogo obshchestva (1859–1909)* (St. Petersburg: Tipografiia Glavnogo Upravleniia Udelov, 1909), 100.
88. Teliakovskii, "Imperatorskie teatry," 310.
89. "A." [E. A. Solov'ev], "Teatr i sobytiia," *Teatral'naia Rossiia/Teatral'naia gazeta* 22 (May 28, 1905): 375.
90. Quoted in A. Ia. Al'tshuller, ed., *Ocherki istorii russkoi teatral'noi kritiki* (Leningrad: Iskusstvo, 1975), 36.
91. "Ot redaktsii," *Teatr i iskusstvo* 22 (May 29, 1905): 343.
92. "Ot redaktsii," *Teatr i iskusstvo* 2 (January 8, 1906): 17.

Even after the February Revolution of 1917, some radicals, including the Menshevik (later Bolshevik) Lev Trotskii, harangued audiences with such lines as "the blood of the people is running in the gutters, and you, you thickheads and vulgarians, you lower yourselves to listen to the stupidities and banalities that a pack of rotten actors spew at you."[93] The collapse of the monarchy did not stop the avant-garde director Vsevolod Meierkhol'd from decrying "the silent, passionless parterre where people come for a rest."[94] Politics and performance were not, in their view, moving in the same direction.

For some radical critics, the memory, or at least the imagination, of an earlier, more politically actualized audience inspired little hope in the late imperial cultural universe. "Look at the image of the contemporary theater hall," one disappointed commentator challenged his readers, "compare it with the old descriptions of Belinskii and Aksakov.... What an abyss!... Gloomy people attend to kill time somehow.... Coldness and apathy are felt more and more here. The electrical current between the stage and the spectator's hall has ceased to function."[95] Another editorial comment observed the sesquicentennial of the Imperial Theaters in August 1906 by bemoaning, just a month after the new State Duma's first dissolution by the tsar, "the complete indifference of society; the complete indifference of the theatrical world."[96] The phenomenon of politicized court trials led one observer to praise their enthusiastic spectators over theater audiences who "long ago lost the feeling."[97]

More inventive commentators wrote at length about their impressions of theater's role in the French Revolution, hoping that the history lesson would inspire readers to transpose its values to their own times. As Fedor Komissarzhevskii, Vera's brother and director, later wrote, "the Russian revolutionaries have not forgotten that the Theatre played a very important part in preparing the Great French Revolution."[98] One editorialist recalled the impact of Marie-Joseph Chénier's antimonarchical and anticlerical play *Charles IX*, the November 1789 premiere of which provoked a public demonstration.[99] "Theater," another critic insisted in a way that may have struck his readers as encouragement,

---

93. Quoted in Feodor Chaliapin, *Man and Mask: Forty Years in the Life of a Singer*, trans. Phyllis Mégroz (New York: Knopf, 1932), 241–42.
94. Quoted in Edward Braun, *The Theatre of Meyerhold: Revolution and the Modern Stage* (New York: Drama Book Specialists, 1979), 146.
95. N[ikolai] Arbenin, "Kakoi teper' nuzhen teatr?" *Teatr i iskusstvo* 5 (January 29, 1906): 75.
96. "Ot redaktsii," *Teatr i iskusstvo* 35 (August 27, 1906): 526.
97. "Teatr i sud," *Teatr i iskusstvo* 11 (March 17, 1913): 253–54.
98. Komisarjevsky, *Myself and the Theatre*, 5–6.
99. "Ark. Press," "Teatr vo vremia frantsuzskoi revoliutsii," *Teatr i iskusstvo*, 44–45 (October 29, 1905): 1261–62.

"sounded the beat of the *Marseillaise,* like a faithful drum major of revolutionary inspiration."[100]

Such wishful thinking led nowhere and was in any case rather exaggerated. As the most thorough study of the Parisian stage during the French Revolution has argued, "politics [was] not the most telling characteristic of that theatre, nor the most revealing of its audiences. . . . Comedy prevailed over tragedy, laughter over rhetoric, in the 1790s."[101] An earlier study of French popular theater has observed that "the enduring repertoire of the popular stage only stood in the way" of "the revolutionaries of 1793–1794[, who] had to neutralize and repress what they could of traditional dramatic culture."[102] Even when radicals sought out politicized culture in other contexts, their arguments depended on what the prevailing scholarship now regards as misinformation. Nor did any meaningful movement among Russian theatergoers attempt to answer their challenge.

Despite Soviet claims that "Russian theater was every day an arena of political struggle," audiences overwhelmingly refrained from truculent behavior.[103] Confrontations, protests, and other disruptions in theaters remained infrequent. Avoiding unpleasant and dangerous environments during times of crisis undoubtedly caused many spectators to abandon their theatergoing, along with other nightlife activities that might have put them in harm's way. But pleasant diversion easily trumped the potential for stoking social and political convictions among Russian audiences. Bertenson, who recorded the riot at the Mariinskii Theater, recalled that he "tended to my personal affairs during the day, devoting every evening to family, reading, and theater. I lived far from the revolutionary currents of the time."[104]

Disturbances in the Imperial Theaters, which stood as symbols of state power, were usually the work of agitators. Varlamov's unfortunate Bloody Sunday performance of Ostrovskii's *A Passionate Heart* (described in Chapter 2) was interrupted just after Filosofov and his fellow symbolist thinkers Dmitrii Merezhkovskii and Zinaida Gippius threatened to take measures to stop it if the theater's administration failed to do so.[105] The Imperial Drama Theater's

---

100. "S. T." [S. Timofeev], "Teatr i frantsuzskaia revoliutsiia," *Teatr i iskusstvo* 16 (April 16, 1906) 253–55.

101. Emmet Kennedy et al., *Theatre, Opera, and Audiences in Revolutionary Paris: Analysis and Repertory* (Westport, Conn.: Greenwood, 1996), 87–90. According to this survey, "almost all" of the fifty most frequently performed plays in 1789–99 had nothing to do with the revolution or its "ideals."

102. Michèle Root-Bernstein, *Boulevard Theater and Revolution in Eighteenth-Century Paris* (Ann Arbor: UMI Research Press, 1984), 240.

103. M. Iankovskii, "Teatral'naia obshchestvennost' Peterburga v 1905–1907 gg.," in *Pervaia russkaia revoliutsiia i teatr: Stat'i i materialy,* ed. A. Ia. Al'tshuller (Moscow: Iskusstvo, 1956), 151.

104. Bertenson, *Za 30 let,* 273.

105. Ibid., 282.

cancellation of Ostrovskii's *The Heart Is Not a Stone* at the beginning of the general strike later that year resulted from the radical actor Nikolai Khodotov's agitation and threats rather than from anything the audience did or said (see Chapter 3).[106] The Mariinskii riot recorded by Bertenson was touched off by a cry of "Down with the autocracy!" that resounded suspiciously soon after representatives of a revolutionary meeting demanded that the performance be called off. They had threatened to take matters into their own hands when the request was denied. The disturbance elicited not the audience's agreement or sympathy but panic and a general desire either to get out of the situation or see order restored.

The audience's general response to these disturbances was to attack those who identified with the agitators. Sometimes this included calling for "God Save the Tsar," the enthusiastically received performance of which ended the troubled evening at the Mariinskii. In the days after the incident, Teliakovskii had to listen to a stream of audience members complain about their spoiled time. Ivan Shcheglovitov, who had attended the performance and became Minister of Justice shortly thereafter, informed the Director that "the public was astounded that the theaters had become a place of scandal."[107] The reactionary official was surely not an objective witness, but his high position does not invalidate the outrage felt by Mariinskii spectators who simply wanted an enjoyable evening out.

Comments such as Shcheglovitov's accurately interpreted radical motives to scandalize state cultural institutions and audiences at a crucial political moment. This desire was almost certainly shared that same night by a radical at the Aleksandrinskii's performance of yet another Ostrovskii play, *It's Not Always Shrovetide for a Cat*, who cried, "Down with the monarchy!" when others in the audience asked for "God Save the Tsar." The dramatic theater was spared a riot because much of the audience booed and hissed the agitator, who fled from his seat in the gallery. The show went on to its conclusion, even if the incident caused the actresses on stage to spill the tea that the scene called for them to be drinking.[108]

In the same turbulent period the small "fighting retinue" of radical actors who wanted to force their recalcitrant colleagues to close theaters and adhere to the general strike did not even try to appeal to the public's political sympathies. Instead they relied on its capacity to be terrorized, or at the very least intimidated, to break up the performances of their own recalcitrant colleagues. Gorin-Goriainov, who helped plan and took part in these raids, described using

---

106. N. N. Khodotov, *Blizkoe—dalekoe* (Leningrad: Iskusstvo, 1962), 181.
107. Teliakovskii, "Imperatorskie teatry," 258.
108. Gnedich, *Kniga zhizni*, 289; Teliakovskii, "Imperatorskie teatry," 257.

canisters of pungent hydrogen sulfide because "this means, essentially harmless, allowed for the possibility of acting psychologically on the audience." As we saw in the last chapter, its use at the Suvorin Theater forced the audience to leave in a hurry, while the Panaev Theater's spectators broke into panic.[109]

Even symbolic expressions of opposition to the government could encounter resistance. At a Nevskii Farce performance of a light musical comedy entitled *To the Sounds of Chopin*, spectators who called for the "Marseillaise" were angrily booed by others who wanted to hear "God Save the Tsar." Many people left the theater to avoid the tension.[110]

Nor did audiences show a great deal of sympathy for artists who undertook provocative actions at tense political moments. When Teliakovskii, reacting to the "strike" movement that beset the imperial ballet in 1905, replaced regular dancers with Ballet School pupils in a performance of Chaikovskii's *Eugene Onegin*, the audience was too interested in seeing the new talents perform to object to the absence of the regular performers. The dancer Iosif Kshesinskii's dismissal for assaulting a fellow performer during an argument over whether to strike elicited some calls for him during the intermission of the next performance in which he had been scheduled to appear, but uncaring audience members silenced them by yelling, "They are calling for the shadow of the departed!"[111] As late as February 1917—nearly on the eve of the monarchy's collapse—a Mariinskii audience booed chorus members striking for higher wages when they refused to sing in full voice during a performance of Rimskii-Korsakov's opera *May Night*.[112]

The rare cases in which Russian audiences did exhibit signs of political or social sensitivity only undermine arguments about the politicization of culture. The premiere of Viktor Krylov and Savelii Litvin's virulently anti-Semitic play *The Smugglers* at the Suvorin Theater in November 1900 elicited a stormy protest in which students bombarded the performers with anything that they could throw and created as much noise as possible to prevent the show from going on. Seventy-two were arrested.[113] In March 1901 audience demonstrations confronted an unsuspecting Stanislavskii during the Moscow Art Theater's first Petersburg performance of Ibsen's *An Enemy of the People*.[114] Outraged members

---

109. Gorin-Goriainov, *Aktery*, 109–10.
110. "Skandal iz-za Marsel'ezy," *Peterburgskaia gazeta*, November 15, 1905.
111. Teliakovskii, "Imperatorskie teatry," 252–53, 282.
112. Vasilii Bezpalov, *Teatry v dni revoliutsii, 1917* (Leningrad: Academia, 1927), 11; "K intsidentu s khorom v Mariinskom teatre," *Teatr i iskusstvo* 9 (February 26, 1917): 171.
113. Petrovskaia, *Teatr i zritel' rossiiskikh stolits*, 69; Gnedich, *Kniga zhizni*, 235; Laurence Senelick, "Anti-Semitism and the Tsarist Theatre: The *Smugglers* Riots," *Theatre Survey* 44, no. 1 (2003): 71–84.
114. K. S. Stanislavskii, *Moia zhizn' v iskusstve* (Moscow: Iskusstvo, 1983), 257.

of the intelligentsia angrily protested the September 1904 premiere of Gor'kii's *Summerfolk*.[115]

Yet even in these incidents, the role of dramatic content in provoking discord may be doubted. Many of the demonstrators who rioted at the premiere of *The Smugglers* were not audience members at all but young radicals who forced their way in without paying.[116] At the Art Theater performance of *An Enemy of the People*, the violent dispersal of a student demonstration earlier in the day had fueled the passion of the demonstrators, whom Nemirovich-Danchenko described as "frozen, wrought up, and hungry."[117] Aleksandr Tikhonov, a radical student and frequent theatergoer who left a firsthand account of Gor'kii's 1904 premiere, claimed that he "never saw a performance like *Summerfolk* again." Presumably he included those he attended over the course of the following year, when Russia was rocked by it first revolution.[118] Numerous performances and other productions of all three of these plays went on without recorded incident.

Analogous demonstrations remained isolated events in the late imperial era, even in times of turmoil. Lines made meaningful or ironic by the surrounding circumstances occasionally drew a response. Some spectators cheered such declamations in Sophocles' *Antigone* as "a free land cannot belong to one person."[119] Portraying a cruel Theban despot whose tyranny and lust for power destroy his family, the plot's subtexts touched some spectators to the quick. Nikolai Khodotov, the radical actor who played Hemon in the Aleksandrinskii production, recalled that "the public reacted to any appropriate passage where something was said against the sickening autocracy." Student audiences sometimes applauded their fictional fellow student Petia Trofimov's idealistic monologues about the future in Chekhov's *The Cherry Orchard*.[120] A performance of Schnitzler's *The Green Parrot*, set on the day of the fall of the Bastille, prompted members of Iavorskaia's audience to sing the "Marseillaise."[121] Lines referring to freedom in her production of Schiller's *Wilhelm Tell* generated applause, as did other material that provoked the audience to what the actor Gorin-Goriainov called "a sign

---

115. S. A. Sokolov [S. Krechetov], "'Dachniki' Gor'kogo na stsene Internatsional'nogo teatra," *Vesy* 3 (1905): 94; "Zigfrid" [E. A. Stark], "'Dachniki' M. Gor'kogo," *Teatral'naia Rossiia/Teatral'naia gazeta* 1 (December 11, 1904): 12–13.

116. A. S. Suvorin, *Dnevnik* (Moscow: Novosti, 1992), 299–300. Senelick, "Anti-Semitism and the Tsarist Theatre," 81, accepts this explanation.

117. Nemirovitch-Danchenko, *My Life*, 238.

118. Serebrov [A. N. Tikhonov], *Vremia i liudi*, 95.

119. Khodotov, *Blizkoe—dalekoe*, 169.

120. Ibid., 169–72.

121. A. Brodskii, "Teatral'naia zhizn' Petrograda," *Maski* 1 (1914/1915): 83.

of protest against gloomy reality."[122] Some opera patrons jeered Ivan Susanin's heroic line, "I will lay down my life for the Tsar and for Rus'," during performances of Glinka's *A Life for the Tsar*.[123] Since that work traditionally opened every imperial opera season and had been closely tied to official nationalism since its 1836 premiere, such incidents may have raised concern.

The tsarist government demonstrated sensitivity to the stage's potential for fomenting audience unrest and at times gestured toward trying to control it. In Stanislavskii's opinion the government "feared that the theater would become an arena for propaganda."[124] Altering the repertoire of the Imperial Theaters was one means, however lukewarm, of allaying official fears. At the urging of the Petersburg gendarmerie, Teliakovskii delayed the Aleksandrinskii's production of *Antigone* eleven months beyond its planned premiere because the police had found a copy of the play with incendiary passages allegedly "underlined by Gor'kii himself" and connected it with a rumor that radical activists would disrupt the performance.[125] The Director also decided not to present Glinka's *A Life for the Tsar* after its traditional opening-night performance at the Mariinskii in the difficult 1905–6 season because he "feared public attacks and protests." But despite these concerns and the catcalls following Susanin's line, Teliakovskii added more performances when a number of patrons complained about the patriotic opera's near absence from the repertoire.[126] Whether they made this observation to support the prevailing political order or simply uphold a convention is unknown, but it does belie the notion of an activist-dissenting audience.

Antigone's delayed premiere turned out to be far from effective in stimulating audience radicalism. Reflecting on the production's political connotations, one reviewer found—regardless of Khodotov's memory—that "these hints have already lost their strength." Instead the critic witnessed among the audience "icy indifference and sometimes even a smile."[127] In any case these alterations (a better word than "censorship" since no works were actually removed) paled in comparison to the wholesale deletion of German and Austrian works from the

---

122. I. Osipov [I. O. Abel'son], "Vil'gel'm Tel'," *Teatral'naia Rossiia/Teatral'naia gazeta* 38 (September 17, 1905): 44–45; Gorin-Goriainov, *Aktery*, 100.
123. Teliakovskii, "Imperatorskie teatry," 274.
124. Stanislavskii, *Moia zhizn'*, 258.
125. Teliakovskii, "Imperatorskie teatry," 305–8.
126. Ibid., 274.
127. "Impressionist" [I. F. Bentovin], "Aleksandrinskii teatr," *Teatr i iskusstvo* 5 (January 29, 1906): 67.

repertoire of Russian theaters on nationalist grounds during World War I, a policy often adopted by theaters in response to audience pressure.[128]

State theatrical censorship betrayed some sensitivity to staged controversy. Several works featuring popular or antigovernment uprisings were banned from performance, especially in the years around 1905. This was particularly true for popular theaters, whose ostensibly lower-class audiences were thought to be more impressionable, but it also affected the less controlled imperial and private stages. The Kromy Forest scene in Musorgskii's opera *Boris Godunov* occasionally disappeared from productions because it presents a crowd of rebellious peasants who nearly lynch a boyar and call out for the tsar's death.[129] Godunov was a usurper, but insurrection against even him presented uncomfortable overtones. So, too, did the themes of antimonarchical conspiracy and rebellion in Schiller's *Don Carlos,* Byron's *Sardanapalus,* and Hugo's *Hernani,* all of which were barred from popular stages around the time of the first revolution.[130] Private theaters encountered prohibitions on such works as Büchner's *Danton's Death,* Chirikov's *The Peasants,* and Svirskii's *The Pulse of Life,* among others that depicted prorevolutionary sympathies and violent events.[131]

Despite these measures neither expressiveness during performances nor the potential for it necessarily indicated revolutionary sympathies, serious political commitment, or a permanent haze of implacable dissent. Showing an appreciation of irony, finding hope in moving words, and vocalizing scorn for detestable features of the status quo simply do not go far as indicators of deep political conviction in the way that some scholars cited throughout this study have suggested, nor were they by any means unique to Late Imperial Russia. As we have seen to the contrary, many critics expressed great disappointment with the lack of "consciousness" demonstrated by Russian audiences. Swift has described reactions that were emoted as "rituals of largely symbolic protest ... for the audiences who thumbed their noses at tsarist authorities from the comfort of their theater seats."[132]

No matter what measures the government adopted, its fears that certain works, scenes, or lines would provoke unrest ultimately revealed more about its own distractions and insecurities than what may or may not have catalyzed

---

128. On this phenomenon, see Hubertus Jahn, *Patriotic Culture in Russia During World War I* (Cambridge: Cambridge University Press, 1995), 141–46.

129. James H. Billington, *The Icon and the Axe: An Interpretive History of Russian Culture* (New York: Knopf, 1966), 410. Nikolay Rimsky-Korsakov, *My Musical Life,* trans. Judah A. Joffe (New York: Knopf, 1923), 342.

130. RGIA, f. 776, op. 26, d. 25, l. 118; d. 24, l. 101; d. 26, l. 39.

131. RGIA, f. 776, op. 26, d. 26, l. 100; d. 24, l. 230; d. 25, l. 181.

132. Swift, *Popular Theater,* 95–96.

audience radicalism. The actor Aleksandr Briantsev recalled audiences only attaching importance to lines removed by the censorship *after* they had been deleted, a typical demonstration of the forbidden's inevitable appeal.[133] Even the police official who delivered the request for *Antigone*'s postponement confided to Teliakovskii that he thought evidence of the supposed plot to disrupt the premiere insubstantial and did not attach much importance to it.[134] Gaideburov, who successfully argued with the censorship over the right to perform the same play for popular audiences in 1908, wryly pointed out the disconnect between its political content and audience reactions. The functionary with whom he dealt feared that popular performances of *Antigone* would cause another revolution within two years, but, as the impresario sarcastically observed, 1917 "came significantly later than the official had predicted."[135]

Works with strong political or social content even frightened Russian theatergoers at tense moments. Already worried about violence unfolding around them, their peace of mind could prove fleeting when they went out in public. A slight argument between a train conductor and a man dressed as a student led the theatrical press to report "cries of horror" breaking out at a symphony concert in St. Petersburg's Pavlovsk suburb.[136] As the actress Verigina recalled revolutionary Moscow, "there were times during performances in the theater when panic broke out."[137]

Gor'kii's *Children of the Sun*, the playwright's second searing portrayal of the intelligentsia, whose members are described in the text as "utterly indifferent," "lonely, and unhappy, and petty," and "frightful bores," premiered literally on the eve of the October 1905 general strike to audiences preoccupied with concerns about their physical safety.[138] In Petersburg, where Komissarzhevskaia's Dramatic Theater presented the work, the actor playing the hapless gentleman scientist Protasov had to stand up to reassure hysterical spectators that the final act's angry mob was not a real street mob invading the theater to beat him up.[139] At the play's Moscow Art Theater premiere shortly thereafter, the same scene provoked hysterical cries of, "Stop the play!" and, from those who identified the scene as part of the drama but still related it to their troubled daily lives, "You

---

133. A. A. Briantsev, *Vospominaniia, stat'i, vystupleniia, dnevniki, pis'ma* (Moscow: VTO, 1979), 51–52.
134. Teliakovskii, "Imperatorskie teatry," 305.
135. Gaideburov, *Literaturnoe nasledie*, 224.
136. "Khronika," *Teatr i iskusstvo* 30 (July 24, 1905): 473.
137. Verigina, *Vospominaniia*, 75.
138. Maxim Gorky, *Children of the Sun*, trans. Stephen Mulrine (London: Hern, 2000), 56, 64, 83.
139. Borovsky, *Triptych*, 162.

Fig. 18 Act II of Gor'kii's *Children of the Sun* in a late 1905 production at Vera Komissarzhevskaia's Dramatic Theater. The actress-entrepreneuse is standing on the left. Her chief director, Vsevolod Meierkhol'd, is seated at the extreme right. The play includes a mob scene that convinced frightened spectators in St. Petersburg and Moscow that the political violence of the time was spilling into performance space. From A. Ia. Al'tshuller, ed., *Vera Fedorovna Komissarzhevskaia: Pis'ma aktrisy, vospominaniia o nei, materialy* (Leningrad: Iskusstvo, 1964).

dare not make sport of our nerves!"[140] When calm returned to the Art Theater, some took the mob on stage for a Black Hundred gang and feared that the theater's management was trying to negotiate with it. Many started to leave. According to Nemirovich-Danchenko, they had "no other thought than to save themselves." By the time the performance resumed, "the theatre had been emptied of more than half of its audience."[141] Stanislavskii mourned his "noticeably vacated hall."[142] In early 1906 the censorship reversed its original approval of the play, not for its potential to radicalize audiences, but because "it created such a tremendous impression on the spectators that scandals often broke out in the theater."[143]

Another measure of audience apathy emerged from the lack of popularity that "idea" works enjoyed and the effect of their low appeal on business. Iavorskaia's New Theater, which specialized in the genre with its productions of Gor'kii, Chirikov, Strindberg, and works by other "socially conscious" playwrights, went bankrupt after five tenuous seasons. One of its actors observed that even its modest existence was still impressive, for it "stood apart from all the theaters of Petersburg, having its own public."[144] Iavorskaia's repertoire, in other words, attracted only a small segment of the theatergoing public, one too slim to keep it in long-term operation.

Komissarzhevskaia suffered the same fate as her rival. Confronted with disappointing receipts from a similar repertoire of idea plays, her first enterprise collapsed in the spring of 1906, after just two seasons. According to Brushtein, she found that much of the audience for politicized drama "sympathized with it out of snobbery and fashion," but lost interest when they realized what revolution might really mean for their comfortable radical chic lifestyles.[145] Komissarzhevskaia's second theatrical enterprise, featuring the works of Maeterlinck, Blok, and other symbolist dramatists, a genre that she "adopted . . . as her salvation," also failed after two seasons. The transition, however, indicated a major departure from the tedium of idea plays in favor of a cutting-edge and apolitical repertoire that the actress-entrepreneuse hoped would have greater social significance and audience appeal.[146]

140. Nemirovitch-Danchenko, *My Life*, 262–63.
141. Ibid.
142. Stanislavskii, *Moia zhizn'*, 295.
143. RGIA, f. 776, d. 26, op. 25, l. 60. The ban was in effect between January and March of that year.
144. I. N. Perestiani, *75 let zhizni v iskusstve* (Moscow: Iskusstvo, 1962), 185–86.
145. Brushtein, *Stranitsy*, 81.
146. Borovsky, *Triptych*, 263–88; Laurence Senelick, "Vera Komissarzhevskaia: The Actress as Symbolist Eidolon," *Theatre Journal* 32, no. 4 (1980): 479.

Less-well-known theaters also did poorly with political works, as the director Nikolai Popov discovered when he opened the New Vasileostrovskii Theater in the autumn of 1906. Presenting a repertoire of Gor'kii, Chirikov, and like-minded dramatists, he lasted but one season before bankruptcy.[147] Two separate attempts to revive Iavorskaia's New Theater with a repertoire similar to that of the original enterprise failed after less than a season each.[148]

Audiences who appreciated the politicized repertoire not only fell far short of dominating Russia's theatergoing community but also failed to comprise a critical mass sufficient to sustain even the small number of theaters that specialized in it. Although Soviet historians tended to blame censorship interventions for the failure of enterprises such as Iavorskaia's and Komissarzhevskaia's, the content of their repertoire selections helped them on the way down. If productions of idea plays survived at the box office at all, it was thanks to the popularity and skills of individual performers. As Borovsky has suggested, spectators "went to Komissarzhevskaya's theatre only to see Komissarzhevskaya, and regarded 'productions in which she was not appearing with suspicion.'"[149] In the words of one of the actress's contemporaries, "if Komissarzhevskaia was not featured, ticket sales remained sluggish."[150]

Managers of theaters with broader repertoires, including conventional classics and contemporary works of light entertainment, noticed the difference in audience reactions when idea plays appeared alongside more traditional works. Productions of Schiller's *Don Carlos, Conspiracy and Love,* and *The Robbers*— older yet socially and politically relevant plays whose anti-authoritarian themes caused the censors to ban them at various times—"held little interest for the public" of the Suvorin Theater, for example.[151] The same company's production of Svirskii's *Prison*, an indictment of the criminal justice system that had also been banned by the censorship, drew "far from a full hall" because, in the opinion of its reviewer for *Theater and Art*, "the public has no desire to torture its nerves."[152]

A number of impresarios who pursued higher social purposes came to believe that established classics could entertain, actualize, and "elevate" lower-class spectators more effectively than "conscious" works that beat them over the head

---

147. Petrovskaia, *Teatr i zritel' rossiiskikh stolits*, 92.
148. Petrovskaia and Somina, *Teatral'nyi Peterburg*, 221–23.
149. Borovsky, *Triptych*, 156.
150. M. Prygunov, "Teatr V. F. Komissarzhevskoi," in *Sbornik pamiati V. F. Komissarzhevskoi* (Moscow: GIKL, 1931), 156.
151. Petrovskaia and Somina, *Teatral'nyi Peterburg*, 209–10.
152. "Malyi teatr," *Teatr i iskusstvo* 3 (January 15, 1906): 36.

with tendentious politics. Stanislavskii, no lightweight in the philosophy of Russian theater, certainly thought so: "There is an opinion that for the peasant one must definitely perform plays from his life, adapted to his worldview, and for workers—plays from their daily lives. This is false. The peasant, watching a play from his everyday life, usually declares that he has had enough of this life, that he has seen enough of it, and that it is incomparably more interesting to him to see how other people live, to see a more beautiful life."[153] A Bolshevik critic observed in Gaideburov's General Accessible Theater an attempt "to draw closer to the proletariat and liberate theater from its degrading role as a place of relaxation and fun for the bourgeois strata."[154] Ostrovskii's œuvre accounted for eleven of the sixteen plays performed in the General Accessible's inaugural 1903–4 season.[155] The traditional playwright's presence declined, but it continued to make up about 25 percent of the theater's repertoire for the next several seasons, contributing in no small way to its early success. Gaideburov's subsequent decision to favor the more "political" works of Schnitzler, Ibsen, Andreev, and others coincided with a marked decline in both revenues and, consequently, in the number of works he could stage. The General Accessible's 1909–10 season, its first after a year of presenting no Ostrovskii at all, had the resources to feature only nine productions. In the following year its offerings dropped to just five works (including one Ostrovskii play), a fraction of what the theater had staged seven years earlier and a figure that remained steady until its venue, the Ligovskii People's House, became a military hospital in 1914.[156]

Although a more traditional repertoire continued to dominate the Imperial Theaters in the early twentieth century (and most great theaters before and since), the appearance of works with subversive or potentially subversive messages did little to politicize their audiences. This was certainly the case when the Mariinskii launched its premiere production of Beethoven's opera *Fidelio* in the troubled autumn months of 1905. As the sympathetic story of a political prisoner's liberation from tyranny—and one that ends in a resounding hymn to freedom—the opera's relevance could hardly have been more obvious in the prevailing atmosphere. Yet the reviews, which appeared in journals free from censorship, mentioned nothing of its political implications and commented only on such purely aesthetic details as Napravnik's masterful conducting and

153. Stanislavskii, *Moia zhizn'*, 383.
154. "N. V." [N. V. Vol'skii], "Iubilei obshchedostupnogo teatra," *Za pravdu*, November 27, 1913. Lynn Mally, *Revolutionary Acts: Amateur Theater and the Soviet State, 1917–1938* (Ithaca: Cornell University Press, 2000), 7–35, demonstrates that this sentiment prevailed after 1917.
155. Gaideburov, *Literaturnoe nasledie*, 431.
156. Ibid., 432–38.

the fine singing of Ershov and other principals.[157] The British journalist and travel writer Maurice Baring, who attended a performance that fall, felt out of place in grasping its theme: "I don't think the young lions in the gallery realized that this opera was the complete expression of the 'Liberation movement' in Germany," he confided to his diary.[158] Indeed, *Fidelio* played without recorded incident to a sell-out crowd the next evening after the Mariinskii's October 18 riot, which had occurred during *Lohengrin*, a work with no political text or subtext at all.[159]

Drama on the imperial stage also did little to galvanize audiences. As we have seen, a reviewer of the Aleksandrinskii's production of *Antigone*, which ran for just five poorly sold performances, detected no palpable connection between the spectators and the play's political implications. It merely followed the imperial dramatic stage's earlier and equally unpopular productions from antiquity. Euripides's *Hippolytus* (1902) and Sophocles' *Oedipus at Colonus* (1904) had also failed, as did Euripides' *Iphigeneia at Aulis* when it appeared there in 1909.[160]

If idea plays failed to become Russia's hot tickets, what succeeded? Despite intelligentsia disappointment, the Empire's expanding and diverse audiences readily amused themselves with comedy, melodrama, and other light forms of entertainment mostly devoid of serious political or social content. The Nevskii Farce, where spectators who wanted to hear the "Marseillaise" found themselves confronted by many who did not, specialized in comedies of errors and piquant operettas featuring tales of mistaken identity, clownish moral hypocrisy, and lighthearted adultery plots. Kugel' described its repertoire as "not at all severe, pedantic, or puritanical."[161] Its paucity of social content and attitude that "commentaries on political life were not the goal" helped it become "one of the most financially successful enterprises" in Petersburg.[162] If a prerevolutionary theater's endurance indicated popularity with audiences and attendant commercial

---

157. "I. Ki-skii," "'Fidelio' Betkhovena," *Teatral'naia gazeta/Muzykal'nyi mir* 40 (October 1, 1905): 1201; M. Nesterov, "Mariinskii teatr," *Teatr i iskusstvo* 40 (October 2, 1905): 633–34.

158. Maurice Baring, *A Year in Russia* (New York: Dutton, 1907), 40. South African audiences, however, certainly did a century later. See above, fn10 in Introduction.

159. Teliakovskii, "Imperatorskie teatry," 260. See the sales figures in "Sezon 1905–1906 gg.," *Ezhegodnik Imperatorskikh teatrov* 16 (1905–6, chast' II): 92.

160. "Impressionist" [I. F. Bentovin], "Aleksandrinskii teatr," *Teatr i iskusstvo* 5 (January 29, 1906): 67. See *Antigone*'s dismal receipts in "Sezon 1905–1906 gg.," *Ezhegodnik Imperatorskikh teatrov* 16 (1905–6, chast' II): 110–26. Petrovskaia and Somina, *Teatral'nyi Peterburg*, 198.

161. "Homo Novus," [Aleksandr Kugel'], "Nevskii Fars," *Teatr i iskusstvo* 45–46 (November 13, 1905): 716.

162. Petrovskaia, *Teatr i zritel' rossiiskikh stolits*, 91.

success, the Nevskii Farce's continuous operation from its founding in 1904 until 1917—one of the longest lives of any of Russia's private theaters—speaks for itself.

Even when the farce genre lampooned leading figures and values of the tsarist government, as the Winter Farce did with its production of Leonid Svetov and Vladimir Valentinov's satirical revue *The Days of Freedom* in late 1905, the atmosphere resounded more with frivolity and fun than indignant protests or shrill rhetoric. Featuring scathing couplets, dark humor, and irreverent impressions, *The Days of Freedom* attracted audiences who wanted to laugh at politics rather than foment unrest. In addition to its satirical depictions of prominent government officials, the revue's cast of more than two hundred also included unflattering caricatures of students, workers, intellectuals, liberals, socialists, artists, servants, and "hooligans," among many other targets culled from contemporary society. The theater staged it primarily, and successfully, to make money from its audience's taste for this type of comedy.[163] Like political and social satire in most other contexts, its material quickly became dated and fell out of fashion, at least for anyone other than historians of the Russian Revolution. *The Days of Freedom*'s humor died like so much of yesterday's news, and no other theater ever attempted to revive it.[164] The Winter Farce itself went bankrupt and closed in the spring of 1906.[165]

The appeal of light comedy and similar forms of diversion drew eager crowds to the Suvorin Theater, whose audience was derided in Soviet times as "spiritually and socially passive."[166] Alongside its failed Schiller productions, an entertaining and inoffensive stage adaptation of Sherlock Holmes mysteries ran for more than fifty performances in 1905–6. Demand for the show grew so high that the management rehearsed two casts for its revival in the following season, hoping that it would be an even bigger hit.[167] Suvorin's audiences thus mimicked and overlapped to a significant degree with Russia's evolving reading public, who also became enamored of Holmes, Watson, and a host of other detectives for their mild amusement at around the same time.[168]

These theaters were far from alone in presenting lighter works for their financial benefit. Johann Strauss's undemanding operetta *The Gypsy Baron*, a work

---

163. D. I. Zolotnitskii, "'Dni svobody' russkogo farsa" in *Russkii teatr i dramaturgiia epokhi revoliutsii, 1905–1907 godov: Sbornik nauchnykh trudov*, ed. A. Ia. Al'tshuller et al. (Leningrad: LGITMiK, 1987), 132–36.

164. Ibid., 137.

165. Petrovskaia and Somina, *Teatral'nyi Peterburg*, 233.

166. Petrovskaia, *Teatr i zritel' rossiiskikh stolits*, 71–72.

167. "Khronika," *Teatr i iskusstvo* 35 (August 27, 1906): 526.

168. Jeffrey Brooks, *When Russia Learned to Read: Literacy and Popular Literature, 1861–1917* (Princeton: Princeton University Press, 1985), 141–46, 151.

popular since its Russian premiere in 1886, still drew a "large" audience almost twenty years later.[169] Pavel Tumpakov's benefit gala, an evening of racy songs, produced "an overflowing hall."[170] As *Theater and Art* noticed, Russia's audiences "eagerly attended plays standing on the sidelines of the contemporary movement."[171] Fedor Komissarzhevskii disparaged them as a "grey public" for what he regarded as their unsophisticated tastes.[172]

Despite their government subsidies, institutional commitment to high culture, and growing interest in innovation, the Imperial Theaters also had to appeal to popular taste, a factor taken increasingly into account in repertoire selection. Indeed, both the Directorate of the Imperial Theaters and its artist councils made largely the same recommendations of what to stage in future seasons. Both naturally wanted works that would draw popular interest, big audiences, and generous revenues. Teliakovskii later admitted that "the more superficial, vulgar, and even trite the plays we staged were, the more willingly ... artists would work with them, the better the press would receive them, and the more the public would attend them."[173]

Perhaps unsurprisingly, the most popular works presented on the imperial stages were those involving intricate human relations, love, passion, violence, or simply great art. The Malyi's and Aleksandrinskii's productions of Ostrovskii and Chekhov did extremely well, usually selling out or coming close. In an average season each theater staged more than forty performances of Ostrovskii's plays alone.[174] Over the course of the revolutionary year of 1905, his dramas were so commonplace that a different one was coincidentally on stage on each of the three occasions when the Aleksandrinskii's operations were disrupted by agitators, again revealing a chasm rather than a link between the content of works on stage and expressions of political sentiment. Yet as in other dramatic theaters, changes in popular taste reflected a movement toward the risqué even on the imperial dramatic stage. A highly successful production of a different color, Vladimir Trakhtenberg's *Fimka*, was a boulevard comedy about prostitutes.[175]

Classics reigned in the imperial operatic and ballet repertoires. The Mariinskii Theater's most commonly performed operas in the last decades of the tsarist

---

169. "Khronika," *Teatr i iskusstvo* 20 (May 15, 1905): 314. On Strauss's popularity, see McReynolds, *Russia at Play*, 232.
170. "Khronika," *Teatr i iskusstvo* 6 (February 5, 1906): 83.
171. "Ot redaktsii," *Teatr i iskusstvo* 51–52 (December 18, 1905): 789.
172. Komisarjevsky, *Myself and the Theatre*, 5.
173. Teliakovskii, "Imperatorskie teatry," 310.
174. For detailed listings and box office receipts, see "Sezon 1905–1906 gg.," *Ezhegodnik Imperatorskikh teatrov* 16 (1905–6, chast' II): 84–130.
175. Teliakovskii, "Imperatorskie teatry," 301.

era not only fit the traditional category, but long held—and continue to hold—respected places in the standard international repertoire. Chaikovskii's *The Queen of Spades*, a tale of obsessive love and supernatural revenge, had the most performances of any opera between 1900 and 1910, followed closely by such recognizable works as the same composer's *Eugene Onegin*, Gounod's *Faust*, Bizet's *Carmen*, Wagner's *Die Walküre*, and Verdi's *Aida*.[176] Although the ballet repertoire was becoming more innovative, its new productions and old favorites remained dominated by comparable themes of love, betrayal, and redemption. The box offices validated these choices. Between 1897 and 1913 the Mariinskii's revenue surged by 57.2 percent, while the Aleksandrinskii's receipts shot up 30.3 percent.[177] Revenues for ballet performances at the Bol'shoi, whose troupe had been an anemic force in the 1890s, trebled in the same period.[178]

Stage productions skeptical or even critical of political change also enjoyed popularity, an echo of the reception of such antirevolutionary literary works as Dostoevskii's tragically prophetic *The Devils*.[179] Along with a dramatized version of that novel, other profitable offerings at the Suvorin Theater included Ekaterina Zhukovskaia's *Chaos*, the tale of an unfortunate society lady who wonders what to do next when her revolutionary lover commits suicide after rampaging peasants burn his estate. Another Suvorin production, entitled *The Apostle*, presented a seamy tableau of corruption resulting from parliamentary democracy.[180] F. N. Shchankin's *In the Storm of Socialism*, submitted to the censorship in 1907, centered on a factory conflict in which workers reject the arguments of a socialist agitator who appears in their midst.[181] P. P. Pecherin-Tsander's *Afterward* (1909) offered a sympathetic depiction of an elderly landowning widow who lives in fear after rebellious peasants sack her estate and murder her daughter and son-in-law.[182]

Along with its ideals and actions, the progressive intelligentsia found itself subjected to prominently staged scorn. Gor'kii criticized it openly in *Summerfolk* and *Children of the Sun*, works designed to show intelligentsia haplessness. Nikolai Evreinov, a noted director and theorist who also wrote drama, castigated it in his play *The Beautiful Despot*. Regarded as "provocative and insolent" by a recent student of Russian modernist theater, the work, set in 1904, depicts a

---

176. Frame, *Imperial Theatres*, 106–7.
177. Calculations based on figures in Teliakovskii, *Vospominaniia*, 76.
178. Komisarjevsky, *Myself and the Theatre*, 35.
179. For a study of antirevolutionary sentiments in the Russian literary tradition, see Charles A. Moser, *Antinihilism in the Russian Novel of the 1860s* (The Hague: Mouton, 1964).
180. Petrovskaia and Somina, *Teatral'nyi Peterburg*, 209–10.
181. RGIA, f. 776, op. 26, d. 26, l. 243.
182. RGIA, f. 776, op. 26, d. 26, l. 43.

disenchanted liberal who lives on and operates his family estate in the same way that his great-grandfather had nearly a century earlier.[183] When a friend who has remained part of the "engaged" intelligentsia arrives to convince him to return to the political struggle, he not only fails but ends the play by becoming entranced with the charms of the estate's carefully cultivated anachronism. At the final curtain the audience is left wondering whether he can muster the will to leave it. A. I. Stoikin, in his aptly entitled 1911 play *The Intelligentsia*, portrayed a priggish revolutionary student whose fervor causes him frequent disappointment in life. Taking a job as a pett y bureaucrat and descending into alcoholism, he is reduced to a "feckless failure, whose extremist views are now held up to ridicule."[184] In Evtikhii Karpov's *Glow* (1912) an idealistic female student (*kursistka*) who helps organize a group of revolutionary workers is raped and murdered by one of them.[185] The outbreak of World War I added to this repertoire such works as *The Blaze of War*, a popular theater melodrama in which a socialist student character calls out for national unity and the abandonment of partisan political differences.[186]

Just as they derided audiences for their "passivity," leftist critics denounced this repertoire and its popularity. Gor'kii's *Summerfolk* was labeled "an accusatory act" and "a merciless whipping."[187] An offended reviewer of *The Apostle* complained that "we don't sleep at night, awaiting a rendezvous with our citizenship like people in love—and the first thing we get from the stage is this bucket of cold water."[188] Suvorin's repertoire selections made him "odious in the eyes of the opposition."[189] Not even Komissarzhevskaia's theater was immune to such criticism. Her successful production of Stanisław Przybyszewski's play *The Eternal Fairy Tale*, a love story about a king and consort who live in blissful ignorance of their royal power, led one reviewer to observe that it "should have been met with a passionate explosion of indignation, [but] was received

---

183. The phrase "provocative and insolent" is from Betsy F. Moeller-Sally, "The Theater as Will and Representation: Artist and Audience in Russian Modernist Theater, 1904–1909," *Slavic Review* 57, no. 2 (1998): 364.

184. McReynolds, *Russia at Play*, 69.

185. RGIA, f. 776, op. 26, d. 30, l. 194. Karpov had himself sympathized with political radicalism and spent time in prison and exile for his involvement in the Populist Movement, but the subject of this play might raise doubts about his convictions.

186. Jahn, *Patriotic Culture*, 133.

187. S. A. Sokolov [S. Krechetov], "'Dachniki' Gor'kogo na stsene Internatsional'nogo teatra," *Vesy* 3 (1905): 94; "Zigfrid" [E. A. Stark], "'Dachniki' M. Gor'kogo," *Teatral'naia Rossiia/Teatral'naia gazeta* 1 (December 11, 1904): 12–13.

188. "Impressionist" [I. F. Bentovin], "Malyi teatr," *Teatr i iskusstvo* 39 (September 25, 1905): 619–20.

189. Petrovskaia and Somina, *Teatral'nyi Peterburg*, 201.

with passionate ecstasy."[190] Whatever the critic thought, it was hardly the only case of an audience caring much more about the art than the politics.

Regardless of their capacity to frighten and agitate audiences, explosions of political unrest had little lasting effect on their appetites. The waning years of the tsarist era witnessed the public's even stronger attraction to light social satires, spoofs on bureaucracy, parodies of "serious" art, vaudeville, and more and more, eroticism and criminality. In Brushtein's words "light plays and playlets filled the theater ... spectators sought relaxation and diversion ... an exit from reality, a renunciation of social themes and themes of struggle."[191] Paléologue found that even as 1917 loomed, "the Russians go to music for the effects of opium."[192] Just as the reading public became enthralled with the amoral exploits of the title character in Mikhail Artsybashev's novel *Sanin* (1907), who is not coincidentally bored by politics, and the tawdry love affairs of Anastasiia Verbitskaia's *The Keys of Happiness* (1908–13), theater audiences craved staged depictions of moral challenges, open sexuality, and other sources of shock.[193]

Themes of eroticism and decadence, however, were hardly confined to the period after the Revolution of 1905. Works employing them only followed on the success of Lev Tolstoi's *The Power of Darkness*, a tale of adultery and infanticide presented so successfully at the Suvorin Theater in 1895 that in Gnedich's jealous view, "if Suvorin had been an experienced entrepreneur, he would have opened a subscription for *The Power of Darkness* and given it five times a week."[194] Two years later the first conference of the Russian Theatrical Society opened with a speech despairing that "an important part of the public is given to bloody melodrama and crude farces."[195] Russia's first performance of Oscar Wilde's incestuous and necrophilic *Salome*—the quintessential dramatic work of decadent modernism—was given (under a different billing and with censorship permission) in 1903. With such titillating titles as *The Female Samson, An Artist and His Model*, and *Modern Amazons*, each new outrage merely created the threshold for the next.

Eroticism strongly influenced the repertoire selections of Russian artistic endeavors operating beyond the Empire's borders. Ida Rubinshtein's fully nude

---

190. V. Azov [V. A. Ashkinazi], "Teatr V. F. Komissarzhevskoi," *Rech'*, December 6, 1906.
191. Brushtein, *Stranitsy*, 82.
192. Paléologue, *Memoirs*, 3:27.
193. For a description of these tastes, see Laura Engelstein, *The Keys to Happiness: Sex and the Search for Modernity in Fin-de-Siècle Russia* (Ithaca: Cornell University Press, 1992).
194. Gnedich, *Kniga zhizni*, 206.
195. Al. P. Lenskii, "Prichiny upadka teatral'nogo dela," *Teatr i iskusstvo* 11 (March 16, 1897): 203.

interpretation of *The Dance of the Seven Veils*, part of her production of Wilde's *Salome* and choreographed by Fokin, made her a Petersburg sensation after its performances in November 1908. When she performed the role in Paris four years later, she catapulted to international stardom. A contemporary critic described Rubinshtein's technique as "the suppleness of a serpent in the physical form of a woman" and marveled at the "undulating movements of her body," a description amply captured by Valentin Serov's portrait.[196] Fokin's production of *Schéhérazade* for the 1912 season of the Ballets Russes included the seduction of a queen by a male concubine and an orgy followed by the slaughter of its participants.[197]

Vatslav Nizhinskii's creations, first staged for the Ballets Russes in 1912–13, also tantalized audiences with frenzied sensuality. His initial production, set to Claude Debussy's *Prélude à l'après-midi d'un faune*, dealt with adolescent sexual awakening. *Jeux* playfully depicted a ménage-à-trois flirtation with thinly disguised homoerotic undertones.[198] The scandalous premiere of *Le Sacre du printemps*, which famously provoked a riot at its Paris premiere, embraced the fashionable primitivist school of art and the young composer Igor' Stravinskii's dissonant music to present stunned audiences with sexualized fertility rites, masturbation, and staged human sacrifice.

These works may have constituted a revolution in dance, but they reflected and appealed to the increasingly prurient proclivities of international cultural taste (to say nothing of Rubinshtein's and Nizhinskii's own sexual personae; both were openly bisexual) rather than the tortured world of Russian politics, an arena that held little interest for the artists and their admirers. They and

---

196. Valerian Svetlov, *Sovremennyi balet* (St. Petersburg: Tovarichestvo R. Golike i A. Vil'borg, 1911), 78. Nearly a century later the Salome motif still commands popularity. Recreations of Aubrey Beardsley's illustrations for the Wilde play decorated the walls of the dance floor at St. Petersburg's Absinthe Club, which opened just after absinthe's legalization in Russia in late 2001 and for at least a couple of years remained one of the city's trendiest and most exclusive nightspots.

197. Lynn Garafola, *Diaghilev's Ballets Russes* (New York: Oxford University Press, 1989), 23, claims without evidence that Fokin's *Schéhérazade* presented "the fury of masses unchained" and "the liberation of self through collective action," themes supporting her conclusion that "on-stage, the spirit of [the Revolution of] 1905 continued to live." Since the "unchained masses" are engaging in sex acts, however, one might properly wonder whether the scene represented a political statement of the type Garafola detects. The bloody finale might also lead one to question what, if anything, Fokin really thought about liberation through collective action. The next time such an ambition was attempted in Russia, he stayed far away.

198. The plot of *Jeux* involves a male tennis player trying to choose between two female tennis players. At the end he runs off with both of them. Vaslav Nijinsky, *The Diary of Vaslav Nijinsky*, trans. Romola Nijinsky (London: Quartet Encounters, 1991), 123, confirmed that "the story of this ballet is about three young men," but that it had to be changed because a homosexual love triangle "could not be represented on the stage." Romola Nijinsky, *Nijinsky* (New York: Simon and Schuster, 1934), 199, more ambiguously refers to the characters as "three moderns."

their creations, furthermore, were far from unwelcome within Russia's borders. Rubinshtein's initial success as Salome had after all been in Petersburg. Fokin's appointment as First Ballet Master after Marius Petipa died in 1910 resulted at least partly from the young choreographer's international fame and recognition, which matched his growing renown at home. Several of Fokin's early creations had premiered or originated as productions for the imperial stage. Indeed, the entire program of full-length ballets performed during the Ballets Russes's inaugural visit to Paris in 1909 (*Le Pavillon d'Armide, The Egyptian Nights/Cléopâtre,* and *Chopiniana/Les Sylphides*) consisted of productions that he had previously staged at the Mariinskii Theater.[199] The sets and costumes for the previous year's production of *Boris Godunov* were brought to the Mariinskii for Meierkhol'd's staging of the opera there in 1911.

Nor were the Imperial Theaters the limit of their appeal. The Tsar Nicholas II People's House invited Diaghilev to present *Schéhérazade* and other Ballets Russes productions shortly after they premiered in Paris. Only a devastating fire that damaged the theater prevented their erotic themes from thrilling the audiences of Russia's biggest and most generously subsidized popular stage in the years before World War I.[200]

The growth of miniature theaters and other cabaret forms, sometimes known collectively in Russia as *estrada,* matched the more traditional theaters' apolitical offerings. The Crooked Mirror, the most famous and successful venue in the world of Russian cabaret, represented the fullest expression of this trend when it opened in 1908. Its first program included a parody of modernist dance called *Salome's Funeral,* irreverent songs, and Nadezhda Teffi's bawdy comedy *Love Through the Centuries,* which addressed "concerns with sexual problems, depicting the evolution of love from the time of the apes to the twenty-first century."[201] The Crooked Mirror's most famous production, *Vampuka, African Bride,* which premiered in January 1909, parodied Verdi's *Aida,* Meyerbeer's *L'Africaine,* and the tradition of nineteenth-century grand opera they represent. A runaway success, it had more than three hundred performances over the next

---

199. According to S. L. Grigoriev, *The Diaghilev Ballet, 1909–1929,* trans. Vera Bowen (Harmondsworth: Penguin, 1960), 26, presenting these ballets was more economical for the young company because they already existed and required much less rehearsal time than new or unfamiliar works. Another part of the 1909 dance program, *Le festin,* was an evening of set pieces from several other existing Mariinskii productions. The 1909 season's opera component was also made up of productions that had been done at the Mariinskii, though Fokin's choreography for the *Polovtsian Dances* in Borodin's *Prince Igor* was original.

200. Nijinsky, *Nijinsky,* 116; Grigoriev, *Diaghilev Ballet,* 58–60.

201. Spencer Golub, *Evreinov: The Theatre of Paradox and Transformation* (Ann Arbor: UMI Research, 1984), 148.

three years.²⁰² "The lack of overtly political content in [its] repertoire" allowed the theater to escape controversy before 1917, survive that year's two revolutions, resume operations after a hiatus from 1918 to 1922, endure its artistic direction's defection to the West in 1925, and last for at least a couple of years into the Stalin era before closing permanently in 1931.²⁰³

Likewise, when Fokin's brother Aleksandr opened the Trinity Theater of Miniatures with a similar repertoire in 1911, he "won the sympathy of the widest public circles, and succeeded brilliantly in financial affairs."²⁰⁴ And why not? A reviewer writing as late as September 1916 appreciated the apolitical atmosphere he found in cabarets, for "in them one relaxes from every 'question' and 'problem.'"²⁰⁵ As a recent study of late tsarist era leisure maintains, "politics figured as only a minor subject in most routines." Cross-dressers (*transformatory*), however, exploded in popularity, in one manifestation of what Hubertus Jahn has plausibly described as an atmosphere of "sophisticated hedonism and ostentatious decadence."²⁰⁶ With the appearance of such venues as Russia's own Moulin Rouge, where "rich Muscovites were entertained with '*Wein, Weib, Gesang, und Tanz*,' particularly with '*Wein und Weib*,'" it is hard to doubt.²⁰⁷

The tastes of Russian audiences only amplified the intelligentsia's pessimism and fear. One sanctimonious critic found popular dramatizations of Sherlock Holmes stories to be "of no use to anyone on earth."²⁰⁸ Another described the popular entertainment commonly offered to the lower classes as "cannibalism."²⁰⁹ The actor Khodotov bitterly lamented the increasing presence of sexuality in the repertoire: "Erotica, taking possession of society,... got through to children, poisoning the younger generation."²¹⁰ Another performer bewailed the Russian stage as a milieu "littered with idealess plays.²¹¹

Some radicals believed that the government was complicit in promoting an apolitical and socially irrelevant role for the performing arts. "Absolutism," one

---

202. Barbara Henry, "Theatrical Parody at the Krivoe zerkalo: Russian 'Teatr Miniatyur,' 1908–1931" (D.Phil. thesis, Oxford University, 1996), 55.
203. Quote is from Petrovskaia and Somina, *Teatral'nyi Peterburg*, 318. Henry, "Krivoe zerkalo," 49n.
204. Petrovskaia, *Teatr i zritel' rossiiskikh stolits*, 102.
205. N. G. Shebuev, "Galochka," *Zritel'* 8 (September 12, 1916): 27.
206. McReynolds, *Russia at Play*, 247, 150–53; Jahn, *Patriotic Culture*, 123.
207. Komisarjevsky, *Myself and the Theatre*, 99.
208. O. Dymov, "Peterburgskie teatry," *Zolotoe runo* 10 (October 1906): 80.
209. "Mim," "Divertisement dlia naroda," *Teatral'naia Rossiia/Muzykal'nyi mir* 16 (April 16, 1905): 243.
210. Khodotov, *Blizkoe—dalekoe*, 216.
211. Tiraspol'skaia, *Iz proshlogo*, 118.

critic insisted, "sought in [theater] distraction and amusement. Art was considered the best means for dispelling civic thought."[212] Clearly he regretted the absence of a sparkling connection between culture and power in his country. A Soviet theater historian later recycled this argument to explain—without evidence—the rationale for the abolition of the Imperial Theaters' performance monopoly in 1882.[213] The Marxist critic Vladimir Friche argued that capitalism was to blame for popular tastes: "If entrepreneurs and directors see theater before all else as a means of making money, then the audience will look above all else for entertainment in performances."[214] This was a self-fulfilling prophecy and an inescapable fact of cultural modernity, but it nevertheless underscored the radical intelligentsia's growing exasperation. It also cast a long shadow. Writing in 1968, the Soviet theater historian Anatolii Al'tshuller complained that before the revolution "the tastes of the public were debauched by numerous farces, variety shows, operettas, and miniature theaters."[215] Even a recent American study has disparaged the "smug conventionality" that its author believed to have been characteristic of late tsarist-era audiences.[216] Value judgments notwithstanding, all these comments reveal a degree of frustration with the noticeable lack of political content in cultural appreciation.

Some government officials shared this dismay and confirmed the critics' views, if in a backhanded way. Prince Nikolai Shakhovskoi, head of the Interior Ministry's Press Affairs Office, the Empire's main censorship organ, felt that "the audience of [popular] theaters need only be defended from operettas, ditties, couplets, and other such works of the light genre that cause bad taste and corrupt spectators."[217] Presumably political dissent and ideological agitation were less of a threat. Teliakovskii, who delegated some of his authority over repertoire selection to administrative subordinates, upbraided Gnedich for showing Aleksandrinskii audiences Ippolit Shpazhinskii's play *The Little Nightingales*, which the Director derided as "filth" (*gadost'*).[218]

---

212. "Ot redaktsii," *Teatr i iskusstvo* 1 (January 1, 1906): 1. There is no evidence that the tsarist government tried actively to influence the repertoire selection of private theaters for this or any other purpose.

213. S. S. Danilov, *Ocherki po istorii russkogo dramaticheskogo teatra* (Moscow: Gosudarstvennyi Nauchno-Issledovatel'skii Institut Teatra i Muzyki, 1948), 421.

214. V. Friche, "Teatr v sovremennom i budushchem obshchestve," in *Krizis teatra: Sbornik statei*, ed. Iurii Steklov (St. Petersburg: Problemy iskusstva, 1908), 159.

215. A. Ia. Al'tshuller, "Aleksandrinskii teatr v 1895–1907 godakh," in *Russkaia khudozhestvennaia kul'tura kontsa XIX–nachala XX veka (1895–1907)*, 4 vols. (Moscow: Nauka, 1968–81), 1:133.

216. Catherine A. Schuler, *Women in the Russian Theatre: The Actress in the Silver Age* (New York: Routledge, 1996), 173.

217. Quoted in "Ot redaktsii," *Teatr i iskusstvo* 20 (May 15, 1905): 311.

218. Gnedich, *Kniga zhizni*, 277.

Nevertheless, other observers saw the proliferation of apolitical light entertainment in positive terms. Shcheglov, a prominent theorist and advocate of the popular theater movement, regarded its Ostrovskii-laden repertoire as a "preventative valve against the poisonous alien sprouting of social fermentation."[219] Rather than proving government complicity in creating popular tastes, his comment suggests that society was using the performing arts to avoid expressions of political discontent.

Whatever one thought of the prevailing content of the Russian stage, it was thriving and it was unavoidable. As Thurston has argued in reference to popular theater's prodigious growth in the decades before 1917, "the masses began to appear less assimilable and some of the most sophisticated of the intelligentsia began to fear that their own values would be the ones engulfed."[220] Jeffrey Brooks has demonstrated that this anxiety was equaled by the intelligentsia's reactions to popular literary tastes, of which it also strongly disapproved and that sometimes (e.g., Sherlock Holmes) provided direct inspiration for what was appearing on Russian stages.[221] The more audiences sought diversion and entertainment in culture, the less likely they were to embrace stimuli for change, reform, and revolution. The "pessimism" commonly associated with the interrevolutionary period between 1905 and 1917 revealed not the defeat of the intelligentsia's values in accomplishing a political transformation but the sinking realization that they were a spent force of declining vitality and marginal interest.

If the political climate of Late Imperial Russia proved anything about Russia's audiences, it was the importance of their role in facilitating the commercialization, rather than the politicization, of the performing arts. To the consternation of reformers and radicals (and some historians), the Empire's spectators engaged with culture almost exclusively as a sour ce of entertainment and diversion. They craved the melodrama, suspense, human relations, comedy, and general "decadence" inherent in the newer and more explicit themes of sex and violence. In other words they wanted everything that made a theatrical enterprise successful and, as was frequently the case, profitable enough to remain in business.

Regardless of how much theater attendance contributed to self-fashioning and changing ideas of entertainment, Russia's audiences were not establishing new spaces for the expression of political and social thought, let alone active

---

219. Quoted in Petrovskaia and Somina, *Teatral'nyi Peterburg*, 269.
220. Thurston, *Popular Theatre*, 251.
221. Brooks, *When Russia Learned to Read*, 328–33.

dissent. By offering popular apolitical works, theaters vied with film, the "staple product" of which consisted of "dysfunctional families, sexual manipulation and deception, violent solutions to insoluble problems," and "deeply violent eroticism."[222] Opposition politics made a pale impression in that new medium as well. As late as 1917, Russian filmgoers were still enjoying such works as Evgenii Bauer's *The Revolutionary*, in which the radical title character's father persuades him to abandon his antiwar political views and enlist in the army.[223]

Even at the most contentious moments, the few disruptions of performances before 1917 resulted from either factors external to what appeared on stage or the actions of agitators whose antics never attracted much sympathy from audiences. The latter were considerably less than "not ready for day-to-day resistance."[224] Gor'kii's supposition that the era "gave birth to real people, to barbarians like those who knocked the legs out from under Rome," becomes untenable in light of real audience tastes. Indeed, the appearance of works that questioned the virtues of revolutionary aspirations and intelligentsia values suggests that Russian audiences may actually have wanted to prevent such births.[225] Iurii Lotman's observation that "at the beginning of nineteenth century . . . the dividing line between art and the everyday behavior of the audience was expunged," hardly appears applicable to the early twentieth.[226] A more instructive comparison could be made to British audiences, who, as Marc Baer has argued, may have promoted order in theaters through their collective restraint and self-control.[227]

Nevertheless, some critics and innovators, including many of the leading minds at work in Russia's Silver Age, took the fact of a commercialized performing arts universe as a challenge and looked for meaningful alternatives to the permanent, growing, and, in their opinion, crass and counterproductive features of modern urban life. The currents of unrest and uncertainty that coursed through the late imperial era offered some hope of stimulating their experiments, which were beginning to take shape under the surfaces of the Empire's mainstream culture. It is with the role and fate of that phantasmagorical world that the main body of this study will conclude.

222. Youngblood, *Magic Mirror*, 75, 107.
223. Ibid., 119–20.
224. Senelick, "Anti-Semitism and the Tsarist Theatre," 94.
225. Quoted in Iu. N. Chirva, "O p'esakh M. Gor'kogo i L. Andreeva epokhi pervoi russkoi revoliutsii," in Al'tshuller, *Russkii teatr i dramaturgiia epokhi revoliutsii*, 27.
226. Jurij M. Lotman, "The Theater and Theatricality as Components of Early Nineteenth-Century Culture," in Ju. M. Lotman and B. A. Uspenskij, *The Semiotics of Russian Culture*, ed. A. Shukman (Ann Arbor: Michigan Slavic Contributors, 1984), 145.
227. Marc Baer, *Theatre and Disorder in Late Georgian London* (Oxford: Clarendon, 1992), 241–42.

6

"A NEW BAYREUTH WILL SAVE NO ONE":
RUSSIAN MODERNISM AND ITS DISCONTENTS

On December 30, 1906, following a performance of Maeterlinck's *The Miracle of St. Anthony*, Vera Komissarzhevskaia's Dramatic Theater presented an unusual play by the young symbolist poet Aleksandr Blok. Entitled *The Fairground Booth* (*Balaganchik*), the short one-act farce features masks of the Italian commedia dell'arte form: Pierrot, Columbine, and Harlequin. In Blok's version, staged that evening by Komissarzhevskaia's chief director Vsevolod Meierkhol'd, the curtain opens on a group of intellectual mystics headily discussing whether a female figure they perceive is a symbol of death. Pierrot, played by Meierkhol'd himself in the premiere production, sees her as Columbine, the amour whom commedia dell'arte convention never allows him to possess. In the next scene a masquerade begins, and several young couples dance, laugh, and flirt. Pierrot morosely wonders whether the female figure is real or made of cardboard. Harlequin, Pierrot's stock rival for Columbine's affection, wistfully complains that life is a dream and that no one knows true love. Seeking escape from his blasé existence, he exclaims that he wants to live in the real world and tries to leap through a window in the paper staging, which tears apart and shows him the floor. Harlequin's leap prompts the arrival of a hooded figure of death, which scares the assembled masquerade into flight. Pierrot remains, however, and sees (or imagines) the figure morphing into a beauty, possibly his Columbine reappearing. A character representing the play's author then comes on stage, feigning disbelief at what he claims to be a distortion of his work by mischievous actors. He attempts to set things right, but just when he feels he has succeeded, Harlequin bleeds to death, claiming that his blood is cranberry juice, while

Pierrot decides that the Death/Columbine figure really is a cardboard illusion. The paper sets rise above the proscenium, the characters disappear, and the audience is left contemplating an empty stage.

No one knew with certainty what either Blok's play or Meierkhol'd's staging of it meant or was intended to mean. Depending on one's perspective, it may have worked on many levels or none at all. The critic Aleksandr Kugel', hardly a conservative, mocked the performance as "*Bedlamchik*" and described it as "impossible to consider" and "ungifted and hopeless."[1] Some scholars have suggested that the farcical romance at the heart of the drama parodied Blok's unhappy marriage to Liubov' Mendeleeva, daughter of the famous chemist, who had begun a long-lasting and deeply emotional affair with his correspondent, sometime friend, and fellow symbolist poet Andrei Belyi.[2] Belyi took it that way, describing *The Fairground Booth* as "a bitter ridicule of my own past" and "constant blasphemy."[3] One theater historian has attempted to read the play as a metaphoric text, which parodied traditional theater in order to expose "outworn structures of society."[4] The actress Valentina Verigina, who appeared in the premiere production as one of the masked revelers, had a much simpler view. Recalling the cast party, which became known as "the evening of paper ladies" because the performers remained in their flimsy costumes, she reminisced that "we entered into a magical circle of play, in which our youth whirled." This was the St. Petersburg of masquerades and parties, of nightlife and fun, the colorful metropolis that Anna Akhmatova remembered and mourned in her *Poem Without a Hero*. Who needed deep meaning, and, as far as *The Fairground Booth* was concerned, who cared if there was "a public that did not understand it at all and that would not accept it in any way?"[5]

A more common interpretation might be that Blok's use of the grotesque expressed frustration with the intelligentsia's ineffectual role in society, a theme that had begun to appear on Russian stages with increasing bitterness after the

---

1. A. Kugel', "Teatral'nye zametki," *Teatr i iskusstvo* 1 (January 7, 1907): 18.
2. Iu. Rybakova, *Komissarzhevskaia* (Leningrad: Iskusstvo, 1971), 152, refers to the play's "romantic irony." Spencer Golub, *The Recurrence of Fate: Theatre and Memory in Twentieth-Century Russia* (Iowa City: University of Iowa Press, 1994), 61, makes this point and suggests the love triangle parody may also have applied to the curious relationship among Dmitrii Merezhkovskii, his wife Zinaida Gippius, and their friend Dmitrii Filosofov. For details on both situations, see Olga Matich, *Erotic Utopia: The Decadent Imagination in Russia's Fin de Siècle* (Madison: University of Wisconsin Press, 2005), 89–125, 162–211.
3. Quoted in Konstantin Rudnitsky, *Meyerhold the Director*, trans. George Petrov (Ann Arbor: Ardis, 1981), 109.
4. J. Douglas Clayton, *Pierrot in Petrograd: The Commedia dell'Arte/Balagan in Twentieth-Century Russian Theatre and Drama* (Montreal: McGill-Queen's University Press, 1993), 81.
5. V. P. Verigina, *Vospominaniia* (Leningrad: Iskusstvo, 1974), 106–8.

Revolution of 1905. Politicized *intelligenty* naturally should have been disappointed by the events of the two years following Bloody Sunday. By the time of *The Fairground Booth*'s premiere, the tsarist government had regained the upper hand in domestic politics, restored order, and largely set its own agenda for reform. As we have seen throughout this study, neither stage performers nor audiences had, to the intelligentsia's audible consternation, grasped onto the performing arts as a locus for political expression. The performers wanted first and foremost to perform, and the audiences almost invariably wanted to be entertained. Harlequin's leap—his face-flattening attempt to break out of a mundane two-dimensional world and reach a more meaningful universe that did not exist for him—gestured toward the intelligentsia's sense of helplessness and generated whatever resonance the play may have had among its members in the audience.

Intellectuals who "saw theatrical revolution as the midwife of the political" were only bound to be disappointed.[6] Spencer Golub, probably giving the Russian intelligentsia more credit than it was due, has characterized Blok's play as "a 'mea culpa' for intellectual self-absorption," defined (however pretentiously) by "socio-spiritual entrapment in its semiotic dialogue."[7] "After the cruel suppression of the Revolution of 1905," some recent Russian scholarship has maintained, "the intelligentsia . . . survived a sharp crisis [and] felt confusion, and more than that, fear before elements of the mass movement, a feeling of fear about the destruction of culture, about the future of Russia."[8] All the "committed" intelligentsia needed to do to feel that way was read the theater listings and survey popular literature, but it may well have been its insecurity and hyperbolic sense of apocalypse that drove Blok to look for a way to stage its haplessness.

What had the depressed creative intelligentsia expected of the relationship between culture and power? Most of those working in or appreciating the performing arts abjured politics, but even those who expected great change in response to events did not necessarily view that transformation in political terms. As Bernice Rosenthal has written, for many intellectuals political upheaval represented "primarily a religious and cultural crisis."[9] Meierkhol'd's production

6. Katerina Clark, *Petersburg, Crucible of Cultural Revolution* (Cambridge: Harvard University Press, 1995), 75.
7. Golub, *Recurrence of Fate*, 36, 58.
8. T. A. Prozorova, "A. M. Gor'kii," and M. Iu. Khmel'nitskaia, "A. A. Blok," both in *Russkii dramaticheskii teatr kontsa XIX–nachala XX vv.*, ed. A. Nazarova and N. Orekhova (Moscow: GITIS, 2000), 95.
9. Bernice Glatzer Rosenthal, *New Myth, New World: From Nietzsche to Stalinism* (University Park: Pennsylvania State University Press, 2002), 41.

of *The Fairground Booth*, ground zero for symbolist theatrical innovation, "did not espouse any political position or de al with any social controversy."[10] In March 1905 Sergei Diaghilev, whose assertiveness had led to his dismissal from the Imperial Theaters during Prince Sergei Volkonskii's tenure as Director but later made him the effective impresario of the Ballets Russes, announced:

> We are witnesses to one of the greatest moments of conclusion and endings in history, of a new, unknown culture which will grow from us, but which will toss us aside. And this is why, without fear or disbelief, I raise my glass to the shattered walls of beautiful palaces as well as to the new principles of a new aesthetic. And the only wish that I, as an unrepentant sensualist, can express, is that the battle before us will not offend the aesthetics of life, and that death would be as bea utiful and radiant as the Resurrection.[11]

Despite his allusion to shattered palaces, Diaghilev's "battle" was a cultural one. A man who always "professed himself a monarchist" and "began cursing the revolutionaries of every country" in 1917, he gave the speech at a banquet honoring his most recently organized art exhibition, a collection of eighteenth-century aristocratic portraiture.[12] It was displayed in Petersburg's neoclassical Tauride Palace, a lesser property belonging to the imperial household, and enjoyed the "Most August Protection" of the tsar himself. Writing to Aleksandr Benua during the October 1905 general strike, Diaghilev's principal concern was for the safety of the paintings and their unhindered return to their noble owners.[13] If the theorists and other theatrically minded intellectuals received any inspiration from revolutionary events, it was not to embrace political upheaval, agitate for reform, or espouse radical ideologies. Diaghilev added to his concerns about the exhibit that "there's nothing to do, only wait around and waste time.... Like a hurricane, [the unrest] is causing many disasters."[14] Blok boasted (perhaps prematurely) in a 1906 New Year's greeting that he would "never become a revolutionary."[15] According to Belyi, his friends Zinaida Gippius and

---

10. Clayton, *Pierrot in Petrograd*, 77.
11. "V chas itogov," *Vesy* 4 (April 1905): 45–46.
12. Quotes taken from S. L. Grigoriev, *The Diaghilev Ballet, 1909–1929*, trans. Vera Bowen (Harmondsworth: Penguin, 1960), 130, 143.
13. Diaghilev to Benua, in I. S. Zil'berstein and V. A. Samkov, *Sergei Diagilev i russkoe iskusstvo*, 2 vols. (Moscow: Izobrazitel'noe iskusstvo, 1982), 2:95.
14. Ibid.
15. Aleksandr Blok, *Sobranie sochinenii*, 8 vols. (Moscow: Gosudarstvennoe izdatel'stvo khudozhestvennoi literatury, 1960–63), 8:144. Blok's alleged sympathies for the Bolshevik Revolution

Dmitrii Merezhkovskii, the symbolist intellectuals who had requested and possibly helped cause the cancellation of the Aleksandrinskii Theater's evening performance on Bloody Sunday, described talk of an uprising later in 1905 as "crazy." They reacted to such political events as the arrest of the St. Petersburg Soviet's deputies with "disinterest."[16]

Many intellectuals looked upon political turmoil as a potential source of social and spiritual renewal. Their abstract commitment to higher artistic truths hardly amounted to a defense of the tsarist status quo, but it did contribute to their view of the arts—especially theater—as a socially integrative force that could help restore unity and dispel conflict, a philosophy that directly contradicted the notions of social and political struggle prevailing in oppositionist thought. A time of political upheaval was not a call to arms but a promise of hope. As a contributor to *Theatrical Russia* wrote in its first issue in December 1904, when increased labor agitation and the Liberation Movement's banquet campaign portended more serious unrest: "Such moments favor art. The best works appear exactly at a moment of rising social consciousness.... The time is not far off when the hard realization will again strike us that theater is not an empty game, [but] that its definite calling is to serve the immortal ideals of truth and beauty.... New forces are being born, which in their works will call out to truth, love, and light."[17] Nearly two years later, after Russia had experienced its first revolution, another writer argued that "with the changes in the social order the theater must now also, as an expression of the people's soul, be reborn and become a social institution."[18]

Revolutionary times surely raised the hopes of those who appreciated these sentiments, but it is a mistake to identify politics as a catalyst for social reform through the performing arts. The development of Western theater as a social instrument falls far beyond the parameters of this study, but it is worth noting that its inventors in antiquity, revivers in the Middle Ages, innovators in the Renaissance, and modern-era idealists all looked to it to varying degrees as an instrument of education, stimulant for social unity, and builder of communion. The roots of modern theater evolved largely from religious rituals—the

---

and single instance of carrying a red flag in a 1905 street demonstration are often mentioned, but the statement in his letter suggests confusion, to say the least. According to Matich, *Erotic Utopia*, 101, Blok spent much of 1905 in the throes of a psychological crisis caused by his sexual neuroses and, perhaps consequently, his troubled marriage.

16. Andrei Belyi, *Mezhdu dvukh revoliutsii* (Moscow: Khudozhestvennaia literatura, 1990), 66.
17. M. Gorodetskii, "Nadezhdy russkogo teatra," *Teatral'naia Rossiia/Teatral'naia gazeta* 1 (December 11, 1904): 15.
18. Anatolii Nelidov, "Teatr, kak obshchestvennoe uchrezhdenie," *Teatr i iskusstvo* 33 (August 6, 1906): 502.

passion plays, liturgical music, and moral dramas performed to celebrate and exalt acts of Christian faith. Nothing special about late tsarist-era political unrest served as a magical, or perhaps more appropriately, mystical light bulb to illuminate Russian minds about these deeper origins.

Diaghilev's choice of religious imagery ("Resurrection") to describe the emerging culture that he toasted was no accident or meaningless rush of words. Indeed, the identification of theater with religious unity was as common a trope in Russian discussions of the role of the arts as it had been in earlier contexts throughout the Western cultural world. The importance of German idealist philosophy and the French symbolists to earlier generations of Russian thought grafted the European Romantic era's values onto Slavophile enthusiasm for communal social structures, Orthodox Christian *sobornost'* (conciliarism), and the natural, peaceful order they were thought to govern. Nietzsche, who had much currency in Russian intellectual circles, placed the ultimate artist in the realm of divinity when he wrote that "existence and the world seem justified only as an aesthetic creation."[19] Vladimir Solov'ev, the great religious philosopher and spiritual godfather of Russian symbolism (Blok was his nephew), had looked to art as a device with a "solemn and prophetic religious role" that would "incarnate the absolute ideal."[20]

Symbolist artists embraced this theologizing in their approach to the performing arts. Konstantin Stanislavskii inaugurated the Moscow Art Theater's first rehearsal with a solemn religious service.[21] The novelist and critic Aleksei Remizov compared theater attendance to taking Holy Communion.[22] In an article aptly entitled "A Theater of One Will," the writer Fedor Sologub described the art form as "a liturgical act" and "religious rite."[23] When Meierkhol'd prepared in late 1905 to come to Petersburg to explore theatrical opportunities, he was convinced that "only now is it possible to commence the building of a new altar."[24]

Although these theorists and their fellow believers "fully expected a vital new

---

19. Friedrich Nietzsche, "The Birth of Tragedy," in *Basic Writings of Nietzsche*, trans. and ed. Walter Kaufmann (New York: Random House, 2000), 141. For Nietzsche's role in the Russian symbolist aesthetic, see Irina Paperno, "The Meaning of Art: Symbolist Theories," in *Creating Life: The Aesthetic Utopia of Russian Modernism*, ed. Irina Paperno and Joan Delaney Grossman (Stanford: Stanford University Press, 1994), 13–23. For solid studies of Nietzsche's impact in Russia, see Rosenthal, *New Myth*, and idem, ed., *Nietzsche in Russia* (Princeton: Princeton University Press, 1986).

20. Vladimir Solov'ev, "Obshchii smysl iskusstva," in Solov'ev, *Sobranie sochinenii*, 12 vols. (St. Petersburg: Prosveshchenie, 1911–14), 6:90. The essay originally appeared in 1890.

21. Jean Benedetti, *Stanislavski: A Biography* (London: Methuen, 1988), 68.

22. A. Remizov, "Tovarichestvo Novoi Dramy," *Vesy* 4 (April 1904): 36.

23. Fedor Sologub, "Teatr odnoi voli," in *"Teatr": Kniga o novom teatre. Sbornik statei* (St. Petersburg: n. p., 1908), 177–98.

24. RGALI, f. 998, op. 626, l. 256. The collapse of Moscow's theatrical life as a result of the December uprising doubtlessly reinforced that conviction.

theater of religious creativity and religious activity to materialize," they were far from alone in approaching the performing arts in religious terms.[25] The conservative imperial stage actress Mariia Savina referred to the Aleksandrinskii as "our church."[26] Lev Tolstoi, nobody's idea of a symbolist, spoke of theater as "the most powerful pulpit of our times" and, taking a cue from the Slavophiles, identified religious consciousness as the main feature of "the art of the whole people."[27] According to Rosenthal, in what is probably an understatement, the desirability of social integration through mysticism, love, art, and other high-minded philosophical concepts was "fairly widespread" among Russian intellectuals.[28]

The immense popularity of Richard Wagner's operas and theoretical works—virtually defined by their mystical and spiritual qualities—should be neither discounted nor overstated. His œuvre was popular with many in Russian and, indeed, international cultural life, including the tsar, some of his most determined opponents, and a great number in between. Nicholas II, who intervened to have the four operas of his *Ring of the Nibelung* staged at the Mariinskii every season from 1907, ranked only Chaikovskii as a composer of equal greatness.[29] Wagnerian themes appeared in Vrubel's painting, Blok's poetry, Rimskii-Korsakov's operas, Meierkhol'd's dramatic theories, and Nizhinskii's choreography.[30] Stanislavskii toured behind the scenes of Wagner's theater in Bayreuth to seek inspiration for his own projects.[31] Liubov' Blok is alleged to have begun her affair with Belyi, possibly a subtext of her cuckolded husband's mockery in *The Fairground Booth,* after the two attended a concert performance of the first

25. Bernice Glatzer Rosenthal, "Theatre as Church: The Vision of the Mystical Anarchists," *Russian History/Histoire Russe* 4, pt. 2 (1977): 136.
26. Quoted in Catherine A. Schuler, *Women in the Russian Theatre: The Actress in the Silver Age* (New York: Routledge, 1996), 61. Perhaps ironically, she used "church" to refer to the status quo that innovators were attacking.
27. Lev Tolstoi, "Chto takoe iskusstvo?" *Sobranie sochinenii,* 21 vols. (Moscow: Gosudarstvennoe izdatel'stvo khudozhestvennoi literatury, 1960–64), 15:109–10, 152. The line about the pulpit is quoted in Steven G. Marks, *How Russia Shaped the Modern World: From Art to Anti-Semitism, Ballet to Bolshevism* (Princeton: Princeton University Press, 2002), 209–10.
28. Bernice Glatzer Rosenthal, "The Transmutation of the Symbolist Ethos: Mystical Anarchism and the Revolution of 1905," *Slavic Review* 36, no. 4 (1977): 626.
29. A. A. Mossolov, *At the Court of the Last Tsar: Being the Memoirs of A. A. Mossolov, Head of the Court Chancellery, 1900–1916,* trans. E. W. Dickes (London: Methuen, 1935), 20.
30. For a comprehensive description of these influences, see Rosamund Bartlett, *Wagner and Russia* (Cambridge: Cambridge University Press, 1995), and Simon Morrison, *Russian Opera and the Symbolist Movement* (Berkeley and Los Angeles: University of California Press, 2002). Vrubel' painted his patroness Princess Mariia Tenisheva as a Valkyrie, a mythical character brought to life in Wagner's *Der Ring des Nibelungen.* Blok's poetry included verse about Siegfried, the major hero of that work. Rimskii-Korsakov's operas included numerous musical citations from Wagner. Robert Leach, *Vsevolod Meyerhold* (Cambridge: Cambridge University Press, 1989), 31, calls Wagner's influence on Meierkhol'd "pervasive."
31. Benedetti, *Stanislavski,* 118.

act of *Parsifal*.³² When the Imperial Theaters Directorate gave Aleksandr Benua the daunting task of staging *Götterdämmerung* as his first production in 1902, the young artist was ecstatic because it was one of his favorite operas. Feliia Litvin, the soprano singing Brünnhilde in the production, prepared for the role "as for a sacred act."³³ The tenor and director Vasilii Shkafer "found a cult of Richard Wagner" awaiting him when he arrived at the Mariinskii.³⁴ Critics embraced the Wagner fad as well. Eduard Stark wrote under the pseudonym "Siegfried" (Zigfrid), after the ill-fated hero of the last two *Ring* operas. The publicist Emil Medtner signed himself "Wolfing" (Wölfing), one of the names used by Siegfried's even less fortunate father before he is renamed Siegmund at the end of the first act of *Die Walküre*. The Marxist critic Vladimir Friche referred to the composer as a "prophet."³⁵

It was probably no coincidence that the most influential of Wagner's rambling theoretical works, *Art and Revolution* and *Opera and Drama*, first appeared in Russian translation in 1906.³⁶ Their emphasis on creating a "total work of art" (*Gesamtkunstwerk*) from expressive forms that had grown apart since their synthesis in antiquity gestured toward the unity for which many Silver Age Russians strived. But how was the adaptation of theater for purposes of social integration to be achieved? This question's answer proved very difficult, for, like most other aspects of Russian symbolism, no unified theory or dominant movement emerged to address it.³⁷

Perhaps the most obvious means of reforming society through theater lay in the physical structure of the auditorium itself. Wagner's theater at Bayreuth, which the composer personally designed, offered one solid model. An updated version of a Greek amphitheater, his so-called "festival playhouse" (*Festspielhaus*) attempted to equalize the audience by removing the standard hierarchy in seating (or at least most of it—he retained a royal box for his patron) and to direct the maximum attention of all spectators to the stage by eliminating decorative ostentation and other sources of visual distraction. Intensifying the interaction

---

32. Bartlett, *Wagner*, 159.
33. Aleksandr Benua, *Moi vospominaniia*, 2 vols. (Moscow: Zakharov, 2003), 2:1372; "as for a sacred act" is from page 1377.
34. V. P. Shkafer, *Sorok let na stsene russkoi opery: Vospominaniia, 1890–1930 gg.* (Leningrad: Izdatel'stvo Teatra Opery i Baleta imeni S. M. Kirova, 1936), 192.
35. V. Friche, "Teatr v sovremennom i budushchem obshchestve," in *Krizis teatra: Sbornik statei*, ed. Iurii Steklov (St. Petersburg: Problemy iskusstva, 1908), 157.
36. Bartlett, *Wagner*, 83. The Russian titles were *Iskusstvo i revoliutsiia* and *Opera i drama*.
37. According to James West, *Russian Symbolism: A Study of Viacheslav Ivanov and the Russian Symbolist Aesthetic* (London: Methuen, 1970), 3, what we conveniently refer to as "Russian symbolism" was "a confusing and considerably less than coherent body of theory."

between performance and audience became a major innovation of modernist theater, and many of its conventions—dimming the lights, discouraging talking during performances, excluding latecomers, limiting curtain calls, and so on— were widely advocated in Western stage culture in the late nineteenth and early twentieth centuries and remain with us today. Another and more far-reaching change was the evolution of naturalism and realism in staging and direction to the iconic qualities of expressionism and symbolism.

In the Russian cultural context politics played a paltry role in facilitating the development of these new creative schools. Stanislavskii embarked on his projects to indulge his love of theater and explore the belief that it should be executed in a more genuine and intuitive manner than nineteenth-century affectations had allowed. Chekhov, the Art Theater's closest collaborator among Russian dramatists, had already begun developing surreal themes in his plays and short stories during the 1880s and 1890s. His character Treplev, one of the central personae in *The Seagull* (1896), stages a symbolist play that expounds on dreamy ideas about the universality of humanity only to have them shot down by his boorish mother, a famous actress and virtual stereotype lifted from nineteenth-century realist theater. Appropriately enough, the mother character may have been based on Lidiia Iavorskaia, with whom the playwright had an affair. The play was so instrumental in launching the Art Theater on the path to viability that the image of a seagull became its symbol. Chekhov's innovations, albeit situated within traditional forms, prompted Gor'kii to exclaim: "Do you know what you are doing? You are killing realism. . . . This form has outlived its times—and that is a fact!"[38]

In 1902 the poet Valerii Briusov, influenced by the World of Art group, which favored symbolism and abstraction in painting and other media, argued in favor of definitively abandoning artistic realism. Instead of its "unnecessary truth," Briusov advocated what he called "stylization" (*uslovnost'*), a concept that has been confusingly rendered as "conventionality" or "a theater of conventions."[39] Referring to the literal definition of dramatic convention, which involves the audience's suspension of disbelief to accept action on stage as truth, Briusov wanted to use performance for depictions of the psychological and, especially, the spiritual essences of the works and characters presented. In effect, and yet without too much originality, he was calling for theater to adopt the abstractions and

---

38. Quoted in A. Nazarova and N. Orekhova, "Vvedenie," in Nazarova and Orekhova, *Russkii dramaticheskii teatr*, 5.
39. Briusov's article originally appeared in *Mir iskusstva* 1 (1902). For an English translation, see Valerii Briusov, "Against Naturalism in the Theater," in *The Russian Symbolist Theater: An Anthology of Plays and Critical Texts*, ed. and trans. Michael Green (Ann Arbor: Ardis, 1986).

Fig. 19 A prelude to symbolism: a scene from the Moscow Art Theater production of Anton Chekhov's *The Seagull*. Vsevolod Meierkhol'd (third from left), then a young actor with the company, portrayed the dreamy and suicidal Treplev. Stanislavskii, in the role of Trigorin, is fifth from left. From Konstantin Stanislavskii, *Moia zhizn' v iskusstve* (Moscow: Iskusstvo, 1983).

emotive qualities then coming to the forefront in the international artistic world, particularly in music, poetry, and painting. And he was doing it fifteen years before the revolutions of 1917 and fourteen years after Stanislavskii had begun formal experimentation with discovering the inner motivations of characters.

Neither the philosophical endowment of art with spiritual values, nor Chekhov's plays, nor Briusov's denunciation of "unnecessary" realism established a definite program of *how* theater was to be transformed, but all these ideas found expression outside a visible political context. Meierkhol'd, whose theatrical work embraced stylization more thoroughly than any other Silver Age director, left his position as an actor at the Moscow Art Theater, where he had portentously appeared as Chekhov's Treplev, to found a new experimental company. Opening in 1902 and renamed the Comradeship of New Drama the following year, it presented a repertoire of mostly realist plays, at first conceived in accordance with Stanislavskii's ideas, but later altered in the hope of conveying more stylized meanings.

Meierkhol'd never left a conclusive record of his artistic inspiration, but at various times he became aware of and was influenced by the work and ideas of such European innovators as Max Reinhardt, Adolphe Appia, Georg Fuchs, and Gordon Craig, some of whose ideas, as well as those of some nineteenth-century American directors, resembled his own. Similar values employed in Japanese theater, known to Russia through a touring troupe that Meierkhol'd encountered, also informed his concepts.[40] Regardless of where he found inspiration, however, no director could approach theater as a holistic medium without imposing a unified "concept" designed to coordinate the acting styles, blocking, sets, costumes, lighting, music, and everything else that makes a performance happen. Indeed, the Moscow Art Theater itself proved to be something of an inspiration. Stanislavskii's business partner Vladimir Nemirovich-Danchenko, Meierkhol'd's early acting teacher, had stressed the novelty of the Moscow Art Theater by claiming that "a single will reigns in our theatre."[41] This idea, which the Germans have come to call *Regietheater* (director's theater), also had strong Wagnerian connotations. Wagner, after all, even designed his own theater in addition to writing his libretti, designing the sets, casting and directing the performers, and, of course, composing and (often in his lifetime) conducting the music.

In the cultural milieu of Russia's Silver Age, aspirations to these concepts placed limits on what an innovative young director could accomplish. For the twenty-eight-year-old Meierkhol'd, founding a new theatrical company dominated by his own directorial designs effectively excluded work with well-established performers, who demanded higher salaries than he could afford and whose fame depended on their status as stars or, in the case of the Moscow Art Theater from which he had sprung, as part of synergetic ensembles of their own formation. Meierkhol'd's Comradeship was filled with young actors of little experience and no major reputation, people whom he described as "performers who have trained at my school," even though he was still under thirty and had only been acting for four years when he broke with the Art Theater.[42] The experimental aspects of his theater failed to attract much attention or sustain appreciable success as the Comradeship toured southern Russia. One

---

40. Edward Braun, *The Theatre of Meyerhold: Revolution on the Modern Stage* (New York: Drama Book Specialists, 1979), 54, suggests that Meierkhol'd was aware of Fuchs's work. Leach, *Meyerhold*, 4, argues that he had very limited knowledge of European developments, but may have known about Reinhardt. For the similar developments in American theater, see Lawrence W. Levine, *Highbrow/Lowbrow: The Emergence of Cultural Hierarchy in America* (Cambridge: Harvard University Press, 1988), 184–94.

41. Vladimir Nemirovitch-Danchenko, *My Life in the Russian Theatre,* trans. John Cournos (London: Bles, 1937), 156.

42. Vsevolod Meierkhol'd, *Perepiska, 1896–1939* (Moscow: Iskusstvo, 1976), 44.

theatergoer claimed that Meierkhol'd "bored the Kherson audience" with his innovations.[43] In Tiflis he presented Stanisław Przybyszewski's *Snow* in complete darkness, to perhaps understandable popular and critical consternation.[44] Taking on Chekhov's *The Cherry Orchard*, he attempted to convey not the comedy that the author had intended to write but "gaiety with overtones of death" and "something terrifying."[45]

By late 1904 or early 1905 Meierkhol'd was ready to return to Moscow. Stanislavskii, with whom he remained on good terms, initially showed some interest in rekindling their professional relationship. Already thinking of ways to invigorate Art Theater productions and interpretations of his acting "System," the impresario agreed to give Meierkhol'd the opportunity to open a studio theater to develop his ideas. The young director, he felt, "had already found new paths and methods, but he could not bring them into being in full measure, partly because of material circumstances, partly in view of the weak condition of the actors of the troupe."[46]

Bringing experimental theater to Moscow, however, spelled disaster. Stanislavskii turned resolutely against the idea after watching several rehearsals of Meierkhol'd's studio. When he attended one of Maeterlinck's *The Death of Tintagiles*, also shrouded in complete darkness, he is said to have yelled, "Lights! Lights!" thinking that there was a technical problem.[47] Meierkhol'd's performers impressed Stanislavskii even less. "Everything became clear," the impresario realized by mid-1905, "the youths had displayed their childlike powerlessness." Although the disturbances surrounding the October general strike prompted Stanislavskii to abbreviate his season and take the Art Theater on its first foreign tour, he also used them as an excuse to shut down Meierkhol'd's studio before its opening-night performance.[48] Meierkhol'd himself admitted some responsibility, confessing that he had approached the project with too much of his "usual haste and heedlessness."[49]

Having failed in Moscow, Meierkhol'd looked to Petersburg as the next incubator of his ideas, his proverbial "altar." He remained far from embracing the capital as the seat of social fermentation and political revolt, if for the simple reason that Moscow abounded with street violence and civic unrest. Observing

---

43. Quoted in Rudnitsky, *Meyerhold*, 48.
44. "Provintsial'naia letopis'," *Teatr i iskusstvo* 42 (October 17, 1904): 749–50.
45. Meierkhol'd, *Perepiska*, 45.
46. K. S. Stanislavskii, *Moia zhizn' v iskusstve* (Moscow: Iskusstvo, 1983), 289–90.
47. Leach, *Meyerhold*, 5.
48. Stanislavskii, *Moia zhizn'*, 292–94.
49. Quoted in Rudnitsky, *Meyerhold*, 74.

the disorders surrounding both the cancellation of the Studio Theater's projected October 1905 opening and the December uprising, the ambitious young director hoped to find relative quiet in the official capital. As he wrote to the actress Verigina, "I have in mind to build here [Petersburg] what could not be done in Moscow: the theaters are all working, in Moscow even the Art Theater is closed."[50] Far from complementing each other, in Meierkhol'd's view, political turmoil and theatrical innovation could not exist in the same place at the same time; however radical the innovation, it still depended on all the day-to-day operations required to execute a sophisticated work of art. Like any other impresario, at a practical level Meierkhol'd needed social and political stability as a prerequisite for his creative work.

Meierkhol'd's arrival in Petersburg occurred amid heated discussions of an innovative new theatrical enterprise within a circle of symbolist intellectuals meeting at the poet and classical Greek scholar Viacheslav Ivanov's weekly literary salon. Its members included Blok, with whom Meierkhol'd later collaborated on *The Fairground Booth,* as well as Belyi, who felt satirized by it. Tentatively calling their theater "The Torches," a name they also adopted shortly thereafter for an unsuccessful literary journal, Ivanov's circle succeeded neither in making the logistical arrangements nor in developing a coherent concept for the theater. Some argued in favor of endowing it with a realist coloration, the opposite of what Meierkhol'd and other innovators wanted to achieve. Gor'kii, who took part in the discussions, looked to theatrical synthesis not for a spiritual unity of art but for a union of creative artists. He wanted the project to "be realized on a great scale. It must be a theater club, which could unite all literary factions."[51] Another participant traveled to Tolstoi's estate at Iasnaia Poliana to commission a play from the elderly writer, whose work, despite the author's philosophical commitment to theologizing theater, belonged to the realist school.[52] Verigina recalled that concepts of innovation were "simply juggled" and "frivolously spoken at the tea table." Meierkhol'd's motto, she thought, was to "say the words first, and then believe in them."[53] Belyi compared him to "a motorboat speeding away."[54] Mikhail Narokov, an actor who had worked with Meierkhol'd in the Comradeship of New Drama, recalled that "confused disputes were kindled in connection with these 'theories.'"[55] According to the radical critic

50. Meierkhol'd, *Perepiska,* 58.
51. Ibid., 59.
52. Georgii Chulkov, *Gody stranstvii* (Moscow: Ellis Lak, 1999), 227.
53. Verigina, *Vospominaniia,* 98.
54. Belyi, *Mezhdu dvukh revoliutsii,* 62.
55. Mikhail S. Narokov, *Biografiia moego pokoleniia: Teatral'nye memuary* (Moscow: VTO, 1956), 152.

Georgii Chulkov, "lively debates" characterized the discussions, but in the end no financial backing could be found.[56]

Despite the incoherence of this approach, Komissarzhevskaia, then in her second season of deficit-producing "idea" plays at her Dramatic Theater, invited Meierkhol'd to assume the direction of its new incarnation, planned to open on Ofitserskaia Street the following season. Meierkhol'd had already returned to Tiflis—the only other place he could find steady work despite his earlier poor reception there—to stage a mainly traditional repertoire, but he eagerly accepted the actress-entrepreneuse's offer: "In the depths of my soul I so want the capital, I so fear cheap provincial laurels, and I so fear the vulgarity of provincial psychopaths. And suddenly [while in the provinces] the dream of being at the head of an impressionist theater slips from my hands." A week later he conveyed an even greater sense of disappointment to his wife: "Here there is no satisfaction. I am inspired to show in the repertoire many interesting nuances, but no one accepts anything, everyone is inattentive, obtuse, and even unscrupulous.... I dream of a theater-school and of much else that will never exist in the provinces.... Now it is clear to me that the provinces are a trash dump [*pomoinaia iama*]."[57]

As Meierkhol'd discovered, however, largely the same disappointments awaited him in the capital. His first production at the Dramatic Theater, Ibsen's *Hedda Gabler*, set the general tone. Presenting a play that demanded a slight, ethereal heroine was no difficult task, for roles of the *femme fragile* type had long been Komissarzhevskaia's specialty. But despite praise for the actress's individual performance, many observers expressed deep reservations about Meierkhol'd's technique, which relied heavily on abstraction, cool colors, unusual curtains, and other visual novelties. In their view these characteristics only created obstacles to understanding the social message of the play: the impossible situation of a woman trapped in a decidedly unenviable bourgeois existence. Verigina recalled that the premiere "was boring and did not enjoy great success." The cast party "left a sad memory," for "Vera Fedorovna was in such grief over the public's cold reaction that she could not control herself even in a crowded gathering. Tears streamed down her cheeks."[58] Several critics sounded the alarm that Meierkhol'd had placed unnatural controls on one of the capital's favorite actresses. Forcing Komissarzhevskaia to conform to his unified concept constrained her beloved

---

56. Chulkov, *Gody stranstvii*, 226–27. Braun, *Meyerhold*, 53, attributes this failure directly to the deleterious effects of 1905 on Petersburg's theater business, discussed in detail in Chapter 2.
57. Meierkhol'd, *Perepiska*, 61–62, 62–63.
58. Verigina, *Vospominaniia*, 90.

expressive talent.⁵⁹ One reviewer called her "a cold horror" under Meierkhol'd's direction.⁶⁰

Although Meierkhol'd scored a modest success—his only important one at the Dramatic Theater—with a production of Maeterlinck's *Sister Beatrice* two days after *Hedda Gabler*'s dismal premiere, it failed to change the course of his fortunes. Many observers felt that the only reason *Sister Beatrice* succeeded was the extraordinary suitability of its title role for Komissarzhevskaia's talents in the *femme fragile* repertoire.⁶¹ Beatrice, a wayward nun who flees her convent with a dashing suitor only to be abandoned by him, is saved in the end by an animated statue of the Virgin Mary. According to one of Komissarzhevskaia's Soviet biographers, "not one role of the Meierkhol'd period, except for Beatrice, pleased the spectators, the critics, or [Komissarzhevskaia] herself."⁶² The actress's brother and director Fedor believed that "seventy-five per cent of [the production's] success was without doubt due to my sister's acting."⁶³ Verigina could still mourn that "Komissarzhevskaia's fire, all of her feelings, were enclosed in strict forms given by the author and director."⁶⁴ Regardless of how observers reacted, the theater's box office receipts fell, negative reviews continued to appear, and Meierkhol'd felt rejected. "Petersburg has greeted us without caresses," he wrote an actor friend, "the press does not understand us—Ah! How it does not understand."⁶⁵

The symbolist repertoire did nothing to help Komissarzhevskaia's theater. Many close to the actress-entrepreneuse identified the turn away from social dramas, the stuff of her enterprise's first incarnation, as the root cause of her downfall, even though that repertoire had not enjoyed great success either. The avid spectator Aleksandra Brushtein believed that "by a tragic mistake she fell into the barren quagmire of stylized [*uslovnyi*]-symbolist theater . . . this mistake cost Komissarzhevskaia dearly: she paid for it with her life."⁶⁶ Vladimir Gardin, the actor who had not understood what Lenin meant by "revolution" when he met him in Switzerland, saw in the symbolist repertoire not an attempt to

---

59. N. Tamarin, "Teatr V. F. Komissarzhevskoi," *Slovo*, November 21, 1906; Vlad[imir] Azov, "Gedda Gabler," *Rech'*, November 12, 1906; A. Kugel', "Teatral'nye zametki, *Teatr i iskusstvo* 47 (November 19, 1906): 730–34.
60. "Zigfrid" [E. A. Stark], "Eskizy," *Sankt Peterburgskie vedemosti*, November 12, 1906.
61. Schuler, *Women in the Russian Theatre*, 176.
62. Rybakova, *Komissarzhevskaia*, 156.
63. Theodore Komisarjevsky, *Myself and the Theatre* (London: Heinemann, 1929), 76.
64. Verigina, *Vospominaniia*, 92.
65. Meierkhol'd, *Perepiska*, 79.
66. A. Ia. Brushtein, *Stranitsy proshlogo* (Leningrad: Iskusstvo, 1952), 79–80, 86. The fatal judgment was not an exaggeration: Komissarzhevskaia died of smallpox in 1910 at the age of forty-six while taking her earlier repertoire on tour to Turkestan to make money.

fulfill or revitalize theater's social mission but rather an abdication from its earlier, more engaged role:

> The activity of our life in those years was so horribly interrupted by violence, hypocrisy, and terrors that leaving it behind for the fantastic and little understood mysteries of Maeterlinck, the fruitless examples of Sologub and Przybyszewski, and the abyss of Andreev became the usual refuge of the burned out [*iznervlennykh*] intelligentsia.... I am absolutely certain that if Vera Fedorovna had remained alive, she would have returned to the bright, vivid truth of the Dramatic Theater's first season productions.[67]

Narokov, whom Meierkhol'd had brought to Komissarzhevskaia's theater, confessed his disappointment with "the fragility of doubtful theatrical development." "Rotten [*gniloe*] 'innovation,'" he lamented, "was but a cover for the utmost inner devastation of bourgeois artists.... Our Comradeship of New Drama still continued to live, although signs of its approaching collapse had already appeared."[68]

The most objectionable feature of Meierkhol'd's technique emerged less from the works he chose than from the constraints he placed on the performers and their talents, a problem manifest from his first productions at the Dramatic Theater. Increasingly, critics, audiences, and the actors and actresses themselves found it difficult to reconcile the subordination of the performers' individuality to "concept" productions and total directorial control. It has even been suggested that some critics, including *Theater and Art*'s editor Aleksandr Kugel', may have objected to the unified theory of direction because they found it antithetical to ideals of individual freedom.[69] But regardless of the possible—and even then rather abstract—political implications, virtually all the actors resented the amount of power that the new style allowed directors to wield over them. Komissarzhevskaia admitted that "Meierkhol'd always controlled us. I saw that in this theater, there was nothing for us performers to do.... With each rehearsal I noticed the fruitlessness of my own and my colleagues' work."[70] She told an understanding Aleksandr Tikhonov, a frequent spectator of hers, that under Meierkhol'd "we have been led into a dead end." She shared the complaints of several Dramatic Theater actors who held that the director's ideas were "making marionettes out of us."[71] The actress-entrepreneuse's brother Fedor, though

---

67. V. R. Gardin, *Zhizn' i trud artista* (Moscow: Iskusstvo, 1960), 81.
68. Narokov, *Biografiia*, 152.
69. I. F. Petrovskaia, *Teatr i zritel' rossiiskikh stolits: 1895–1917* (Leningrad: Iskusstvo, 1990), 26.
70. Quoted in D. Tal'nikov, *Komissarzhevskaia* (Moscow: Iskusstvo, 1939), 34.
71. A. Serebrov [A. N. Tikhonov], *Vremia i liudi: Vospominaniia, 1898–1905* (Moscow: Moskovskii rabochii, 1955), 98.

possibly speaking with filial ardor, resented Meierkhol'd for "confining the actors and making them dependent upon the settings," for such an automaton, "having no will of its own, would be much better material with which to express the producer's intentions than an actor."[72] Brushtein, who sat through many of their performances, lamented that "the actor in this new theater turned out to be more suppressed and crushed [*zaslonennym i zadavlennym*] than he had ever been before. He was forged by the dictatorship of the director, which turned the live actor into a soulless puppet."[73]

A sympathetic biographer of Meierkhol'd reveals that "differences" in the director's creative partnership with Komissarzhevskaia "emerged as early as the close of the first season."[74] In addition to other problems, the deleterious financial impact of Meierkhol'd's productions demanded that the Dramatic Theater tour the provinces with a more traditional repertoire. Despite the urgent fiscal necessity behind this step and the director's role in creating it, he lost no time expressing his indignation: "What a terrible mistake Vera Fedorovna made when she toured Russia with the old repertoire," he wrote, "this compromises her as a figure at the head of the new theater."[75] Rumors of Meierkhol'd's imminent departure circulated even before the theater opened its second season.[76] Fedor Komissarzhevskii later judged that his sister "had to part with him, realizing how he cramped and limited the actors with his methods, and how his ideas at that time were leading the Theatre of living actors to a certain end."[77]

The most important production of the new season, Maeterlinck's *Pelléas and Mélisande*, sealed Meierkhol'd's fate. Its October 1907 premiere was greeted by "the laughter and catcalls of the public." Meierkhol'd cast the forty-three-year-old Komissarzhevskaia as a naïve girl, and his sets and costumes only made her look ridiculous. As an actor appearing in the production, he also banalized his own role. Playing Mélisande's aged father-in-law, he injudiciously wore a false beard made of cardboard, totally destroying any gravitas his role might have imparted, or so thought a critic who titled his review "Not Quite."[78] Kugel' compared the performers to "marionettes" and "mosquitoes."[79] I. O. Abel'son, editor of the *Review of Theaters* (and formerly editor of the by then defunct *Theatrical*

---

72. Komisarjevsky, *Myself and the Theatre*, 78.
73. Brushtein, *Stranitsy*, 85. Her use of the term "dictatorship" need not necessarily be taken as metaphoric.
74. Rudnitsky, *Meyerhold*, 116.
75. Meierkhol'd, *Perepiska*, 87.
76. Rudnitsky, *Meyerhold*, 119.
77. Komisarjevsky, *Myself and the Theatre*, 79.
78. A. Rostislavov, "Ne to," *Teatr i iskusstvo* 43 (October 28, 1907): 701.
79. Quoted in Rudnitsky, *Meyerhold*, 121.

Russia), called the production "theatrical sadism."[80] Even Blok, who had soured on Meierkhol'd's ideas since the premiere of *The Fairground Booth* the previous December, criticized "the production's utter lack of substance."[81] Catastrophe also surrounded the autumn visit of the Dramatic Theater to Moscow, where Meierkhol'd's old boss Stanislavskii cuttingly declared that he "would have given 40,000 rubles for this [the new stylized productions] not to have been shown to the public."[82]

Shortly after the Moscow debacle Komissarzhevskaia fired her collaborator, reasoning that "the theater must recognize that all its past work was a mistake, and the director must either abandon his method of producing plays or must leave the theater."[83] The letter of dismissal, which she read to a meeting of the troupe, informed him that: "I have done a lot of thinking and come to the deep conclusion that you and I look at theater differently and that what you are seeking is not what I am seeking.... I am looking the future straight in the eye and say that we cannot go on this path together.... I do not want the people working with me to be working with closed eyes."[84] Meierkhol'd sued Komissarzhevskaia for breach of contract, but an arbitration committee found his claim "baseless."[85] Most of the theatrical press supported the actress-entrepreneuse's decision as well, though some—in another sign of the theatrical world's rising commitment to professionalization and legal standards—objected to the abrogation of Meierkhol'd's contract.[86]

The Dramatic Theater's financial plight only highlighted the absence of public interest in the symbolist repertoire, whether it appeared at Komissarzhevskaia's theater or elsewhere. According to Victor Borovsky, "the theatre in Ofitserskaya Street remained empty and when Komissarzhevskaya was not playing it was even worse."[87] Brushtein noted that the actress's enterprise "began to lose a significant part of its former spectators, unimpressive in number though they may have

---

80. I. Osipov [I. O. Abel'son], "Teatr V. F. Komissarzhevskoi," *Obozrenie teatrov* 217 (October 12, 1907): 12.

81. Quoted in Rudnitsky, *Meyerhold*, 122.

82. I. Osipov [I. O. Abel'son], "Teatr V. F. Komissarzhevskoi," *Obozrenie teatrov* 219–20 (October 14–15, 1907): 16.

83. Quoted in Rybakova, *Komissarzhevskaia*, 166.

84. Meierkhol'd, *Perepiska*, 108.

85. "Rezoliutsiia treteiskogo suda po delu V. F. Komissarzhevskoi s V. E. Meierkhol'd," *Obozrenie teatrov* 287–88 (December 22–23, 1907): 13.

86. "Ot redaktsii," *Teatr i iskusstvo* 46 (November 18, 1907): 751, for example, considered "Meierkhol'd's conduct to be incorrect and, from our point of view, harmful to the theater," but still complained about the contract issue.

87. Victor Borovsky, *A Triptych from the Russian Theatre: An Artistic Biography of the Komissarzhevskys* (Iowa City: University of Iowa Press, 2001), 177.

been."[88] In Narokov's general recollection of experimental performance, "all of the newly born theaters remained empty. The spectator left them aside."[89] In Russia's ever more commercialized and consumerized performing arts universe, the most significant product of the symbolist repertoire was six-figure debt.

As Narokov's observation suggests, most attempts to establish viable symbolist theaters fell flat. Ivanov and some of his acolytes believed that dramas that had remained in humanity's creative consciousness for centuries or millennia could serve the integrative function that Russian symbolists were seeking in the arts. "True symbolism," Ivanov wrote with communitarian flair, "must reconcile the poet and the crowd in a great, universal act."[90] Proponents of this ideal advocated the revival of plays and the recreation of theatrical forms from antiquity. The unpopularity of Sophocles' *Antigone* and other ancient Greek dramas, however, portended their disappointment.

A conscious attempt to explore the creative and social potential of plays from the remote past emerged in a uniq ue enterprise opened by the director Nikolai Evreinov in 1907. Fittingly called the "Ancient Theater," it staged works from antiquity, medieval times, and the Renaissance, emphasizing passion plays, courtly romances, and other styles in which Evreinov envisioned the drama's absorption of the audience.[91] In the radical critic Chulkov's words its "main purpose" was "the restoration of scenic productions from different eras, beginning with the epoch of ancient theater and ending with the theater of Molière."[92] Its first production was based on the tale of Robin Hood. Enamored of the communitarian role, or at least what he imagined to have been the communitarian role, that such works had employed to dissolve boundaries between public performance and religious ritual, Evreinov urged his audiences to participate in the action by watching from on stage and attending in costume.[93]

But just as Meierkhol'd's ideas had firm antecedents in cultural life prior to the rising tide of political crisis, so too did Evreinov's interest in combining theater with public ceremony predate the upheavals of the early twentieth century. A trained lawyer, he had written his university thesis on the history of corporal punishment and was fascinated by the ritualization of public executions,

88. Brushtein, *Stranitsy*, 81.
89. Narokov, *Biografiia*, 152.
90. Viacheslav Ivanov, *Po zvezdam* (St. Petersburg: n.p., 1909), 41–42. For a detailed explanation of these ideas, see Rosenthal, "Theatre as Church," 127–29.
91. Spencer Golub, *Evreinov: The Theatre of Paradox and Transformation* (Ann Arbor: UMI Research, 1984), 108–15.
92. Chulkov, *Gody stranstvii*, 239.
93. Golub, *Evreinov*, 122.

which he found theatrical.⁹⁴ This morbid curiosity led to a pronounced interest in the role of all public rituals, especially those that he believed could morph from religious observance to spectacle without losing their communal effect. Nietzsche's (and Ivanov's) idolization of the Greeks and desire to recover the lost synthesis of their art forms lent heavily to Evreinov's idea of resurrecting older theater idioms. So too did the French philosopher Henri Bergson's notions of social evolution, which argued that human happiness would ultimately arise from new modes of vitality and creativity.⁹⁵

Although Evreinov's approach foreshadowed the mass "festivals" that commemorated the events of 1917 in the early Soviet period and tried to foster a sense of revolutionary community, it was doomed to failure in the freer society that preceded Bolshevism.⁹⁶ The expectation of audience participation in performances offered little to theatergoers who sought diversion. As we have seen, Russian spectators wanted primarily to be entertained, not educated, preached to, or forced to participate in an *Überdirektor*'s socioanthropological experiment. The theatrical styles themselves, already familiar in the Western (and Westernized Russian) cultural experience and devoid of the stimulating content of cutting-edge works and beloved classics, seemed outmoded and boring. Benua, who declined an offer to work with the Ancient Theater, found "something paradoxical and unnecessary in such a museum-like resurrection of dead forms."⁹⁷ Evreinov's experiment collapsed after one season.⁹⁸ He revived the idea for short performance series, but "ancient theater" was as moribund as the civilizations it sought to recreate. All its defenders could do was crow about its importance and bewail the "obtuseness" of Russian audiences for not dashing to embrace it. The sympathetic critic Eduard Stark claimed rather baselessly that the Ancient Theater "left results that no other theatrical institution could have left after functioning for many seasons." Nevertheless, he explained its failure with quasi-religious sanctimoniousness: "Obviously, we have not yet grown up to the happiness of mastering such cultural values, we are not yet worthy of eternally guarding the holy flame in the temple of beauty."⁹⁹ "The current theater," another observer lamented, "laughs boorishly at the sacred word 'inspiration.'"¹⁰⁰

94. Sharon M. Carnicke, "The Theatrical Instinct: A Study of the Work of Nikolaj Evreinov in Early Twentieth Century Russia" (Ph.D. diss., Columbia University, 1979), 75.
95. Golub, *Evreinov*, 20–22. For the philosophical background, see Henri Bergson, *L'évolution créatrice* (Paris: Presses universitaires de France, 1966).
96. For a thorough explanation of these developments, see James von Geldern, *Bolshevik Festivals, 1917–1920* (Berkeley and Los Angeles: University of California Press, 1993), 3–38.
97. Benua, *Vospominaniia*, 2:1500.
98. Carnicke, "Theatrical Instinct," 80.
99. E. A. Stark, *Starinnyi teatr* (St. Petersburg: Izdanie N. I. Butkovskoi, 1912), 41–42, 48.
100. N. Gossov, "Antichnost' i sovremennost'," *Teatr i iskusstvo* 46 (November 11, 1912): 896.

Advocates of popular theater also wanted to promote social harmony through the performing arts, but they spurned the symbolist œuvre in all its forms as inaccessible and abstruse. Symbolist plays and productions "never gained a foothold in the popular theater."[101] Gaideburov, whose General Accessible Theater moved from a strictly classical repertoire to one embracing (to its peril) contemporary social dramas, never saw much in the avant-garde repertoire. He once staged a friend's symbolist work out of kindness but realized that "his play was not profitable before a mass audience, it was too unusual in form and in its philosophical contents, without any noticeable internal intrigue."[102] Assessing the overall impact of symbolist innovation on Russian tastes, a recent student of tsarist-era leisure has described its works as "symbolist weirdness" that "audiences avoided."[103] However lofty its philosophical goals, symbolist innovation simply did not attract broad popular interest, an essential asset were it to effect social transformation. As one critic looked back on Russia's prerevolutionary cultural life, "symbolism, however rich in lyricism, could not lead theater to new paths."[104]

Nor, conversely, did the avant-garde have much use for popular theater. The simple, traditional staging that most popular enterprises employed and their repertoires' heavy reliance on melodrama and classics—to say nothing of the realist tableaux staged by such venues as the Nicholas II People's House—turned it off. Meierkhol'd described one leading exponent of popular theater (and well-known political radical) in these terms: "Where Evtikhii Karpov begins, art ends."[105] The young director may have regarded Blok's *The Fairground Booth* and its carnivalesque trappings as a means of connecting with ordinary people, but the oddness of his production and its esoteric meditation on the nature of consciousness and reality failed to communicate with a mass audience—or, as the reviews showed to a significant degree, even with an elite one.[106]

Perhaps more telling, the symbolist repertoire caused experimental theatrical

101. E. Anthony Swift, *Popular Theater and Society in Tsarist Russia* (Berkeley and Los Angeles: University of California Press, 2002), 129.
102. P. P. Gaideburov, *Literaturnoe nasledie. Vospominaniia. Stat'i. Rezhisserskie eksplikatsii. Vystupleniia* (Moscow: VTO, 1977), 177–78.
103. Louise McReynolds, *Russia at Play: Leisure Activities at the End of the Tsarist Era* (Ithaca: Cornell University Press, 2003), 73. The passage applies these judgments directly to Andreev's *The Life of Man,* another failed production that Meierkhol'd staged at Komissarzhevskaia's Dramatic Theater.
104. E. A. Znosko-Borovskii, *Russkii teatr nachala XX veka* (Prague: Plamia Praga, 1925), 293.
105. Quoted in G. A. Tarnavskaia, "Aleksandrinskii teatr," in Nazarova and Orekhova, *Russkii dramaticheskii teatr,* 153.
106. Rosenthal, "Theatre as Church," 131, describes it as a "search for common ground with the people." Geldern, *Bolshevik Festivals,* 59, sees it as an early effort to break down barriers between elite and popular culture.

enterprises to fail, while the popular venues that eschewed it simultaneously experienced healthy growth. Meierkhol'd's dismissive opinions notwithstanding, most Russian theaters did not need "stylization" to succeed, at least not in a financial and, that is to say, an existential sense. Despite the fiscal dilemmas confronting the performing arts as a consequence of the Revolution of 1905, the Temperance Trusteeship opened no fewer than fifty-nine new popular theaters over the next four years, including ten in Petersburg alone.[107] Although Gaideburov reluctantly staged a few symbolist plays at the Ligovskii People's House, its mainstay repertoire of Ostrovskii and other classics entertained an audience that grew by more than 50 percent between the 1906–7 and 1911–12 seasons.[108]

Evreinov, who authored traditional plays in addition to his experimental work, balanced innovative projects with an adaptation to the commercial demands of Russian theater when he established his long association with the Crooked Mirror, the satirical cabaret where he worked from its opening in December 1908 until his emigration to the West in 1925. A large part of its repertoire, and of the standard repertoire of Russian cabaret, adhered to Harold Segel's observation that "literary symbolism and the Symbolist drama in particular were favorite targets of parody and satire."[109] Ironically, the Crooked Mirror opened to an enthusiastic reception immediately after Meierkhol'd presented his unsuccessful symbolist enterprise, the Strand, in the same theater on the same night.[110]

In an even greater irony Meierkhol'd, despite his failures on the private stage, attracted the interest of the Imperial Theaters, which, "to the complete bewilderment" of many performers, gave him the opportunity to continue his pioneering work until the end of the tsarist era.[111] The theaters' Director Vladimir

---

107. G. A. Khaichenko, *Russkii narodnyi teatr kontsa XIX–nachala XX veka* (Moscow: Nauka, 1975), 98; Patricia Herlihy, *The Alcoholic Empire: Vodka and Politics in Late Imperial Russia* (New York: Oxford University Press, 2002), 18, has the Petersburg figure. According to Lynn Mally, *Culture of the Future: The Proletkult Movement in Revolutionary Russia* (Berkeley and Los Angeles: University of California Press, 1990), 13, popular theaters "mushroomed in the years after 1905." For a detailed discussion of the expansion of popular theater, see Gary Thurston, *The Popular Theatre Movement in Russia, 1862–1919* (Evanston: Northwestern University Press, 1998), 211–56.

108. Petrovskaia, *Teatr i zritel' rossiiskikh stolits,* 83. As we have seen, however, the operations of Gaideburov's General Accessible Theater declined as a result of its less traditional repertoire.

109. Harold B. Segel, *Turn-of-the-Century Cabaret: Paris, Barcelona, Berlin, Munich, Vienna, Cracow, Moscow, St. Petersburg, Zurich* (New York: Columbia University Press, 1987), 296. For the best study of the Crooked Mirror's repertoire, see Barbara Henry, "Theatrical Parody at the Krivoe zerkalo: Russian 'Teatr Miniatyur,' 1908–1931" (D.Phil. thesis, Oxford University, 1996).

110. Meierkhol'd's theater gave only two performances and then vanished.

111. This reaction is recorded by Shkafer, *Sorok let,* 217. Feodor Chaliapin, *Man and Mask: Forty Years in the Life of a Singer,* trans. Phyllis Mégroz (New York: Knopf, 1932), 128, accused "innovators" of "violating the canons of art" and recorded his secret desire to hang at least one of them. He did not mention a name, but he worked with Meierkhol'd at least once.

Teliakovskii, who presided over operations funded by healthy subsidies from the Court, could indulge his expectation that by hiring Meierkhol'd, "something interesting and new would doubtlessly turn out ... we would not be bored."[112] The young director used the stable employment to pursue other experimental projects, establishing an alter ego known on Petersburg/Petrograd theater boards as "Doctor Dapertutto," after the quack physician/demon who wreaks havoc in E. T. A. Hoffmann. Contrary to the slanders of Soviet historians and mischaracterizations of others, and perhaps paradoxically, the state arts establishment thus figured among prerevolutionary Russia's most generous, indulgent, and enduring sponsors of experimental trends in theatrical art.[113] If for no other reason it could afford to be. As we have seen throughout this study, no serious political or ideological guidelines prevented it from assuming that role, despite the bad reviews and performer hostility that Meierkhol'd's productions could generate. Fedor Komissarzhevskii, who worked in Moscow's Imperial Theaters after the collapse of his sister's enterprise, recalled that "the annual subsidy ... made it possible to experiment and to wait until the public grew accustomed to and accepted new plays, new actors, new producers and scenic artists."[114]

Despite the imperial stage's willingness to take risks with experimentation, the widening world of Russian modernist theater refocused its efforts to take the art form back to Stanislavskii's original emphasis on capturing truth through the rigorous development of performers seeking the purest realism. Blok, despite his initial eagerness to write and stage symbolist drama, began to regret his association with stylized performance. "Everything concerning Meierkhol'd pains me," he wrote not long after the premiere of *The Fairground Booth*.[115] Observing more of the director's work with Komissarzhevskaia, he warned that "the theater must turn to a new path if it does not want to kill itself. Saying that

---

112. V. A. Teliakovskii, *Vospominaniia* (Leningrad: Iskusstvo, 1965), 168.
113. Nikolai Volkov, "Teatr v epokhu krusheniia monarkhii," in Ia. O. Boiarskii, *Sto let: Aleksandrinskii teatr—teatr gosdramy, 1832–1932. Sbornik stat'ei* (Leningrad: Direktsiia Leningradskikh gosudarstvennykh teatrov, 1932), 306, maintained that their "bureaucratic apparatus and irresponsible influences ... often paralyzed any reformist initiative and doomed the imperial stage to routine and conservatism." V. M. Bogdanov-Berezovskii, *Leningradskii gosudarstvennyi akademicheskii ordena Lenina teatr opery i baleta im. S. M. Kirova* (Leningrad: Iskusstvo, 1959), 23, denounced "the leadership of the Imperial Theaters, this citadel of autocracy in the area of theatrical art, always more penetrated by militant conservatism." Edith W. Clowes, "Social Discourse in the Moscow Art Theater," in *Between Tsar and People: Educated Society and the Quest for Public Identity in Late Imperial Russia*, ed. Edith W. Clowes, Samuel D. Kassow, and James L. West (Princeton: Princeton University Press, 1991), 273, has unfairly characterized the Imperial Theaters as "top-heavy with bureaucracy and short on innovative spirit and professional seriousness."
114. Komisarjevsky, *Myself and the Theatre*, 34.
115. A. A. Blok, *Zapisnye knizhki* (Moscow: Izdatel'stvo khudozhestvennoi literatury, 1965), 209.

embitters me, but I cannot do otherwise, it is all too clear . . . if there is no new path, the old path is better—a hundred times better altogether."[116]

Many directors, including Meierkhol'd, were willing to listen. Perhaps his failures with full directorial control led him back to a more traditional approach, but Meierkhol'd's youthful ardor showed signs of mellowing in the final years of the Empire and even in the far less certain early Soviet period. Rather than fight against the rising "acmeist" movement, which—as advocated by Akhmatova and such prominent "preservationist" aesthetes as Aleksandr Benua—favored art for its own sake, he developed "close links" to them while still preserving avant-garde connections.[117] His 1911 Mariinskii production of *Boris Godunov* even paid homage to the "star" casting system by setting Shaliapin's title role in sharp relief to the faceless chorus, a concept that the bass found inadvertently unflattering when the chorus members used it to deliver its "protest" for higher wages during a performance attended by the tsar.

Meierkhol'd's next permanent private venture after the failed Strand cabaret, a studio theater founded in Petersburg in 1912–13, focused extensively on actor training. Its didactic purpose was "not to control performers through sweeping social or philosophical imperatives," but to shape the physicality of their performance in ways that could deliver what he believed to be greater artistic truth.[118] In the same season he dismissed the politicization of theater as something that "destroys its theatricality."[119] The Aleksandrinskii's conservative grande dame Mariia Savina could not have said it better.

During the war Meierkhol'd adapted his style to support patriotic efforts. A pantomime entitled *The Triumph of the Powers* propagandized from the Mariinskii stage, while the director employed public carnival-style entertainments to drum up investment in war bonds.[120] He also staged an adaptation of Maupassant's *Mademoiselle Fifi* at the Suvorin Theater, a production described as a "completely patriotic manifesto." All the Allied ambassadors attended.[121] The reputation of the theater's deceased founder (Suvorin died in 1912) for having

---

116. Blok, *Sobranie sochinenii*, 5:202.
117. Clark, *Petersburg*, 95. He may have been attracted by their widespread belief that autocracy favored art, especially architecture, because it had the power to create united visions of urban landscape, just as master directors hoped to create united visions of stage production. See Clark, *Petersburg*, 62–65, on the acmeist attraction to autocracy.
118. Alma Law and Mel Gordon, *Meyerhold, Eisenstein, and Biomechanics: Actor Training in Revolutionary Russia* (Jefferson, N.C.: McFarland, 1996), 24.
119. Quoted in Braun, *Meyerhold*, 146.
120. Jahn, *Patriotic Culture*, 134; Clark, *Petersburg*, 99.
121. "Teatr A. S. Suvorina," *Teatr i iskusstvo* 33 (August 17, 1914): 678.

become "odious in the eyes of the opposition" did not stand in the way of his willingness to work there.[122]

Meierkhol'd's last tsarist-era production, Lermontov's *Masquerade* for the Aleksandrinskii in February 1917, was lavish, opulent, expensive (twenty-eight thousand rubles!), and, at least superficially, realistic. True to the play's title, Meierkhol'd may have intended to "mask" imperial decadence with ironic ostentation, but his means of imputing social significance were far more subtle than they had been a decade earlier.[123] In any case he was criticized for being outlandish at a time of worsening material deprivation. Kugel' thought the production "a Babylon of unthinkably absurd luxury" and compared its director to "some pharaoh building the pyramids." "What is this," the critic demanded to know about his country's performing arts culture, "Rome of the Caesars?"[124] Ironically, given Blok's earlier disenchantment with the director, Meierkhol'd claimed that *Masquerade* represented an attempt to escape the playwright's philosophical influence over his work.[125] Although he reembraced the avant-garde and revolutionary cultural projects after 1917, artistic backtracking led the director to design some of his early Soviet-era productions in a "more humanized and realistic" manner than the experimental work he had executed before the revolution.[126]

Meierkhol'd's evolving concept of acting, elements of which came to be called "biomechanics," was in many ways a variant of the same process he had learned as a twenty-something actor at the Moscow Art Theater. Lecturing to a group of young students in the 1930s, Meierkhol'd compared Stanislavskii's system to his own approach, which he described in "more modest" but hardly less significant way as a "manual."[127] Not unlike his first employer's system, Meierkhol'd's concept focused on developing performance techniques that could be applied to any theatrical genre or idiom. In the words of the phenomenon's most astute scholars, he "accepted Stanislavsky's basic analysis of the special problems of the actor: inspiration and expression."[128] Indeed, he even identified himself with it by telling people proudly through the 1920s: "I am a pupil of Stanislavski."[129] The ideological strictures that militated against experimentation

---

122. I. F. Petrovskaia and V. Somina, *Teatral'nyi Peterburg: Nachalo XVIII veka-oktiabr' 1917 goda: obozrenie-putevoditel'* (St. Petersburg: RIII, 1994), 201.

123. For this interpretation, see Clark, *Petersburg*, 95–99.

124. "Homo novus" [Aleksandr Kugel'], "Zametki," *Teatr i iskusstvo* 10–11 (March 12, 1917): 192.

125. Braun, *Meyerhold*, 140.

126. James M. Symons, *Meyerhold's Theatre of the Grotesque: The Post-Revolutionary Productions, 1920–1932* (Coral Gables: University of Miami Press, 1971), 118.

127. Law and Gordon, *Meyerhold, Eisenstein, and Biomechanics*, 131.

128. Ibid., 2.

129. Quoted in Benedetti, *Stanislavski*, 238.

on the Soviet stage may have forced Meierkhol'd to continue down more conventional roads, but he had already set out on them before the revolution, as soon as he realized that a zealous reading of Briusov would lead nowhere without substantial modification. The full unfolding of Meierkhol'd's "manual" grew out of the naturalist school of acting that he had rebelled against in his artistic youth.

The Moscow Art Theater, which continued the experimental edges that it had begun to explore from the time of Meierkhol'd's ill-fated return to found its Studio Theater, nevertheless remained rooted in its or iginal concepts. It offered a traditional repertoire for most of its pre- and postrevolutionary eras, though it attempted innovations in its studios and, later, occasionally in political plays suggested by its Soviet minders. The Art Theater's influential tour of the United States in 1923–24, the event that directly inspired Lee Strasberg, Elia Kazan, and others in the rising generation of American actors to adapt Stanislavskii's "System" into the pseudo-Freudian "Method" so familiar to us today, mostly presented works from the Art Theater's early seasons. Russia's greatest impact on American stagecraft thus came in the form of *Tsar Fedor Ivanovich* (1898), *Uncle Vania* (1899), *The Cherry Orchard* (1903), and other plays of what had by then become part of Russia's traditional dramatic repertoire.[130] In the words of one of the subject's most knowledgeable students, the tour "presented the image of a theatre that had stopped developing around 1904."[131]

The rising generation of modernist directors joined their mentors in pursuing art for its own sake, a goal that harmonized their aesthetic vision with the acmeists and others interested in creativity as an expr ession of pleasure. Aleksandr Tairov, who acted under Meierkhol'd at Komissarzhevskaia's Dramatic Theater in his early twenties and played in *The Fairground Booth*, also developed an approach designed to train artists rather than control them. His 1921 theatrical manifesto, *Notes of a Director,* assailed both outmoded realist theater and the "stylized" (*uslovnyi*) concepts closely identified with Meierkhol'd's early work.[132] Instead, Tairov pursued a renewed focus on the actor as the primary source of creativity in theater, a role that he believed to require rhythm and musicality. Awareness of this concept led him to leave Komissarzhevskaia for Gaideburov's Wandering Theater, some other rather conventional enterprises,

---

130. This could even be said to be true of Gor'kii's *The Lower Depths,* which premiered at the Art Theater in 1902 and was famed both then and during the U.S. tour for its char acter studies.

131. Jean Benedetti, "Stanislavsky and the Moscow Art Theatre, 1898–1938," in *A History of Russian Theatre,* ed. Robert Leach and Victor Borovsky (Cambridge: Cambridge University Press, 1999), 273.

132. Aleksandr Tairov, *Zapiski rezhissera* (Moscow: GITIS, 2000).

and then, in 1914, to his own Chamber Theater, which he founded in Moscow with his wife, the Art Theater actress Alisa Koonen.[133]

The work of the Chamber Theater, though not devoid of an avant-garde dimension (one of Tairov's preferred exercises was a pantomime of shirtless men), hearkened back in meaningful ways to Stanislavskii. Like Tairov, the grand old man of the Moscow Art Theater advocated and had undergone formal training in music and dance. Now Tairov, who sought "to forge a theatre of pure aesthetics, founded on the 'master actor,'" was attempting a new approach to the same goal.[134] Its pursuit distanced him from the social purposes that other members of the avant-garde had hoped to find in theater. Reflecting on the Bolshevik Revolution in the dangerous year of 1936, he argued that it was "an illusion" to identify the development of Russia's performing arts culture as part of the political upheaval.[135] Nearer to the time of the October coup, he had insisted "that a 'pure temple of the arts' had no place for 'tendentious spectacle.'"[136]

Even closer to Stanislavskii was the rising Armenian director Evgenii Vakhtangov, who, like Meierkhol'd, got his start at the Moscow Art Theater. Stanislavskii hired him as an actor in 1911 and found him so in tune with his dramatic teachings that within only a few months he began employing the new arrival as a coach for younger performers.[137] Despite Vakhtangov's attraction to mass spectacle and popular theater as potential conduits for social messages, he also returned to a more traditional concept of his medium, an approach that he described as "imaginative realism." In such prewar productions as Hauptmann's *Festival of Peace*, he sought to present "the personal rather than the social."[138]

After the revolution, which Vakhtangov greeted with no small degree of skepticism and doubt, he thought of establishing a kind of "theatrical monastery" to shield dramatic art from politics.[139] His final and most important production, a Moscow staging of Carlo Gozzi's *Princess Turandot* (the inspiration for Puccini's more famous opera) mounted shortly before his premature death from cancer in 1922, revealed fancy, color, and frivolity to entertain the depressed residents of the dreary revolutionary capital. Although some observers interpreted the production as the herald of a bright communist future, its message

---

133. Nick Worrall, *Modernism to Realism on the Soviet Stage: Tairov—Vakhtangov—Okhlopkov* (Cambridge: Cambridge University Press, 1989), 19–30.
134. Ibid., 15.
135. Quoted in Konstantin Rudnitsky, ed., *Istoriia sovetskogo dramaticheskogo teatra*, 6 vols. (Moscow: Nauka, 1966), 1:164.
136. Quoted in Worrall, *Modernism to Realism*, 34–35.
137. Benedetti, *Stanislavski*, 207.
138. Worrall, *Modernism to Realism*, 85.
139. Ibid., 96–101.

of optimism at a time of disaster resonated for far longer and to much greater effect.[140] In a fitting tribute that illustrated Vakhtangov's creative debts, Stanislavskii rushed from the premiere's finale to offer his terminally ill pupil personal congratulations and then rushed back to continue taking part in the thunderous applause.[141]

Those who had encouraged symbolist theater often reacted to its failures with doubt about the role of art in imparting social change or associated "mystical" qualities. They had been "tempted to exaggerate the claim that symbolist art had by its very nature transforming power and this pretension began to run thin."[142] Perhaps prophetically, Chekhov's *The Seagull*, which in the 1890s suggested theatrical innovation as the wave of the future, ends with a report of the dreamy but ultimately unsuccessful, disillusioned, and unhappy Treplev's suicide. Its original description as a comedy was thus more than a bit ironic. Komissarzhevskaia, despite her willingness to hire Meierkhol'd, could nevertheless write to the director's nemesis Karpov (under whom she had worked at the Aleksandrinskii) that "Nietzsche should be regarded as a man of genius, but if one takes his philosophy as a symbol of faith, one will never go any further."[143] Of course she both took theatrical modernism as something close to faith and found herself more or less stopped in her artistic tracks, but as Laurence Senelick has observed, she "encountered the symbolists and instantly, almost unthinkingly, adopted them as her salvation, without fully comprehending their aesthetic principles."[144] Clearly it was a decision she regretted. During World War I the symbolist playwright Fedor Sologub arrived at this rather unoriginal conclusion: "There is nothing surprising in that the public thirsts for happy shows."[145] "Why make the theater into a temple when we already have temples?" Belyi asked.[146] "Stylization," he believed, "turns a personality into a mannequin. Such a transformation is the first and decisive step toward the destruction of the theater."[147] "A new Bayreuth," the symbolist intellectual Dmitrii Filosofov sardonically concluded in the same spirit with reference to Wagner's theater, "will save no one."[148] The last decades of the tsarist era proved them more right than wrong.

140. Ibid., 127–39. A revival was staged as late as 1963 and continued to be produced at least until the late 1980s.
141. Ibid., 138.
142. West, *Russian Symbolism*, 184.
143. Quoted in Borovsky, *Triptych*, 137.
144. Laurence Senelick, "Vera Komissarzhevskaia: The Actress as Symbolist Eidolon," *Theatre Journal* 32, no. 4 (1980): 479.
145. Fedor Sologub, "Ten' tragedii," *Teatr i iskusstvo* 48 (November 30, 1914): 922.
146. Quoted in Rosenthal, "Theatre as Church," 138.
147. Quoted in Rybakova, *Komissarzhevskaia*, 163.
148. Dmitrii Filosofov, "Khudozhestvennaia zhizn' Peterburga," *Zolotoe runo* 10 (October 1906): 63–64.

"ART MUST BE APOLITICAL":

A CONCLUSION

In March 2005 the Bol'shoi Theater presented Leonid Desiatnikov's new opera *The Children of Rosenthal*, the first world premiere mounted on Moscow's principal state stage since 1979. Composed to a libretto by the postmodernist writer Vladimir Sorokin, the production provoked a flash of controversy. Sorokin's previous literary works featured a society whose people rely for nourishment on a "substance" that looks and smells like feces; those who do not partake are branded dissidents. His novel *Blue Lard* includes a gay sex scene in which a clone of Soviet leader Nikita Khrushchev sodomizes a clone of his predecessor Iosif Stalin. Little public notice of Sorokin's work for the Bol'shoi became known, however, until a few weeks before the premiere when Sergei Neverov, a Duma deputy belonging to President Vladimir Putin's loyal United Russia Party, demanded government action to stop it. Invoking the "pride of Russian culture," Neverov declared, "we can't allow Sorokin's vulgar plays to be staged."[1] Protesters from a pro-Putin youth group called Moving Together held a small but noticed public demonstration against the opera on Moscow's Theater Square, where they tore up and trampled on copies of the novelist's printed works.[2] One of their leaders intoned: "We must cleanse Russian culture of the parasites like Sorokin who have stuck to it during the so-called democratic years of [former

1. Arkady Ostrovsky, "Attacks on New Bolshoi Opera Revive Russia's Memories of Stalinism: A Rising Tide of Intolerance Towards Russian Artists Is Seen to Be Linked with a Wider Nationalistic Trend," *Financial Times*, April 5, 2005.
2. Andrew Osburn, "Putin Youth Protest at Vulgar 'Pornography' on Show at the Bolshoi," *Independent*, March 15, 2005.

President Boris] Yeltsin's government. This will be the first step towards reviving great Russian culture. There is no place for pornography at the Bolshoi."[3]

The fracas seemed exaggerated when the opening-night spectators found no evidence of pornography in the opera. Its plot revolves around a music-loving German scientist who found refuge in Stalin's Soviet Union and was put in charge of cloning experiments. Ordered to produce model workers, he has also created clones of five great composers: Mozart, Verdi, Wagner, Musorgskii, and Chaikovskii. Abandoned by their underfunded government laboratory after the fall of communism and the death of their creator, the clones are left to wander the streets of Moscow, living as itinerant musicians among the city's down and out. When the Mozart clone marries a prostitute, her jealous pimp poisons the wedding vodka, killing all those present except the bridegroom, who ends the opera consumed by madness in a hospital ward.

Garish though the opera may have been, it failed to shock the "new" Russia's public morals. Desiatnikov described his principal theme as life's absurdity for those incapable of adapting to radical change of the type that his country has experienced since 1991.[4] The only reported disturbance in the theater came from a spectator annoyed by a mime sequence that went on for several minutes without music.[5] An American critic found the opera innocuous and doubted whether its artistic merits would have attracted any attention at all but for the controversy around Sorokin.[6] Neverov undermined his own case by admitting that he had read neither the libretto nor any of the novelist's other works.[7]

Nevertheless, the absence of explicit pornography failed to satisfy Sorokin's enemies. A member of the Duma's cultural affairs committee who attended a dress rehearsal found it "diabolical" that a chorus of prostitutes should appear on the stage of the venerable Bol'shoi.[8] Some of her colleagues demanded the dismissal of the theater's general director, Anatolii Iksanov.[9] A controversial billion-dollar project to renovate the Bol'shoi, announced less than a month before the premiere, cast a shadow over the whole affair.[10] Sorokin compared

---

3. Quoted in Ostrovsky, "Attacks on New Bolshoi."
4. Vadim Prokhorov, "Genetically Modified Mozart: A New Opera About Clones Is Raising Hell at the Bolshoi—and It Hasn't Even Opened Yet," *Guardian*, March 16, 2005.
5. Sophia Kishkovsky, "Bolshoi Opens Controversial Opera," *New York Times*, March 24, 2005.
6. George Loomis, "Murky Doings at the Bolshoi: Misguided Attacks on 'The Children of Rosenthal' Are Just One Aspect of a Complicated Story," *Financial Times*, April 1, 2005. My thanks to Dr. Loomis for sharing his impressions with me in person.
7. Raymond Stults, "Big Scandal at the Bolshoi," *St. Petersburg Times*, March 25, 2005.
8. Nick Allen, "Bolshoi's 'Porn Opera' Upsets the Russians," *Daily Telegraph*, March 24, 2005.
9. Kishkovsky, "Bolshoi Opens."
10. Loomis, "Murky Doings."

the uproar to Stalinist cultural politics: "It's reminiscent of the 1930s," he said of the protests, "the authorities should be ashamed."[11] Generations after the events described in the preceding pages, Russia is still experiencing an evolution in its relationship between culture and power.

What did that relationship mean for Russians in the late imperial era? As I hope to have demonstrated in this study, with only a handful of exceptions that usually proved the rule, politics and the performing arts largely stood apart. Theaters, administrators, performers, audiences, and critics almost uniformly revealed that their involvement in politics and development of a greater social "consciousness" faced major limitations. The venerated connection between dissent and artistic expression, a common trope in Russian cultural history, was becoming ever more attenuated during a prolonged period of modernization that challenged its potency, curtailed its boundaries, and ultimately exposed its weakness.

This fact was particularly manifest in the institutional structures administered by the tsarist government. Theatrical censorship, perhaps the greatest potential vehicle for state power over cultural life, functioned neither strictly nor efficiently. Even before the loosening of censorship in 1905–6, the Empire's overworked theatrical censors approved nearly nine out of every ten works submitted for their consideration. Many of the works that they did not approve nevertheless appeared on stage, including, in the case of the largest popular theater, nearly 40 percent of its inaugural season's repertoire. The consequences of disobeying censorship directives ranged from light to nonexistent. In most ways it resembled Western censorship regimes of the time more closely than it did the stricter Soviet theatrical censorship that replaced it.[12] In some cases, including its favorable decisions on such plays as Strindberg's *Miss Julie*, Maeterlinck's *Monna Vanna*, Ibsen's *Ghosts*, the dramatization of Daudet's *Sapho*, and, despite extralegal interference in the Dramatic Theater production, Wilde's *Salome*, Imperial Russia's theatrical censorship outdid its Western counterparts in permissiveness.

---

11. Osborn, "Putin Youth."

12. For a comprehensive study of early Soviet theatrical censorship, see Steven D. Richmond, "Ideologically Firm: Soviet Theater Censorship, 1921–1928" (Ph.D. diss., University of Chicago, 1996). From 1923 Soviet theatrical censorship required both preliminary approval of works and strict scrutiny to make sure that the actual content produced on stage was acceptable and obeyed censorship directives. Unlike Imperial Russia's censorship laws, the 1923 charter also expressly empowered the secret police (called the GPU at the time) to sanction violations of censorship directives with arrest and the forcible closing of theaters. In practice secret police officials came to be active in the censorship process as well. After World War II a formal licensing mechanism was added to allow Ministry of Culture officials to vet stage productions. For a description of the process, see Birgit Beumers, "Commercial Enterprise on the Stage: Changes in Russian Theatre Management between 1986 and 1996," *Europe-Asia Studies* 48, no. 8 (1996): 1404.

Political challenges to the state led only to the diminution of the censorship's authority. Although its powers of preliminary review remained in place, few critics or political figures seriously advocated its abolition or major diminutions of its power. Many of those who objected to the moral content of what they saw on stage complained that the censorship was not strict enough. Others publicly commented on its weakness and objected to the arbitrariness to which that quality led. Rather than producing a reaction that endowed the censorship with renewed strength, political crisis and revaluations of what was considered taboo substantially lowered the bar on what the censors felt compelled to prohibit. As the Kobeko Commission's discussions made clear, they openly doubted the efficacy and relevance of their own powers. Many prohibited works, including some critical of the status quo or presenting themes and metaphors recommending such criticism, met with and retained official government approval as time went on. The reduced number of works that remained proscribed usually featured incendiary depictions of mass violence, incitements to it, or explicit sexuality—subjects that rarely meet with any government's approval regardless of whether it is confronted by political instability or revolutionary unrest. Enforcing this declining number of bans was another matter altogether; often it was an exercise in futility.

State intervention in theatrical operations was marked more by its casual application and pettiness than by its frequency and strength. When it did occur, it resulted not from a predetermined or systematic policy of repression but from the temporary fear that certain cultural activities would fan the flames of unrest. This was the reason why St. Petersburg's Governor General Dmitrii Trepov issued a circular, transient and ineffectual though it was, to prohibit performances of Rimskii-Korsakov's music in 1905. The scandal caused by the composer's dismissal from St. Petersburg Conservatory had made him—largely against his own wishes and inclination—into a symbol for the opposition and a stimulus for political demonstrations. But no matter what the police organs did, their actions were far from the last word. Entrepreneurs could freely challenge them in courts of law and expect positive results. Practical limitations on the powers of the police, together with their far greater priorities in late imperial times, often made such interventions unenforceable. Svetov and Valentinov's incendiary satirical revue *The Days of Freedom* continued to be performed with impunity for weeks after the Council of Ministers prohibited it by special circular. Many performers and impresarios found that they could ignore legal and extralegal prohibitions altogether or defuse them through willful dialogues with the authorities.

The imperial predecessors of contemporary Russia's state theatrical administrators were no strangers to controversies of the type current a century later.

But rather than becoming wary or censorious of radical performers, politicized works, techniques imbued with explicit social purposes, or content susceptible to moral criticism, the Imperial Theaters Directorate readily accommodated them. As Mikhail Fokin, Boris Gorin-Goriainov, Tamara Karsavina, Nikolai Khodotov, Ekaterina Korchagina-Aleksandrovskaia, Valentina Kuza, Vsevolod Meierkhol'd, Anna Pavlova, Fedor Shaliapin, and others discovered, it gladly employed, promoted, and gave favorable treatment to a number of artists associated—sometimes tangentially and sometimes not—with oppositionist ideas and sentiments. Khodotov, one of the very few imperial performers who actively engaged with the revolutionary movement, appeared on stage more frequently than all but one of his colleagues in the contentious 1905–6 season, got a raise, and thereafter had his own radical (but tellingly unsuccessful) plays produced at the Aleksandrinskii. Fokin, Pavlova, Karsavina, and most other participants in the abortive October 1905 ballet "strike"—itself far more artistic and professional than political or revolutionary in character—were subsequently promoted to positions of greater power and prestige. Fokin was named First Ballet Master upon Marius Petipa's death just five years later. Pavlova and Karsavina both received the coveted "Ballerina" title. If the government worried about subversion in cultural life, its concerns were not reflected in its personnel decisions.

Nor were the Directorate's repertoire choices determined by political considerations. Under Vladimir Teliakovskii's leadership the Imperial Theaters staged a broad range of works, including some, such as Beethoven's *Fidelio*, Sophocles' *Antigone*, Rimskii-Korsakov's *The Snow Maiden*, and Strauss's *Elektra*, that observers expected, hoped, and/or feared might provoke revolutionary sentiment. By and large, however, they did not. At the same time many who followed the imperial dramatic stage commented on the Directorate's willingness to feature works distinguished by their "vulgarity," including one, Vladimir Trakhtenberg's *Fimka*, whose plot about prostitutes featured the same type of characters that Duma members did not like to see on the state stage a century later in very different political circumstances. Few works other than Glinka's largely ceremonial opera *A Life for the Tsar* (1836) offered political connotations explicitly favorable to autocracy, and no evidence suggests that either the Imperial Theaters' top officials or their superiors at Court advocated or promoted such works at any time after the reign of Nicholas I.

Despite their ostensible goals of reshaping society and redefining theater's social role, the emerging symbolist and "stylized" currents in stagecraft also found a welcome home on the imperial stages. Their avatar Meierkhol'd, whom Teliakovskii enthusiastically hired in 1908, remained a respected employee of the Imperial Theaters for the rest of the tsarist era. His art and politics did not adversely affect his career in them, nor did politics appear to be a tremendous source of his inspiration. Meierkhol'd's major concern on the eve of the February Revolution of 1917 was whether his lavish new production of Lermontov's *Masquerade* would go on and attract a substantial audience.[13] In another example of official permissiveness, the Imperial Theaters willingly accommodated Hamsun's *At the Gates of the Kingdom,* Andreev's works, and Khodotov's politicized plays, all in productions that failed to attract large or sympathetic audiences.

Two main implications arise from these developments. First, in the case of censorship and state intervention in the performing arts, the tsarist government approached what was happening on the Empire's stages as a low priority. Although some authority figures wanted to neutralize potentially incendiary works, material, and personages at chaotic moments, the overall picture unfolding in the decades before 1917 was one of ambivalence, if not neglect. The censorship became looser, and its top officials talked far more apprehensively of morally unsound content than of political challenges from under the proscenium arch.

Second, in the case of the government's stages, personnel and repertoire choices were largely divorced from political realities. Teliakovskii's reluctant decision to postpone the Aleksandrinskii premiere of *Antigone* and initial hesitancy to offer the usual number of performances of *A Life for the Tsar* in the 1905–6 opera season were the only tepid signs registering the impact of domestic political unrest as it emerged in a series of events unparalleled at any other time before 1917. The effect of World War I on repertoire choices was much greater and shared with other nations at war with Germany. Nor was the tsarist government isolated in its anti-German sentiment domestically.

The Directorate's gentle handling of artists associated with the revolutionary movement and radical ideas revealed its priorities further. As Teliakovskii demonstrated when he threatened to resign if Shaliapin were dismissed for singing *The Little Cudgel* on the Bol'shoi stage, government officials could be quite protective of performers when they became the subject of controversy. The state's chief interest in culture leaned mostly toward questions of aesthetics. Even at times when the autocracy came under determined political assault, its institutions and officials revealed only marginal concern with cultural life. Nizhinskii's poor professionalism and revealing costume brought about a swifter and more definitive dismissal from service than any political act by imperial stage artists, including Iosif Kshesinskii's physical assault of another dancer.

The disconnect between politics and the performing arts was no less pronounced outside the realm of the state. Private and popular theaters, which had

---

13. N. V. Petrov, *50 i 500* (Moscow: VTO, 1950), 137.

blossomed since (and outside the capitals before) their legalization in 1882, usually, and understandably, tried to present works that drew audiences and produced revenue. Regardless of what was happening in the political realm, most management decisions revolved around financial considerations. The urban instability and declining attendance that characterized theatrical life during the Revolutions of 1905 and 1917—prolonged and extreme cases of political unrest—magnified these woes, as did the impact of World War I. At these times the theatrical press hemorrhaged with accounts of low box office receipts, closing theaters, laid-off actors, and canceled performances. With their livelihoods and businesses threatened, entrepreneurs almost uniformly worried about avoiding trouble and weathering periods of turmoil (as, despite their generous state subsidies and other advantages, did the Imperial Theaters). With only a handful of exceptions, notably the capricious Iavorskaia and the small number of short-lived drama circles formed by radical workers whose undertakings usually failed in short order, impresarios remained far removed from embracing radical ideas or turning their theaters into loci of discontent or rebellion. As did any group of entrepreneurs in Imperial Russia or elsewhere, they regarded urban stability as crucial to their success and survival. If political crisis proved anything about the administrative side of show business, it was the thoroughness of its commercial development and consumer orientation. Disturbances in the status quo raised fears rather than hopes.

The performers who brought Russia's stages to life demonstrated little attachment to the great "questions" of the day. To the recollection, regret, pride, or consternation of virtually every firsthand observer, the politicization of the Empire's stage artists remained a decidedly unaccomplished fact. Most wanted nothing to do with politics and, as Mariia Savina and others publicly declared, instead saw political engagement as incompatible with their métier. Many actively opposed political radicalism and its supporters. As Gorin-Goriainov and his "fighting retinue" comrades learned during the October 1905 general strike, some performers were willing to resist with violence.

As a component of Imperial Russia's urban middle, stage performers articulated their identity through a strong commitment to improving their professional status, a category that included material concerns, employment conditions, and cohesion as a community. Political and social turmoil threatened only to impede the pursuit of these goals. Performers in the Imperial Theaters saw little advantage in assisting or sympathizing with those who attacked the sources of their prestige and comparative prosperity. Almost all of them spurned it. To the derision of radical critics, on several occasions they declared their loyalty to the tsarist government. Less-well-off private and popular stage performers normally resisted developments that threatened their jobs and wages, however meager they could be. Many performers declined to pursue active political engagement because they were uninterested in, ill informed about, or even repulsed by politics. Shaliapin's "whole nature revolt[ed] against them."[14] Nizhinskii equated them with death.[15] The political "semi-literacy" that the actor Mikhail Narokov ascribed to his fellow performers has met no sustainable refutation.[16] Indeed, virtually every press comment on the matter decried the performers' lack of social commitment and placed them squarely "on the sidelines." Students of the performing arts, many of whom aspired to join the ranks of those who entertained the Empire's theatergoers, also largely avoided politics. Their most dramatic demonstrations, which disrupted St. Petersburg Conservatory's operations in 1905, called for better living conditions and greater educational opportunities, and even these demands did not represent the sentiments of a majority of students.

The most significant impact of political events on the lives and careers of Russian stage performers emerged not from their ideological meanings or social messages but from economic crises that worsened their already precarious position and accelerated their drive toward professionalization. This trend could be observed as early as the 1870s, when Russian performers began to form charitable organizations to care for their impoverished colleagues. It continued with the founding of the Russian Theatrical Society in 1894. The Theatrical Society's more hands-on product, the Union of Stage Performers established in 1906, resulted directly from the difficult material circumstances caused by the revolutionary events of the preceding year. Intended to protect economic interests and codify conditions of employment, these associations resembled other professional groups created in the late imperial era. Like many of them, the arts organizations avoided politicization and sought hopefully to negotiate the best opportunities and advantages for their members within the existing order. For stage performers professionalization was chiefly an economic development. Political crises worked as fulcra that propelled this development through practical effects.

As I argued in Chapter 5, political strife both illustrated and reinforced the apolitical mentalities of Russian audiences. For as long as Russians enjoyed a

14. Feodor Chaliapin, *Man and Mask: Forty Years in the Life of a Singer*, trans. Phyllis Mégroz (New York: Knopf, 1932), 175.
15. Vaslav Nijinsky, *The Diary of Vaslav Nijinsky*, trans. Romola Nijinsky (London: Quartet Encounters, 1991), 26.
16. Mikhail S. Narokov, *Biografiia moego pokoleniia: Teatral'nye memuary* (Moscow: VTO, 1956), 99.

modern theatrical life, they had been cultivating a strong interest in melodrama, comedy, romance, human dilemmas, detective stories, and other genres that quenched their thirst for diversion and entertainment, still relative novelties for many living through the last decades of the tsarist era. A common view among the middle and lower classes regarded theater as an entrée into a more refined world of ideas, education, and higher social status. Rather than embracing the stage as a medium for social and political agitation, they usually avoided situations that could have involved them in civic disturbances, exposed them to harm, or, by implication, threatened a valuable vehicle of social mobility. Audiences who panicked because they believed that incidents of mass violence depicted on stage were real, as they did during performances of the final-act mob scene in Gor'kii's *Children of the Sun,* or who angrily confronted radicals calling out for the "Marseillaise" and other revolutionary statements were not likely agents to politicize cultural life. Like Dr. Bertenson, who chronicled the riot that broke out at the Mariinskii Theater during a performance of Wagner's fairy tale opera *Lohengrin,* most wanted to forget their troubles by staying "far from the revolutionary currents of the time."[17]

Theaters catered to the tastes of these audiences, which were marked to an overwhelming degree by their craving for pure entertainment and indifference to tendentious works imbued with themes of social and political struggle. The traditional repertoire that dominated popular theater and drew millions of spectators every year illustrated this fact all too clearly, as did the popularity of new works that fueled modern vogues. A number of crowd-pleasing productions, such as the Suvorin Theater's dramatization of Dostoevskii's *The Devils* and the variety of plays that mocked the intelligentsia and its values, not only eschewed political engagement, but presented receptive audiences with negative depictions of radicalism, reform, revolution, and their sympathizers.

The quest to stimulate ideals of social unity through art—the distillation of an enduring theme in Russian literary and philosophical thought—also attracted little mass interest. Enterprises that adopted them invariably failed, and even many of their onetime proponents—including Aleksandr Blok, whose play *The Fairground Booth* practically defined the genre—ceased to see much value in their pursuit. When Dmitrii Filosofov judged with Wagnerian gravitas that "a new Bayreuth will save no one," he spoke for many who believed that innovation had failed in its main goals.[18] Blok certainly subscribed to that sentiment when he remarked that earlier modes of performance were "a hundred times

---

17. V. B. Bertenson, *Za 30 let (listki iz vospominanii)* (St. Petersburg: n.p., 1914), 273.
18. Dmitrii Filosofov, "Khudozhestvennaia zhizn' Peterburga," *Zolotoe runo* 10 (October 1906): 63–64.

better" than the available innovative ones.[19] The philosophical bases, theoretical groundwork, and first practical applications of such experiments were in most cases international rather than peculiar to Russia and developed largely outside periods of political unrest. Experimental currents normally identified with the period after the Revolution of 1905 were already in development and practice in the years leading up to that event. Chekhov introduced shades of what came to be called "stylization" (*uslovnost'*) into his plays in the 1890s. Meierkhol'd's first experimental theater troupe began to perform in 1902, the same year in which Briusov launched his appeal for more "stylization" and attacked "unnecessary truth." Fokin's new dance concepts, which mainly involved coordinating movement with music and design, formed years before Bloody Sunday. Nizhinskii's more athletic approach, tailored to dissonance and sensuality, evolved years after it. As much as 1917 mattered in terms of power politics, the endurance (however harried) of experimental trends thereafter—and their coexistence with the predominant traditional repertoire—belied that year's significance as a cultural watershed.

Many radical critics registered their disappointment with theatrical presentations and the popular tastes that supported them—facts of cultural life also often decried by government officials and political conservatives as well. But the volume of their complaints only revealed the yawning chasm between quasi-messianic ideals about the role of the arts in society and the plain reality of what Russian theatergoers wanted to take in. If they preferred *Vampuka, African Bride* (performed more than three hundred times in 1909–12 alone) or cross-dressers to the symbolist pastiche of Meierkhol'd's Strand cabaret (performed twice before bankruptcy in December 1908) or plays about the politics of factory labor, their tastes are not hard to determine. The Russian Empire's large, diverse audiences failed to embrace radical social, political, and philosophical messages presented to them from the stage, and, along with the strength of their commitment to revolutionary ideals, one may properly doubt the strength of their identification of culture with power.

Referring to what he called Russia's "unrealized civil society," Samuel Kassow has argued that "solving problems by dialogue, process, law, and debate requires certain shared beliefs that did not flourish in an atmosphere of suspicion and mistrust."[20] Insofar as the performing arts were concerned, however, all those

---

19. Aleksandr Blok, *Sobranie sochinenii*, 8 vols. (Moscow: Gosudarstvennoe izdatel'stvo khudozhestvennoi literatury, 1960–63), 5:202.

20. Samuel D. Kassow, "Russia's Unrealized Civil Society," in *Between Tsar and People: Educated Society and the Quest for Public Identity in Late Imperial Russia*, ed. Edith W. Clowes, Samuel D. Kassow, and James L. West (Princeton: Princeton University Press, 1991), 370–71.

exchanges were an important part of public life in the last decades of the tsarist era, even at the most difficult moments. Nothing in my research has led me to doubt the sincerity of Aleksandr Benua's description of it as "a time of all sorts of enterprises and every kind of bliss."[21] "The origins of Stalinist cultural policy"—the full and oppressive development of which Sorokin compared to the atmosphere in which he found himself in 2005—were not "firmly embedded in the nature of the pre-revolutionary relationship between culture and power."[22]

It is more accurate to think of that relationship as a strand in Imperial Russia's ongoing evolution from autocracy to pluralism. In this respect the performing arts represented a highly visible and relatively successful aspect of the Empire's burgeoning civil society. Its participants actively worked for the realization of their goals within existing frameworks, which included an expanding and increasingly diverse community of cultural interests, a free commercial economy that offered a substantial entertainment industry, a professional sphere in which those who derived a living from performance sought and gained a recognized place, and a state that both willingly accommodated them and for the most part remained reluctant or unable to amplify its powers of control. In the case of the abolition of the Imperial Theaters' performance monopoly in 1882, the autocracy found common ground with civic interests that wanted a stronger national tradition of Russian theater and the legal right to bring one into being through private initiative. The Russian Theatrical Society, formally styled "Imperial" from 1904, enjoyed steady government financial support and high-level patronage, as did the Russian Musical Society, whose founding preceded it. During the Revolution of 1905, theatrical entrepreneurs (and entrepreneuses) who felt maltreated by police authorities sued them in courts of law and received at least some redress of their grievances. Throughout the late imperial era many figures active in cultural life simply ignored government restrictions and dictates on their art and got away with it.

In these ways Russia's performing arts culture illustrated and contributed to an evolutionary process that in the absence of World War I may well have precluded the events of 1917. The weak politicization of cultural life suggests enough public confidence in the status quo to preclude the performing arts' development into a venue of political dissent or radical identity formation. Unlike imperial

21. Aleksandr Benua, *Vospominaniia*, 2 vols. (Moscow: Zakharov, 2003), 2:1504.
22. Murray Frame, *The St. Petersburg Imperial Theatres: Stage and State in Revolutionary Russia, 1900–1920* (Greensboro, N.C.: McFarland, 2000), 175. To his credit Frame later revised this thought to suggest that after 1917 "the state had taken complete control and transformed the stage into a political tribune," a goal to which no tsar ever aspired. Frame, *School for Citizens: Theatre and Civil Society in Imperial Russia* (New Haven: Yale University Press, 2006), 202.

peripheries, traumatized postcolonial societies, repressive dictatorships, and other cultural contexts that deny their populations viable public spheres, the Russian Empire developed one durable enough that seeking a "virtual" alternative failed to become a compelling imperative or popular goal. Regardless of how loudly disgruntled radicals complained about this fact—and complain they did—its stamina through the decades before 1917 bears witness to how strongly realized the Empire's civil society truly was. If, as much of the recent work presented in the introduction to this study suggests, a prominent, alternative, and politicized role for the performing arts grows naturally within oppressive political environments, then Late Imperial Russia fails any test that would define it in those terms.

Although some work has been done, evaluating the full implications of the relationship between politics and the performing arts during and after the Revolution of 1917 belongs to another study, one that I hope this book will encourage. For our purposes it is useful to note that Russia's evolving prerevolutionary cultural milieu did not survive intact. As Louise McReynolds has convincingly written, "the opportunities for pluralism were significantly greater before 1917 than after."[23] Writing specifically about expressive culture, Katherine Bliss Eaton has made the apt and far from inaccurate observation that "the brilliant art born in Russia at the beginning of the [twentieth] century collapsed entirely" after the Bolshevik Revolution.[24]

In perhaps the most telling outcome, a large number of the people mentioned in these pages who lived through that traumatic event permanently emigrated from their homeland, whose Soviet experience they found hostile to their lives, careers, and creativity. However sad it was, this trend had great significance for the performing arts in Europe and the United States. Twentieth-century music and dance, the leading American and British schools of acting, modern stage direction and technique, and the general vitalization of artistic performance all have strong roots in the Russian emigration.[25] Those who left or failed to return included many cultural figures who were active and important

---

23. Louise McReynolds, *Russia at Play: Leisure Activities at the End of the Tsarist Era* (Ithaca: Cornell University Press, 2003), 299.

24. Katherine Bliss Eaton, introduction to *Enemies of the People: The Destruction of Soviet Literary, Theater, and Film Arts in the 1930s*, ed. Katherine Bliss Eaton (Evanston: Northwestern University Press, 2002), xxiv.

25. For solid assessments of this impact, see Marc Raeff, *Russia Abroad: A Cultural History of the Emigration, 1919–1939* (New York: Oxford University Press, 1990), and Steven G. Marks, *How Russia Shaped the Modern World: From Art to Anti-Semitism, Ballet to Bolshevism* (Princeton: Princeton University Press, 2002). One might also add culinary influences—New York's famous Russian Tea Room was founded by exiled artists of the imperial ballet.

in late tsarist times: Andreev, Artsybashev, Benua, Diaghilev, Evreinov, Fokin, Gippius, Glazunov, Iavorskaia, Karsavina, Fedor Komissarzhevskii (Theodore Komisarjevsky), Kshesinskaia, Kuznetsova-Benua, Litvin, Merezhkovskii, the Nizhinskiis, Pavlova, Ol'ga Preobrazhenskaia, Ida Rubinshtein, Remizov, Shaliapin, Trefilova, Volkonskii, and Ziloti, to give only a partial list.[26] Fedor Lopukhov, who professed his complete lack of interest in politics, felt virtually alone among ballet dancers in his decision to remain in Soviet Russia.[27] Even his own sister Lidiia, famous in the West as the dancer Lydia Lopokhova and later as Lady Keynes (wife of the economist), did not return home after the revolution.

Some of the smaller number who emigrated for a while after 1917 and then returned did so in curious circumstances. Gor'kii, who left Soviet Russia in disenchantment in 1921 but moved back ten years later, required an enormous amount of official flattery, including the renaming of Moscow's main thoroughfare and the playwright's hometown in his honor. New evidence suggests that Prokof'ev, who lived abroad between 1918 and 1936, returned because he was threatened by the NKVD.[28] His estranged Spanish wife disappeared into the gulag after World War II, and his children by her were made wards of the state, possibly to ensure the composer's good behavior.[29] Igor' Stravinskii, stranded abroad by the outbreak of World War I and wholly unsympathetic to the revolution that followed at home three years later, refused all invitations to return (however insistent) apart from a brief visit in 1962.

Nor was life too easy for those artists who attempted to soldier on under the Soviets. The composer Dmitrii Shostakovich, who was denied permission to emigrate in the mid-1920s, lived in prolonged fear of arrest, suffered frequent criticism of his music on political grounds, and, despite a lively controversy about the possible meanings of his works and personal actions, faced many obstacles to reconciliation with the regime.[30] Blok, who imbued the Bolshevik Revolution with an improbable (or ironic) Christian messianism in his poem

---

26. A number of leading tsarist-era cultural figures died before 1917; they included Dalmatov, Vera Komissarzhevskaia, Liadov, Napravnik, Rimskii-Korsakov, Savina, and Varlamov. It is impossible to say exactly how they would have reacted to Bolshevism in power, but an educated guess might conclude that they would not have reacted well.

27. Fedor Lopukhov, *Shest'desiat let v balete: Vospominaniia i zapiski baletmeistera* (Moscow: Iskusstvo, 1966), 188.

28. Personal communication from Professor Simon Morrison, Princeton University Department of Music, December 9, 2004.

29. Norman Lebrecht, *The Companion to 20th Century Music* (New York: Simon and Schuster, 1992), 267.

30. The debate over Shostakovich is passionate and acrimonious. A posthumously published memoir, *Testimony: The Memoirs of Dmitri Shostakovich*, ed. Solomon Volkov, trans. Antonina W.

The Twelve and held positions in the early Soviet cultural establishment, narrowly avoided execution in 1919 and died of an illness brought on by malnutrition two years later at the premature age of forty—after the regime refused him permission to seek medical treatment abroad.[31] Gor'kii perished in suspicious circumstances in the early phases of Stalin's purges. Meierkhol'd developed major artistic differences with the socialist realist aesthetic that dominated the new regime's cultural policies and denied him creative freedom. After denouncing these policies publicly as "stupefying" and "monstrous," he was arrested, suffered the brutal murder of his wife and leading lady, Zinaida Raikh, while imprisoned, and was gruesomely tortured by the secret police. In February 1940 he was shot.[32] These cases were exceptionally tragic, but there is every indication that many Russian artists knew of the potential outcomes they faced under communism. As Sheila Fitzpatrick has acknowledged, "almost all" members of the artistic community "were determined to boycott the new government."[33] Amy Nelson's more recent words about musicians seem broadly applicable to most performers: they "were at least mistrustful, if not overtly hostile to, the new Bolshevik regime."[34]

Hostility certainly appeared to be the rule of the day in the former Imperial Theaters. Indeed, the period immediately after the Bolshevik coup d'état of October 1917 witnessed the first real strikes by performers of the state stage. For several months its artists boycotted the new regime and refused to meet with or acknowledge Soviet officials, whom they officially regarded as "imposters." Nizhinskii, formerly of the imperial ballet, referred to them from abroad as "godless animals."[35] The Aleksandrinskii's drama troupe sought "consciously

---

Bouis (New York: Harper and Row, 1979), suggested that he despised the regime bitterly and coded antigovernment messages into his works. Its authenticity has been contested. More recent studies, Elizabeth Wilson, *Shostakovich: A Life Remembered* (Princeton: Princeton University Press, 1995), and Laurel E. Fay, *Shostakovich: A Life* (New York: Oxford University Press, 2005), argue that his attitudes were more nuanced and ambiguous. No one, however, suggests that the composer's life was easy.

31. According to Olga Matich, *Erotic Utopia: The Decadent Imagination in Russia's Fin de Siècle* (Madison: University of Wisconsin Press, 2005), 276, Blok and others, despite their general aversion to politics, attached "apocalyptic meaning" to the revolution once it happened, a value that further signifies their interpretation of the phenomenon as a spiritual rather than political crisis.

32. On Meierkhol'd's fate, see Robert Conquest, *The Great Terror: A Reassessment* (New York: Oxford University Press, 1990), 306–7.

33. Sheila Fitzpatrick, *The Commissariat of Enlightenment: Soviet Organization of Education and the Arts under Lunacharsky, October 1917–1921* (Cambridge: Cambridge University Press, 1970), 110.

34. Amy Nelson, *Music for the Revolution: Musicians and Power in Early Soviet Russia* (University Park: Pennsylvania State University Press, 2004), 14.

35. D. Zolotnitskii, *Akademicheskie teatry na putiakh oktiabria* (Leningrad: Iskusstvo, 1982), 32–33. For a more detailed analysis of this period, see Richard G. Thorpe, "The Management of Culture

to separate itself from the political struggle," while Petrograd opera soloists insisted that "art must be apolitical."[36] The tenor Vasilii Bezpalov, who had become one of the Provisional Government's chief administrative officials of the former Imperial Theaters, recalled a large group of artists who stood "against the new regime" established by the October coup.[37] Lopukhov remembered that "fear and panic tore apart the artists," who were ever more inclined to leave the country.[38] The director Vasilii Shkafer recalled that his colleagues simply "awaited future events."[39] In January 1918 a group of Mariinskii soloists demanded the dismissal of "pro-Bolshevik" artists, including Meierkhol'd and the tenor Ivan Ershov. The Soviet musicologist Abram Gozenpud alleged that some protesters, "influenced by counterrevolutionary propaganda, resorted to sabotage and the disruption of performances."[40]

Individual stories testify to the contentiousness of the situation. Sergei Rakhmaninov, the noted composer, left Russia immediately after the Bolshevik coup to settle in the United States. The soprano Marianna Cherkasskaia resigned from the Mariinskii's opera troupe in December 1917, declaring: "Now that politics is interfering with the theater, consciously ruining it, there is nothing more for me to do there."[41] Shaliapin, who continued to perform in Soviet Russia, wearied of the regime's bad treatment of him as a "bourgeois," an experience that included having his apartment ransacked, bank account confiscated, friends senselessly murdered, and family subjected to petty humiliations.[42] Imperial Russia's highest-paid artist was said to collect his postrevolutionary performance fees in flour and eggs.[43] Developing what he later called an "inner revulsion against the kind of life created by the new régime," he emigrated in 1922, as soon as he felt it safe for him and his family to do so.[44] Fedor Komissarzhevskii resented the subordination of his directorial work on the state stage to a "theater committee" that included porters, coat check girls, and a bad conductor.

---

in Revolutionary Russia: The Imperial Theaters and the State, 1897–1928" (Ph.D. diss., Princeton University, 1990), 79–118. The "imposters" comment and a formal declaration of a performance strike is recorded in RGIA, f. 497, op. 6, ed. khr. 5129, l. 3. For Nizhinskii's quote, see Nijinsky, *Diary*, 86.

36. "Konflikt v Gosudarstv[ennykh] teatrakh," *Teatr i iskusstvo* 51 (December 17, 1917): 847.
37. Vasilii Bezpalov, *Teatry v dni revoliutsii, 1917* (Leningrad: Academia, 1927), 30–31.
38. Lopukhov, *Shest'desiat let v balete*, 187–88.
39. V. P. Shkafer, *Sorok let na stsene russkoi opery: Vospominaniia, 1890–1930 gg.* (Leningrad: Izdatel'stvo Teatra Opery i Baleta imeni S. M. Kirova, 1936), 230.
40. Abram Gozenpud, *Ivan Ershov: Zhizn' i stsenicheskaia deiatel'nost': Issledovanie*, 2nd ed. (St. Petersburg: Kompozitor, 1999), 275.
41. "Khronika," *Teatr i iskusstvo* 52 (December 24, 1917): 862.
42. Chaliapin, *Man and Mask*, 252–68.
43. H. G. Wells, *Russia in the Shadows* (Westport, Conn.: Hyperion, 1973), 47
44. Chaliapin, *Man and Mask*, 264.

When he complained, he was told that he was unworthy of working there because of his gentry origins.[45] Ziloti, the concert impresario who had become the Mariinskii Theater's chief administrator under the Provisional Government, found himself jailed by the Cheka for refusing to turn over the keys to the tsar's box.[46] Both he and Komissarzhevskii thought it best to leave their country forever. Albert Coates, who had succeeded the late Eduard Napravnik as the Mariinskii's chief conductor in early 1917, threatened to halt any performance under his baton if his nominal new boss, the Bolshevik commissar of enlightenment Anatolii Lunacharskii, set foot in the theater. He also left, eventually settling in South Africa.[47] Sergei Kusevitskii (Koussevitzky), another accomplished conductor, fled in 1920, after the regime confiscated his fine musical library, and went on to become a famed director of the Boston Symphony.

Such reactions did not go unreciprocated in the new conditions. Rakhmaninov's music remained banned in his home country for many years, as did Stravinskii's and most of what Prokof'ev composed while abroad. Some of these composers' works were only performed in Russia in the early twenty-first century.[48] Artists who had achieved material success before 1917, the "bourgeois" Shaliapin among them, quickly found themselves classified as "former people" (*byvshie liudi*) and suffered all the discrimination, deprivations, and civic disabilities that went along with that peculiar Soviet category.[49] Stanislavskii lost his home, factory, and fortune, if not his renown and desire to continue serving his homeland's art as best h e could.[50] The great actress Mariia Ermolova found herself impoverished and confined to the attic of her spacious Moscow home, most of which was given over to her servants and the urban poor. In the hard winter months of 1918, she barely managed to avoid being drafted—at age sixty-four—to shovel snow.[51] The younger composer Nikolai Miaskovskii went to jail for refusing to perform the same task.[52] Aleksandr Tairov was officially cautioned for producing plays that Soviet censors identified as "the banner of the imperialist, reactionary bourgeoisie." This was a prelude to decades of official

---

45. Theodore Komisarjevsky, *Myself and the Theatre* (London: Heinemann, 1929), 11–12.
46. Charles F. Barber, *Lost in the Stars: The Forgotten Musical Life of Alexander Siloti* (Lanham, Md.: Scarecrow, 2002), 173; Fitzpatrick, *Commissariat of Enlightenment*, 110.
47. Fitzpatrick, *Commissariat of Enlightenment*, 118. Coates's appointment as chief conductor is noted in "Khronika," *Teatr i iskusstvo* 2 (January 8, 1917): 27.
48. Stravinskii's 1923 ballet *Les Noces*, for example, only received its Mariinskii Theater premiere in 2003.
49. Lopukhov, *Shest'desiat let v balete*, 187, recalled that "numerous" fellow artists fell into this category.
50. Jean Benedetti, *Stanislavski: A Biography* (London: Methuen, 1988), 235.
51. R. I. Ostrovskaia et al., *Mariia Ermolova* (Moscow: Russkaia kniga, 2001), 231.
52. Nelson, *Music for the Revolution*, 24.

trouble, which, as Shostakovich also experienced, included having his work personally trashed by Stalin.[53] An official of the new regime publicly charged that another theater director who stayed on after th e revolution was "a repellent manifestation of a class that has had its day, a sycophant [who] ... hates everything Communist, every value that the working class and the party inculcates [sic]."[54] These attitudes never fully di sappeared. As late as 1990 the Bol'shoi's artistic director, the choreographer Iurii Grigorovich, had to face challenges to his leadership from his theater's party cell, the secretary of which was a secondrate tenor no longer employed on the stage.[55]

Although the radical actor Iakov Maliutin recalled intense frustration because so few of his colleagues sympathized with the revolution, given their day-to-day experiences one might wonder whether he was truly sur prised.[56] At the same time Maliutin felt his disappointment, Lunacharskii suffered serious embarrassment when artists working in all media ignored his invitation to a state arts conference: of 120 figures invited, just five appeared. Only one of them, Meierkhol'd, was a theater artist.[57] In 1927—ten years after the revolution and despite a politically motivated purge of arts education faculties carried out in the meantime—just four M oscow Conservatory professors belonged t o the Communist Party. None were musicians and all taught recently added "social science" courses.[58] Indeed, the departure of artists belonging to younger generations, including Aleksandr Cherepnin, Mikhail and Ol'ga Chekhov, Mariia Uspenskaia (Ouspenskaya), Georgii Balanchivadze (George Balanchine), Aleksandra Danilova, Igor' Iushkevich (Youskevitch), Vladimir Horowitz, Rudol'f Nureev, Natal'ia Makarova, Valeryi Afanas'ev, Mstislav Rostropovich, Galina Vishnevskaia, Mikhail Baryshnikov, Andrei Tarkovskii, and Iurii Liubimov—to name only the most sensational cases from the realm of high culture—did little to indicate the emergence of a creative community receptive to communism.[59]

---

53. Marc Slonim, *Russian Theater: From the Empire to the Soviets* (Cleveland: World Publishing, 1961), 260–63. Stalin literally called Tairov's work "trash."

54. Quoted in Sheila Fitzpatrick, *Tear Off the Masks! Identity and Imposture in Twentieth-Century Russia* (Princeton: Princeton University Press, 2005), 59.

55. Anna Kisselgoff, "For the Bolshoi Ballet Director, Politics Looms as Large as Art," *New York Times*, July 11, 1990.

56. Ia. O. Maliutin, *Aktery moego pokoleniia* (Leningrad: Iskusstvo, 1959), 351.

57. Slonim, *Russian Theater*, 229. Alma Law and Mel Gordon, *Meyerhold, Eisenstein, and Biomechanics: Actor Training in Revolutionary Russia* (Jefferson, N.C.: McFarland, 1996), 27.

58. Nelson, *Music for the Revolution*, 160–61.

59. Cherepnin, a composer, fled Soviet power twice along with his father, the composer Nikolai Cherepnin—to independent Georgia in 1918 and again to France after Georgia's conquest by the Red Army in 1921. The Chekhovs (he was the playwright's nephew) divorced in 1919 and left separately. Ol'ga went to Germany in 1920 and became a famous screen actress adored by none other than Adolf Hitler and Joseph Goebbels. Mikhail left seven years later and ended up in Hollywood

Instead, in the words of a leading current Russian history textbook, they "defected to Europe and America in embarrassing numbers." A popular joke asked for a definition of a Soviet string quartet; the answer was a Soviet orchestra that had toured the West.[60] Liubimov, the late Soviet era's most famous stage director, told the Western press upon his departure in 1983: "I simply don't have the time to wait until these government officials finally arrive at an understanding of a culture that is worthy of my native land."[61] The phenomenon of artistic emigration continued, moreover, despite preventative and more than occasionally repressive measures taken by Soviet cultural and police authorities.

Russia's commercial theatrical culture disappeared for more than seventy years, until *glasnost'* tentatively allowed its reemergence.[62] All theaters were declared state property less than three weeks after the Bolshevik coup d'état—months before industry and most other private enterprises—and then either nationalized or placed under government financial control. In some cases, such as that of the Moscow Art Theater, their former proprietors were kept on in a management or advisory capacity, a gesture toward officially promised "autonomy." State-sponsored theatrical projects briefly experimented with some of the innovations advocated by the prerevolutionary avant-garde, but they failed to achieve much long-term success.[63] Meierkhol'd's early Soviet experimental

---

as a character actor and noted teacher of drama. Ouspenskaya defected during the Moscow Art Theater's 1923 tour of the United States. The twenty-year-old Balanchine and Danilova, along with two other young dancers on tour with them in the West in 1924, refused to return to the USSR and spent the rest of their lives abroad. Youskevitch immigrated to Monte Carlo in 1938 and later became a distinguished ballet teacher in New York. Horowitz spent much time in the West and ultimately settled in the United States in 1940. Nureev sought political asylum in Charles de Gaulle airport in Paris at the end of a 1961 tour, after being warned about having too much personal contact with the French. Makarova, a leading Mariinskii (Kirov) ballerina, defected in London in 1970. Afanas'ev, a pianist, followed suit two years later and became a Belgian citizen. Rostropovich and Vishnevskaia, a married conductor/cellist and soprano, immigrated to the United States for political reasons in 1974. Baryshnikov defected to the United States the same year. Tarkovskii, the preeminent postwar Soviet filmmaker, who also staged theatrical productions, went to Italy for professional reasons in 1982 and later requested asylum there. Liubimov, founder of Moscow's Theater on the Taganka, likewise went to work abroad in 1983 but did not return and was stripped of his citizenship. Antony Beevor, *The Mystery of Olga Chekhova* (New York: Viking, 2004), has argued that the actress may have been a spy for the Soviets during World War II but maintains that her motivation was to protect her family remaining in the USSR. In any case she tried to start a Hollywood career after the war and, when that failed, moved to West Germany rather than return to the Soviet Union. A number of film actors, including Ivan Mozzhukin and Mariia Ulianova, can be added to this list.

60. Catherine Evtuhov et al., *A History of Russia: Peoples, Legends, Events, Forces* (New York: Houghton Mifflin, 2004), 763.

61. Dusko Doder, "Soviet Director Is Fired After Staying in the West: Loss Is Major Blow for Avant-Garde Theater," *Washington Post*, March 7, 1984.

62. Beumers, "Commercial Enterprise," 1405–10, discusses this transition.

63. For discussions of these experiments, see James von Geldern, *Bolshevik Festivals, 1917–1920* (Berkeley and Los Angeles: University of California Press, 1993), and Richard Stites, *Revolutionary*

theaters and workshops quickly fell into disfavor and were closed down. Ironically, given the ideological circumstances, the main institution under his direction was dissolved for losing money.[64] Eventually the Soviet regime—as well as artists who wished to avoid difficult interactions with it—decided that culture should rigidly emphasize the classics or at least imitations of classical forms. "Back to Ostrovskii!" an official Soviet arts slogan declared as early as 1923. However uninspired it may have been, socialist realism was after all a kind of realism.

The urban upper and middle classes noted among prerevolutionary theater audiences either disappeared or were transformed beyond recognition by the events of 1917 and after. In the early days of the new regime, theater halls became the preserve of trade union members, Red Army soldiers, party officials, students, and others who received preferential treatment in ticket distribution and, in at least some cases, orders to attend.[65] In the words of the actor Aleksandr Usachev, "we played for a new spectator forged by the revolution. The old 'imperial' structure of theatrical life had disappeared into the irretrievable past."[66] According to Stanislavskii "the theater received a new mission: it was to open its doors to the widest stratum of spectators, for those millions of people who until that time did not have the possibility to make use of cultural satisfaction."[67] Given the palpable social diversity of audiences before 1917, who also numbered in the millions, this statement probably reflected the zeal of official cultural policy more than historical fact. But it did reveal its writer's view of the new situation.

Nevertheless, the "new" Soviet audiences turned out for many of the same works popular in tsarist times, though they were largely denied the sexual themes, gender role reversals, "decadent" subjects, and other politically taboo forms of entertainment. As Lynn Mally has found, both existing theaters that endured under Soviet state management and new enterprises parroting goals similar to those of the prerevolutionary popular theater movement "chose the same plays that had been common ... before the revolution." Lists of "suitable

---

Dreams: Utopian Vision and Experimental Life in the Russian Revolution (Oxford: Oxford University Press, 1989), 79–100.

64. Edward Braun, *The Theatre of Meyerhold: Revolution on the Modern Stage* (New York: Drama Book Specialists, 1979), 162. The theater, RSFSR (Russian Soviet Federated Socialist Republic) Theater No. 1, closed in September 1921. The New Economic Policy had withdrawn subsidies to theaters of its type and thus made its existence unjustifiable to the Moscow Soviet.

65. Chaliapin, *Man and Mask*, 245, noted this about some of his early Soviet-era audiences.

66. A. A. Usachev, *Povest' ob odnom aktere: Vospominaniia* (Leningrad: Gosudarstvennyi akademicheskii teatr dramy, 1935), 97.

67. K. S. Stanislavskii, *Moia zhizn' v iskusstve* (Moscow: Iskusstvo, 1983), 382.

plays" for performance—part of Soviet Russia's much stricter theatrical censorship regime—were dominated by nineteenth-century classics.[68] Gaideburov kept working at the Ligovskii People's House, now under state administration rather than the harassed and exiled Countess Panina's, with the same traditional repertoire.[69] Early Soviet film registered little divergence from the melodramatic and "bourgeois" themes that pervaded Russian cinema in its first, prerevolutionary decade, though, as in theaters, the risqué and "immoral" content vanished.[70] Overwhelmingly it was Chekhov and Ostrovskii, Chaikovskii and Rimskii-Korsakov whose works provided the backbone of Soviet cultural offerings. In 1940 and 1944, respectively, the Moscow and Leningrad (Petersburg) Conservatories, which had been nationalized along with all other Russian Musical Society institutions in July 1918, were symbolically named for the two composers to honor the centenaries of their births.

Regardless of communism's social goals, no amount of political or ideological control succeeded in the long-term "proletarianization" of Soviet theater audiences, most of whom represented (at least in the Soviet context) the urban middle and upper middle. A series of sociological surveys conducted from the 1960s through the 1980s found that white-collar employees and intellectuals accounted for some 70 percent of Soviet theatergoers, while only 5 percent were workers.[71] According to one analysis these results betrayed "broad similarity" to audiences in Britain and the United States.[72] Nor, despite heady Soviet claims, could the new regime succeed in making the performing arts available to appreciably greater numbers of people. In the late 1960s only 7.5 percent of the USSR's urban population attended the theater more than once a year.[73]

There has been no comprehensive study, but in its immediate post-Soviet experience Russia has succeeded in restoring something resembling its prerevolutionary cultural environment. The issues at the forefront of the scandal over *The*

---

68. Lynn Mally, *Revolutionary Acts: Amateur Theater and the Soviet State, 1917–1938* (Ithaca: Cornell University Press, 2000), 34–35.

69. Ibid., 7–8. According to Katerina Clark, *Petersburg, Crucible of Cultural Revolution* (Cambridge: Harvard University Press, 1995), 112, his "understanding of people's theater in Soviet Russia was virtually unaltered from his prerevolutionary position." For the fate of Countess Panina, see Adele Lindenmeyr, "The First Soviet Political Trial: Countess Sofia V. Panina Before the Petrograd Revolutionary Tribunal," *Russian Review* 60, no. 4 (2001): 505–25.

70. For an overview, see Denise Youngblood, *Movies for the Masses: Popular Cinema and Soviet Society in the 1920s* (Cambridge: Cambridge University Press, 1992).

71. Beumers, "Commercial Enterprise," 1412, relies on the most complete figures. Soviet social identities were often subjective, but the results of the surveys can at least be taken as an indication of how the Soviet government itself regarded the situation.

72. Mikhail Deza and Mervyn Matthews, "Soviet Theater Audiences," *Slavic Review* 34, no. 4 (1975): 723.

73. Ibid., 716. Unfortunately, no such studies exist for prerevolutionary Russia.

Children of Rosenthal in 2005 resembled those current a century earlier, when critics and government officials worried, among other issues, about the performing arts' potential to corrupt public morals. But like their tsarist antecedents, post-Soviet Russia's cultural purists are fighting a losing ba ttle. Ultimately Desiatnikov's opera was produced, no one involved was punished, Russian culture was not "cleansed," and at this writing the Bol'shoi is spending its billion-dollar renovation budget.

At the same time a few productions imbued with political subtexts have been appearing on Russia's state stages. A 1999 Mariinskii production of Prokof'ev's *Semen Kotko*, a socialist realist-style opera that extols a simple young soldier's fight against the White armies and their German supporters during the Russian Civil War, transforms its strident finale identifying the Bolshevik Revolution with freedom into an ironic comment on the bland conformity imposed by communism. In the production's last scene its entire cast shed their original period costumes for identical gray Mao suits and hold up copies of what appears to be the *Red Book*. In 2003 the main theater of provincial Saratov was reportedly scheduling the premiere of an opera called *Monica in the Kremlin*, a satirical work in which a character resembling U.S. President Bill Clinton's infamous paramour Monica Lewinsky ("Monika Levinson") arrives in Moscow on a spy mission to seduce the Russian president, "Krutin." After a comedy of errors, she is revealed to be a Russian double agent who has successfully carried out a mission to seduce and disgrace the president of the United States. At the end of the opera, she falls for "Krutin's" security chief. Russia's real-life president was said to be amused, though the opera's composer claimed that members of the presidential staff had warned him to "be careful."[74] A 2004 staging of *A Life for the Tsar*—the title of Glinka's opera now restored from such Soviet-era alternatives as *Ivan Susanin* (still used at the Bol'shoi), *A Life for the Soviet*, and *Hammer and Sickle*—portrayed the heroic martyr as an ordinary contemporary Russian eking out an exi stence and the invading Poles as ostentatious "new Russians" who bark into cell phones and inhabit a revealingly modern-looking Kremlin palace. Most other post-Soviet productions have avoided such political connotations, however mild, and there seems to be n either any call for th em nor, despite recent political developments, any serious pressure for productions flattering to the current government and its values. In another echo of prerevolutionary artistic inclinations and a potential portent of controversy given some

---

74. "Monica au Kremlin doit sortir en décembre 2003," *France-CEI*, August 17, 2003. The "be careful" admonition was reported in "Monica's Back—and This Time She's Stalking the Kremlin," *Guardian*, September 18, 2002.

of the bleaker moments in Russia's twentieth-century history, its main operatic stages again present healthy amounts of Wagner. Eight of the composer's ten mature works—several of which had not been heard in Russia since before World War I—had appeared in much heralded new productions by May 2005.

Just as the prerevolutionary art world worried about market pressures and attracting top talent, so have the post-Soviet theaters sought ways to adapt to the times. Lucrative foreign tours and foreign contracts for star artists have direct prerevolutionary precedents and are now updated and expanded by faster means of transportation and communication. The frenetic foreign touring activity of Russia's major opera and ballet companies, along with their huge popularity and high prices abroad, evokes memories of the Ballets Russes. At home marketed ticket sales, commercial advertising, private loans, charitable donations, regular performance festivals, gala benefits (for ballet dancers only at this writing), and, resuming at the Mariinskii in the 2007–8 season, subscription ticket sales all figure prominently in financing the new Russia's performing arts culture. So do some rather idiosyncratic measures, such as the Mariinskii Theater's continuing insistence on charging foreign tourists several times more than Russians.

Imperial symbolism has also made a strong comeback. The Soviet penchant for renaming culturally significant public spaces has encountered substantial reversals in the new Russia. Just as Leningrad reverted to its pre–World War I name, after 1991 the Kirov and Pushkin Theaters quickly became the Mariinskii and Aleksandrinskii again, even if the Mariinskii long used its old Soviet designation on tours abroad to benefit in a very capitalist way from name recognition.[75] In 1995 the gilded imperial crown that had adorned the Mariinskii's tsar's box before the revolution reappeared as the result of private sponsorship, as did its imperial coats of arms.

Contemporary Russian popular culture—which like most modern popular cultures tends to be national or international—also resounds with echoes of tsarist times. Just as prerevolutionary theaters presented eager audiences with

---

75. The Mariinskii was renamed the National Academy of Opera and Ballet in 1920 and then, in 1935, for the Soviet party boss of Leningrad Sergei Kirov, who had been mysteriously assassinated late in the previous year. After a period of redesignation as the State Theater of Drama, in 1937 the Aleksandrinkii was renamed for the famed nineteenth-century writer Aleksandr Pushkin to commemorate the centenary of his death. The Soviet symbolism is, however, fading. During a 2001 visit to the John F. Kennedy Center for the Performing Arts, a Washington doyenne was overheard praising a young "Kirov" dancer whose talent she believed to have sprung, however improbably, from having "danced with Kirov himself." The Soviets converted the "French" Mikhailovskii Theater for use as a lesser opera and ballet venue and renamed it for the composer Modest Musorgskii, a designation that it retains along with the sometimes used Malyi ("Small"). Moscow's state theaters retained their apolitical and noncontroversial prerevolutionary names, Bol'shoi ("Great") and Malyi ("Small").

sex, crime, moral intrigue, and violence, so have modern Russians begun to embrace them in a broad acceptance of what was at least publicly unthinkable in the Soviet cultural experience. One alliterative comment recently asserted that "Russian theater has fallen into a state of stress and landed in a swamp of sin."[76] Outside the more traditional forms, the years since 1991 have seen an explosion of "erotica" (pornography remains formally illegal), prostitute-filled bars and clubs, ever more explicit advertisements and venues for "*striptiz,*" and film and television industries racing to present updated versions of the same risqué subjects common on prerevolutionary stages and screens. One television station has courted viewers by featuring an attractive female reporter who takes off her clothes while delivering the news. The teenage pop duo Tatu, whose manager is rumored to have started professional life as a child psychologist, rocketed to international fame by affecting a lesbian chic. The violent, profane, sexualized—and thoroughly entertaining—American gangster series *The Sopranos* has appeared in Russia on prime time network television.

As we draw further and further away from 1991, Russia seems to be returning to the more permissive, more interesting, more diverse, and less politicized performing arts culture that it enjoyed before 1917. Regardless of how that culture is best defined, many of the early twenty-first-century Russians who produce and consume it are again indulging in entertainment for its own sake, devoting increasing amounts of energy and resources to creativity and leisure, and fueling a commercial milieu that, whatever its artistic merits or lack thereof, is both reflecting and contributing to the reemergence of a civil society. Despite ominous signals to the contrary, this momentum might continue.

76. Nina Velekhova, "The State of Russian Theater in the 1990s," in *Eastern European Theater after the Iron Curtain,* ed. Kalina Stefanova (Amsterdam: Harwood, 2000), 209.

Bibliography

PRIMARY SOURCES

Archives

Gosudarstvennaia Teatral'naia Biblioteka Sankt Peterburga (GTB SPb)
Gosudarstvennyi Tsentral'nyi Teatral'nyi Muzei imeni A. A. Bakhrushina (GTSTMB)
Rossiiskii Gosudarstvennyi Arkhiv Literatury i Iskusstva (RGALI)
Rossiiskii Gosudarstvennyi Istoricheskii Arkhiv (RGIA)
Sankt Peterburgskii Gosudarstvennyi Teatral'nyi Muzei (SPb GTM)

Periodicals

Apollon
Birzhevye vedomosti
Daily Telegraph
Ezhegodnik Imperatorskikh teatrov
Financial Times
Guardian
Independent
Maski
Mir iskusstva
New York Times
Novaia zhizn'
Novoe vremia
Obozrenie teatrov
Pereval
Peterburgskaia gazeta
Rampa i zhizn'
Rech'
Sankt Peterburgskie vedomosti
Slovo
St. Petersburg Times
Teatr
Teatral'naia Rossiia
Teatr i iskusstvo
The Times (London)
Vesy
Washington Post
Za pravdu
Zhizn' i iskusstvo
Zolotoe runo
Zritel'

Memoirs and Documentary Collections

Al'tshuller, A. Ia., ed. *Vera Fedorovna Komissarzhevskaia: Pis'ma aktrisy, vospominaniia o nei, materialy*. Leningrad: Iskusstvo, 1964.

Baring, Maurice. *A Year in Russia*. New York: Dutton, 1907.

Belyi, Andrei [Boris Bugaev]. *Mezhdu dvukh revoliutsii*. Moscow: Khudozhestvennaia literatura, 1990.

Benua, Aleksandr [Alexandre Benois]. *Moi vospominaniia*. 2 vols. Moscow: Zakharov, 2003.

Bertenson, V. B. *Za 30 let (listki iz vospominanii)*. St. Petersburg: n.p., 1914.

Bezpalov, Vasilii. *Teatry v dni revoliutsii, 1917*. Leningrad: Academia, 1927.

Blok, A. A. *Sobranie sochinenii*. 8 vols. Moscow: Gosudarstvennoe izdatel'stvo khudozhestvennoi literatury, 1960–63.

———. *Zapisnye knizhki*. Moscow: Izdatel'stvo khudozhestvennoi literatury, 1965.

Briantsev, A. A. *Vospominaniia, stat'i, vystupleniia, dnevniki, pis'ma*. Moscow: VTO, 1979.

Brushtein, Aleksandra Ia. *Stranitsy proshlogo*. Leningrad: Iskusstvo, 1952.

Chaliapin, Feodor. *Man and Mask: Forty Years in the Life of a Singer*. Translated by Phyllis Mégroz. New York: Knopf, 1932.

———. *Pages from My Life: An Autobiography*. Translated by H. M. Buck. New York: Harper and Brothers, 1927.

Chulkov, Georgii. *Gody stranstvii*. Moscow: Ellis Lak, 1999.

Duncan, Isadora. *My Life*. New York: Boni and Liveright, 1927.

Findeizen, N. F. *Ocherk deiatel'nosti S.-Peterburgskogo otdeleniia Imperatorskogo russkogo muzykal'nogo obshchestva (1859–1909)*. St. Petersburg: Tipografiia Glavnogo Upravleniia Udelov, 1909.

Fokine, Michel [Mikhail Fokin]. *Fokine: Memoirs of a Ballet Master*. Translated by Vitale Fokine. Boston: Little, Brown, 1961.

———. *Protiv techeniia: Vospominaniia baletmeistera. Stat'i, pis'ma*. Leningrad: Iskusstvo, 1962.

Gaideburov, P. P. *Literaturnoe nasledie. Vospominaniia. Stat'i. Rezhisserskie eksplikatsii. Vystupleniia*. Moscow: VTO, 1977.

Gardin, V. R. *Zhizn' i trud artista*. Moscow: Iskusstvo, 1960.

Gnedich, P. P. *Kniga zhizni: Vospominaniia, 1855–1918*. Moscow: Agraf, 2000.

Gorin-Goriainov, B. A. *Aktery: Iz vospominaniia*. Moscow: Iskusstvo, 1947.

Gor'kii, Maksim. [A. M. Peshkov]. *Polnoe sobranie sochinenii*. 25 vols. Moscow: Gosudarstvennoe Izdatel'stvo khudozhestvennoi literatury, 1968. *See also* Gorky, Maxim.

———. *Zhizn' Klima Samgina*. 4 vols. Moscow: Sovetskii pisatel', 1947.

Gorky, Maxim. *Children of the Sun*. Translated by Stephen Mulrine. London: Hern, 2000. *See also* Gor'kii, Maksim.

Grigoriev, S. L. *The Diaghilev Ballet, 1909–1929*. Translated by Vera Bowen. Harmondsworth: Penguin, 1960.

Iur'ev, Iu. M. *Zapiski*. 2 vols. Leningrad: Iskusstvo, 1963.

Ivanov, Viacheslav. *Po zvezdam*. St. Petersburg: n. p., 1909.

Karsavina, Tamara. *Theatre Street: The Reminiscences of Tamara Karsavina*. New York: Dutton, 1931.

Khodotov, N. N. *Blizkoe—dalekoe*. Leningrad: Iskusstvo, 1962.

Komisarjevsky, Theodore [F. F. Komissarzhevskii]. *Myself and the Theatre*. London: Heinemann, 1929.

Korchagina-Aleksandrovskaia, E. P. *"Stranitsy zhizni," stat'i i rechi, vospominaniia*. Moscow: Iskusstvo, 1955.
Kshessinska, Mathilde [Matil'da Kshesinskaia]. *Souvenirs de la Kschessinska, prima ballerina du Théâtre impérial de Saint-Pétersbourg*. Paris: Plon, 1960.
———. *Vospominaniia*. Moscow: Olimp, 2002.
Legat, Nicolas [N. G. Legat]. *Ballet Russe: Memoirs of Nicolas Legat*. Translated by Sir Paul Dukes. London: Methuen, 1939.
Lieven, Prince Peter. *The Birth of the Ballets-Russes*. Translated by L. Zarine. New York: Dover, 1973.
Litvin, Feliia. *Moia zhizn' i moe iskusstvo*. Leningrad: Muzyka, 1967.
Lopukhov, Fedor. *Shest'desiat let v balete: Vospominaniia i zapiski baletmeistera*. Moscow: Iskusstvo, 1966.
Maliutin, Ia. O. *Aktery moego pokoleniia*. Leningrad: Iskusstvo, 1959.
Meierkhol'd, Vsevolod. *Perepiska, 1896–1939*. Moscow: Iskusstvo, 1976.
Mgebrov, A. A. *Zhizn' v teatre*. 2 vols. Leningrad: Academia, 1929.
Michurina-Samoilova, V. A. *Shest'desiat let v iskusstve*. Leningrad: Iskusstvo, 1946.
Mossolov [Mosolov], A. A. *At the Court of the Last Tsar: Being the Memoirs of A. A. Mossolov, Head of the Court Chancellery, 1900–1916*. Translated by E. W. Dickes. London: Methuen, 1935.
Nabokov, Vladimir. *Pnin*. New York: Vintage, 1989.
Napravnik, E. F. *Avtobiograficheskie, tvoricheskie materialy, dokumenty, pis'ma*. Leningrad: Gosudarstvennoe muzykal'noe izdatel'stvo, 1959.
Narokov, Mikhail S. *Biografiia moego pokoleniia: Teatral'nye memuary*. Moscow: VTO, 1956.
Nemirovitch-Danchenko, Vladimir. *My Life in the Russian Theatre*. Translated by John Cournos. London: Bles, 1937.
Nietzsche, Friedrich. *Basic Writings of Nietzsche*. Translated and edited by Walter Kaufmann. New York: Random House, 2000.
Nijinska, Bronislava. *Early Memoirs*. Translated by Irina Nijinska and Jean Rawlinson. New York: Holt, Rinehart, and Winston, 1981.
Nijinsky [Nizhinskaia], Romola. *Nijinsky*. New York: Simon and Schuster, 1934.
Nijinsky, Vaslav. *The Diary of Vaslav Nijinsky*. Translated by Romola Nijinsky. London: Quartet Encounters, 1991.
Orlenev, Pavel [P. N. Orlov]. *Zhizn' i tvorchestvo russkogo aktera Pavla Orleneva opisannye im samim*. Moscow: Academia, 1931.
Paléologue, Maurice. *An Ambassador's Memoirs*. 3 vols. Translated by F. A. Holt. London: Hutchinson, 1923–25.
Patrusheva, N. G. *Tsenzura v Rossii v kontse XIX–nachale XX veka: Sbornik vospominanii*. St. Petersburg: Bulanin, 2003.
Perestiani, I. N. *75 let zhizni v iskusstve*. Moscow: Iskusstvo, 1962.
Petipa, Marius. *Materialy. Vospominaniia. Stat'i*. Leningrad: Iskusstvo, 1971.
Petrov, N. V. *50 i 500*. Moscow: VTO, 1950.
Plany i tseny v Imperatorskikh teatrakh. St. Petersburg: Tipografiia Imperatorskikh Sankt Peterburgskikh teatrov, 1913.
Pleshcheev, A. A. *Pod seniiu kulis*. . . . Paris: VAL, 1936.
Pokhitonov, D. I. *Iz proshlogo russkoi opery*. Leningrad: VTO, 1949.
Prokof'ev, Sergei S. *Avtobiografiia*. Moscow: Sovetskii Kompozitor, 1982.
Prygunov, M. "Teatr V. F. Komissarzhevskoi." *Sbornik pamiati V. F. Komissarzhevskoi*. Moscow: GIKL, 1931.

Rimskii-Korsakov, N. A. *Letopis' moei muzykal'noi zhizni, 1844–1906.* St. Petersburg: Glazunov, 1909. See also Rimsky-Korsakov, Nikolay.
Rimsky-Korsakov, Nikolay. *My Musical Life.* Translated by Judah A. Joffe. New York: Knopf, 1923. See also Rimskii-Korsakov, N. A.
Serebrov, A. [A. N. Tikhonov]. *Vremia i liudi: Vospominaniia, 1898–1905.* Moscow: Moskovskii rabochii, 1955.
Shaliapin, Fedor. *Literaturnoe nasledstvo. Pis'ma. Stat'i. Vyskazyvaniia. Vospominaniia o F. I. Shaliapine.* 2 vols. Moscow: Iskusstvo, 1960. See also Chaliapin, Feodor.
———. *Povesti o zhizni.* Moscow: Iskusstvo, 1960.
Shchepkina-Kupernik, T. L. *Iz vospominanii o russkom teatre.* Moscow: Iskusstvo, 1956.
———. *Teatr v moei zhizni.* Moscow: Iskusstvo, 1948.
Shkafer, V. P. *Sorok let na stsene russkoi opery: Vospominaniia, 1890–1930 gg.* Leningrad: Izdatel'stvo Teatra Opery i Baleta imeni S. M. Kirova, 1936.
Shostakovich, Dmitri. *Testimony: The Memoirs of Dmitri Shostakovich.* Edited by Solomon Volkov and translated by Antonina W. Bouis. New York: Harper and Row, 1979.
Skorobogatov, K. [V.] *Zhizn' i stsena.* Leningrad: Lenizdat, 1970.
Solov'ev, Vladimir. *Sobranie sochinenii.* 12 vols. St. Petersburg: Prosveshchenie, 1911–14.
Stanislavskii, Konstantin[K. S. Alekseev]. *Moia zhizn' v iskusstve.* Moscow: Iskusstvo, 1983. See also Stanislavsky, Konstantin.
Stanislavsky, Konstantin[K. S. Alekseev]. *My Life in Art.* New York, 1956. See also Stanislavskii, Konstantin.
Stark, E. A. *Starinnyi teatr.* St. Petersburg: Izdanie N. I. Butkovskoi, 1912.
Steklov, Iurii, ed. *Krizis teatra: Sbornik statei.* St. Petersburg: Problemy iskusstva, 1908.
Suvorin, A. S. *Dnevnik.* Moscow: Novosti, 1992.
Svetlov, Valerian. *Sovremennyi balet.* St. Petersburg: Tovarichestvo R. Golike i A. Vil'borg, 1911.
Tairov, Aleksandr. *Zapiski rezhissera.* Moscow: GITIS, 2000.
"Teatr": *Kniga o novom teatre. Sbornik statei.* St. Petersburg: n.p., 1908.
Teliakovskii, V. A. *Dnevniki direktora Imperatorskikh teatrov, 1898–1901: Moskva.* Moscow: Artist. Rezhisser. Teatr., 1998.
———. *Dnevniki direktora Imperatorskikh teatrov, 1901–1903: Sankt-Peterburg.* Moscow: Artist. Rezhisser. Teatr., 2002.
———. *Vospominaniia.* Leningrad: Iskusstvo, 1965.
Tiraspol'skaia, N. L. *Iz proshlogo russkoi stseny.* Moscow: VTO, 1950.
———. *Zhizn' aktrisy.* Leningrad: Iskusstvo, 1962.
Tolstoi, Lev. *Sobranie sochinenii.* 21 vols. Moscow: Gosudarstvennoe izdatel'stvo khudozhestvennoi literatury, 1960–64.
Trudy pervogo Vserossiiskogo s"ezda stsenicheskikh deiatelei, 9.3–23.3 1897. 2 vols. St. Petersburg: Nadezhda, 1898.
Trudy Vserossiiskogo s"ezda deitalei narodnogo teatra v Moskve, 27 dekabria 1915–5 ianvaria 1916. Petrograd: Tipografiia L. Ia. Ganzburga, 1919.
Usachev, A. A. *Povest' ob odnom aktere: Vospominaniia.* Leningrad: Gosudarstvennyi akademicheskii teatr dramy, 1935.
Vassilyev, A. T. *The Ochrana: The Russian Secret Police.* London: Harrap, 1930.
Velizarii, M. I. *Put' provintsial'noi aktrisy.* Leningrad: Iskusstvo, 1938.
Verigina, V. P. *Vospominaniia.* Leningrad: Iskusstvo, 1974.
Villari, Luigi. *Russia of To-Day.* Boston: Millet, 1910.
Volkonskii, Prince Sergei. *Moi vospominaniia.* Moscow: Iskusstvo, 1992.
———. *Rodina: Vospominaniia.* Moscow: Zakharov, 2002.

Yastrebtsev, V. V. *Reminiscences of Rimsky-Korsakov*. Translated by Florence Jonas. New York: Columbia University Press, 1985.

SECONDARY SOURCES

Adams, Laura L. "Modernity, Postcolonialism, and Theatrical Form in Uzbekistan." *Slavic Review* 64, no. 2 (2005): 333–54.
Al'tshuller, A. Ia., ed. *Ocherki istorii russkoi teatral'noi kritiki*. Leningrad: Iskusstvo, 1975.
———, ed. *Pervaia russkaia revoliutsiia i teatr: Stat'i i materialy*. Moscow: Iskusstvo, 1956.
Al'tshuller, A. Ia., et al., eds. *Russkii teatr i dramaturgiia epokhi revoliutsii, 1905–1907 godov: Sbornik nauchnykh trudov*. Leningrad: LGITMiK, 1987.
Al'tshuller, A. Ia., et al., eds. *Russkii teatr i dramaturgiia nachala XX veka : Sbornik nauchnykh trudov*. Leningrad: LGITMiK, 1984.
Andreeva, M. I., et al., eds. *Russkii dramaticheskii teatr: Entsiklopediia*. Moscow: Bol'shaia Rossiiskaia Entsiklopediia, 2001.
Ascher, Abraham. *The Revolution of 1905: Authority Restored*. Stanford: Stanford University Press, 1992.
———. *The Revolution of 1905: Russia in Disarray*. Stanford: Stanford University Press, 1988.
Baer, Marc. *Theatre and Disorder in Late Georgian London*. Oxford: Clarendon, 1992.
Balme, Christopher B. *Decolonizing the Stage: Theatrical Syncretism and Post-Colonial Drama*. Oxford: Clarendon, 1999.
Balmuth, Daniel. *Censorship in Russia, 1865–1905*. Washington, D.C.: University Press of America, 1979.
Balzer, Harley D., ed. *Russia's Missing Middle Class: The Professions in Russian History*. Armonk, N.Y.: M. E. Sharpe, 1996.
Barber, Charles F. *Lost in the Stars: The Forgotten Musical Life of Alexander Siloti*. Lanham, Md.: Scarecrow, 2002.
Bartlett, Rosamund. *Wagner and Russia*. Cambridge: Cambridge University Press, 1995.
Becker, Seymour. *Nobility and Privilege in Late Imperial Russia*. DeKalb: Northern Illinois University Press, 1985.
Beevor, Antony. *The Mystery of Olga Chekhova*. New York: Viking, 2004.
Benedetti, Jean, ed. *The Moscow Art Theatre Letters*. London: Methuen, 1991.
———. *Stanislavski: A Life*. London: Methuen, 1988.
Bergson, Henri. *L'Évolution créatrice*. Paris: Presses universitaires de France, 1966.
Beumers, Birgit. "Commercial Enterprise on the Stage: Changes in Russian Theatre Management Between 1986 and 1996." *Europe-Asia Studies* 48, no. 8 (1996): 1403–16.
Bhabha, Homi K. *The Location of Culture*. New York: Routledge, 1994.
Billington, James H. *The Icon and the Axe: An Interpretive History of Russian Culture*. New York: Knopf, 1966.
Bogdanov-Berezovskii, V. M. *Leningradskii gosudarstvennyi akademicheskii ordena Lenina teatr opery i baleta im. S. M. Kirova*. Leningrad: Iskusstvo, 1959.
Boiarskii, Ia. O., ed. *Sto let: Aleksandrinskii teatr—teatr gosdramy, 1832–1932. Sbornik stat'ei*. Leningrad: Direktsiia Leningradskikh gosudarstvennykh teatrov, 1932.
Bonnell, Victoria. *Roots of Rebellion: Workers' Politics and Organizations in St. Petersburg and Moscow, 1900–1914*. Berkeley and Los Angeles: University of California Press, 1983.
Borovsky, Victor. *Chaliapin: A Critical Biography*. New York: Knopf, 1988.

———. *A Triptych from the Russian Theatre: An Artistic Biography of the Komissarzhevskys.* Iowa City: University of Iowa Press, 2001.
Bourdieu, Pierre. *Distinction: A Social Critique of the Judgement of Taste.* Translated by Richard Nice. Cambridge: Harvard University Press, 1984.
Bradley, Joseph. "Subjects into Citizens: Societies, Civil Society, and Autocracy in Tsarist Russia." *American Historical Review* 107, no. 4 (2002): 1094–123.
Braun, Edward. *The Theatre of Meyerhold: Revolution on the Modern Stage.* New York: Drama Book Specialists, 1979.
Braun, Kazimierz. *A History of Polish Theater, 1939–1989: Spheres of Captivity and Freedom.* Westport, Conn.: Greenwood, 1996.
Brooks, Jeffrey. *When Russia Learned to Read: Literacy and Popular Literature, 1861–1917.* Princeton: Princeton University Press, 1985.
Buckler, Julie A. *The Literary Lorgnette: Attending Opera in Imperial Russia.* Stanford: Stanford University Press, 2000.
———. *Mapping St. Petersburg: Imperial Text and Cityshape.* Princeton: Princeton University Press, 2005.
Burian, Jarka M. *Modern Czech Theatre: Reflector and Conscience of a Nation.* Iowa City: University of Iowa Press, 2000.
Carlson, Marvin. *Theatre Semiotics: Signs of Life.* Bloomington: Indiana University Press, 1990.
Carnicke, Sharon M. "The Theatrical Instinct: A Study of the Work of Nikolaj Evreinov in Early Twentieth-Century Russia." Ph.D. diss., Columbia University, 1979.
Clark, Katerina. *Petersburg, Crucible of Cultural Revolution.* Cambridge: Harvard University Press, 1995.
Clayton, J. Douglas. *Pierrot in Petrograd: The Commedia dell'Arte/Balagan in Twentieth-Century Russian Theatre and Drama.* Montreal: McGill-Queen's University Press, 1993.
Clowes, Edith W., Samuel D. Kassow, and James L. West, eds. *Between Tsar and People: Educated Society and the Quest for Public Identity in Late Imperial Russia.* Princeton: Princeton University Press, 1991.
Conquest, Robert. *The Great Terror: A Reassessment.* New York: Oxford University Press, 1990.
Conroy, Mary Schaeffer, ed. *Emerging Democracy in Late Imperial Russia: Case Studies on Local Self-Government (the Zemstvos), State Duma Elections, the Tsarist Government, and the State Council Before and During World War I.* Niwot: University of Colorado Press, 1998.
Crow, Brian, with Chris Banfield. *An Introduction to Post-Colonial Theatre.* Cambridge: Cambridge University Press, 1996.
Danilov, S. S. *Ocherki po istorii russkogo dramaticheskogo teatra.* Moscow: Gosudarstvennyi Nauchno-Issledovatel'skii Institut Teatra i Muzyki, 1948.
Davis, Jim, and Victor Emeljanow. *Reflecting the Audience: London Theatregoing, 1840–1880.* Iowa City: University of Iowa Press, 2001.
Degen, Arsen, and Igor Stupnikov, eds. *Peterburgskii balet, 1903–2003: Spravochnoe izdanie.* St. Petersburg: Baltiskii dom, 2003.
Deza, Mikhail, and Mervyn Matthews. "Soviet Theater Audiences." *Slavic Review,* 34, no. 4 (1975): 716–30.
Donald, Moira. "Russia, 1905: The Forgotten Revolution." In *Reinterpreting Revolution in Twentieth-Century Europe,* edited by Moira Donald and Tim Rees, 41–54. New York: St. Martin's, 2001.

Donald, Moira, and Tim Rees, eds. *Reinterpreting Revolution in Twentieth-Century Europe.* New York: St. Martin's, 2001.
Eaton, Katherine Bliss, ed. *Enemies of the People: The Destruction of Soviet Literary, Theater, and Film Arts in the 1930s.* Evanston: Northwestern University Press, 2002.
Elizarova, N. A. *Teatry Sheremetevykh.* Moscow: Iskusstvo, 1944.
Emmons, Terrence. "Russia's Banquet Campaign." *California Slavic Studies* 10 (1977): 45–86.
Engelstein, Laura. *Castration and the Heavenly Kingdom: A Russian Folktale.* Ithaca: Cornell University Press, 2003.
———. *The Keys to Happiness: Sex and the Search for Modernity in Fin-de-Siècle Russia.* Ithaca: Cornell University Press, 1992.
Engelstein, Laura, and Stephanie Sadler, eds. *Self and Story in Russian History.* Ithaca: Cornell University Press, 2000.
Erenberg, Lewis A. *Steppin' Out: New York Nightlife and the Transformation of American Culture, 1890–1930.* Westport, Conn.: Greenwood, 1981.
Evtuhov, Catherine, et al. *A History of Russia: Peoples, Legends, Events, Forces.* New York: Houghton Mifflin, 2004.
Fay, Laurel E. *Shostakovich: A Life.* New York: Oxford University Press, 2005.
Figes, Orlando. *Natasha's Dance: A Cultural History of Russia.* New York: Metropolitan, 2002.
———. *A People's Tragedy: The Russian Revolution, 1891–1924.* New York: Penguin, 1997.
Figes, Orlando, and Boris Kolonitskii. *Interpreting the Russian Revolution: The Language and Symbols of 1917.* New Haven: Yale University Press, 1999.
Fitzpatrick, Sheila. *The Commissariat of Enlightenment: Soviet Organization of Education and the Arts Under Lunacharsky, October 1917–1921.* Cambridge: Cambridge University Press, 1970.
———. *Tear Off the Masks! Identity and Imposture in Twentieth-Century Russia.* Princeton: Princeton University Press, 2005.
Fitzpatrick, Sheila, and Lynne Viola, eds. *A Researcher's Guide to Sources on Soviet Social History in the 1930s.* Armonk, N.Y.: M. E. Sharpe, 1990.
Frame, Murray. "Commercial Theatre and Professionalization in Late Imperial Russia." *Historical Journal* 48, no. 4 (2005).
———. "'Freedom of the Theatres': The Abolition of the Russian Imperial Theatre Monopoly." *Slavonic and East European Review* 83, no. 2 (2005).
———. *The St. Petersburg Imperial Theatres: Stage and State in Revolutionary Russia, 1900–1920.* Greensboro, N.C.: McFarland, 2000.
———. *School for Citizens: Theatre and Civil Society in Imperial Russia.* New Haven: Yale University Press, 2006.
———. "Theatre and Revolution in 1917: The Case of the Petrograd State Theatres." *Revolutionary Russia* 12, no. 1 (1999).
Frierson, Cathy A. *All Russia Is Burning! A Cultural History of Fire and Arson in Late Imperial Russia.* Seattle: University of Washington Press, 2002.
Galai, Shmuel. *The Liberation Movement in Russia, 1900–1905.* Cambridge: Cambridge University Press, 1972.
Garafola, Lynn. *Diaghilev's Ballets Russes.* New York: Oxford University Press, 1989.
Gasparov, Boris. *Five Operas and a Symphony: Word and Music in Russian Culture.* New Haven: Yale University Press, 2005.
Gauss, Rebecca B. "Lydia Borisovna Yavorskaya: Her Life, Her Work, Her Times." M.A. thesis, University of Colorado, 1992.

Geifman, Anna. *Thou Shalt Kill: Revolutionary Terrorism in Russia, 1894–1917*. Princeton: Princeton University Press, 1993.

Geldern, James von. *Bolshevik Festivals, 1917–1920*. Berkeley and Los Angeles: University of California Press, 1993.

George, Arthur, and Elena George. *St. Petersburg: Russia's Window to the Future, The First Three Centuries*. Lanham, Md.: Taylor, 2003.

Gladkov, Aleksandr. *Meierkhol'd*. 2 vols. Moscow: Soiuz teatral'nikh deiatelei, 1990.

Golub, Spencer. *Evreinov: The Theatre of Paradox and Transformation*. Ann Arbor: UMI Research, 1984.

———. *The Recurrence of Fate: Theatre and Memory in Twentieth-Century Russia*. Iowa City: University of Iowa Press, 1994.

Gorchakov, N. A. *The Theater in Soviet Russia*. Translated by Edgar Lehrman. New York: Columbia University Press, 1957.

Gozenpud, Abram. *Ivan Ershov: Zhizn' i stsenicheskaia deiatel'nost': Issledovanie*. 2nd ed. St. Petersburg: Kompozitor, 1999.

Green, Michael, ed. and trans. *The Russian Symbolist Theater: An Anthology of Plays and Critical Texts*. Ann Arbor: Ardis, 1986.

Habermas, Jürgen. *The Structural Transformation of the Public Sphere: An Inquiry into a Category of Bourgeois Society*. Translated by Thomas Burger. Cambridge: MIT Press, 1989.

Haimson, Leopold, ed. *The Politics of Rural Russia, 1905–1914*. Bloomington: Indiana University Press, 1979.

———. "The Problem of Social Stability in Urban Russia, 1905–1914." *Slavic Review* 23, no. 4 (1964), and 24, no. 1 (1965).

Harcave, Sidney. *First Blood: The Revolution of 1905*. New York: Macmillan, 1964.

Hemmings, F. W. J. *Theatre and State in France, 1760–1905*. Cambridge: Cambridge University Press, 1994.

Henry, Barbara. "Theatrical Parody at the Krivoe zerkalo: Russian 'Teatr Miniatyur,' 1908–1931." D.Phil. thesis, Oxford University, 1996.

Herlihy, Patricia. *The Alcoholic Empire: Vodka and Politics in Late Imperial Russia*. New York: Oxford University Press, 2002.

Houchin, John H. *Censorship of the American Theatre in the Twentieth Century*. Ithaca: Cornell University Press, 2003.

Hunt, Lynn. *Politics, Culture, and Class in the French Revolution*. Berkeley and Los Angeles: University of California Press, 1984.

Iankovskii, M. O. *Rimskii-Korsakov i revoliutsiia 1905 goda*. Moscow: Gosudarstvennoe muzykal'noe izdatel'stvo, 1950.

Jahn, Hubertus. "Fun, Leisure, and Entertainment in Russian History." *Kritika: Explorations in Russian and Eurasian History* 6, no. 4 (2005).

———. *Patriotic Culture in Russia During World War I*. Cambridge: Cambridge University Press, 1995.

Jelavich, Peter. *Munich and Theatrical Modernism: Politics, Playwriting, and Performance, 1890–1914*. Cambridge: Harvard University Press, 1985.

Kara, S. *Varlamov*. Leningrad: Iskusstvo, 1969.

Kassow, Samuel D. *Students, Professors, and the State in Tsarist Russia*. Berkeley and Los Angeles: University of California Press, 1989.

Kennedy, Emmet. *A Cultural History of the French Revolution*. New Haven: Yale University Press, 1989.

Kennedy, Emmet, et al. *Theatre, Opera, and Audiences in Revolutionary Paris: Analysis and Repertory*. Westport, Conn.: Greenwood, 1996.
Kershaw, Baz. *The Politics of Performance: Radical Theater as Cultural Intervention*. New York: Routledge, 1992.
Khaichenko, G. A. *Russkii narodnyi teatr kontsa XIX–nachala XX veka*. Moscow: Nauka, 1975.
Kholodov, E. G., et al., eds. *Istoriia russkogo dramaticheskogo teatra*. 7 vols. Moscow: Iskusstvo, 1977–87.
Korros, Alexandra. *A Reluctant Parliament: Stolypin, Nationalism, and the Politics of the Russian Imperial State Council, 1906–1911*. Lanham, Md.: Rowman and Littlefield, 2002.
Kotz, David M., and Fred Weir. *Revolution from Above: The Demise of the Soviet System*. New York: Routledge, 1997.
Kruger, Loren. *The Drama of South Africa: Plays, Pageants, and Publics Since 1910*. New York: Routledge, 1999.
———. *Post-Imperial Brecht: Politics and Performance, East and South*. Berkeley and Los Angeles: University of California Press, 2004.
Kuromiya, Hiroaki. "Guide to Émigré and Dissident Memoir Literature." In *A Researcher's Guide to Sources on Soviet Social History in the 1930s*, edited by Sheila Fitzpatrick and Lynne Viola, 255–67. Armonk, N.Y.: M. E. Sharpe, 1990.
———. "Soviet Memoirs as a Historical Source." In *A Researcher's Guide to Sources on Soviet Social History in the 1930s*, edited by Sheila Fitzpatrick and Lynne Viola, 233–54. Armonk, N.Y.: M. E. Sharpe, 1990.
Lauchlan, Iain. *Russian Hide-and-Seek: The Tsarist Secret Police in St. Petersburg, 1906–1914*. Helsinki: Suomalaisen Kirjallisuuden Seura, 2002.
Laue, Theodore von. *Why Lenin? Why Stalin? A Reappraisal of the Russian Revolution, 1900–1930*. Philadelphia: Lippincott, 1971.
Law, Alma, and Mel Gordon. *Meyerhold, Eisenstein, and Biomechanics: Actor Training in Revolutionary Russia*. Jefferson, N.C.: McFarland, 1996.
Leach, Robert. *Vsevolod Meyerhold*. Cambridge: Cambridge University Press, 1989.
Leach, Robert, and Victor Borovsky, eds. *A History of Russian Theatre*. Cambridge: Cambridge University Press, 1999.
Lebrecht, Norman. *The Companion to 20th Century Music*. New York: Simon and Schuster, 1992.
Leikina-Svirskaia, V. R. *Russkaia intelligentsiia v 1900–1917 godakh*. Moscow: Mysl', 1981.
Levine, Lawrence W. *Highbrow/Lowbrow: The Emergence of Cultural Hierarchy in America*. Cambridge: Harvard University Press, 1988.
Lincoln, W. Bruce. *Between Heaven and Hell: The Story of a Thousand Years of Artistic Life in Russia*. New York: Viking, 1998.
———. *Sunlight at Midnight: St. Petersburg and the Rise of Modern Russia*. New York: Basic, 2000.
Lindenmeyr, Adele. "The First Soviet Political Trial: Countess Sofia V. Panina Before the Petrograd Revolutionary Tribunal." *Russian Review* 60, no. 4 (2001): 505–25.
———. *Poverty Is Not a Vice: Charity, Society, and the State in Imperial Russia*. Princeton: Princeton University Press, 1996.
Lotman, Ju. M., and B. A. Uspenskij. *The Semiotics of Russian Culture*. Edited by A. Shukman. Ann Arbor: Michigan Slavic Contributors, 1984.
Mally, Lynn. *Culture of the Future: The Proletkult Movement in Revolutionary Russia*. Berkeley and Los Angeles: University of California Press, 1990.

———. *Revolutionary Acts: Amateur Theater and the Soviet State, 1917–1938*. Ithaca: Cornell University Press, 2000.

Manning, Roberta. *The Crisis of the Old Order in Russia: Gentry and Government*. Princeton: Princeton University Press, 1982.

Marks, Steven G. *How Russia Shaped the Modern World: From Art to Anti-Semitism, Ballet to Bolshevism*. Princeton: Princeton University Press, 2002.

Matich, Olga. *Erotic Utopia: The Decadent Imagination in Russia's Fin de Siècle*. Madison: University of Wisconsin Press, 2005.

Mayer, Charles S. "Ida Rubinstein: A Twentieth-Century Cleopatra." *Dance Research Journal* 20, no. 2 (1989): 33–51.

McCaffray, Susan P. *The Politics of Industrialization in Tsarist Russia: The Association of Southern Coal and Steel Producers, 1874–1914*. DeKalb: Northern Illinois University Press, 1996.

McCormick, John. *Popular Theatres of Nineteenth-Century France*. New York: Routledge, 1993.

McDowell, Nicholas. *The English Radical Imagination: Culture, Religion, and Revolution, 1630–1660*. Oxford: Oxford University Press, 2004.

McReynolds, Louise. *The News Under Russia's Old Regime: The Development of a Mass-Circulation Press*. Princeton: Princeton University Press, 1991.

———. *Russia at Play: Leisure Activities at the End of the Tsarist Era*. Ithaca: Cornell University Press, 2003.

Mikheeva, Marina. "Sankt Peterburgskaia Konservatoriia i 1905 god." http://www.conservatory.ru/rus/ history_cons1905.shtml.

Moeller-Sally, Betsy F. "The Theater as Will and Representation: Artist and Audience in Russian Modernist Theater, 1904–1909." *Slavic Review* 57, no. 2 (1998): 350–71.

Money, Keith. *Anna Pavlova: Her Life and Art*. New York: Knopf, 1982.

Morrison, Simon. *Russian Opera and the Symbolist Movement*. Berkeley and Los Angeles: University of California Press, 2002.

Moser, Charles A. *Antinihilism in the Russian Novel of the 1860s*. The Hague: Mouton, 1964.

Napravnik, V. E. *Eduard Frantsevich Napravnik i ego sovremenniki*. Leningrad: Muzyka, 1991.

Nazarova, A., and N. Orekhova, eds. *Russkii dramaticheskii teatr kontsa XIX–nachala XX vv.* Moscow: GITIS, 2000.

Nelson, Amy. *Music for the Revolution: Musicians and Power in Early Soviet Russia*. University Park: Pennsylvania State University Press, 2004.

Neuberger, Joan. *Hooliganism: Crime, Culture, and Power in St. Petersburg, 1900–1914*. Berkeley and Los Angeles: University of California Press, 1993.

Nicholson, Steve. *British Theatre and the Red Peril: The Portrayal of Communism, 1917–1945*. Exeter: University of Exeter Press, 1999.

———. *The Censorship of British Drama, 1900–1968*. 2 vols. Exeter: University of Exeter Press, 2003.

———. "Unnecessary Plays: European Drama and the British Censor in th e 1920s." *Theatre Research International* 20, no. 1 (1995): 30–41.

Orlov, Iu. M., ed. *Teatr mezhdu proshlym i budushchim. Sbornik nauchnykh trudov*. Moscow: Gos. in-t teatral'nogo iskvsstva, 1989.

Ossipova, Erika V. "Culture and Theatre as Foundation for National Identity in the Russian far East." *Nationalities Papers* 33, no.1 (2005).

Ostrovskaia, R. I., et al. *Mariia Ermolova*. Moscow: Russkaia kniga, 2001.

Ostwald, Peter. *Nijinsky: A Leap into Madness*. New York: Lyle Stuart, 1991.
Ozouf, Mona. *La fête révolutionnaire, 1789–1799*. Paris: Gallimard, 1976.
Palat, Madhavan K., ed. *Social Identities in Revolutionary Russia*. New York: Palgrave, 2001.
Paperno, Irina, and Joan Delaney Grossman, eds. *Creating Life: The Aesthetic Utopia of Russian Modernism*. Stanford: Stanford University Press, 1994.
Petrovskaia, I. F. *Istochnikovedenie istorii russkogo dorevoliutsionnogo dramaticheskogo teatra*. Leningrad: GITMK, 1971.
———. *Muzykal'noe obrazovanie i muzykal'nye obshchestvennye organizatsii v Peterburge, 1801–1917: Entsiklopediia*. St. Petersburg: RIII, 1999.
———. *Teatr i zritel' provintsial'noi Rossii, vtoraia polovina XIX v.* Leningrad: Iskusstvo, 1979.
———. *Teatr i zritel' rossiiskikh stolits: 1895–1917*. Leningrad: Iskusstvo, 1990.
Petrovskaia, I. F., and V. Somina. *Teatral'nyi Peterburg: Nachalo XVIII veka–oktiabr' 1917 goda: Obozrenie-putevoditel'*. St. Petersburg: RIII, 1994.
Raeff, Marc. *Russia Abroad: A Cultural History of the Emigration, 1919–1939*. New York: Oxford University Press, 1990.
Rawson, Don C. *Russian Rightists and the Revolution of 1905*. Cambridge: Cambridge University Press, 1995.
Resing, Mary C. "Vera Fedorovna Kommissarzhevskaia [sic]: A Life in Performance." Ph.D. diss., University of Michigan, 1997.
Richardson, William. "*Zolotoe Runo*" *and Russian Modernism, 1905–1910*. Ann Arbor: Ardis, 1986.
Richmond, Steven D. "Ideologically Firm: Soviet Theater Censorship, 1921–1928." Ph.D. diss., University of Chicago, 1996.
Rigberg, Benjamin. "The Efficacy of Tsarist Censorship Operations, 1894–1917." *Jahrbücher für Geschichte Osteuropas* 14, no. 3 (1966): 327–46.
Rogger, Hans. *Russia in the Age of Modernisation and Revolution, 1881–1917*. New York: Longman, 1983.
Roosevelt, Priscilla. *Life on the Russian Country Estate: A Social and Cultural History*. New Haven: Yale University Press, 1995.
Root-Bernstein, Michèle. *Boulevard Theater and Revolution in Eighteenth-Century Paris*. Ann Arbor: UMI Research Press, 1984.
Rosenthal, Bernice Glatzer. *New Myth, New World: From Nietzsche to Stalinism*. University Park: Pennsylvania State University Press, 2002.
———, ed. *Nietzsche in Russia*. Princeton: Princeton University Press, 1986.
———. "Theatre as Church: The Vision of the Mystical Anarchists." Pt. 2. *Russian History/Histoire russe* 4, pt. 2 (1977): 122–41.
———. "The Transmutation of the Symbolist Ethos: Mystical Anarchism and the Revolution of 1905." *Slavic Review* 36, no. 4 (1977).
Rudnitsky, Konstantin, ed. *Istoriia sovetskogo dramaticheskogo teatra*. 6 vols. Moscow: Nauka, 1966.
———. *Meyerhold the Director*. Translated by George Petrov. Ann Arbor: Ardis, 1981.
Russkaia khudozhestvennaia kul'tura kontsa XIX–nachala XX veka (1895–1907). 4 vols. Moscow: Nauka, 1968–81.
Ruud, Charles A. *Fighting Words: Imperial Censorship and the Russian Press, 1804–1906*. Toronto: University of Toronto Press, 1982.
Rybakova, Iu. *Komissarzhevskaia*. Leningrad: Iskusstvo, 1971.

Sablinsky, Walter. *Father Gapon and the St. Petersburg Massacre of 1905.* Princeton: Princeton University Press, 1976.

Said, Edward W. *Culture and Imperialism.* New York: Knopf, 1993.

Sanderson, Michael. *From Irving to Olivier: A Social History of the Acting Profession in England, 1880–1983.* New York: St. Martin's, 1984.

Sargeant, Lynn. "*Kashchei the Immortal:* Liberal Politics, Cultural Memory, and the Rimsky-Korsakov Scandal of 1905." *Russian Review* 64, no. 1 (2005): 22–43.

———. "Middle-Class Culture: Music and Identity in Late Imperial Russia." Ph.D. diss., Indiana University, 2001.

———. "A New Class of People: The Conservatoire and Musical Professionalization in Russia, 1861–1917." *Music and Letters* 85, no. 1 (2004): 41–61.

Schrader, Abby M. *Languages of the Lash: Corporal Punishment and Identity in Imperial Russia.* DeKalb: Northern Illinois University Press, 2003.

Schuler, Catherine A. *Women in the Russian Theatre: The Actress in the Silver Age.* New York: Routledge, 1996.

Segel, Harold B. *Turn-of-the-Century Cabaret: Paris, Barcelona, Berlin, Munich, Vienna, Cracow, Moscow, St. Petersburg, Zurich.* New York: Columbia University Press, 1987.

Senelick, Laurence. "Anti-Semitism and the Tsarist Theatre: The *Smugglers* Riots." *Theatre Survey* 44, no. 1 (2003): 68–101.

———, ed. *National Theatre in Northern and Eastern Europe, 1746–1900.* Cambridge: Cambridge University Press, 1991.

———. *Serf Actor: The Life and Art of Mikhail Shchepkin.* Westport, Conn.: Greenwood, 1984.

———. "Vera Komissarzhevskaia: The Actress as Symbolist Eidolon." *Theatre Journal* 32, no. 4 (1980): 475–87.

Seregny, Scott. *Russian Teachers and Peasant Revolution: The Politics of Education in 1905.* Bloomington: Indiana University Press, 1989.

Shellard, Dominic. *British Theatre Since the War.* New Haven: Yale University Press, 1999.

Shellard, Dominic, and Steve Nicholson. *The Lord Chamberlain Regrets: A History of British Theatre Censorship.* London: British Library, 2004.

Shneiderman, I. I. *Mariia Gavrilovna Savina, 1854–1915.* Leningrad: Iskusstvo, 1956.

Slonim, Marc. *Russian Theater: From the Empire to the Soviets.* Cleveland: World Publishing, 1961.

Stefanova, Kalina., ed. *Eastern European Theater after the Iron Curtain.* Amsterdam: Harwood, 2000.

Stites, Richard. *Revolutionary Dreams: Utopian Vision and Experimental Life in the Russian Revolution.* Oxford: Oxford University Press, 1989.

———. *Serfdom, Society, and the Arts in Imperial Russia: The Pleasure and the Power.* New Haven: Yale University Press, 2005.

Stokes, Gale. *The Walls Came Tumbling Down: The Collapse of Communism in Eastern Europe.* New York: Oxford University Press, 1993.

Sukhanov, N. N. *The Russian Revolution.* Edited and translated by Joel Carmichael. London: Oxford University Press, 1955.

Surh, Gerald D. *1905 in St. Petersburg: Labor, Society, and Revolution.* Stanford: Stanford University Press, 1989.

Svetaeva, M. G. *Mariia Gavrilovna Savina.* Moscow: Iskusstvo, 1988.

Swift, E. Anthony. "Fighting the Germs of Disorder: The Censorship of Russian Popular Theater, 1888–1917." *Russian History/Histoire russe* 18, no. 1 (1991): 1–49.

———. *Popular Theater and Society in Tsarist Russia*. Berkeley and Los Angeles: University of California Press, 2002.

———. "Workers' Theater and 'Proletarian Culture' in Prerevolutionary Russia, 1905–1917." In *Workers and Intelligentsia in Late Imperial Russia: Realities, Representations, Reflections*, edited by Reginald Zelnik, 260–91. International and Area Studies Research Series No. 101. Berkeley and Los Angeles: University of California, 1999.

Symons, James M. *Meyerhold's Theatre of the Grotesque: The Post-Revolutionary Productions, 1920–1932*. Coral Gables: University of Miami Press, 1971.

Tal'nikov, D. *Komissarzhevskaia*. Moscow: Iskusstvo, 1939.

Thorpe, Richard G. "The Management of Culture in Revolutionary Russia: The Imperial Theaters and the State, 1897–1928." Ph.D. diss., Princeton University, 1990.

Thurston, Gary. "The Impact of Russian Popular Theatre, 1886–1915." *Journal of Modern History* 55, no. 2 (1983): 237–67.

———. *The Popular Theatre Movement in Russia, 1862–1919*. Evanston: Northwestern University Press, 1998.

Tikhvinskaia, Liudmila. *Kabare i teatry miniatur v Rossii, 1908–1917*. Moscow: Kul'tura, 1995.

Tsivian, Yuri. *Early Cinema in Russia and Its Cultural Reception*. Translated by Alan Bodger. New York: Routledge, 1994.

Tucker, Robert C., ed. *The Lenin Anthology*. New York: Norton, 1975.

Tumanova, A. S. *Samoderzhavie i obshchestvennye organizatsii v Rossii, 1905–1917 gody*. Tambov: Izdatel'stvo TGU imeni G. R. Derzhavina, 2002.

Turkin, N. V. *Komissarzhevskaia v zhizni i na stsene*. Moscow: Zolotosvet, 1910.

Vdovin, V. A. "Neopublikovannoe pis'mo V. F. Komissarzhevskoi." *Sovetskie arkhivy* 3 (1970): 116–19.

Velekhova, Nina. "The State of Russian Theatre in the 1990s." In *Eastern European Theater after the Iron Curtain*, edited by Kalina Stefanova. Amsterdam: Harwood, 2000.

Volkov, Solomon. *St. Petersburg: A Cultural History*. New York: Free Press, 1995.

Wagner, William G. *Marriage, Property, and Law in Late Imperial Russia*. New York: Oxford University Press, 1994.

Weinberg, Robert. *The Revolution of 1905 in Odessa: Blood on the Steps*. Bloomington: Indiana University Press, 1993.

Wells, H. G. *Russia in the Shadows*. Westport, Conn.: Hyperion, 1973.

West, James. *Russian Symbolism: A Study of Viacheslav Ivanov and the Russian Symbolist Aesthetic*. London: Methuen, 1970.

Wiley, Roland John. *Tchaikovsky's Ballets: "Swan Lake," "Sleeping Beauty," "Nutcracker."* Oxford: Clarendon, 1985.

Wilson, Elizabeth. *Shostakovich: A Life Remembered*. Princeton: Princeton University Press, 1995.

Wirtschafter, Elise Kimerling. *The Play of Ideas in Russian Enlightenment Theater*. DeKalb: Northern Illinois University Press, 2003.

———. *Social Identity in Imperial Russia*. DeKalb: Northern Illinois University Press, 1997.

Wood, Gordon S. *The Radicalism of the American Revolution*. New York: Knopf, 1991.

Worrall, Nick. *Modernism to Realism on the Soviet Stage: Tairov—Vakhtangov—Okhlopkov*. Cambridge: Cambridge University Press, 1989.

Wortman, Richard S. *Scenarios of Power: Myth and Ceremony in Russian Monarchy from Peter the Great to the Abdication of Nicholas II*. Princeton: Princeton University Press, 2006.

Yekelchyk, Serhy. "The Nation's Clothes: Constructing a Ukrainian High Culture in the Russian Empire, 1860–1900." *Jahrbücher für Geschichte Osteuropas* 49, no. 2 (2001).

Youngblood, Denise. *The Magic Mirror: Moviemaking in Russia, 1908–1918*. Madison: University of Wisconsin Press, 1999.

———. *Movies for the Masses: Popular Cinema and Soviet Society in the 1920s*. Cambridge: Cambridge University Press, 1992.

Zelnik, Reginald E., ed. and trans. *A Radical Worker in Tsarist Russia: The Autobiography of Semën Ivanovich Kanatchikov*. Stanford: Stanford University Press, 1986.

———, ed. *Workers and Intelligentsia in Late Imperial Russia: Realities, Representations, Reflections*. International and Area Studies Research Series No. 101. Berkeley and Los Angeles: University of California, 1999.

Zil'berstein, I. S., and V. A. Samkov. *Sergei Diagilev i russkoe iskusstvo*. 2 vols. Moscow: Izobrazitel'noe iskusstvo, 1982.

Znosko-Borovskii, E. A. *Russkii teatr nachala XX veka*. Prague: Plamia Praga, 1925.

Zolotnitskii, D. *Akademicheskie teatry na putiakh oktiabria*. Leningrad: Iskusstvo, 1982.

Index

Abel'son, I. O., 112, 231–32
Absinthe Club (St. Petersburg), 209 n. 196
Adam, Adolphe, *Giselle*, 128
The Adventures of Sherlock Holmes (Sir Arthur Conan Doyle), dramatizations of, 204, 211, 213
advertising (theatrical), 185
Afanas'ev, Valerii, 259, 260 n. 59
Aga Khan, The, 31
Akhmatova, Anna, 238
  Poem Without a Hero, 217
Aksakov, Konstantin, 191
Albee, Edward, *Who's Afraid of Virginia Woolf?*, 53
Aleksandra, Empress (reigned 1894–1917), 131
Aleksandrinskii Theater (St. Petersburg), 16, 22, 32, 33, 43, 50, 51 n. 186, 56–57, 57 n. 3, 63, 64, 66, 75 n. 97, 78, 86, 87, 103, 106, 108, 110, 111, 119–25, 128, 129, 130, 135, 140, 142, 142 n. 37, 146, 162, 167, 168, 177, 178, 179, 181 n. 48, 184, 186, 192–93, 195, 196, 202, 203, 205, 206, 212, 219, 221, 238, 239, 242, 256–57, 264
  repertoire council of, 122, 123–25
Alekseev family, 60
Aleksei, Tsar (reigned 1645–76), 16 n. 6
Aleksei Aleksandrovich, Grand Duke, 43
Alexander I, Tsar (reigned 1801–25), 44
Alexander II, Tsar (reigned 1855–81), 1, 17, 25, 35, 44
Alexander III, Tsar (reigned 1881–94), 17–18, 25, 47, 63
Alfonso XIII, King of Spain, 31
Ancient Theater (St. Petersburg), 233–34. *See also* Evreinov, Nikolai
Andreev, Leonid, 33, 64, 202, 230, 248, 255
  Anathema, 81
  To the Stars, 73
Anna, Empress (reigned 1730–40), 38
anti-Semitism, 148, 159, 194, 195
The Apostle (play), 206, 207
Appia, Adolphe, 225
Arbatov, Nikolai, 154
Arbenin, Nikolai, 162

Arbenin, G. A., 25
Arcadia (pleasure garden, St. Petersburg), 35
The Artist and His Model (theatrical), 208
Artsybashev, Mikhail, 255
  Sanin, 208
Astruc, Gabriel, 31
Auber, Daniel, *La muette de Portici*, 49

Bakhrushin family, 27, 30
Bakst, Lev, 32
Balanchine, Georges (Georgii Balanchivadze), 259, 260 n. 59
Baletta, Elise, 43, 109–10
balletomanes, 174–76, 176 n. 29, 181
Ballets Russes, 6, 15, 30, 31, 31 nn. 81–82, 35, 53 n. 202, 86, 126, 135, 142, 209–10, 218, 264
Baranskii, Grigorii, 141
Bariatinskii, Prince Vladimir, 26, 47, 146, 165
Baring, Maurice, 53, 61, 203
Baryshnikov, Mikhail, 259, 260 n. 59
Batiushkov, Fedor, 86–87, 125, 130
Bauer, Evgenii, *The Revolutionary*, 214
Bauman, Nikolai, 147
Beardsley, Aubrey, 209 n. 196
Beaumarchais, Pierre Augustin Caron de, *The Barber of Seville*, 69
Beethoven, Ludwig van
  Fidelio, 4 n. 10, 74 n. 94, 131–32, 132 n. 171, 202–3, 247
  Third Symphony, 77
Bekefi, Alfred, 111 n. 57, 114
Belarus, 5
Belinskii, Vissarion, 191
Belyi, Andrei (Boris Bugaev), 188–89, 217, 218–19, 221–22, 227, 242
Benois, Alexandre. *See* Benua, Aleksandr
Benua, Aleksandr (Alexandre Benois), 19, 22, 32, 107, 108, 109, 218, 222, 234, 238, 253, 255
Benua, Iurii, 36
Bergson, Henri, 234
Berngard, A. R., 92–93, 97
Bernhardt, Sarah, 26
Bertenson, Vasilii, 171–73, 177, 192, 193, 251
Beyerlein, Franz Adam, *Lights Out*, 54

Bezpalov, Vasilii, 257
Bhabha, Homi, 4
biomechanics, 239–40. *See also* Meierkhol'd, Vsevolod
Bizet, Georges, *Carmen*, 206
Black Hundreds, 118
The Blaze of War (melodrama), 207
Blok, Aleksandr, 165, 200, 218–19 n. 15, 220, 221, 221 n. 30, 237–38, 239, 251–52, 256 n. 31
    The Fairground Booth (*Balaganchik*), 215–18, 227, 232, 235, 237, 240, 251
    The Twelve, 255–56
Bloody Sunday. *See* "Revolution of 1905"
Blumenfel'd, Feliks, 93
Boito, Arrigo, *Mefistofele*, 133
Bolshevik (Communist) Party, 87–88, 148, 259
Bol'shoi Dramaticheskii Teatr (Leningrad), 25
Bol'shoi Kammenyi Theater (Moscow), 16, 41
Bol'shoi Theater (Moscow), 16, 106, 111, 131, 131 n. 166, 142, 243–45, 263, 264 n. 75
    ballet company of, 40, 62, 118, 176, 206
    opera company of, 118
    orchestra of, 84, 86
Bonaparte, Napoleon, 38, 77
Borodin, Aleksandr
    Polovtsian Dances, 210 n. 199
    Prince Igor', 210 n. 199
Borovsky, Victor, 177
Boston Symphony, 84, 258
Bourdieu, Pierre, 3, 184
Braque, Georges, 32
Bravich, Kazimir, 147, 152, 159, 160
Brecht, Bertolt, 3
Brenko, Anna, 24, 28
Briantsev, Aleksandr, 52, 155, 198
British Actors' Association, 153 n. 95
Briusov, Valerii, 223–24, 240, 252
Brushtein, Aleksandra, 166, 168, 179, 186, 200, 208, 229, 231, 232–33
Büchner, Georg, *Danton's Death*, 71, 197
Bulygin, Aleksandr, 73
Byron, Lord (George Gordon), *Sardanapalus*, 71, 197

Castellane, Count Boniface de, 31
Catherine II, "the Great," 70
censorship, 11, 44–54, 65–76, 87, 111, 145, 197–98, 200, 201, 245–46
    in the Soviet Union, 246 n. 12, 261–62
Chaikovskii, Petr (Peter Ilyich Tchaikovsky), 20, 114, 221, 244, 262
    Eugene Onegin, 46, 90, 106, 116, 194, 206
    The Queen of Spades, 114, 116, 127, 206
Chaliapin, Feodor. *See* Shaliapin, Fedor

Chamber Theater (Moscow), 241
Chanel, Coco, 32
Charin, A. I., 140 n. 21
charity, 132–34, 166–69
Chekhov, Anton, 36, 40, 205, 252, 262
    The Cherry Orchard, 70, 85, 195, 226, 240
    The Seagull, 168, 223, 224, 242
    Uncle Vania, 70, 89, 240
Chekhov, Mikhail (nephew of above), 259, 259 n. 59
Chekhov, Ol'ga (sometime wife of above), 259, 259 n. 59
Chénier, Marie-Joseph, *Charles IX*, 191
Cheremisinov, P. N., 95, 98
Cherepnin, Aleksandr, 259, 259 n. 59
Cherepnin, Nikolai (father of above), 259 n. 59
Cherkasskaia, Marianna, 257
Chirikov, Evgenii, 149–50, 200, 201
    Ivan Mironych, 74
    The Jew, 53
    Peasants, 71, 197
Chulkov, Georgii, 60, 233
civil society, 14, 94, 164, 252–54
Coates, Albert, 258
Cocteau, Jean, 32
Comradeship of New Drama, 224–26, 227. *See also* Meierkhol'd, Vsevolod
Constitutional Democratic Party, 130, 162
Contemporary Theater, 60
Corps des pages, 20
Council of Ministers, 80, 81, 246
Craig, Gordon, 225
The Crooked Mirror (*Krivoe zerkalo*, St. Petersburg), cabaret, 33, 70, 82, 210–11, 236
Cuba (restaurant, St. Petersburg), 110

Dalmatov, Vasilii, 124, 153, 167–68, 255 n. 26
Dal'skii, Mamont, 43
The Dance of the Seven Veils, 80, 209
Danilova, Aleksandra, 259, 260 n. 59
Daudet, Alphonse, *Sapho*, 54, 245
Davydov, Vladimir, 39 n. 125, 121, 123
Debussy, Claude, 32
    Prélude à l'après-midi d'un faune, 209
Dediulin, V. A., 121
Deich, Lev, 147
Desniatnikov, Leonid, *The Children of Rosenthal*, 243–45, 263
Diaghilev, Sergei, 15, 15 nn. 3–4, 30–31, 31 n. 79, 32, 34–35, 126, 128, 210, 218, 220, 255
Didelot, Charles, 39
Dolina, Mariia, 167
Donizetti, Gaetano, *The Elixir of Love*, 17

Dostoevskii, Fedor
  The Devils, 206, 251
  The Village of Stepanchikovo, 47
Dramatic Theater (St. Petersburg), 27, 32, 58, 63, 77, 95, 137, 141, 142, 143, 144, 159, 165, 166, 168, 198, 199, 215, 228–33, 240, 245
Duma, 62, 75, 79, 80, 139, 164, 191, 243, 247
Duncan, Isadora, 39, 175, 179
Durnovo, Petr, 45 n. 151
Duse, Eleanora, 26
Dymov, Osip, 146

Egarev, V. N., 27
Eisenshtein, Sergei, 131 n. 166
Elena Pavlova, Grand Duchess, 40
Eliseev (department store), 26, 27
Elizabeth, Empress (reigned 1741–61), 16
emigration, 254–55
Ermolova, Mariia, 40, 258
Ershov, Ivan, 131–32, 136, 181, 203, 257
estrada (vaudeville), 189, 210–11
Euripides
  Iphigeneia at Aulis, 203
  Hippolytus, 203
Evreinov, Nikolai, 33, 144, 233–34, 236, 255
  The Beautiful Despot, 206–7

The Female Samson (theatrical), 208
Feoktistov, Evgenii, 47
Figner-Mei, Medea, 133
La fille mal gardée (ballet), 110
film industry (Russian), 75, 214
  audiences of, 181, 188–89
  censorship of, 87
  Soviet film, 262
Filosofov, Dmitrii, 190, 192, 242, 251
Finland, Grand Duchy of, 44 n. 149
Finnish Life Guards Regiment, 167
Fireflies (operetta), 156
Fokin, Aleksandr (brother of below), 211
Fokin, Mikhail [Michel Fokine], 39, 113, 114–16, 127–28, 181, 209, 209 n. 197, 247, 252, 255
  Chopiniana (*Les Sylphides*), 127, 210
  The Dying Swan, 127
  The Egyptian Nights (*Cléopâtre*), 127, 210
  Eunice, 127
  Le Pavillon d'Armide, 127, 210
Fokine, Michel. *See* Fokin, Mikhail
fon Derviz (von der Witz), V. N., 36
Frederiks, Baron Vladimir (Minister of the Imperial Court), 16, 62, 131, 133, 172
Friche, Vladimir, 212, 222
Fuchs, Georg, 225, 225 n. 40

Gaideburov, Pavel, 36, 52, 58, 76, 84, 150–51, 155, 167, 188, 198, 202, 235, 236 n. 108, 262
Gapon, Father Georgii, 58, 109
Gardin, Vladimir, 137, 147, 149, 229–30
Garin-Mikhailovskii, Nikolai, *A Village Drama*, 70
Ge, Grigorii, 124, 124 n. 124
Gedeonov, Stepan (dramatist and Director of the Imperial Theaters, 1867–75), 19, 71 n. 81
  Vasilisa Melent'eva (with Aleksandr Ostrovskii), 70–71
General Accessible Theater (Wandering Theater, St. Petersburg), 36, 52, 58, 76, 84, 155, 202, 235, 240
George V, King of Great Britain, 31
Ginzburg family, 26
Gippius, Zinaida, 192, 218–19, 255
glasnost', 260
Glazunov, Aleksandr, 93, 98, 255
Glinka, Mikhail, *A Life for the Tsar*, 18, 37, 65 n. 55, 78, 134, 188, 196, 247, 263
Gnedich, Petr, 23 n. 34, 43–44, 63, 86, 103, 111, 122, 128, 162, 177, 208, 212
  The Assembly, 75 n. 97
  Winter, 110
"God Save the Tsar" (imperial national anthem), 17, 82, 118, 119, 122, 132, 135, 172, 173, 193, 194
Goethe, Johann Wolfgang von, *Faust*, 46, 69
Golovin, Aleksandr, 32
Goncharova, Natal'ia, 32
Gorin-Goriainov, Boris, 130, 137–38, 148, 150, 155–56, 187, 193–94, 195–96, 247, 249
Gor'kii, Maksim [A. M. Peshkov], 36, 135, 149, 158, 168, 200, 201, 214, 223, 227, 255, 256
  Children of the Sun, 71 n. 85, 154, 165, 198, 199, 206, 251
  The Life of Klim Samgin, 107 n. 28
  The Lower Depths, 47, 51, 71, 72
  Summerfolk, 77, 186–87, 195, 206, 207
Gounod, Charles, *Faust*, 206
Gozzi, Carlo, *Princess Turandot*, 241–42
Great Reforms, 1
Greffuhle, Countess Elisabeth de, 31
Griboedov, Aleksandr, *Woe from Wit*, 69
Grigorovich, Iurii, 259

Habermas, Jürgen, 9
Hamsun, Knut, *At the Gates of the Kingdom*, 63, 130, 248
Hauptmann, Gerhart
  Festival of Peace, 241
  Hannele, 79
  The Weavers, 49, 52

Havel, Václav, 5, 6
Hermitage Gardens (Moscow), 35
Hermitage (museum), 15 n. 1
Hermitage Theater (St. Petersburg), 22
Hoffmann, E. T. A., 237
Holy Synod (Most Holy Synod), 63, 73, 79
Horowitz, Vladimir, 259, 260 n. 59
Horse Guards Regiment, 20, 122
House of Interludes (*Dom intermedii*), 33
Hugo, Victor, *Hernani*, 71–73, 197
The Humpbacked Horse (ballet), 19

Iakovlev, Kondrat, 140 n. 23
Iavorskaia, Lidiia, 26, 32, 33, 34, 47, 52–53, 54, 58, 62, 77, 136, 137, 146, 148, 165, 166, 187, 195, 200, 201, 223, 249, 255
Ibsen, Henrik, 158, 202, 245
  An Enemy of the People, 52, 100–101, 148, 194, 195
  Ghosts, 54
  Hedda Gabler, 228
Iksanov, Anatolii, 244
Imperial Academy of Fine Arts, 41, 110–11
Imperial Ballet School (later Vaganova Ballet Academy), 38–39, 85, 88, 89–91, 116, 181, 194
Imperial Court Orchestra, 84
Imperial Drama School, 39, 88, 90, 111, 116
Imperial Russian Musical Society (RMO), 20, 27, 40, 41, 59, 88, 89, 91–93, 95–96, 98–99, 253, 262
Imperial Russian Theatrical Society (RTO), 66, 68, 75, 105, 138–40, 139 n. 12, 145, 146, 148, 150, 151, 152–54, 161–63, 190, 208, 250, 253
  Actors' Mutual Aid Circle, 153, 154, 157, 158, 167
Imperial Senate, 76, 77, 145
Imperial Theaters Directorate, 10, 11, 18, 19, 20, 22, 25, 32, 38, 40, 51, 59, 62, 63, 64, 88, 90, 97, 102, 105, 112, 113, 114, 116, 122, 125, 126, 127, 128–29, 132, 139, 142, 176, 185, 205, 222, 247
Ionafan, Metropolitan of Iaroslavl', 79
Iur'ev, Iurii, 20–21, 124, 179, 183
Iushkevitch, Igor' (Igor Youskevitch), 259, 260 n. 59
Iusupov, Prince Nikolai, 23, 24
Iuzhin-Sumbatov, Prince Aleksandr, 125, 130, 162
Ivan IV, "the Terrible," Tsar (reigned 1533–84), 71
Ivanov, Viacheslav, 227, 233, 234

Jeux (ballet), 209, 209 n. 198

Kamenskaia, Mariia, 106
Kanatchikov, Semen, 50 n. 185, 182–83
Karpov, Evtikhii, 34, 67, 125, 130, 142, 142 n. 34, 162, 207 n. 185, 235, 242
  Glow, 207
Karsavina, Tamara, 19, 106, 112, 114–16, 117, 127, 175, 247
Kartavov, A. F., 25
Kashirin, Aleksandr, 112 n. 61
Katkov, Mikhail, 25
Kazan, Elia, 240
Kazanskii, V. A., 26
Khar'kov Conservatory, 99
Khodotov, Nikolai, 46 n. 157, 78, 108, 119–21, 122, 124, 128, 130, 132, 133, 135, 146, 147, 149, 160, 167–68, 193, 195, 196, 211, 247–48
  At the Crossroads, 129
  Miss Vulgarity, 129
Khrushchev, Nikita, 243
Khrustalev-Nosar, Georgii, 169
Kiev Conservatory, 89, 99
Kiev Municipal Theater, 51
Kirov, Sergei, 264 n. 75
Kiselev, Vasilii, 117
Klement'ev, Lev, 157
Knipper, Ol'ga, 40
Kobeko, Dmitrii, 66, 246
Kobeko commission, 66, 68, 74, 78, 130
Kollontai, Aleksandra, 166
Komissarzhevskaia, Vera, 26–27, 27, 30, 32, 34, 36, 40, 58, 62, 63, 71, 77, 78, 79, 80, 95, 103, 130, 140, 141, 142, 142 n. 37, 143, 144, 146 n. 54, 153, 154, 159, 160, 165–69, 179, 186, 191, 198, 199, 200, 201, 207, 215, 228–33, 229 n. 66, 237, 240, 242, 255 n. 26
Komissarzhevskii, Fedor (Theodore Komisarjevsky), 21, 27, 34, 79, 168, 179, 191, 205, 229, 230–31, 237, 255, 257–58
Komissarzhevskii, Fedor (tenor, father of above two entries), 40
Koonen, Alisa, 241
Korchagina-Aleksandrovskaia, Ekaterina, 130, 146, 165, 247
Korovin, Konstantin, 32, 109
Korsh, Fedor, 27, 28, 30
Korsh Theater (Moscow), 27, 28, 30, 82, 140 n. 21, 186
Koussevitzky, Serge. *See* Kusevitskii, Sergei
Krasin, Leonid, 168–69
Krehbiel, Henry, 81
Kruglova, Agrippina, 168
Krupenskii, Aleksandr, 128–29
Krylov, Viktor, *The Smugglers* (with Savelii Litvin), 148, 194, 195

Kshesinskaia, Matil'da, 16, 43, 61, 107, 109, 110, 118, 126 n. 138
Kshesinskii, Iosif, 108, 113, 116, 117–18, 126, 194, 248, 255
Kugel', Aleksandr, 86, 146, 153, 155, 156, 157–58, 162, 188, 203, 217, 230, 231, 239
Kuprin, Aleksandr, *The Duel*, 71
Kusevitskii, Sergei (Serge Koussevitzky), 84, 258
Kuza, Valentina, 108, 126, 247
Kuznetsova-Benua, Mariia, 105, 119, 132, 140 n. 23, 255

labor unrest, 57–58
Lamkert, Oskar, 48, 71
Landé, Jean-Baptiste, 38
Legat, Nikolai, 103, 106, 117
Legat, Sergei, 116, 136
Leifert, A. V., 153
Lenin, Vladimir Il'ich (Uli'anov), 1, 8, 132, 137, 147, 149
Leningrad Conservatory. *See* St. Petersburg Conservatory
Lenskii, Aleksandr, 40
Lenskii, Pavel (Prince Pavel Telepnev-Ovchina-Obolenskii), 121
Lent, theatrical performances during, 63
Lentovskii, Mikhail, 30, 35
Lermontov, Mikhail, *Masquerade*, 239, 248
Liadov, Anatolii, 20, 93, 255 n. 26
Liberation Movement, 112, 148, 157–58, 219
Ligovskii People's House (St. Petersburg), 36, 84, 202, 236, 262
Likhosherstova, Varvara, 39
Lintvarev, A. A., 62, 144, 151, 164
Liteinyi Theatrical Club, 27
Literary-Artistic Circle (later Literary-Artistic Society), 25, 26, 30
"The Little Cudgel" ("*Dubinushka*," revolutionary song), 106, 131, 248
Litvin, Feliia, 61, 110, 222, 255
Litvin, Savelii, *The Smugglers* (with Viktor Krylov), 148, 194, 195
Liubimov, Iurii, 259, 260, 260 n. 59
Liven, Prince Petr (Prince Peter Lieven), 15 n. 4, 27, 42, 176
Lopukhov, Fedor, 90, 113, 114, 117, 132, 255, 257
Lopukhova, Lidiia (Lopokhova, Lady Keynes), 255
Lord Chamberlain's Office (Britain), 53
Lotman, Iurii, 3, 214
Lunacharskii, Anatolii, 258, 259
Lutugin, L. I., 120, 147
Lutugin, V. I., 120

Maeterlinck, Maurice, 200, 230
  The Death of Tintagiles, 226
  The Miracle of St. Anthony, 215
  Monna Vanna, 54, 245
  Pélleas et Mélisande, 231
  Sister Beatrice, 229
Main Office for Press Affairs (*Glavnoe upravlenie po delam pechati*), 11, 44, 44 n. 150, 45, 45 n. 151, 46, 48, 50, 51, 52, 65, 69, 74, 87, 145, 212
Makarova, Natal'ia, 259, 260 n. 59
Maliutin, Iakov, 119, 259
Malyi Theater (Moscow), 16, 24, 40, 61, 86, 87, 125, 129, 130, 160, 205, 264 n. 75
Mamontov, Savva, 28, 95, 141
Mariinskii Theater (St. Petersburg), 16, 27, 44, 51, 51 n. 186, 61, 64, 84, 90, 97, 105, 107, 111, 126, 127, 128, 131, 131 n. 166, 134, 139 n. 16, 140 n. 23, 170–73, 175, 177, 180, 188, 190, 192, 193, 202, 203, 210, 210 n. 199, 221, 238, 251, 257, 258, 263, 264
  ballet company of, 113–18, 132, 181, 206
  chorus of, 118, 194
  opera company of, 118, 133, 205–6
  orchestra of, 118
"*La Marseillaise*" (revolutionary song), 133, 157, 194, 203, 251
Massenet, Jules, *Don Quichotte*, 187
Masur, Kurt, 5
Matisse, Henri, 32
Maupassant, Guy de, *Mademoiselle Fifi*, 238
Medtner, Emil, 222
Medvedev, Petr, 66, 67, 123, 124
Medvedeva, Nadezhda, 139
Meierkhol'd, Vsevolod, 33, 40, 63, 64, 65, 130, 131, 131 n. 166, 141, 142, 150, 166, 191, 199, 210, 215–18, 220, 221, 224–33, 235, 236, 236–40, 242, 247–48, 252, 256, 257, 259, 260–61
Mendeleeva, Liubov, 217, 221–22
Menshevik Party, 148
Merezhkovskii, Dmitrii, 87, 192, 219, 255
  Emperor Paul I, 87
Mérimée, Prosper, *La Jacquerie*, 49
Metropol' (restaurant, Moscow), 106
Metropolitan Opera (New York), 3 n. 4, 81, 176 n. 26
Meyerbeer, Giacomo
  L'Africaine, 210
  Le Prophète, 47
Mgebrov, Aleksandr, 129, 129 n. 155
Miaskovskii, Nikolai, 258
Michael I, Tsar (reigned 1613–45), 18
Michurina-Samoilova, Vera, 112
Mikhailov, Petr, 113–14

Mikhailovskii Theater (St. Petersburg), 16, 43, 51 n. 186, 62, 85, 107, 132, 182, 264 n. 75
Miliukov, Pavel, 75 n. 99
Ministry of Education, 44
Ministry of Finance, 37, 51, 52
Ministry of the Imperial Court, 19
Ministry of the Interior, 22, 44, 44 n. 149, 45, 50, 65, 87, 160, 162
Mirzoev, Vladimir, 131 n. 166
Modern Amazons (theatrical), 208
Molchanov, Anatolii, 66, 105
Molière (Jean-Baptiste Poquelin), 233
  Don Juan, 69
  Tartuffe, 52
Monakhov, Aleksandr, 117–18
Monakhov, Grigorii, 41
Monica in the Kremlin (satirical opera), 263
Morozov, Savva, 28, 30, 60, 168
Moscow Art Theater, 26, 27, 28, 30, 32, 40, 60, 61, 62, 78, 79, 82, 84, 85, 100, 140, 167, 184–86, 194, 195, 198–200, 220, 223, 224, 225, 239, 241, 260
  Studio Theater of, 226–27, 240. *See also* Meierkhol'd, Vsevolod
Moscow Conservatory, 20, 41, 85, 259, 262
Moscow Drama School, 40
Moscow Hunting Club, 26
Moscow People's House (theater), 51
Moscow Philharmonic Society, 39–40
Moscow Soviet, 85, 261 n. 64
Mosolov, Aleksandr, 42
Moulin Rouge (Moscow), 211
Moving Together, youth group, 243
Mozart, Wolfgang Amadeus, 244
Munte, Suzanne, 109–10
Musorgskii, Modest, 31, 104, 118, 197, 210, 238, 244, 264 n. 75
  Boris Godunov, 31, 104, 118, 135, 197, 210, 238

Nabokov, Vladimir, 119
Napravnik, Eduard, 21, 23 n. 34, 24, 172, 202, 255 n. 26, 258
Narokov, Mikhail, 137, 150, 155–56, 159, 227, 233, 250
Naryshkin, Aleksandr (Director of the Imperial Theaters, 1799–1819), 19
Nemetti, V. A., 27
Nemirova-Ral'f, Anastasiia, 121
Nemirovich-Danchenko, Vladimir, 28, 40, 67, 78, 79, 138, 146, 184–86, 195, 200, 225
Neverov, Sergei, 244
Nevolin, Boris, 153
Nevskii Farce Theater (St. Petersburg), 26, 59, 156–57, 194, 203, 204

Nevskii Society for the Support of Popular Entertainment, 35, 60
New Admiralty Theater (St. Petersburg), 59
New Economic Policy, 261 n. 64
New Summer Theater (St. Petersburg), 188
New Theater (Moscow), 26
New Theater (St. Petersburg), 26, 32, 34, 47, 52, 53, 58, 136, 137, 141, 142, 148, 165, 187, 200, 201
New Times (*Novoe vremia*), newspaper, 33
New Vasileostrovskii Theater, 201
Nezlobin Theater (Moscow), 167
Nicholas I, Tsar (reigned 1825–55), 19, 129, 247
Nicholas II, Tsar (reigned 1894–1917), 16, 17, 18, 42, 43, 45, 47, 56, 61, 65, 97, 102 n. 4, 103, 127, 131, 170–71, 191, 221, 242
Nietzsche, Friedrich, 220, 234
Nijinsky, Vaslav. *See* Nizhinskii, Vatslav
Nikolai Mikhailovich, Grand Duke, 109
Nizhinskaia, Bronislava, 126
Nizhinskii, Vatslav (Vaslav Nijinsky), 34–35, 90, 126, 126 n. 136, 128, 209, 221, 248, 250, 252, 255, 256
Noailles, Countess Anne de, 31
Nureev, Rudol'f, 259, 260 n. 59

Obolenskii, Prince Nikolai, 121, 131
Obukhov factory (St. Petersburg), 36, 37, 121, 141, 149, 177, 179
October Manifesto (1905), 61, 117, 118, 122, 157, 170–71, 205
Octobrist Party, 164
Offenbach, Jacques, 53
Okhrana (tsarist secret police), 129
Omon (Aumont) Theater (Moscow), 28
Order of St. Anne, 102, 102 n. 6
Order of St. Stanislav, 102, 140 n. 21
Orlenev, Pavel, 140
Orthodox Church (Russian), 79
Ostrovskii, Aleksandr, 19, 24, 25, 36, 37, 129, 129 n. 159, 202, 213, 236, 262
  The Forest, 121, 122
  The Heart is Not a Stone, 120, 193
  It's Not Always Shrovetide For a Cat, 193
  A Passionate Heart, 56, 58, 107, 192
  Vasilisa Melent'eva (with Stepan Gedeonov), 70–71
Otradinaia, N. N., 60

Paléologue, Maurice, 65 n. 55, 83, 175, 179, 187, 208
Panaev Theater (St. Petersburg), 27, 58, 84, 156, 157, 158, 168
Panina, Countess Sofiia, 36, 262

Passage (department store), 27
Patriotic Society, 133
patriotism in theater, 65
Pavlova, Anna, 32, 108, 114–16, 117, 126, 127, 247, 255
Pecherin-Tsander, P. P., *Afterward*, 206
Peck, Harry Thurston, 53
Perestiani, Ivan, 136, 137
Peter I, "the Great," Tsar (reigned 1682–1725), 19 n. 16, 37, 41, 45, 65 n. 55
Peterhof (palace), 114
Petersburg Conservatory. *See* St. Petersburg Conservatory
Petipa, Mariia, 117, 210, 247
Petipa, Marius, 39, 103, 107, 114, 117, 127
Petrograd Soviet, 85
Petrov, Nikolai, 140–41, 150
Picasso, Pablo, 32
Piscator, Erwin, 3
Pisemskii, Aleksei, *The Partition*, 70
Pleshcheev, Aleksandr, 20, 127, 179
Plevitskaia, Nadezhda, 167
Pobedonostsev, Konstantin, 45 n. 151, 73
Pokhitonov, Grigorii, 42, 106
Poor Jonathan (operetta), 79
Popov, Nikolai, 201
popular theaters, 1–2, 12, 13, 35–38, 44–45, 49, 69, 188, 213, 235–36
Populist Movement, 130, 207 n. 185
Port Arthur, 57
Potocki, Count, 31 n. 82
Preobrazhenskaia, Ol'ga, 107, 108, 110, 255
professional and civic associations, 57, 94
Prokof'ev, Sergei, 88, 91, 98, 175, 177, 255, 258, 263
  Semen Kotko, 263
Provisional Government. *See* Revolutions of 1917 (Russia)
Przbyszewski, Stanisław, 230
  The Eternal Fairytale, 207–8
  Snow, 226
Pulszky, Romola [Romola Nizhinskaia], 35, 111 n. 57, 117, 128
Purishkevich, Vladimir, 79, 80, 81, 129
Pushkin, Aleksandr, 46, 82, 264 n. 75
  Boris Godunov, 46
Putilov plant, 58, 121
Putin, Vladimir, 243, 263

Raikh, Zinaida, 256
Rakhmaninov, Sergei, 32, 257, 258
Rasputin, Grigorii, 42, 79
Ravel, Maurice, 32
Reinek, A. K., 84

Reinhardt, Max, 225, 225 n. 40
Remizov, Aleksei, 220, 255
Repin, Il'ia, 171
  October 17, 1905, 171 n. 2
Review of Theaters (*Obozrenie teatrov*), journal, 231–32
Revolution of 1789 (France), 191
Revolution of 1830 (Belgium), 49
Revolution of 1848 (France), 57 n. 6
Revolution of 1905 (Russia), 1, 8, 12, 56–62, 69–76, 78, 83, 89–99, 106–24, 189–94, 219, 226–27, 236, 250, 253
  "Bloody Sunday," 56, 65, 68, 69, 76, 77, 89–91, 105, 107, 108, 110–11, 141, 144, 192, 195, 205, 217, 219, 252
  general strike, 71, 73, 74, 98, 112–17, 130, 154–59, 164, 165, 167, 171, 193, 198, 218, 226, 249
  October Days, 113, 117–24, 171
  December rising (Moscow), 159, 220–21 n. 24
Revolutions of 1917 (Russia), 1, 11, 12, 224, 241, 249, 254
  February Revolution, 85, 87, 118, 125, 130, 191, 247
  July days, 85
  Provisional Government, 85, 86, 87, 125, 258
  October Revolution, 85, 125, 163, 166, 241, 254, 255, 256–59, 260
Rimskii-Korsakov, Nikolai, 59, 61, 64, 95, 131, 221, 221 n. 30, 246, 255 n. 26, 262
  St. Petersburg Conservatory in 1905 and, 91–99
  The Golden Cockerel, 97
  The Legend of the Invisible City of Kitezh and Maiden Fevroniia, 46, 97
  Lord Governor (*Pan Voevoda*), 97
  Kashchei the Immortal, 95–97
  May Night, 118, 194
  Mlada, 19
  Sadko, 97
  The Snow Maiden, 97, 131–32, 247
  The Tsar's Bride, 97
Ripon, Marchioness of, 31
Romanov dynasty, 64, 87
Rossi, Ernesto, 26
Rossini, Giaochino, *Wilhelm Tell*, 47
Rostropovich, Mstislav, 259, 260 n. 59
Rouselle, Henri, 109–10
Rubinshtein, Anton, 20, 41
Rubinshtein, Ida, 80, 208–9, 210, 255
Rubinshtein, Nikolai (brother of Anton), 20, 24, 41
Russian Dramatic Theater, 84
Russian Private Opera (Moscow), 28, 95

Russian Tea Room (restaurant, New York), 254
Russo-Japanese War, 57, 84, 97–98, 108, 133

Said, Edward, 3
Salome's Funeral (parody), 210
Samoilov, Pavel, 112 n. 61, 142, 142 n. 36
Sanin, Aleksandr, 32–33, 142
Saratov Conservatory, 99
Satie, Erik, 32
Savina, Mariia, 40, 102 n. 4, 103, 105, 107, 112, 113, 119, 121, 123, 124, 130, 132, 135, 142, 168, 221, 238, 249, 255 n. 26
Sazonov, Sergei, 187
Schéhérazade (ballet), 209, 210
Schiller, Johann Christoph Friedrich von, 202, 204
   Don Carlos, 71, 197, 201
   Intrigue and Love, 52, 69, 201
   Mary Stuart, 69
   The Robbers, 201
   Wilhelm Tell, 195–96
Schnitzler, Arthur, *The Green Parrot*, 52, 195
Scriabin, Alexander. *See* Skriabin, Aleksandr
The Severing of a Live Person's Head (hypnotist act), 76
Sergeev, Nikolai, 113
Sergei Aleksandrovich, Grand Duke, 140
Serov, Valentin, 110–11, 209
Sex (play), 81
Shakespeare, William
   Hamlet, 69
   Julius Caesar, 46
   King Lear, 69
   Othello, 69
   A Winter's Tale, 69
Shakhovskoi, Prince Nikolai, 49, 49 nn. 175–76, 66, 68, 74, 145, 212
Shaliapin, Fedor (Feodor Chaliapin), 21, 31, 41, 43, 104, 105, 106–7, 109, 131, 133–35, 141, 177, 188, 238, 247, 248, 250, 255, 257, 259
Shaw, George Bernard, *Mrs. Warren's Profession*, 81
Shchankin, F. N., *In the Storm of Socialism*, 206
Shcheglov, Ivan, 146, 188, 213
Shcheglovitov, Ivan, 193
Shchepkin, Mikhail, 33, 40, 165
Shchepkina-Kupernik, Tat'iana, 33, 165, 186
Shiriaev, Aleksandr, 111 n. 57, 114, 114 n. 74
Shkafer, Vasilii, 21, 141, 222, 257
Sheremetev, Count Aleksandr, 27
Sheremetev, Count Nikolai, 23
Shostakovich, Dmitrii, 88–89, 255, 259

Shpazhinskii, Ippolit
   The Little Nightingales, 212
   Princess Tarakanova, 70
      film version of, 75
Shtiurmer, Boris, 43
Shuvalova, Liubov', 108
Sipiagin, Dmitrii, 49 n. 176
Skar'skaia, Nadezhda, 36
Skobolev, Mikhail, 133
Skorobogatov, Konstantin, 36, 37, 141, 149, 177, 179
Skriabin, Aleksandr, 32
Slavophiles, 220–21
Smirnova, Elena, 108, 116
Social Democratic (SD) Party, 148, 165, 168
Socialist Revolutionary (SR) Party, 76, 129, 148
Society for Arts and Literature, 28
Sologub, Fedor, 220, 230, 242
Solov'ev, E. A., 158–59, 189, 190
Solov'ev, Vladimir, 220
Sophocles
   Antigone, 26, 195, 196, 198, 202, 233, 247, 248
   Electra, 64
   Oedipus at Colonus, 203
   Oedipus Rex, 26, 49
The Sopranos (television series), 265
Sorokin, Vladimir, 243–45, 253
   Blue Lard, 243
Soviet secret police (Cheka, GPU, NKVD), 245 n. 12, 255, 258
The Spark (*Iskra*), newspaper, 168
The Splendid Pearl (ballet), 18
St. Petersburg Conservatory, 20, 27, 41, 85, 88, 89–96, 98–99, 157, 246, 250, 262
St. Petersburg Nobleman's Club, 24, 27
St. Petersburg Philharmonic, 24, 27
St. Petersburg Society for the Care of the Mentally Ill, 118
St. Petersburg Soviet, 113, 156, 168, 173 n. 3, 219
Stalin, Iosif (Djugashvili), 11, 243, 244, 256, 259
Stanislavskaia, Mariia, 26 n. 52
Stanislavskii, Konstantin [Konstantin Alekseev], 26, 28, 36, 40, 42, 47, 60, 62, 72, 82, 100, 101, 138, 146, 148, 194, 196, 200, 202, 220, 221, 223, 224, 225, 226, 232, 237, 241, 242, 258, 261
Stark, Eduard, 222, 234
State Council, 139, 139 n. 17
Stock Exchange Gazette (*Birzhevye vedomosti*), newspaper, 141
Stoikin, A. I., 207
Stolypin, Petr, 51
Stoppard, Tom, 6

The Strand (*Lukmor'e*, St. Petersburg), cabaret, 33, 238, 252. *See also* Meierkhol'd, Vsevolod
Strasberg, Lee, 240
Strauss, Johann, 82
  The Gypsy Baron, 204–5
Strauss, Richard
  Elektra, 64, 247
  Der Rosenkavalier, 64
  Salome, 81
Stravinskii, Igor', 32, 255, 258
  The Firebird, 86
  Le sacre du printemps, 209
The Stray Dog cabaret (St. Petersburg), 167
Strindberg, August, 200
  Miss Julie, 53, 245
student unrest, 57, 58, 88, 99, 100–101, 195
stylization (*uslovnost'*), 223, 240, 252
subscription sales (in theaters), 87, 174–76, 184, 184 n. 60, 264
Supreme Soviet, 130
Susanin, Ivan, 18, 196
Suvorin, Aleksei, 30, 33, 34, 46–47, 49, 66, 67, 154, 207, 208
Suvorin (Malyi) Theater (St. Petersburg), 25, 30, 47, 84, 87, 140, 142, 142 n. 34, 144, 148, 154, 156, 157, 167, 186, 194, 201, 204, 206, 208, 238–39, 251
Suvorov, Aleksandr, Marshal, 38
Svetov, Leonid, *The Days of Freedom* (with Vladimir Valentinov), 73, 80–81, 204, 246
Svetlov, Sergei, 149, 152, 153
Sviatopolk-Mirskii, Prince Petr, 66 n. 59
Svirskii, Aleksei
  Prison, 71, 201
  The Pulse of Life, 73, 197
"System" ("Method") acting, 226, 239–40. *See also* Stanislavskii, Konstantin

Table of Ranks, 19 n. 16, 41
Tairov, Aleksandr, 240–41, 258–59
  Notes of a Director, 241
Tarkovskii, Andrei, 259, 260 n. 59
Tartakov, Ioakim, 44
Tatu (pop group), 265
Tauride Palace, 218
Teatro alla Scala (Milan), 177 n. 37
Teffi, Nadezhda, *Love through the Centuries* (theatrical), 210
Teliakovskii, Vladimir (Director of the Imperial Theaters), 15 n. 3, 20, 22, 22–23, 23, 30, 39, 41, 42, 43, 44 n. 147, 51, 62, 63, 83, 87, 90, 97, 103, 109, 111, 113, 114, 116–18, 120, 121–22, 123, 124, 125, 128, 130, 131, 132, 133, 141–42, 142 n. 37, 173, 174, 176, 176 n. 29, 177, 181, 183, 190, 193, 194, 196, 198, 205, 212, 236–37, 247–48
Temperance Trusteeship, 37, 51, 52, 236
Tenisheva, Princess Mariia, 36, 221 n. 30
Theater and Art (*Teatr i iskusstvo*), journal, 10, 68, 86, 145, 146, 149, 151, 153, 161, 162, 188, 190, 201, 205, 230
Theatrical Russia (*Teatral'naia Rossiia*), journal, 10, 68, 95, 112, 144, 158, 159, 219, 231–32
Thornton textile plant, 52
Tikhonov, Aleksandr, 195, 230
Tiraspol'skaia, Nadezhda, 78, 166
Tiufiakin, Prince Mikhail (Director of the Imperial Theaters, 1819–22), 19
To the Far East (play), 45
To the Sounds of Chopin (musical comedy), 194
Tolstoi, Aleksei
  The Death of Ivan the Terrible, 46
  Tsar Fedor Ivanovich, 45, 240
Tolstoi, Dmitrii, 45 n. 151
Tolstoi, Count Lev, *The Power of Darkness*, 37, 47, 70, 208
Tolstoi, Mikhail, 52
"The Torches" (*Fakely*), theater project and journal, 227
Trakhtenberg, Vladimir, *Fimka*, 205, 247
Trefilova, Vera, 107, 255
Trepov, Dmitrii, 73, 96, 122, 171, 172, 246
Trinity Theater of Miniatures (St. Petersburg), 211
The Triumph of the Powers (pantomime), 65, 238
Trotskii, Lev (Bronshtein), 191
Tsar Nicholas II People's House, 37, 51–52, 58–59, 59, 82, 85, 144, 146 n. 54, 157, 187, 210, 235
Tsereteli, Prince Aleksei (and his private opera company), 27, 34, 59, 144, 157, 160
Tumpakov, Pavel, 204

Union of the Archangel Michael, 80
Union of Stage Performers (*Soiuz stsenicheskikh deiatelei*), 112, 145, 151, 157, 160, 161–63, 250
Union of Unions, 163
United Russia, 243
University Charter of 1884, 98
Usachev, Aleksandr, 261
Uspenskaia, Mariia (Maria Ouspenskaya), 259, 259–60 n. 59

Vakhtangov, Evgenii, 241–42
Valentinov, Vladimir, *The Days of Freedom* (with Leonid Svetov), 73, 80–81, 204, 246

Vampuka, African Bride (operatic parody), 210–11, 252
Varlamov, Konstantin, 56, 58, 59, 60, 105, 107, 108, 120, 123, 135, 192, 255 n. 26
"*La Varsovienne*" (revolutionary song), 133
Vasileostrovskii Theater, 60
Vasil'eva, Nadezhda, 107–8
Veinberg, Petr, 26, 160
Vekhter, Nikolai, 148, 148 n. 64
Velizarii, Mariia, 33–34, 141, 151, 164–65
Verbitskaia, Anastasiia, *The Keys of Happiness*, 208
Verdi, Giuseppe, 243
  Aida, 206
Vereshchagin, Sergei, 46, 66, 73, 74, 160–61, 162
Verigina, Valentia, 60, 137, 147, 154, 177, 198, 217, 227, 228, 229
Villari, Luigi, 187
Vishnevskaia, Galina, 259, 260 n. 59
Vitte, Count Sergei, 157
Vladimir, Metropoltian of Moscow, 79
Vladimir Aleksandrovich, Grand Duke, 111
Volkonskii, Prince Sergei (Director of the Imperial Theaters, 1899–1901), 15, 15 n. 3, 15–16, 16, 19, 87, 103, 218, 255
Vrubel', Mikhail, 221, 221 n. 30
Vsevolozhskii, Ivan, (Director of the Imperial Theaters, 1881–99), 15, 15 n. 1, 19, 25, 129, 140

Wagner, Richard, 82, 83, 202, 225, 243, 264
  Bayreuth, theater in, 221, 222, 242, 251
  Musical works:
  Götterdämmerung, 222
  Lohengrin, 118, 170–71, 177, 203, 251
  Die Meistersinger, 139 n. 16
  Parsifal, 222
  The Ring of the Nibelung, 62, 131 n. 166, 221, 222
  Tannhäuser, 127
  Tristan and Isolde, 131, 177
  Die Walküre, 131 n. 166, 206, 222
  Theoretical works:
  Art and Revolution, 222
  Opera and Drama, 222
Wagnerism, 31, 221–23
Wandering Theater. *See* General Accessible Theater
West, Mae, 81
Wilde, Oscar, 3, 209 n. 196
  Salome, 79, 80, 81, 129 n. 155, 209, 245
William II, German Emperor, 31
Winter Bouffe, 27
Winter Farce Theater (St. Petersburg), 58, 73, 203
Winter Palace, 22, 38
The Word (*Slovo*), newspaper, 145
World of Art Group, 36, 223
World War I, 74–75, 82–85, 127, 133, 134, 144, 161, 167, 196–97, 207, 242, 248, 249, 253

Yearbook of the Imperial Theaters (*Ezhegodnik Imperatorskikh teatrov*), journal, 10, 15, 111, 175
Yeltsin, Boris, 244

Zhdanov, Lev, *In the Struggle*, 77
Zhukovskaia, Ekaterina, *Chaos*, 206
Zhuleva, Ekaterina, 123
Ziloti, Aleksandr, 27, 30, 61, 62, 255, 258
Zimin, Sergei, 26, 34, 84, 85, 98, 184 n. 60

www.ingramcontent.com/pod-product-compliance
Lightning Source LLC
Chambersburg PA
CBHW021356290426
44108CB00010B/263